Y0-BRV-482

TECHNOLOGY AND SOCIETY

TECHNOLOGY AND SOCIETY

Advisory Editor
DANIEL J. BOORSTIN, author of
The Americans and Director of
The National Museum of History
and Technology, Smithsonian Institution

THE STORY OF THE
BALTIMORE & OHIO RAILROAD
1827∼1927

BY

EDWARD HUNGERFORD

Volume I

ARNO PRESS
A NEW YORK TIMES COMPANY
New York • 1973

Reprint Edition 1972 by Arno Press Inc.

Reprinted from a copy in
The University of Illinois Library

Technology and Society
ISBN for complete set: 0-405-04680-4
See last pages of this volume for titles.

Manufactured in the United States of America

————————

Library of Congress Cataloging in Publication Data

Hungerford, Edward, 1875-1948.
    The story of the Baltimore & Ohio Railroad, 1827-1927.

    (Technology and society)
    1. Baltimore and Ohio Railroad. I. Title.
II. Series.
HE2791.B3H8 1972b   385'.0974   72-5054
ISBN 0-405-04735-5

THE STORY OF THE

BALTIMORE & OHIO RAILROAD

1827∼1927

BUILDERS OF THE BALTIMORE AND OHIO.

The men who in the first half century of the company's existence brought it to a high standard of development.

From a painting by Francis B. Mayer, made in 1891, which hangs in the Board Room of the Baltimore and Ohio Central Headquarters Building in Baltimore.

THE STORY OF THE
BALTIMORE & OHIO RAILROAD
1827‿1927

By

EDWARD HUNGERFORD

PROFUSELY ILLUSTRATED WITH MAPS,
PRINTS, PHOTOGRAPHS, ETC., ETC.

G. P. PUTNAM'S SONS
NEW YORK — LONDON
The Knickerbocker Press
1928

FOREWORD

THE record of any large railroad is apt to be the record of the social and economic life of the territory it serves. Baltimore and Ohio is no exception to this. In the first one hundred years of its life—coincident with the first hundred years of the railroad, itself, here in the United States —its record becomes that of the great industrial area that it serves. Crossing or entering thirteen of the states of the Union, reaching eight out of the ten largest cities of the nation, its history automatically becomes that of a very considerable part of America. Its first span of an even century is the span of one of the most interesting periods of social and industrial development that the world has known. With the history of that development, its own is entwined, irrevocably.

The idea of this book, originally, was that of its author. He went to the officers of the Baltimore and Ohio Railroad and sought their coöperation in finding records and other source materials upon which to fabricate it. This help was given quickly. Yet, nothing more was proffered nor imposed. The author was left perfectly free to write this history as he himself chose to write it. At no time has he been asked to change nor to deflect it. The record is his own. The comments upon the men and events that go to make up the long chronicle of one hundred years likewise are his own. At all times he has tried to speak without malice or without prejudice. His desire has been a simple one—to spread the story of the development of a single far-reaching American enterprise as a detailed history; with here and there, perhaps, an unjudicial comment as to the effect of that record upon the life and growth of the community in general.

To make that record, he has had access to reports, letters, documents of every sort. He has read the daily files of many years of the newspapers of Baltimore and elsewhere. He has perused many of the books already written upon the history of the company. Its bibliography, already carefully compiled, is far too extensive to be placed here in full. Printed, it would make a volume quite as large as either of these that go to make the present record. Precise accuracy in this history, he cannot guarantee. That ever has been his aim. But, in the passing of many years, conflicting statements arise. One man's guess is as good as another's. And even records, themselves, are sometimes conflicting and misleading.

All of which is offered not as apology, but as explanation. . . . It has been a hard task, compiling this record and making it as accurate as is humanly possible. But it has been a pleasant work. A task made pleasant by the unending help given by so many folk—the officers of the Baltimore and Ohio Railroad, the librarians of the Maryland Historical Society, of the Library of Congress and of the Bureau of Railway Economics; the late Colonel John M. Schoonmaker, Mr. J. B. Yohe, Mr. W. W. Shock, many, many others. Finally, the author would speak a special word for the interest and energy of his secretary, Miss Doré Hough, who has helped him greatly in the preparation of this book.

E. H.

BALTIMORE, March, 1928

CONTENTS

CHAPTER I

CHAPTER II

CHAPTER III

CHAPTER IV

CHAPTER V

CONTENTS

CONTENTS

ILLUSTRATIONS

ix

THE STORY OF
THE BALTIMORE AND OHIO RAILROAD

THE STORY OF
THE BALTIMORE AND OHIO RAILROAD

CHAPTER I

BALTIMORE FACES A CRISIS

The Growing Young City of Baltimore Comes to a Real Crisis—
The New Transport Advantages of Her Rivals, New York and
Philadelphia—The Opening of the Erie Canal—The Great
Era of the National Road.

ON the twenty-eighth day of February, 1927, the Baltimore
and Ohio Railroad Company celebrated its one-hundredth
birthday, and a second century in the history of the railroad
in the United States was begun. For an older railroad company than this does not today exist in the United States, if
anywhere. When the Maryland Legislature, under the peti-
tions of citizens of Baltimore, was chartering the company,
only one other railroad, for the public transport of passengers and of goods, had as yet been incorporated. . . . The
Mohawk and Hudson Railroad, connecting Albany and Schenectady, was chartered two months earlier than the Baltimore
and Ohio. But it was not until the summer of 1830 that
ground for this pioneer railroad in the state of New York first
was broken. By that time, the Baltimore and Ohio was
operating its first regular trains for the reception of passengers.

True it was, too, that the Delaware and Hudson Canal
Company had been incorporated four years before, April 23,

1823. But the original purpose of that company was, as its name indicates, merely to construct an artificial waterway—to run from Rondout, upon the Hudson, into the anthracite hills of northeastern Pennsylvania. It was not until 1826 that the Delaware and Hudson laid down, as an accessory to its canal, its first railroad; an ingenious series of levels and of inclined planes, extending from Carbondale, in the heart of the coal beds, up over Moosic Mountain and down again to the head of the canal at Honesdale. It was upon this stretch of coal-carrying railroad that Horatio Allen, in August, 1829, operated the first steam locomotive ever to turn wheels upon American soil: the *Stourbridge Lion*, built by the George Stephenson works upon the English Tyne and brought in a sailing vessel to the United States.

Gridley Bryant, in 1826, opened his railroad from the quarries at Quincy, Massachusetts, to a dock three miles distant, in order that the huge stones for the Bunker Hill Monument, then building, might be the more easily transported. . . . The picturesque Mauch Chunk Railroad, in the valley of the Lehigh in Pennsylvania, already was under construction. . . . There were other colliery lines, technically railroads, here and there within the United States. But all of these were small and isolated. They were planned merely as accessories to far more important industrial enterprises.[1]

.   .   .   .

Of larger caliber, however, were the transportation plans which the Atlantic coast cities, New York and Philadelphia, were just putting into effect. . . . The Erie Canal, extending from Albany, close to the head of tidewater upon the Hudson, to Buffalo, at the foot of Lake Erie, had been completed and was open for business. It was, and still is, the longest artificial waterway in the world. Traffic began to sweep toward it. It made a vital link of connection between salt water and the

[1] These very early railroads were all designed for operation with horses or cables as motive power. The steam locomotive still was some distance away.

great inland seas of North America, the first real key to the development of her interior territory.

New York City, at the mouth of the Hudson, sat at the entrance to this new water path. It was keeper of the gate. The traffic that the new canal bore, bound to increase rapidly, would pay tribute to its harbor. As the hinterland grew— that unknown region of vast possibilities which Baltimore knew chiefly as the Ohio country—more and more would grow that traffic upon the Erie Canal; more and more in size and in importance would grow the city of New York. . . . There would seem to be no damming of the floods of business that would come in upon her.

Philadelphia, too, was preparing to thrust an eager arm into the Ohio country. Pennsylvania offered no such easy pathway to the West as that which nature had provided across the state of New York; through the valley of the Mohawk, Oneida Lake and along the shelving southern slope of Lake Ontario. All the way north and south across Pennsylvania, the Alleghenies thrust a grim wall of shadows. Yet, just beyond this great barrier were the headwaters of the navigable Ohio, leading straight toward the father of all rivers, the Mississippi, and a new land, seemingly of an almost interminable vastness.

The men of Philadelphia refused to be daunted by mountain barriers. Recognizing all the practical difficulties that confronted them, they nevertheless set about to create a pathway across their commonwealth, which, like the then new Delaware and Hudson, should be an ingenious combination of canal, of level railroad and of inclined plane. With much wealth at their command, they began, and eventually finished, this curious pathway; successfully utilized it for a number of years, until the great railroad which today bears the name of Pennsylvania came to replace it.

.   .   .   .

Against these new pathways of the cities that were its commercial rivals, what had Baltimore to offer; what, save the

National Road? And what was the National Road? When one came to compare it with the great Erie Canal or even that combined project of canal and railroad upon which Pennsylvania had already embarked.

The National Road was an enterprise in which, from the first, Baltimore had a lively interest. It had its beginnings, in 1808, in Maryland. It had thrust itself westward from Cumberland, a small city at the headwaters of the Potomac, through toward Wheeling; which was not reached, however, until 1817. After which the National Road sprang into immediate favor.

For Wheeling meant the Ohio, and the Ohio meant navigation. By 1817 the steamboat had already begun to pass out from its period of uncertainty and experimentation and was a recognized and valued agent of transport. . . . The first steamer to sail down the Ohio—Nicholas Roosevelt's *New Orleans*—made the journey in 1811. After which there was an increasing and unending procession of these craft; bound down the Ohio to Cairo and then up the Mississippi to St. Louis or down to the Crescent City.

.   .   .   .

Thomas Jefferson was the first really powerful sponsor for the National Road, although Albert Gallatin had urged it even earlier. President Jefferson foresaw that, once it had been extended to the banks of the Ohio, it would afford a comparatively easy route toward an undeveloped interior section of the land. . . . The Federal decision to join the Atlantic coast and the interior country by this highway was not reached until 1806. After which it was made part of the fundamental law of the land that the Federal government had the right to build roads when and where it pleased. Ohio, Indiana, Illinois and Missouri were admitted to statehood only after accepting this principle.

The Washington government having formulated this policy and having completed the road between Cumberland and Wheeling as a road of much pretense—with its stout stone bridges, its substantial toll houses[1] and even its trim white mileposts—it apparently stood committed to an almost indefinite extension of a national highway system until President Monroe, in 1822, vetoed an act "for the preservation and repair of the Cumberland road." Monroe stated that he had grave doubts as to the constitutional rights of Congress to impose such a highway system, willy-nilly, upon the face of the country. . . .

Here was a firm stand, firmly taken. And one of far-reaching consequences. For by this step, just before the dawn of the railroad era, James Monroe unquestionably saved the United States from being committed to a general governmental ownership and operation of the railroads from the outset. . . . Federal highways easily might have led to federal railways. Nevertheless the President did not succeed in allaying a very general national sentiment in favor of enlarging the highway structure of the land. After all, the railroad had not yet been born. Travel, in those portions of the United States not reached by waterways, was an extremely tedious and arduous thing. The transport of goods inland was so difficult a thing as seemingly to preclude all hope of development of regions well back from navigable waters. No wonder that the nation clamored for better roads.

Henry Clay voiced this feeling. It was one of the factors in the presidential campaign of 1824. With the result, after all, that one of James Monroe's last official acts—on the third of March, 1825—was the signing of a bill appropriating $150,000 for the extension of the National Road through Ohio, Indiana and Illinois. . . . John Quincy Adams, as President, approved eight bills, which together set aside another $750,000 for this same purpose. . . . After which, a flood of these

---

[1] Some of these bridges and toll houses still stand. The bridges were the so-called "S" structures, so built as best to withstand floods and flood débris. Their masonry was of the most durable sort and their stout stone arches carry easily the heavy motor traffic of today over the National Road; even though their double curves do not always excite the admiration of the motorist.

statutes came pouring in upon the White House—not only for roads but also for canals, railroads and river improvements—until Andrew Jackson, gathering his courage together, vetoed a measure appropriating aid for the building of a sixty-mile turnpike wholly in Kentucky; purely a state improvement. . . . By this time, these proposed transport helps were asking $63,000,000 in federal aid; with others, in a less tangible form, but aggregating more than $200,000,000, just behind them. And this of a nation whose total annual revenues were then less than $24,000,000!

Yet, in the long run, even Andrew Jackson weakened. And approved an appropriation of $250,000 for further extension of the National Road, which finally came into Columbus, Ohio, in 1833. . . . St. Louis and the Mississippi were never reached, officially. By 1852, the National Road had only struggled through as far as Vandalia, where it connected with rather ordinary dirt roads through to the West. . . . There it was abandoned. There was no need of going through with it any further. The railroad had come into its own. The workmen were laying the iron of what later was to be one of the westerly extensions of the Baltimore and Ohio, through southern Illinois and almost directly past Vandalia, the ancient capital of the state, up to the east bank of the Father of Waters, directly opposite the city of St. Louis.

.   .   .   .

Yet, the National Road served its own part in the upbuilding of the land—and a very great part it was. From about 1820 up to at least 1845, it was all that its name implies. To find its counterpart, one would have had to recall the road-building triumphs of the Romans or to journey far overseas and discover something, for instance, like the great North Road of England, running from London up to York and on to Edinburgh.

Over this National Road of the United States, for two decades and a half, there poured a vast vehicular traffic. It was all but unending. Wagon trains, stage coaches, post chaises and men on horseback. . . . Droves of cattle, or of sheep, sending up choking clouds of dust as they made their weary progress. . . . A dusty way at many times; and, at others, a quagmire through which wheeled vehicles struggled wearily.

An unending procession of traffic. . . . Often in a single grouping, more than two dozen four-horse coaches passed together along the road.[1] Farms and towns and taverns and comfortable cities sprang into existence upon it. . . . It was not, in the ordinary sense, a road. In all of its confusion, its bustle and its noise, it was a city thoroughfare. . . . It was no place for sleep. At times, the racket was deafening. Travelers who passed along the National Road remembered it; for a long time afterwards, and with a shudder.

And, yet, it had its recompenses. In the pleasant hills and in the mountains of Maryland and of southwestern Pennsylvania, fair vistas, and many of them. . . . The road dipped over the hills and across the valleys, rarely swerving its course for any of these. The taverns that lined it were of a rather uniform grade of excellence. The carters who drove the hundreds and hundreds of Conestoga wagons and the mule pack trains from one end of the road to the other—year in and year out—had their own resting places. Resting places for man and for beast. Rather rough and ordinary places, these. With meals at twelve cents each and whiskey at three cents a glass. . . . The stage houses, however, were of a different sort. . . . Aristocrats. . . . Roadside swells. . . . Famed for their eating. . . . And for their drinking. . . .

[1] Thomas B. Searight's *The Old Pike; A History of the National Road*, etc., says: " . . . As many as twenty four-horse coaches have been counted at one time on the road, and large broad-wheeled wagons, covered with white canvas stretched over bows, laden with merchandise and drawn by six Conestoga horses, were visible all the day long at every point, and many times until late in the evening, besides innumerable caravans of horses, mules, cattle, hogs and sheep. It looked more like a leading avenue of a great city than a road through rural districts. . . ."

So, in their way, were the fleet stage coaches that pulled up to their aristocratic doors, aristocrats. Patriotic fellows— one hundred per cent Americans. You could see that, at first glance. By just looking at the names upon the gaily painted panels of their doors. . . . The *Washington*, the *Lafayette*, the *General Wayne*, the *General Harrison*, the *Rough and Ready*, the *Madison*, the *Monroe*, the *Henry Clay*. Sometimes, the coaches were named for cities or for states or for nations. . . . There was the *Erin Go Bragh*. . . . Even the names of the stage lines reflected a delicacy of sentiment. Think of the *National Line*, to say nothing of the *June Bug* one. Or of the *Shake Gut*. One might get a slight thrill in riding on the *Good Intent;* but the *Oyster Line*, as its name implies, was given over quite largely to the transport of that delicate article of food.

.   .   .   .

Sometimes, they made swift speed upon the old National Road. . . . The regular running time for the mail stages from Baltimore to Wheeling was three and a half days; with changes of horses every twelve to fourteen miles. . . . Always when a President-elect was ready to travel to his inauguration, a special coach was builded for him, which bore either his name or else the proud title of *The President*. Andrew Jackson refused to ride, free of charge, or at all, over the National Road, but finally permitted his family to use the coach which was prepared for him. General Harrison had no such qualms. Neither had James K. Polk, who rode in one of the very handsomest coaches ever put on the great highroad. . . . General Taylor made the trip over it to Washington when it was encrusted with ice, and it was said that the only reason that he ever got through with his neck unbroken was because his driver was Montgomery Demming.

Demming, who was reputed to weigh 465 pounds, was of a race which has long since disappeared. It had its final flicker of brilliancy out in the far West when its last survivors

A TOLLGATE ON THE NATIONAL ROAD.

Still standing (1927) on that ancient highway, near Frostburg, Maryland.

From a recent photograph.

STAGE COACH DAYS.
A scene along the National Road.
From a painting by H. D. Stitt.

drove the Concord coaches of Ben Halliday and of Wells
Fargo. . . . Yet, Montgomery Demming's glory was shared;
with Homer Westover, who once drove from Uniontown to
Brownsville, twenty miles, up and down the hills, in forty-five
minutes; and with Redding Bunting, six feet six and straight as
the proverbial ramrod, who drove six horses 131 miles in twelve
hours, carrying President Polk's message notifying the country
that the war with Mexico had been begun. . . . Truly an
unusual race of men, these stage drivers.

.   .   .   .

Baltimore was the eastern gateway of the National Road.
. . . Not officially, but practically. Officially, as has been
said, the road began its way at Cumberland. . . . Up toward
Cumberland, from the growing city at the head of Chesapeake
Bay, ran—and still runs—through the fairest fields of Maryland, the Frederick Pike. . . . Through Frederick, just below
Hagerstown, and then on to Cumberland. The great traffic
of the National Road all passed over the Frederick Pike. And
it began at Baltimore.

In 1827, Baltimore, with a population of nearly 80,000 folk,
had come to be the third city of the Union. Her recent growth
had been heralded as hardly less than phenomenal. Of her,
Jared Sharp was writing, in 1825:

. . . Among all the cities of America, or of the Old World,
in modern or ancient times, there is no record of any one which
has sprung up so quickly to so high a degree of importance as
Baltimore. . . .

At this time, the population of the town was about five times
what it had been five years before. In a similar proportion,
had its commerce increased. One factor alone had contributed
greatly to the wealth of its merchants—the San Domingan
trade. The bartering in tobacco and in flour already had come
to large proportions. . . . And, assuredly, the completion of

the National Road through to Wheeling had been a fine thing for the town. No wonder that her citizens looked with jealous eyes upon anything that menaced the prosperity of that highway.

This, then, was the enterprising, ambitious city wherein the Baltimore and Ohio Railroad was born. . . . A gay, brave town, rising on the steep banks of the Patapsco, almost at the very point where that swiftly running stream comes to tidewater—in that great estuary of the sea known to mariners the world over as the Chesapeake Bay. . . . A town already famed for its progress, as well as for its growth. Since the days of the Revolution, Baltimore had indeed come to a real position in the land. On the heights back of the inner harbor, where in 1782 Rochambeau had encamped his victorious French army, after Yorktown, there already was a neat pattern of streets and houses. . . . Back of all these, Howard Park with the tall granite shaft of the Washington Monument, then as now, rising above the town and majestically overlooking it.

There were tall church spires, and many of them, in the Baltimore of 1827. The new cathedral had been finished and dedicated. The town had a theater. A theater lighted by gas—in that day described by the newspapers as the "aeriform fluid"! Occasionally, the weak new illuminant puffed itself out, leaving the audience in a Stygian darkness, but that was thought of as nothing; merely as an ordinary difficulty incident to the adoption of any new illuminating medium. . . .

A brave, gay, busy town. . . . Throbbing with all its businesses. Ships coming into and going out from its pretty harbor. Beautiful ships, with their hulls coppered and copper-fastened; and making much of that. Line ships for Liverpool and Amsterdam and Le Havre and Boston and New York and Halifax—and frequent ones for Havana and Vera Cruz and Bordeaux and many, many other ports, both of the West Indies and the Mediterranean. . . . By 1827, steamboats a-plenty running daily to Annapolis, to Norfolk, down the Bay and up the Potomac to Washington City. . . .

By land, the great tradings of the highroads. Baltimore was, and still is, the hub of a giant wheel whose spokes are the hard-surfaced pikes, running away from her in every direction; to Havre de Grace and to Philadelphia, to York, to Reisterstown, to Annapolis, to Washington—and greatest of all, by far, that Frederick Pike, leading off straight to the West and the wonderful National Road.

Upon all the spokes of this mighty wheel, there moved at all times an unending traffic. It did not seem even remotely possible that this could ever be seriously threatened. So much bustle and confusion. Wagons coming and wagons going. Gay stage coaches vying with one another for traffic. The busy scenes in the taverns of the town. . . . So many of these—in 1827. . . . The earlier ones in Old Town, east of Jones Falls. The *Bull's Head*, the *Rising Sun* and *Habbersett's* were great favorites there; the last one, particularly so, with Harford County farmers. The *Fountain Inn*, with a famous limpid, gushing sign, was always a pet of the men from the Eastern Shore; it remained so, long after the Presidents of the United States had ceased to favor it with their patronage and turned toward Gadsby's newer *Indian Queen*. . . .

But the more westerly portions of Baltimore were now gaining in popularity. Along Franklin Street swung the gaudy signs of the *Golden Horse*, the *White Swan*, the *Golden Lamb* and the *Black Horse*. Paca Street had its own quota of these inns: the *General Wayne*, the *May Pole* and the *Three Tuns*. The fact that both Paca and Franklin streets were convenient of access to the great highway leading toward the West rendered them popular for tavern sites. . . . As long as the National Road flourished, these old inns hung on, bravely. When it went down in favor, they went down. And Baltimore came quickly to the era of such showier hostelries as Barnum's Hotel and the Eutaw House; large caravansaries that, from the first, wholly discarded the old-fashioned index of a gay, swinging sign. . . .

The older inns were something more than mere taverns;

eating and drinking and sleeping places. Many of them made
a business of booking passengers and freight and, so, acting as
terminals for the coach and wagon lines. . . . The ones on
the western side of the town, in particular, generally were filled
with staunch, rough teamsters and drovers; their yards
occupied with cattle for the shambles, and fine big horses for
sale or for swap. . . . The streets were fairly choked at times
with the Conestoga wagons; curious affairs, some of which survive to this very day. This old type of wagon, set in ponderous wheels, with tires from four to six inches in width, was
hauled by six powerful horses adorned with jingling bells.
Their very coming made a great howdy-do. . . . Their relays
at the wagon stands were times of great noise and confusion, as
well as gayety. . . . Whiskey at three cents a glass.

.   .   .   .

A great road, the National; a very great road. A highway
to be reckoned with. But one whose very existence, as early as
1827, was seriously threatened. That strange-looking highway, whose chief factors were two long, narrow strips of rail,
was creeping into being upon the broad face of the world. . . .
Some day, the National Road would have to look to itself—not
merely as a king among highways, but for bare existence.

A group of Baltimore men foresaw that day. And, fore-
seeing—understanding quite well what both New York and
Philadelphia were doing—began to grope blindly, like men in
the dark, toward that strange new thing, the rail highway. . . .

The Baltimore and Ohio Railroad was born as much out of
fear as out of high ambition.

CHAPTER II

ORGANIZING THE BALTIMORE AND OHIO

Some February Evenings in Mr. George Brown's House and What
Comes of Them—The Birth of a Railroad—The Brilliant
McMahon and His Charter—The Company Organized—The
Rush for Its Shares—Discussion as to the Location of the New
Line.

A BRAVE, gay town, bustling and full of many businesses,
yet faced with possible disaster, unless it quickly should take
stock of its menace. The wiser men of Baltimore were now
quite aware of what the inevitable success of the new transport
routes across New York and across Pennsylvania would mean
to the National Road; to their own community, the chief
beneficiary of that early artery of travel; to themselves. They
began to see, in their imagination, grass growing in the pretty
streets of Baltimore City. A few families already had mi-
grated from it. . . . These men of Baltimore were not
asleep to the situation. . . . They fell into much discussion.

For a time, this took the form of a plan finally to build the
Chesapeake and Ohio Canal, which was to parallel the
Potomac, all the way from Washington to Cumberland—
eventually, to Pittsburgh. . . . Washington, himself, had
been the first sponsor of this project. In his papers one may
find references to it. But, in the press of many other things
upon a young nation, it had become forgotten. And was only
remembered when the astonishing success of the Erie Canal
focussed national attention upon waterways of that sort. . . .

For Baltimore, there was a particular fly in the ointment
of the Chesapeake and Ohio Canal scheme. In case it were

built, it obviously would follow the watercourse of the Potomac and so would come to navigable waters, logically, at Washington City, not at Baltimore. Various schemes were entertained—as late as 1842—for a connection canal from the Chesapeake and Ohio across country to Baltimore, either from the Point of Rocks or from Washington itself. But the engineering difficulties to be encountered never brought these into a very serious consideration. . . . There was at no time a necessity for such an expensive link of canal. . . . It was clear that Baltimore would have to find some other pathway out of her dilemma.

·   ·   ·   ·   ·   ·   ·   ·

Nevertheless, for a time, she gave serious attention to the revival of the Chesapeake and Ohio Canal project. In 1825, a meeting of delegates from all parts of the state decided that "the practicability of a canal from Baltimore to intersect and unite with the Chesapeake and Ohio Canal, thence to Pittsburgh, and thence to Lake Erie, no longer admitted of a doubt and should be carried," and induced the Maryland Legislature to subscribe $500,000 to the stock of the canal company. In the following summer, a report, prepared under the direction of General Bernard, Chief of the United States Corps of Engineers and President of the Board of Internal Improvements, stated that to dig a canal, forty-eight feet in width at the surface and thirty-three feet at the bottom, and five feet deep, all the way from Georgetown (at Washington City) through Cumberland, and on to Pittsburgh, 341 miles, would cost $22,375,427; exclusive of land purchases, condemnations and unforeseen contingencies. The same report estimated that, with tolls fixed at $5.85 a ton from tidewater through to Pittsburgh, the canal in the first six years after its projected opening, in 1838, would earn an average of $1,173,696 a year; thereafter, up to a maximum of $5,570,791 annually. . . . It is interesting, at this date, to see the precision of the optimism of the Army engineers of that day. Even though Bernard's report was, at the time, regarded as requiring so much money as to make the construction of the Chesapeake and Ohio Canal a financial impossibility. (The Erie Canal had cost but $7,000,000.)

The proposed canal was to have inclined planes, in addition to 398 locks; also a tunnel four miles in length through the summit of the Alleghenies. It was suggested that the chief commodities that it would carry would be wheat, corn, flour and meal, rye, tobacco, hemp, flaxseed, beef, pork, bacon, lard, tallow, whiskey, iron and glass. Of secondary importance in tonnage would be coal (it is evident that the engineers could not have foreseen the dominance of coal-carrying by rail at the present day), lime, timber, plank, slate, marble and freestone.

Coincident with the authorized subscription by the state of Maryland to the stock of the Chesapeake and Ohio Canal Company, a citizen of Baltimore, Mr. Philip E. Thomas, was made the commissioner representing the state in that company. . . . Yet, within a twelvemonth, he had resigned that post. He had convinced himself of the absolute futility of the canal enterprise, particularly as one affording any commercial relief to Baltimore. Neither did he believe that the alternative project, sometimes brought forward, of digging a canal across the country to the north, through York, and to the Susquehanna and the new Pennsylvania system of canals and railroads combined, afforded any better solution of the problem. As far as Baltimore was concerned, Philip E. Thomas felt that the correct answer must come in some other way.

.   .   .   .

And yet, the answer must be found. This was imperative. . . . General Bernard's report was focussing attention upon the Chesapeake and Ohio Canal, and Baltimore was out of it. . . . The business men of the town who gathered almost daily upon the floor of its fine new Exchange discussed the thing —informally and at length. But to no definite end. It was

difficult to formulate a really practicable form of relief to the
situation by any canal to be builded inland from Baltimore.

Then, for the first time, came into discussion the railroad—
this strange new thing that was beginning its existence on two
sides of the Atlantic.   According to Mr. John H. B. Latrobe,[1]
the railroad was first given serious attention at a dinner held
one evening in the fall of 1826 at Belvedere, the home of
Colonel John Eager Howard at Baltimore.   Evan Thomas, a
brother of Philip E. Thomas, had just returned from England,
where he had inspected the Stockton and Darlington Railroad,
upon which coal trains were being drawn by cumbrous engines
from the mines to the coal docks where they were unloaded.
Although possessing no determined views, Mr. Thomas gave a
vivid picture of the new enterprise.   The dinner guests listened
to him with great interest.

Yet, it is possible that most of the men who sat around that
table would have quite forgotten about the Stockton and Darlington, had it not been for the persistence of the other Thomas.
. . .   Philip E. Thomas had oft been remarked in Baltimore
for his self-possession, his energy, his clearness of perception
and his rare judgment.   Of the Quaker faith, he had the calm
serenity of this religion. . . .   These things together had
brought him fortune and position in the community.   Already
he was president of the Merchants Bank.

> Here [wrote Mr. Latrobe in later years] he was associated
> with men who, like himself, were prosperous merchants and
> whose confidence in him was unbounded.   His persuasiveness
> was remarkable.   Never thrown off his balance, quiet in his
> speech, laborious in his search for facts, and above all, as giving
> him influence with the community, eminently successful in his
> own business, people listened to him with conviction who
> listened to Evan Thomas in kindness. . . .

[1] For sixty-four years the counsel of the Baltimore and Ohio and a local historian of no mean worth.

THE BALTIMORE OF A HUNDRED YEARS AGO.
"A brave, gay town, bustling and full of business."

From a contemporary painting.

THEY MET AT THE HOME OF GEORGE BROWN, ESQ.

The merchants of Baltimore conferred repeatedly in February, 1827, on the fascinating project of a new railroad to the West.

From a painting by H. D. Stitt.

This was the manner of man who presently was to become the first president of the Baltimore and Ohio Railroad.

．　　　．　　　．　　　．　　　．　　　．　　　．

Gradually these discussions increased. The persistence of Philip E. Thomas counted for much. The opinion of his brother that the scheme of drawing carriages upon iron rails would succeed—whether drawn by the steam locomotive, still in a highly experimental stage, or by horses, in the long run probably far more trustworthy—he carried again and again to his fellow business leaders of Baltimore.

Gradually all of this fell upon fertile soil. With the result that on the evening of February 2, 1827, a memorable meeting of these business men of Baltimore was held in the residence of one of the most influential of them all; in the house of George Brown, also a banker of the town and a son of Alexander Brown, one of its most famous early merchants. At this meeting the two Thomas brothers assumed leadership, quite easily and naturally. . . . After some extended discussion of the advantages to Baltimore of a through trade route to the West, these men adjourned to meet again, ten days later.

Some twenty-five of the men of Baltimore came to this meeting, also at George Brown's house. Of what they discussed, there is no record. The call to the meeting read that it would "take under consideration the best means of restoring to the city of Baltimore that portion of the western trade which has recently been diverted from it by the introduction of steam navigation and by other causes." . . . It is evident, indeed, that the inroads of the Erie Canal already were making themselves felt.

At this assemblage, William Patterson—another well-known merchant of the town, whose daughter, Betsy, had married Prince Jerome Bonaparte, the so-called King of Naples—was made the chairman, and David Winchester was the secretary. After discussion, a committee was appointed to make a report on the practicability of a railroad from

Baltimore to the Ohio. It consisted of Philip E. Thomas, Benjamin C. Howard, George Brown, Talbot Jones, Joseph W. Patterson, Evan Thomas and John V. L. McMahon. This last was a brilliant young attorney of North-of-Ireland stock who had graduated from Princeton in the class of 1817, and one who was destined to play a most important rôle in the launching of the Baltimore and Ohio Railroad.

One week later, this committee reported back to the larger group. It recommended, without hesitation, that immediate steps be taken to construct, by the most eligible and direct route, a "double railroad" between the city of Baltimore and some suitable point upon the Ohio River. It also asked that a charter to incorporate the company to prosecute this great work be sought from the Legislature, at the earliest practical opportunity.

The report of this sub-committee remains to this day— over a hundred years after its writing—a real tribute to the vision and the ability of the men who brought it into being. . . . After presenting and enforcing the position of Baltimore in regard to the proposed canals, both to the Potomac and to the Susquehanna, it goes forward, saying:

> . . . But important as this trade is to Baltimore, it is certainly of minor consideration, when compared with the immense commerce which lies within our grasp to the West, provided we have the enterprise to profit by the advantages which our local situation gives us in reference to that trade. Baltimore lies 200 miles nearer to the navigable waters of the West than New York, and about 100 miles nearer to them than Philadelphia, to which may be added the important fact, that the easiest, and by far the most practicable route through the ridges of mountains that divide the Atlantic from the western waters is along the depression formed by the Potomac in its passage through them. Taking then into the estimate the advantages which these important circumstances afford to Baltimore, in regard to this immense trade, we again repeat that nothing is wanted to secure a great portion of it to our

city, but a faithful application of the means within our own power.

The only point from which we have anything to apprehend is New Orleans; with that city, it is admitted, we must be content to share this trade, because she will always enjoy a *certain portion* of it in defiance of our efforts; but from a country of such vast extent, and whose productions are so various and of such incalculable amount, where will be a sufficient trade to sustain both New Orleans and Baltimore; and we may feel fully contented if we can succeed in securing to ourselves that portion of it which will prefer to seek a market east of the mountains.

Of the several artificial means which human ingenuity and industry have devised to open easy and economical communications between distant points, turnpike-roads, canals and railroads have unquestionably the advantage over all others. When turnpike-roads were first attempted in England they were almost universally opposed by the great body of the people; a few enterprising citizens, however, succeeded, after a severe struggle, in constructing them.   The amount of traveling was then so limited that this means of transportation was found abundantly sufficient for all the exigencies of the then trade of that country; in a little time, however, so great was the increase of commerce there . . . that even the turnpikes were found insufficient to accommodate the growing trade of the country, and the substitution of canals in place of roads was the consequence. . . .

It was soon ascertained that in proportion to the increased facilities afforded to trade by the canals in England was the increase of trade itself, until even this means of communication was actually, in many of the more commercial parts of the country, found insufficient for the transportation required.

Railroads had upon a limited scale been used in several places in England and Wales for a number of years and had in every instance been found fully to answer the purposes required. . . . The idea of applying them upon a more extended scale appears, however, only recently to have been suggested in that country; but notwithstanding so little time has elapsed since the attempt was first made, yet we find that so decided have been their advantages over turnpike-roads, or even over canals, that already 2000 miles of them are actually completed or in a train of rapid progress in Great Britain, and that the experiment of their construction has not in one case failed, nor has there been one instance in which they have not fully answered the most sanguine expectations of their projectors. Indeed, so completely has this improvement succeeded in England that it is the opinion of many judicious and practical men there that these roads will, for heavy transportation, supersede canals as effectually as canals have superseded turnpike-roads. . . .

The report then proceeds to say that in England owing to the milder climate canals have a far greater opportunity than in the greater part of the United States. . . . Although the facts in regard to the British railway system were not so extensive as the committee desired to present, they declared that they had gleaned from the documents they examined on the subject enough to leave no doubt upon their minds that these railroads were far better adapted to their situation and circumstances than a canal across the mountains would be. Therefore came the recommendation toward the immediate construction of a "double railroad" across the Alleghenies to the headwaters of the Ohio, as well as the concurrent one for the immediate securing of a railroad charter.

The report next relates, in some detail, various facts in possession of the sub-committee and concludes after this fashion:

The district of country which would mainly depend upon this route for the conveyance of its surplus produce, it will be recollected, already contains nearly two million inhabitants, that is to say about one-fifth of the whole population of the United States, whilst the population depending upon the New York [Erie] Canal is not estimated to be more than about one million; and the receipts from the latter [the Erie Canal] are stated to be as follows:

Receipts for the year 1824....$340,761.07
1825.... 566,221.51
1826.... 765,000.00

There are a great variety of articles, the product of the country west of the Alleghany Mountains, which are now of little value in those countries on account of the heavy expense unavoidably incurred in the transportation of them to a port whence they could be shipped to a foreign market. With the facilities afforded by this railroad, many of these articles could not only bear a transportation to Baltimore, but, while they would afford a constant and increasing supply of freight upon the proposed road, they would become a source of great wealth to the people of the West.

Hard facts these—and true. They must have appealed to those hard-headed, wise-headed old merchants of Baltimore City, as again they sat in Mr. Brown's house to listen to the reading of the report of their sub-committee. . . . When the report went forward to say that a barrel of flour, which at that time was worth five dollars in Baltimore, was worth but a dollar in Wheeling, because its transport over the National Road cost four dollars, it was speaking a very plain language to them. "Whereas," continued this document, "upon the proposed railroad the whole expense of transportation from the Ohio River to Baltimore being estimated to be only at the rate of ten dollars per ton, the cost of carriage upon a barrel of flour would then be only one dollar; thus at once would its value, as an article of export, be enhanced in Ohio from one dollar to four dollars per barrel." . . . Hard facts these. And enough to make the men of Baltimore listen eagerly as the report proceeded:

The expense of conveying cotton upon the proposed railroad from the Ohio River to Baltimore, including all charges, may be estimated at one-quarter of a cent per pound, certainly not more than half a cent per pound; and coal from the Alleghany Mountains, near to Cumberland, including its cost at the pits, could be delivered at Baltimore at from 11 to 12 cents per bushel. Let us then apply this calculation to the other numerous productions of the Western States, and we shall be at once convinced that there is no scale by which we could venture to calculate the ultimate extent of the trade which would flow into the State of Maryland, upon the proposed railroad, should its results approach anything near to our present expectations.

No part of the country included in these estimates lies nearer to New Orleans than 1200, or perhaps 1500 miles (and that, it should be recollected, is the only market that could compete with us for this trade) whilst a large portion of these districts lie 2000 miles distant from that city. By the estimates here furnished it is manifestly clear that the produce from a large portion of these countries can be delivered at Baltimore at a less expense of transportation than they possibly can be carried to New Orleans.

Admitting the cities of New Orleans and Baltimore to stand competitively, as regards their claims to this trade, Baltimore, to say the least, might be expected to hold its share; but we should not lose sight of the important fact that the productions of these extensive regions, excepting only tobacco and cotton, being breadstuffs, provisions and other perishable articles, cannot be exposed to the deleterious climate of New Orleans without the hazard of great injury; hence we find that considerable portions of the flour and provisions which go by the way of the Mississippi are often so much damaged as to be rendered unfit for exportation to a foreign market. Many valuable lives are also annually sacrificed to the climate, in the prosecution of the trade upon the Mississippi. What then has Baltimore to fear from New Orleans in a conflict on equal terms for their trade?

To convince any one that there is no probability that the trade here estimated will be likely hereafter to decline, it will only be necessary to observe that the population upon which the calculations are founded is rapidly increasing every year, and that it must, for several succeeding generations, continue to increase. The country around the Chesapeake Bay was first settled by Europeans about the year 1632 and in the year 1800 the white population had barely reached as far west as the Ohio River; that is to say, in 160 years it had advanced westward about 400 miles, or at the rate of two and a half miles per year. There is now a dense population extending as far west as the junction of the Osage River with the Missouri; which is about 900 miles west of the Ohio River, at Wheeling; of course the white population has, within the last thirty years, traveled that distance, or more than thirty miles each year and is at this time advancing with as great, if not greater impetus, than at any former period; and according to all probability, if not checked by some unforseen circumstances, it will, within the next thirty years, reach the Rocky Mountains or even to the Pacific Ocean. We have, therefore, no reason to look for any falling off in this trade, but, on the contrary, for an increase of it, to an extent of which no estimate could now be formed.

The accuracy of the vision of these men in 1827 will come sharply to the human mind today; when San Francisco lies less than four days distant by rail from Baltimore and portions of the state of California are as densely settled as any of those of Maryland. . . .

The report of this sub-committee was promptly adopted and a large edition of it, in pamphlet form, ordered printed for general distribution. After some consideration the following resolutions were adopted by the meeting:

Resolved, That immediate application be made to the Legislature of Maryland for an act incorporating a joint stock company to be styled "The Baltimore and Ohio Railway Company," and clothing such company with all the powers necessary to the construction of a railroad, with two or more sets of rails, from the city of Baltimore to the Ohio River.

Resolved, That the capital stock of said company be five millions of dollars, but that the company be incorporated, and provision shall be made by the said act for its organization, upon the subscription of one million of dollars to said stock, and that the said company shall have power to increase the capital stock thereof, so far as may be necessary to effect said objects.

Resolved, That it is expedient and proper in said act, to permit subscriptions of stock to the same, to be made by the United States, by States, corporations or individuals; and to provide that as soon as the said act shall have been passed by the Legislature of Maryland, subscription books shall be opened, subscriptions received, the company organized, and the said road constructed, so far as it may lie within the limits of the State of Maryland; and that the assent of the Legislatures of Pennsylvania and Virginia to the said act shall be obtained as speedily as possible, but shall be made necessary only so far as in constructing the said road it shall be found necessary to pass through their respective States.

To prepare the formal application to the Legislature of Maryland, the following gentlemen were appointed a committee:

CHARLES CARROLL,
  OF CARROLLTON
WILLIAM PATTERSON
ISAAC McKIM
ROBERT OLIVER
CHARLES RIDGELY,
  OF HAMPTON
THOMAS TENANT
ALEXANDER BROWN
JOHN McKIM, JR.
TALBOT JONES
JAMES WILSON
THOMAS ELLICOTT
GEORGE HOFFMAN

PHILIP E. THOMAS
WILLIAM STEUART
WILLIAM LORMAN
GEORGE WARNER
BENJAMIN C. HOWARD
SOLOMON ETTING
W. W. TAYLOR
ALEXANDER FRIDGE
JAMES L. HAWKINS
JOHN B. MORRIS
LUKE TIERNAN
ALEXANDER McDONALD
SOLOMON BIRCKHEAD

.   .   .   .

To a final meeting at the house of George Brown and the definite action that it took, came an instant and a hearty response from all Baltimore. The town was now thoroughly aroused. Its tongues were buzzing. The railroad project was being received with a general favor, not only in the city, but throughout all Maryland; and so, when a formal application for a charter for the new company was presented to the Legislature by John V. L. McMahon, little opposition showed itself.

. . . On February 28, 1827, the act which formally sanctioned the incorporation of the Baltimore and Ohio Railroad was passed by the state of Maryland.

.   .   .   .

In a moment we shall come to the laying of the First Stone of this railroad; an elaborate and impressive service on the Fourth of July of the ensuing year. Yet, the real corner stone of Baltimore and Ohio, the one which has served it so faithfully these many years, is its sturdy charter. This document, the work of McMahon, has served as a model for many and many another which has followed it. Yet, it was, in turn, modeled quite frankly upon similar works for the earlier turnpike companies.

It has, however, many unusual phases. For instance, it provided in the beginning that the capital stock of the company should be $3,000,000, in shares of one hundred dollars each, of which 10,000 shares should be reserved, for a period of twelve months, for subscription by the state of Maryland and 5000 for subscription by the city of Baltimore. The remaining 15,000 shares were to be open to individuals or corporations. . . . As soon as 10,000 of these shares had been taken, the company would be declared established, with its full powers, rights and privileges.

If more than 15,000 shares were subscribed, from these sources outside of city and of state, the subscription was to be reduced to that number; automatically, by striking off from the largest number of shares or reducing all subscriptions to one share. If there were more than 15,000 different subscriptions, lots were to be drawn to determine which were to be excluded. . . . Upon this point the charter was very definite. . . . One dollar was to be paid on every share and the residue in installments. Provision was made, however, that not more than one-third of a subscription was to be demanded in any one year from the commencement of the work, nor any actual payment until at least sixty days of advance notice had been given.

After which time, failure to make an installment payment would result in a forfeiture of the shares.

Nine commissioners were appointed to receive the subscriptions to the capital stock and they were to keep the books open for this purpose for at least ten consecutive days. The stockholders were then to elect twelve directors by ballot and these, in turn, were to elect a president. Each stockholder was allowed one vote for each share of stock owned by him, and voting by proxy was authorized. . . . In case the state of Maryland or the city of Baltimore failed to make their proposed subscriptions to the stock, the president and the directors could make any disposition for the benefit of the company they saw fit, provided they did not sell it for less than its par value. . . . Their powers were made very sweeping in most of these matters.

On the other hand, there were some ways in which they were curbed. Restrictions upon the powers of the company were written into its charter. If the road was not actually begun within two years of the time of the passage of its act of incorporation and completed in Maryland within ten years of the beginning of the work, the act was declared "null and void."

The turnpike origin of the charter is shown in provision that the company be allowed to charge "tolls" upon both goods and passengers to be carried over the railroad. These were definitely fixed. . . . Power was given the company to place upon its line "all machines, wagons, vehicles, or carriages of any description whatsoever which they may deem necessary or proper for the purposes of transportation." (This gave full opportunity for the possible use of that strange new device —the steam locomotive—which already was being developed over in England.) On the other hand, the charter said, quite definitely, that no person should travel upon nor use the road of the company for transportation without permission from its officers. . . . The toll-road idea cropping out again. . . . And still again, when the width of the roadbed of the line was not permitted to exceed sixty-six feet. . . . Sixty-six feet was a fixed standard for the width of all main post roads in that day; secondary roads had their width arbitrarily placed at thirty-three feet.

Of vastly greater importance, however, was that provision which exempted the Baltimore and Ohio Railroad in Maryland from all payment of any taxes whatsoever to the state. A tremendous help to the struggling young company. . . . This clause repeatedly has been attacked in the courts. And has stood stoutly throughout all the years. The shrewd McMahon wrought even better than he knew.

Before the charter, as completed in the rough draft, was submitted to the Legislature, it was read by him to the organizing committee of the railroad, for its approval. . . . Slowly McMahon read it aloud to the little group, pausing after each carefully worded provision. Gradually there was unfolded to them this most remarkable railroad document. Before the attorney had come to its end, he was interrupted; by that venerable Baltimorean, Robert Oliver.

"Stop, man," shouted Oliver, in the peculiarly blunt and offhand way for which he was known in the town. "You're asking for more than the Lord's Prayer."

McMahon replied, with a smile, that it was all necessary, and the more they asked for, the more they would get.

"Right, go on," replied the older man to the younger one; and the reading proceeded to its conclusion.

.   .   .   .

The charter of the Baltimore and Ohio Railroad Company being at last formally passed by the Legislature of the state of Maryland, there remained nothing to do but to gain stock subscriptions, formally organize the company, make the first surveys and begin the actual construction of the road. All of which was, of course, much more easily said than done. . . . A vast task was ahead of the Baltimore men who had met those eventful February evenings of 1827 in Mr. George Brown's house.

Yet, when the stock books were opened, there was an instant and a highly practical response. . . . Every one wanted stock. . . . Because of that provision of the charter that the number of shares subscribed were to be apportioned if the limit of the capital should be exceeded, many set about obtaining proxies, in one form or another. Parents subscribed in the names of their children and paid down the dollar on each share that the regulations demanded. They were beginning, even in that day, to have the thing that today we call mob psychology. . . . The remarkable demand for the first stock of the Baltimore and Ohio Railroad was commented upon by newspapers all over the country. . . . The United States immediately entered upon an era of railroad mania—with Baltimore leading—that was not to subside until the great panic of 1837.

The subscription books for the shares of the new railroad company were opened on March 20, at the Mechanics Bank in Baltimore, at the Farmers Branch Bank in Frederick, and at the Hagerstown Bank in Hagerstown. They remained open but twelve days. In that time 36,788 shares were subscribed in Baltimore alone—exclusive of the 5000 shares taken by the city itself. These shares represented more than 22,000 individuals. Similarly large subscriptions came from both Hagerstown and Frederick. But, as only 15,000 shares were to be allotted to individuals at that time, the shares were, as provided by the charter, properly apportioned.

.   .   .   .

The company, itself, was formally incorporated April 24, 1827, when, in accordance with the provisions of its charter, the following men were elected as its first officers and directors:

President, PHILIP E. THOMAS
Treasurer, GEORGE BROWN

Directors

CHARLES CARROLL,
OF CARROLLTON

GEORGE HOFFMAN
PHILIP E. THOMAS

A Very Early Stock Certificate.
Engraved about 1831 and showing the early locomotive and cars of that day.
From the original.

PHILIP E. THOMAS.
First President of the Baltimore and Ohio Railroad Company, 1827–1836.
From a painting.

WILLIAM PATTERSON   THOMAS ELLICOTT
ROBERT OLIVER   JOHN B. MORRIS
ALEXANDER BROWN   TALBOT JONES
ISAAC MCKIM   WILLIAM STEUART
WILLIAM LORMAN

The state of Virginia confirmed the charter of the Baltimore
and Ohio Railroad Company, March 8, 1827; the state of
Pennsylvania, February 22, 1828. Baltimore moved toward
its participation in the enterprise, subscribed to its stock and
prepared to elect two directors to represent the interests of the
city in the company.

Here, then, were the actual beginnings of the Baltimore and
Ohio Railroad!

.   .   .   .

Came next the vast problem of the proper location of the
line. . . . Recourse was had to the engineering resources
of the Federal government.[1] From the Army was taken at the
outset, Colonel Stephen H. Long; while from the National Road
was chosen Jonathan Knight, another member of the Society of
Friends, a profound mathematician, and known as an extremely
honest and able man. With Knight came his superintendent
of construction, Caspar W. Wever, who had built many miles
of the road through Ohio. Wever was given the same title with
the railroad. And a salary of $2000 a year. Colonel Long and
Knight were paid $3000 annually.

Long and Knight were chosen to make the preliminary
surveys for the new railroad. Their ability, their thoroughness, their precision, are shown by the actual work that they
accomplished. . . . Knowing but little of what a railroad was

---

[1] In that early day there was no established school of engineering in the United
States, except the Military Academy at West Point. It was quite customary,
therefore, to call upon its graduates for the technical skill required in the planning
of large internal improvements.

or should be—remember always that as the Baltimore and
Ohio company was organized it was by no means an assured
fact that the steam locomotive would ever be used upon it; the
directors were of the belief that frequent relays of horses all
the way through to the Ohio would be a more economical and
reliable motive power—Messrs. Knight and Long, like
McMahon, worked with a greater vision than they themselves could possibly have appreciated. . . . Mr. Knight
remained with the road as its chief engineer for many years.
He became from the outset one of its great guiding forces and
inspirations. To no small extent, the original line, east of
Harpers Ferry, is to be regarded as his personal handiwork.

A brave enterprise this—building a railroad, in a day when
nothing was known about railroads. So brave, that it easily
might have been deemed foolhardy. Some folk did not hesitate
to call it such—in its beginnings and for many and many a day
thereafter. . . . But these were in the minority. Already we
have seen Baltimore itself, as a brave town and prosperous,
growing like a young reed. . . . It accepted the new enterprise with avidity. Its wisest, its most successful men had
placed themselves behind the railroad. Perhaps even because
it smacked of adventure. Of attaining the impossible. . . .
Youth and courage were with the Baltimore and Ohio; from
the very hour of its birth. It may have been born out of fear,
but fear did not long remain with it.

.   .   .   .

From Knight and Long came glowing reports of the preliminary surveys. It was going to be a fairly difficult country
to traverse; from Baltimore cross-country to the Potomac, in
the neighborhood of the historic Point of Rocks; but by no
means an impossible country for this new marvel of the age—
the Rail Road. . . . A mission of engineers prepared itself to
go to England, to see the things that were being accomplished
over there. Another went to examine the railroads at Honesdale and at Mauch Chunk. . . . At home, the directors of the

company, availing themselves of the vast drift of public favor toward their enterprise, gratified their patrons by permitting them, at a fell swoop, to double their stock subscriptions. . . . A plenty of money was available for the new railroad.

And still no one knew what a railroad really was!

.　　.　　.　　.　　.　　.　　.

It was not all plain sailing, of course. There were rifts in the lute. Human aspirations and human selfishness have a way of cropping out, even in the most glorified moments of the beginnings of great enterprises.

There was the matter of the precise location of the new road. The directors—the most of them being wise old souls of Baltimore—expected that they might have trouble there. In this they were not disappointed.

In all the whirl and excitement of the location of the new railroad—whether it should be builded to the Ohio at Pittsburgh, or at Wheeling; whether this strange new thing over in England, the locomotive which ran by a hot steam vapor, would ever really amount to anything—there were a few hardheaded folk in Baltimore who asked where the line would be built, *in Baltimore*. Whose land—in Baltimore—would be taken by the company, and whose land—in Baltimore—would most be benefited by the new road of rails? And whose interests might possibly be affected . . . favorably . . . unfavorably? Unpleasant questions these, perhaps, but undeniably pertinent ones. And ones that were bound to crop out.

There must have been a good deal of discussion of some of them—in that summer of 1827, as well as in the long months that ensued. Because presently we find the City Council of Baltimore coming to a definite refusal to pay over one single dollar of the $500,000 which the corporation had generously— and in a moment of great enthusiasm—subscribed; unless the railroad at its Baltimore terminus was located at precisely sixty-six feet above tidewater. . . . No more. . . . No less. . . . Put your railroad at sixty-six feet or you do not get the half million. Do you see?

The young railroad saw. And presently set upon the site for its beginning—for the first of the rails that were yet to reach all the way over the distant mountains and to the yellow river that runs its course behind them—at the corner of Pratt Street and Amity Alley, where to this day its great Mount Clare shops cover many, many acres, with all of their varied activities. . . . Pratt and Amity, at just sixty-six feet. . . . Baltimore City then gave its crisp new check to the treasury of the young railroad company.

.   .   .   .

And yet, as in many highly arbitrary rulings, complications presently ensued. After all, it was argued, the purpose of the new railroad was not merely to serve the local necessities of Baltimore, but also the many ships that rubbed their noses against its harbor wharves. . . . To bring the railroad down that sixty-six feet of elevation, from the corner of Pratt Street and Amity Alley, was going to be something of a problem, it was feared. The City Council was appealed to. It remained adamant. It had given its $500,000 check on the condition that the road emerge from the town at a sixty-six-foot level. On that condition the railroad had accepted it. On this point the City Council of Baltimore was to remain fixed—until eternity, if need be.

Discussion arose once again—no two-sided discussion this time. As to the precise path and way of reaching the docks of the town with the rails, a many-sided discussion. Which lasted for long months—even after the construction of the railroad actually was begun.

One popular idea in those days was to tunnel under Howard Street, coming out into what is today Center Street and what was then a part of Howard Park surrounding the shaft of the Washington Monument. From Center Street the railroad would make an easy descent to and across Jones Falls on its way to the shipping at Fells Point. . . . A good idea, this, if it had not been so expensive. The east side of Baltimore did have some rights to the benefits of the new railroad. Some folk realized this point. And suggested, as a far less costly and more practicable route, laying the tracks right down the middle or the sides of Pratt Street, to the docks of the inner harbor.

At this there was fresh outcry. And a memorial was prepared which was sent over to Congress, then sitting at Washington. . . . The memorial took the proposed invasion of Pratt Street by the railroad as a most portentous matter. Assuming, in the first instance, that the tracks would be laid down at the sides of the street and that the cars would probably move with one wheel on the curbings and the other on a single stone rail to be laid in the pavement of the street itself (oh, how very, very little they really knew about a railroad in those beginning days!), it naïvely suggests that this course would necessitate the removal of every pump, hydrant, lamp-post, awning-post, sign-post, tree and feeding trough along that thoroughfare. . . .

Yet, even this was hardly to be compared with the devastation that would arise should the new railroad elect to place its tracks down the center of Pratt Street. The memorial dilates upon these possibilities—after this fashion:

> . . . Make the rail tracks on Pratt Street part of the main street and should it occur that a six-horse wagon, loaded with wheat, should meet a railroad car filled with passengers riding, *for pleasure*, it would seem hard for the law to enact that business should give way to pleasure.

However, the memorial seems to feel far more definitely and more poignantly that the railroad tracks would go upon the sides of Pratt Street, whether one rail was laid—as has just been suggested—or two for each track. In such an event, busy Pratt Street would be narrowed from forty feet to twenty-one; horses would be scared; the piling of firewood along the curbs would be prevented, while (one can almost feel the note of triumph in this point) "no lady would ever shop across a railroad track." . . . It dilates further upon the possibilities of horses being frightened, should the steam locomotive ever come into use, and finally suggests that parents living along Pratt Street "will labor under a constant apprehension for their children and will hesitate to send them to school or upon errands across the street." . . . (One feels that such apprehension would probably *not* be shared by the boys of Baltimore; the coming of the railroad would be far more apt to spell a real joy to their souls.)

In this discussion there was not a little bitterness. A deal of acrimony developed. Richard Caton at one time became so exercised over the situation that he actually started to build a railroad of his own. . . . Finally, some one suggested that a road which was having so much difficulty in getting across the gutters of Baltimore might have some trouble in surmounting the summits of the Alleghenies. At which folk laughed. And the tension was relieved.

The railroad came; and for many years continued to occupy Pratt Street with its main line of communication between the North and the South through Baltimore. Poor Memorial! It was in vain. And yet, not entirely so. For Pratt Street, as we shall see in good time, was barred to the steam locomotive. Horses drew the heavy cars of the railroad through it; singly and in brigades. . . .

The Memorial little knew. But who could know? The Rail Road in those days was so very, very young. . . .

CHAPTER III

On Which a Corner Stone is Laid—There is a Long Procession
Through the Streets of Baltimore City—The Venerable
Charles Carroll of Carrollton Breaks Ground for the Railroad
—The Masons place the First Stone—Fireworks and
Rejoicings Follow.

ABOUT one thing, the directors of the new Baltimore and
Ohio Railroad were quite agreed: There must be a corner
stone. . . . In that day, every institution began its career
with a corner stone; generally laid by the Masonic lodges. . . .
The Masonic lodges were kept very busy, indeed. . . . But
they seemed to thrive upon the traffic.

About many things, the directors of the new railroad might
and did disagree—the precise route that it was to take to the
distant Ohio, the exact forms of locomotion that were to be
used upon its rails, the infinite minor details of the new enterprise. But all were a unit in regard to a corner stone. A
corner stone the Baltimore and Ohio must have. And
presently did have. . . . Even though it was to be forever
known as the First Stone. It was first suggested that Charles
Carroll of Carrollton should lay the stone. He was not merely
a signer of the Declaration of Independence, but, in 1828, the
sole survivor of that distinguished band. More than this,
Mr. Carroll was recognized throughout all Maryland as a
public citizen of the highest worth. No less a man could lay
the First Stone of the Baltimore and Ohio.

As a matter of precise fact, Mr. Carroll did not lay the

stone. That privilege was reserved for the Masons; and he was not a Mason. But he was very much present at the great event and actually took the spade and turned the first bit of soil for the new railroad. After which, the Masonic lodges carried on with the ceremony.

This event took place on the farm of a relative, James Carroll, at Gwynns Falls—not far from the corner of Pratt Street and Amity Alley. That estate long had been known as Mount Clare. The laying of the stone was held upon the Fourth of July, 1828, and was attended by several thousand persons. For weeks Baltimore had lived in an anxious expectancy of the affair. Her civic organizations had vied with one another in their preparations for it. All that was needed to make it a complete success was good weather. And this last was vouchsafed it, in generous degree.

.   .   .   .

The morning of that unforgettable Independence Day dawned bright and crisp and seasonably cool. From sunup on, all Baltimore was in activity. . . . For several days past, folk had been pouring in from the surrounding country. In all her history no such congestion of carriages and wagons and saddled horses in her stable yards and upon her streets as came this day. . . . The town, literally, was packed to overflowing.

After the fashion of that day, the exercises began promptly, in the early morning. The parade was planned to start from the corner of Baltimore and Bond streets at eight o'clock. But, long before that hour, the people were in the streets; lively and incessant crowds everywhere. Rife was the excitement. Great floats—in those days they called them stages or cars—and bands and companies of uniformed men going to their posts in the parade procession. Small boys under foot everywhere; girls in their soft, white dresses, and preened for the occasion. Country lasses and their swains into Baltimore City for the first time—and a tremendous time. . . . The pave-

THE LAYING OF THE FIRST STONE.

Charles Carroll of Carrollton (with the spade) turned the earth and the Masonic lodge laid the marker.

From a painting by Stanley M. Arthurs.

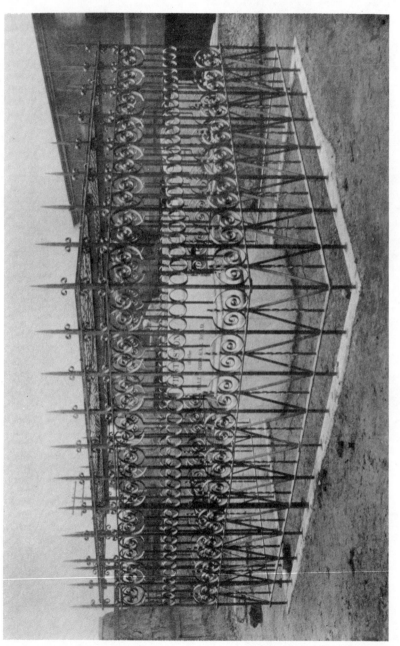

THE FIRST STONE ITSELF.

As it stands today, near Mt. Clare shops, Baltimore.

From a recent photograph.

ments crowded everywhere. . . . And in the windows that looked down upon them, upon the announced line of march of the procession, every seat taken soon after dawn. . . . Window space at a premium. And at a premium also, seats upon the wooden stands which carpenters for a week past had been erecting. . . . Above all, the flags and the bunting; gay, bright, beautiful. . . . What a pity it would have been if it had rained, upon Baltimore's most memorable Independence Day!

.   .   .   .

The procession, itself, a most pretentious thing. Three grand divisions of it; the first led by Captain Cox and his Troop of Horse, followed in quick succession by the Pioneers and by the Grand Lodge of the Masons. After which, the president and the directors of the Baltimore and Ohio Rail Road Company, its military and its civil engineers; the Society of the Cincinnati; the surviving officers and soldiers of the Revolutionary Army—a straggling and pathetic group—and, in high state, the Orator of the Day, the Speaker of the House of Representatives, the Governor of Indiana, the Mayor of Baltimore, members of Congress, of the Legislature and of the Baltimore city government. . . . An impressive array of human importance.[1]

The second division was given over wholly to the trades associations, or guilds, of the city with their various floats. First came the Agricultural Society; then followed in swift succession: the farmers and planters, the gardeners, the plough makers, the millers and inspectors of flour, the bakers, the victuallers, the brewers and distillers, the tailors, the blacksmiths and the whitesmiths, the weavers, the bleachers and dyers and the manufacturers of cotton and of wool. . . . A

[1] Seemingly, the only really high personage that was absent was the President of the United States. Mr. Adams had gone to Georgetown that very day to help lay the first stone of the Chesapeake and Ohio Canal. In after years, the Chesapeake and Ohio Canal and the Baltimore and Ohio Railroad were to lock horns up at the Point of Rocks. But the canal was never to celebrate its centenary.

vast array. . . . The stone cutters, the painters and glaziers, the fancy and Windsor chair makers, the sugar refiners, the glasscutters, the cordwainers and journeymen, the ornamental chair painters.

Trades, almost without number. The saddle and harness makers. The coach makers. The cedar coopers. The ship carpenters. The ship joiners, block and pump makers. The boat builders. The rope makers. The riggers. The sailmakers. The pilots. The ship captains and mates. The seamen. . . . What a multiplex thing was industry, even in that early day!

This list of the participating guilds runs on, seemingly toward infinity. . . . As a matter of real fact, there were about fifty of these trades organizations in the long line; each with its appropriate float, flag-bedecked, and each with from fifty to a hundred and fifty of its members, gaily dressed in honor of the occasion, walking beside it or in front of it.

It was agreed that, while the floats of many of these guilds quite outdid anything that had previously been attempted anywhere, the exhibit of the ship captains, mates and seamen— the miniature ship *Union*—quite overshadowed everything else in the procession. The farmers and planters, almost at the head of the division, had attempted much. A delegation of "twenty-four aged and respectable farmers" (to quote the precise phrasing of the *Baltimore American* of the following day), riding on horseback and in double file, preceded not less than five floats depicting five different phases or episodes in the life of the agriculturist. . . . The millers and flour inspectors were warmly received; these last in drab coats, white hats, vests and pantaloons.

The weavers had a loom upon a float, and upon another the tailors had a miniature shop. During the passage of the procession, the loom of the weavers produced a small bolt of cloth, from which the tailors cut and sewed a coat, which was presented to Mr. Carroll at the conclusion of the laying of the First Stone. The distinguished signer had many such gifts as a result of the day's events; but to General Lafayette, who had been the guest of the city of Baltimore but three years before, went the lady's slippers of white kid that were prepared by the bookbinders in the line on that Fourth of July of 1828.

The carpenters excited a lively admiration for their elaborate float, which showed a miniature temple, with a portico and pediment of the Doric order, all exquisitely rendered. A banner carried at the head of this delegation displayed a railroad station with a Doric arcade and a locomotive engine approaching its center door. . . . The stone cutters were the honor guard of the First Stone itself, which they had prepared and given for the occasion. This huge object of respect and veneration was seated in the outgoing parade on a stout plinth covered with green baize. The people of Baltimore looked upon it with much admiration.

Yet, all of these paled before the coming of the good ship *Union*. What a vast deal of human labor had gone into the preparation of that highly unique float! A miniature brig, twenty-seven feet long and of six-foot beam, had been builded and, with sails set and flags flying, placed in the great procession. The ladies of Fells Point, where she had been constructed, had labored hard in the making of her colors.

Timothy Gardner was the master of this remarkable craft and E. W. R. Sink her pilot. Her officers and crew were composed of distinguished shipmasters. They were all dressed alike. . . . and the jolly dogs seemed so happy in their voyage that smiles and cheers alike greeted them on their way. . . . In the wake of the *Union* came masters, mates and seamen of the port of Baltimore afoot; in their rear, several carriages with the older men of the guild.

Soon after the beginning of the parade, the venerable Charles Carroll came along the line. As he passed the *Union*, riding at anchor in front of the *American* office, he received an official salute from the craft. Thereafter ensued the following dialogue between Henry Thompson, his aide, and Captain Gardner, of the *Union*.

"Ship ahoy!" said the aide.   "What is the name of that ship and by whom commanded?"

"The *Union;* Captain Gardner," came the response.

"From whence came you and where bound?"

"From Baltimore, bound to the Ohio."

"How will you get over the mountains?"

"We've engaged a passage by the railroad." . . .

.   .   .   .

A final division of the parade was given over to still other organizations, these last marching without floats, however. Following Captain Walters' fine band of music, one noted the juvenile associations: the Jefferson, the Jackson, the Franklin, the Carrollton, the Clinton, the Washington, and, finally, the school children themselves, distinguished by a large banner on which were displayed the letters of the alphabet and this motto:

> Large streams from little fountains flow,
> Tall oaks from little acorns grow.

. . . In all, more than five thousand highly enthusiastic folk marched that July day over the pavements of Baltimore, as a token of their faith in the coming of the railroad that was to be the commercial salvation of the town.   While the *Baltimore American* solemnly averred that not less than from fifty to seventy-five thousand persons saw them pass out toward the place of the laying of the First Stone. . . .

The spot for the laying of the stone on James Carroll's farm was designated by a pavilion, gaily decorated, which had been erected on a narrow ridge running north and south across it. This pavilion, the slow-moving, great parade reached at about ten o'clock. . . . On either side of it was ranged the cavalry. In front, toward the east and upon the brow of the ridge, was the place where the First Stone was to go.   The floats were drawn up in a huge grouping at the left; while the Masonic bodies formed a hollow square around the stone. . . .

As we have just seen, this central object was the gift of the stone cutters of Baltimore.   Similarly, the pick, the spade, the stone hammer and the trowel used on this occasion were given by the blacksmiths' guild of the town, as represented by David Whetson, Martin Metter and Robert Buck.   A fascinating little controversy had preceded this last donation.   The directors of the Baltimore and Ohio had begun to despair of obtaining iron in the United States for their new railroad at fair prices; in fact, a bill had been advanced in Congress revoking the import duties upon rails and other metal work for the new line. . . .   A deal of discussion had followed.   And the head of the blacksmiths' guild had written to the president of the railroad, suggesting the gift of the corner stone tools and asking if he preferred to import foreign tools for this purpose. To which the Quaker Thomas had replied with great urbanity that nothing, except possibly the rails for the new line, would be imported and that he still hoped to obtain these within the United States. . . .

The exercises in James Carroll's field were begun with prayer by the Rev. Dr. Wyatt, the Masonic Grand Chaplain; the vast audience uncovering their heads both for this and for the reading of the Declaration of Independence, which immediately followed.   The *Carrollton March*, composed by a Mr. Clifton, was then played by the assembled bands, after which the Orator of the Day, Mr. John B. Morris, performed his portion of the function. . . .   One outstanding paragraph of his address—presumably written with the co-operation of Mr. John H. B. Latrobe—has come down through the years.   In it Mr. Morris said:

> It is but a few years since the introduction of steamboats effected powerful changes.   Of a similar and equally important effect will be the Baltimore and Ohio Railroad.   While the one will have stemmed the current of the Mississippi, the other will have surmounted and reduced the height of the Alleghenies.

Upon the conclusion of this oration, two boys, dressed as Mercuries, advanced toward the canopy and prayed that all the remarks made upon the occasion be printed and distributed to the populace generally. . . .

This was preparation. . . . The great event was still ahead, though close at hand. While the men were yet tinkering with the First Stone, Charles Carroll, accompanied by Mr. Morris and the Grand Marshal of the day, descended from the pavilion and proceeded toward the exact spot designated for the laying. Mr. Carroll, despite his years and the fact that he was carrying the heavy spade, walked with firm step, and with steady hand struck the implement deep into the ground; thus verifying the prediction of a song published that very morning:

> The hand that held the pen
> Never falters, but again
> Is employed with the spade, to assist his fellow-men.

. . . A group of men with great dexterity then brought the stone to its final resting place. The Masonic Grand Master, with the other high officers of that order who were present that day, applied the instruments of it to the stone and pronounced it to be "well-formed, true and trusty." . . . The Grand Chaplain invoked the benediction of Heaven upon the success of the railroad enterprise, the prosperity of the city of Baltimore and the future life of the venerable man who had assisted upon the occasion. As for Mr. Carroll, he did not hesitate to say to a friend who stood close beside him: "I consider this among the most important acts of my life, second only to my signing of the Declaration of Independence, if second even to that." . . . Through the short remaining space of his years, he was to continue an unwavering friend of the railroad, ready at all times to come to its aid. . . .

With the pouring of wine and oil and the scattering of seed corn upon the stone, the ceremony was concluded. . . . The procession turned about and filed its way back toward the town, while Mr. Carroll was induced to become one of the few honored guests who were invited aboard the good ship *Union*.

. . . The reporter of the *Baltimore American* notes the fact that he partook solely of his favorite beverage, water.

Others were not so punctilious. For, in the afternoon, the various guilds held their banquets in the hotels and the taverns of the town; with inordinate speech making and eating; and perhaps a little drinking to boot. In those days, they were not overscrupulous about intoxication. In fact, it was the common custom upon occasions such as this for cities to suspend their police regulations, save as against offenses of the most heinous sort. . . . Drunkenness was not then regarded as particularly heinous. . . .

In the evening, there were more celebrations. Dancing in various places. A play at the theater. The launching by James Beacham of a fine 800-ton ship—at dusk—which was named after Mr. Carroll. . . . And after dark finally was to come, for the joy of the populace, fireworks upon Federal Hill. . . . Peale's Museum displayed transparencies of the railroad and of Mr. Carroll, engaged Captain Roundtree's band, and at eight o'clock exhibited the magic lantern. An Independence Day not easily to be forgotten!

.   .   .   .   .   .

Those curious folk who stayed behind after the ceremony in James Carroll's field or who came shortly after to look at the First Stone, read upon the top of it this inscription:

THIS STONE

Presented by the Stone Cutters of Baltimore
In commemoration of the commencement of the

BALTIMORE AND OHIO RAIL ROAD, was here placed
On the 4th of July, 1828, by the GRAND LODGE OF
MARYLAND

Assisted by CHARLES CARROLL OF CARROLLTON
The last surviving Signer
OF THE DECLARATION OF AMERICAN
INDEPENDENCE

And under the direction of the President and Directors
OF THE RAIL ROAD COMPANY

On each side, the stone bore—and still bears—an inscription stating that it is the "FIRST STONE OF THE BALT. & OHIO RAIL ROAD." The eyes of such visitors could not, of course, penetrate the interior of the block of granite; could not read, in its hermetically sealed cavity, the copy of the charter of the railroad, the newspapers placed beside it, nor the parchment scroll upon which was written:

This stone is deposited in commemoration of the commencement of the Baltimore and Ohio Rail Road, a work of deep and vital interest to the American people. Its accomplishment will confer the most important benefits upon this nation, by facilitating its commerce, diffusing and extending its social intercourse and perpetuating the happy Union of the Confederated States. The first general meeting of the Citizens of Baltimore to confer upon the adoption of proper measures for undertaking this magnificent work, was on the second day of February, 1827. An act of Incorporation by the State of Maryland, was granted February 28th, 1827, and was confirmed by the State of Virginia, March 8th, 1827. Stock was subscribed, to provide funds for its execution, April 1st, 1827. The First Board of Directors was elected April 23d, 1827. The Company was organized 24th April, 1827. An examination of the country was commenced under the direction of Lieutenant Colonel Stephen H. Long and Captain William G. McNeill, United States Topographical Engineers, and William Howard, United States Civil Engineer, assisted by Lieutenants Barney, Trimble and Dillahunty, of the U. S. Artillery, and Mr. Harrison, July 2d, 1827. The actual Surveys, to determine the Route, were begun by the same officers, with the additional assistance of Lieutenants Cook, Gwynn, Hazzard, Fessenden and Thompson, and Mr. Guion, November 20th, 1827. The Charter of the Company was confirmed by the State of Pennsylvania, February 22d, 1828. The State of Maryland became a Stockholder in the Company, by subscribing for half a million of dollars of its stock, March 6th, 1828. And the construction of the Road was commenced July 4th, 1828, under the management of the following named Board of

WORN IN HONOR OF THE COMING OF THE RAILROAD.

A badge worn by the marchers in the parade in the streets of Baltimore,
July 4, 1828.

From the company's archives.

SONG IN HONOR OF THE RAILROAD.

The famous *Carrollton March* which was played in the parade of July 4, 1828.

From the company's archives.

Directors:—Philip Evan Thomas, President; Charles Carroll, of Carrollton, William Patterson, Robert Oliver, Alexander Brown, Isaac McKim, William Lorman, George Hoffman, John B. Morris, Talbot Jones, William Steuart, Solomon Etting, Patrick Macauley; George Brown, Treasurer.

.   .   .   .

The First Stone once laid, was laid—that was all there was of it. . . . Presently, very few folk took the trouble of going out from Baltimore to see it. It was neglected, forsaken. And when, some two score years or more later, the main line of the railroad leading out from the town was deflected two miles to the south and passenger trains ceased to go through Mount Clare, it was forgotten. Not only forgotten, but deeply buried under repeated gradings and regradings of the line into the Mount Clare shops.

It was not until about thirty years ago that the First Stone was exhumed and restored and given a setting at least partly commensurate with its real importance. There is, at this time, little of beauty in that setting. The ragged fringe of a great city does not usually lend itself to the placing of monuments of this sort. But the neatly cut and inscribed stone stands today, clean and legible, carefully fenced off from any vandal hands. It is safe to say that, of all the many monuments of the Monumental City, not one, not even the great Washington shaft, nor the lowly marble slab over the grave of Edgar Allan Poe in Fayette Street, transcends in interest or in importance the simple stone marker of the beginnings of America's first important railroad.

CHAPTER IV

A GREAT TASK IS RIGHT AHEAD

The Directors of the Baltimore and Ohio Face Problems in the Construction of Their Railroad—Arguments and Contentions —The Vagueness of the Plans—Men and Measures—The Latrobes.

AFTER all, it was one thing to lay a corner stone, and another—and quite a more difficult one—to build the railroad itself. To keep Baltimore steadily up to that fine fervor of enthusiasm that had attended its tremendous Fourth of July was quite out of the question. Discussions and dissensions were bound to arise. And presently did arise. . . . The flames of argument as to the precise terminal point for the road in the heart of the town, whether or not Pratt Street was to be used as a part of its right of way, burst forth anew. The rival advocates of steam locomotion and of horse shouted out their demands. Rumors ran throughout all Baltimore that both the board of directors and the engineers of the new road were torn with dispute; that they were having difficulties, not alone in finding a proper location for it, but that the all-important questions of its financing were assuming grave proportions.

Most of this, after the fashion of most rumors, was sheer exaggeration. Yet, to much of it, there was a strong undercurrent of truth. The directors were, indeed, facing many problems; perplexing ones. They were beset here and there by strong oppositions. The friends of the Chesapeake and Ohio Canal, strengthened by the stout support of Washington, both official and unofficial, were making fresh efforts in its behalf. Remember that, on that same glorious Fourth that Charles Carroll was turning the first spadeful of earth for the Baltimore and Ohio Railroad, no less a personage than the President of the United States was engaged in a similar mission for the Chesapeake and Ohio Canal. It was quite plain to see that that ambitious waterway project was not easily to be downed. Federal power already stood behind it.

Of even greater immediate moment possibly, were the squabbles of the Baltimore citizenry as to the placing of the line within their borders. Richard Caton persisted in his determination to build his own railroad through to the Ohio. A number of subscribers threatened to cancel their subscriptions to the company's stock if they could not have their own way as to the location of its rails. Every man wanted his own way. . . . Political pressure was brought upon the authorities, both state and city. . . .

Nor was this sort of conflict entirely confined to Baltimore. Frederick City, which had contributed generously to the new enterprise, learned for the first time that the favored route for the railroad would pass nearly two miles south of the town, and protested, rather vigorously, against this. Some of her townsmen sent a memorial to President Thomas and his associates, saying:

> The enterprise in which you are engaged at all times commanded the approbation of the citizens of Frederick. That Baltimoreans should be benefited in an essential degree corresponded as well with their inclinations as with their sense of policy. But they did not suppose that this was to be done in total disregard of other interests or that a rising town like Frederick, necessarily to be passed within a few miles, would be treated as an object of indifference. . . .

They had a way, in those days, of speaking out rather frankly their innermost thoughts. Here was one "Brindley" writing in the *National Intelligencer* (published in the city of Washington) and saying:

A writer, calling himself a Baltimorean in a series published in the *National Intelligencer* and in a tone of low scurrility, attacked the Baltimore and Ohio Railroad Company, maintaining that it was a scheme got up by a few designing individuals with Mr. Carroll at their head to swindle the community. . . .

"Brindley" had waxed wroth over this suggestion. He answered the correspondent of the Washington paper, point by point, and concluded his letter by a stout opinion that the people of Baltimore had nothing to fear from the final results of the system which they had adopted. . . . Bitterness in the air—seemingly, nearly everywhere.

And atop of all of it, the uncertainty as to the methods of construction to be employed in the building of the new line. Apparently, it was agreed that the tracks would have to be made level, or practically so; with inclined planes, such as were already in use in England—and upon the Delaware and Hudson and at Mauch Chunk in this country—to overcome the ascents and descents of the interior country. This much was a distinct concession to those who argued for the use of the horse—old, safe and reliable—as the best method of locomotion for the Baltimore and Ohio.

Yet, beyond this rather primary principle for the construction and location of the new line, very little was known of the way that it should be builded. . . . John H. B. Latrobe well remembered lending a hand in the preparation of some of the earliest drawings for the new railroad, showing in some detail how it purposed to cross the mountains. Of them he says:

. . . A double track of road was to be constructed up and down them, as straight as an arrow; care being taken that the upper end of one of the tracks should be close to a stream which was to be used to fill water cars, whose weight, as they descended on one track, was to be used to drag up the passenger and burden cars on the other, the two tracks being connected by a rope passing around a pulley at the summit. At the bottom of the mountain the water cars were to be emptied;

but the engineer had forgotten to provide a way for getting them back to the top for the next trip. That a mountain road must necessarily be a serpentine one, and that there would probably be a want of water for any purpose whatsoever on the crest of the Alleghanies never seemed to have entered the head of the distinguished gentleman. . . .

.   .   .   .   .   .

Yet, despite all this argument and contention, the railroad itself very soon was under actual construction. On the seventh of July, 1828, but three days after the laying of the First Stone, Lieutenants Cook, Hazzard and Dillahunty of the Army Engineers, working under the direction of Captain William G. McNeill, began the "definitive location" of the road, and seven days later Messrs. Long and Knight published advertisements saying that proposals for the construction of its first twelve miles of line—from the outskirts of Baltimore to Ellicotts Mills—would be opened at Barnum's Hotel on August 11. These men, forming the board of engineers of the new railroad, stipulated that certificates of character should accompany each tender; whilst the bridge builders and the stone masons would be expected to show testimonials of their professional skill.

For the detailed construction of the line between Baltimore and Ellicotts Mills, it was subdivided into twenty-six separate sections and contracts. These were awarded to different contractors, and on July 28th the *Baltimore Gazette* announced:

It affords us sincere gratification to be able to announce to our readers that the actual commencement of the grading and preparation of the first twelve miles of the Baltimore and Ohio Railroad took place this morning. We further learn that there is a fair prospect that the entire line originally contemplated to be completed within the first year will be under contract in a few days, at very fair and reasonable rates. The real and sound judgment with which this noble enterprise has so far been constructed, the able talents which have been engaged in its construction and the powerful influence which has been happily brought to sustain it, all assure us that nothing will be found wanting which wealth, talents and zeal can effect to secure its early and triumphant success.

The Baltimore and Ohio was not without its firm journalistic friends, even in that early day!

.   .   .   .

Well it needed its friends. The actual proposals for the construction of the first dozen miles of the line showed that the expenditures were far to exceed the roseate first estimates of the engineers. The average cost per mile for grading and masonry alone ran about $17,000; in those days to be regarded as an excessive figure. The fourth and fifth contracts, which included the "Deep Cut" west of Gwynns Run (78 feet deep and some 1300 yards long), alone came to about one-third of the total cost of preparing the line for the rails, all the way to Ellicotts Mills. . . . This cutting was to prove itself literally the chief obstacle to the early progress of the Baltimore and Ohio. Before it was to be passed, the road would have to abandon its original intention to lay an actually level line from the First Stone through to Ellicotts. Not without many pangs of regret. Remember that in the beginning the engineers had hoped to build it all the way through to the Point of Rocks, where it first would touch the waters of the Potomac, with a practically level line. With but one exception; at Parrs Spring Ridge (the present Mount Airy), where it was planned to carry the railroad over four inclined planes, two ascending and two descending. Eventually, these planes were built, although they were never equipped with stationary engines and cables, as originally designed. Before this could come to pass, the steam locomotive was an accepted fact upon the Baltimore and Ohio, and a relief line was being builded roundabout them. To this day, one can see faint traces of their embankments, while a small station upon the old main line of the road still bears the name of Plane Number Four.

The Deep Cut just outside Baltimore might have entirely wrecked the incipient career of the young weakling of a railroad, had it not been for the hard-headed sagacity of Alexander Brown, the shrewd merchant-banker of early Baltimore who had been elected to a position upon its board. Hearing of trouble there, Mr. Brown went out to it in the late autumn of 1828 and found that, while a vast number of cubic yards of earth and stone had already been taken out of the work to bring a part of it to full depth, to carry on, to enable the railroad to go through it at absolute deep level, seemed to be an almost impossible thing. He shook his head, significantly, as the enormity of the task was explained to him by the engineers. And turning to them, he said slowly:

"Stop, stop with your digging. How is that ditch to be drained if you ever get through with it? It will never do. It is against all reason and common sense. Provide a way for the rain and the springs to run off and you will save money by the operation."

The engineers were wise enough to accept his advice. They changed then and there from their original plan of a level line, actually filled up a part of the cut once again, and provided a grade through the place of seventeen feet to the mile, which not only saved many thousands of dollars in construction costs, but provided the necessary drainage. By this step they did more. They earned Brown's enthusiasm and absolute coöperation for the project. With the direct result that, a little time later, when the company had come to another of its fearful financial impasses, it was Alexander Brown who was most instrumental in raising a highly necessary $200,000 to keep the work from ceasing entirely.

Forever was the Baltimore and Ohio company seeking fresh funds for its enterprise, and many, many times was it being rebuffed in its efforts. The fine burst of enthusiasm which had led the citizens of Baltimore, of Frederick and of Hagerstown to oversubscribe its first offerings of shares, did not last long. Thereafter, it often became a real task to raise money for its immediate needs. Stockholders were constantly being called upon for fresh installments of hard cash and were responding with an increasing reluctance. With every energy bended to this end, at the close of the calendar year of 1828 the company had only some $4,000,000 in hand with which to build a railroad from Baltimore City to the Ohio River—more than three hundred miles.

Early in that twelvemonth, the company had presented a memorial to Congress—through William Patterson, George Brown and Ross Winans (this last gentleman here enters these pages for the first time, to reënter them many times before their closing)—praying for help for the nascent enterprise. It already estimated the cost of the line through to the Ohio as between six and seven millions—its first experiences with contractors had been eye openers. . . . Against this it had the paltry four millions, with but little immediate hope of getting more.

The Senate committee, to whom this memorial first was presented, made a flattering report upon the prospects of the new railroad and suggested that the federal government subscribe for a million dollars of its stock. The House refused to do anything, however, and the entire matter went over, until December, 1829, when the question again was brought to the attention of both branches of Congress, but with no eventual result. The friends of the Chesapeake and Ohio Canal were upon the ground at all times and tremendously active in their opposition to the project of the business men of Baltimore. (Incidentally, the president of the canal company was the chairman of the House Committee on Roads.) They succeeded in helping defeat the appeal of the struggling young railroad company to Congress for remission of duties upon the rails and other metals that it felt it must needs import from England, and eventually they succeeded in quashing any warm-hearted attempts on the part of official Washington to subscribe to the company's stock.

These men of Baltimore must go it alone. Eventually,

AMERICA'S EARLIEST RAILROAD STATION.

Mount Clare passenger station still stands—in the shadows of the company's chief shops.

From a recent photograph.

SURVEYING FOR THE RAILROAD.

A pioneer reconnaissance corps in the valley of the Potomac.

From a painting by H. D. Stitt.

they did go it alone and probably came to be glad that they had not accepted governmental help, with all the strings that would have been attached to it. They were a self-reliant lot. Of them, Mr. Latrobe's pen has painted a picture which has come down through the years. Skilled with his brush in the use of both water colors and of oil, the man who was the distinguished legal counsel of the Baltimore and Ohio for many, many years, was not less proficient in his powers of descriptive writing. Witness his glowing picture of the founders of the Baltimore and Ohio as they rode one autumn day in the great year of 1828 out to the gorge of the Patapsco to inspect the route of their new railroad:

First came Mr. Robert Oliver, mounted as should be the proprietor of Harewood and the leader of the hunt in the necks of the Patapsco—a grand looking man, far advanced in years, his few remaining locks snow-white, but with all the vitality and vigor of youth. Straight as an arrow, broad-chested and with the seat of a soldier in a saddle; frank and joyous in his manner, his very voice was inspiration, so cheerful and so resonant—the impersonation of the "fine old English gentleman," all of the olden time. He went at the gap [left by the contractors in the construction of the grade of the railroad] carelessly and gracefully; and when across stood in his stirrups and laughed at the hesitation of those who were to follow. If ever the title of "merchant prince" fitted any one it was Mr. Robert Oliver.

Next came Alexander Brown, with the grand frame of Mr. Oliver, but without that *abandon* which on such an occasion was the latter's peculiar characteristic. To Mr. Brown everything was a matter of business and the hunt at Harewood knew him not. The exchange, the ocean, distant lands gave him his amusement. Warily, yet fearlessly, he crossed the gap, and the two Irishmen stood together watching their companions.

Mr William Lorman followed, with his florid complexion, business aspect, keen bright eye and quiet self-possession. No stranger, he, to horsemanship.

Then came Mr. John McKim, Jr., a large square-built man, with strongly marked Roman features, the character of whose expression was acute intelligence, but who rode with caution, as if the occasion was unfamiliar.

Millions had now crossed, and it came the turn of Mr. Alexander Fridge, whose careful hesitating guidance of his horse showed that an inexpert rider feared an accident; and had one befallen him all Baltimore would have mourned—for a purer man, one of simpler or less ostentatious habits, or of more expanded benevolence, speaking in the tones of his voice and in the kindliest countenance, existed not in our midst.

Following Mr. Fridge came Mr. William Patterson, a small spare man, of dark complexion, with great determination in his quiet look—brief of speech, the very opposite of Mr. Oliver in outward carriage, but his equal in strong intelligence, sagacity and power. Another million crossed the gap when he joined those, who had gone before. Isaac McKim, spare and thin-visaged, acute and cautious, the only merchant of them all who sought political life—who built a ship and sent her, bearing his wife's name, around the world; whose beauty, the ship's not more than the lady's, was the pride of Baltimore. Talbot Jones, a representative man, prudent on horseback as on 'Change—a merchant, too, liberal and enlightened in all his views, and whose whole heart was in the railroad. George Hoffman, refined and eminently courteous in his bearing, prominent as a merchant and the head of a family which was in those days a power in Baltimore. John B. Morris, a gallant horseman, the handsomest of the group, as he was the youngest of the directors. William Steuart, afterwards Mayor of Baltimore, came next; and last, Mr. Philip E. Thomas, the president, on his ambling nag, with a kind word for all, and by all looked up to as the leader in the enterprise, followed in the path, now well beaten, while at his side was George Brown, the treasurer, whose active intellect was devoted to the interests of the company—who made it the hobby of his life, and who, as he rode along, discussed the work, utterly careless of his horsemanship. . . . These were the men, or at all events the most prominent of the men, who planned our great road to the West. They were the true conscript fathers of the city. They represented its wealth—its enterprise—its perseverance. They were the pioneers of the railroad system in America. . . .

At another time Mr. Latrobe had discussed the personality of Charles Carroll of Carrollton, saying that he was:

> . . . a spare attenuated old man, verging on his four score years and ten, small in size but active in his movements, with eyes still bright and sparkling, with a voice thin now and feeble, but clear and distinct, as in emphatic utterances, the venerable and venerated man prophesied the success of the great work [the Baltimore and Ohio Railroad]. . . .

Now, what manner of man was this Latrobe, who, many years ago, had established himself as one of the most intelligent and fascinating of the early historians of the Baltimore and Ohio? In a word it may be said that he attained a most unusual distinction—not reached by any other important officer of an American railroad: For sixty-four years, from the inception of the company, in 1827, until his death in 1891, John H. B. Latrobe was the counsel of the Baltimore and Ohio Railroad Company, although for many years his fees were pitiably inconsequential. Truly a remarkable record.

A brother, Benjamin H. Latrobe, shared distinction with him in the early years of the enterprise. Both were sons of that gifted early American architect, Benjamin H. Latrobe, who had planned in many details the original Capitol at Washington, and so earned for himself an imperishable fame. The elder Latrobe had been called to Washington by President Thomas Jefferson—himself a passionate lover of good architecture—early in the nineteenth century, to finish an edifice far, far from completion. In 1803 he took charge of the building of the Capitol. He was given copies of the original plans for the structure, which were, however, useless to him. He had to work the thing out himself. This he did, with results that are apparent to this day. The exquisite Corinthian capitals in the older part of the building, carved in the details of the American corn and the tobacco, are fanciful reminders of the great architect who for many years engaged himself upon it—at the munificent salary of $1700 a year!

These two sons the federal architect had—Benjamin and John. The first of them was educated to be a lawyer, the other sent to West Point to receive the splendid engineering training which the Military Academy gave, even in that early day. But, alas, for the futility of parental hopes and plans! It was John H. B. Latrobe who shortly became the lawyer; and Benjamin, the engineer. Each in his finally chosen field attained a large distinction. Each for many years was of tremendous service in the moulding of the Baltimore and Ohio Railroad. If the elder Latrobe's imperishable monument is in the walls of the Washington Capitol, not less truly is that of his engineer son in the remarkable stone viaduct at Relay, nine miles west of Baltimore, a bridge originally builded for the lightest form of early locomotives, and today—unchanged in a single detail of its construction—carrying, easily, the heaviest types of locomotives known in the United States. While John H. B. Latrobe's many memorials today rest in the archives of the law department of the Baltimore and Ohio— in the important early papers which he drew up for the company.

The splendid and thorough training which John H. B. Latrobe received at West Point stood him in good stead throughout the rest of his long and very active life. Yet, aside from his appearance—almost to the end of his days he was tall and straight as a ramrod—there was little about him to suggest the military man. Far more to bring to mind the student or the artist. In after years, John K. Cowen was to write of Mr. Latrobe, who was still living, saying:

. . . I ask you to bear with me a moment while I speak of my friend Latrobe, himself. I regard him as one of the most interesting figures in the history of the railroads of this country. He wrote the address delivered at the laying of the corner stone of the Baltimore and Ohio Railroad on the 4th day of July, 1828. He was one of the counsel who prepared its charter. . . . From that day to this he has been its advocate and legal adviser. . . . He is . . . a bright example of what a man can do, who,

while devoting more hours than most of us who have the
physical strength to devote to the arduous labors of a profession, has still been able to cultivate that which is graceful in life.
. . . Within ten years past I have known Mr. Latrobe to be,
at the early hour of six in the morning, at his canvas with the
brush which he handles with such skill and cleverness; and I
know the fact that many an hour which otherwise might have
been an idle one has been filled by him with graceful lines. . . .

. . . .

At most times has the Baltimore and Ohio Railroad been
greater than the men who have guided and directed its fortunes.   Yet, as these have succeeded, individually, the road
has succeeded; as they have failed, the property has failed.
We live today in the great mechanical age of all time; and yet
today our huge intricacies of mechanism remain utterly dependent upon a single factor—the human one.

Because the men who came originally to guide the fortunes
of the Baltimore and Ohio ran true, their enterprise ran true.
In the end, arguments and dissensions mattered not.   The
seeming refusal of Congress to aid the newborn and struggling
rail highway—stupid and politically narrow—was overcome,
and so was the hard and bitter opposition of the Chesapeake
and Ohio Canal Company and others of its sort.   America's
first railroad persevered and prospered because the men who
first instituted it were of the hard, clear-minded sort who do
not know failure.   Mr. Latrobe painted them in none too
glowing colors. . . .

A modern railroad, as we know it in these days, is infinitely
greater than the men who create and who operate it; and yet,
paradoxically, it remains forever dependent upon man; his
ability, his judgment, his foresight, his honesty. . . .   The
Baltimore and Ohio, now past its one-hundredth birthday, is a
living proof of this statement.

CHAPTER V

GETTING DOWN TO HARD WORK

Actual Construction Begins—The Problem of the Bridges—Wood Against Stone—The Carrollton Viaduct—Labor Troubles on the New Road—The Question of Track—The Line Prepares for Business.

EACH of the twenty-six contracts for the construction of the railroad between Baltimore and Ellicotts Mills had not only been let by the first day of October, 1828, but work had actually begun upon all of them. Notwithstanding a nation-wide shortage of labor throughout the United States, because of the many other large public works in progress at just that time, great numbers of workingmen, horses, wagons and other paraphernalia of construction were being assembled. . . . Yet, the work dragged with a painful slowness. There were still more demands upon the citizens of the Maryland towns which were participating in it, for further cash payments upon their subscriptions, and for a long time but little actual construction to be shown them for their money. . . . The men who rode with John H. B. Latrobe out to Gadsbys Run late in that year of 1828, well needed all the enthusiasm that they could summon to their aid. The Gadsbys Run embankment, a huge work in itself—nearly a mile in length and from thirty to fifty feet in height—dragged wearily. . . .

Yet, at no time did construction cease. Nor did the ardor of the small group of men who formed the board of directors of the Baltimore and Ohio Railroad Company die. Not even when there appeared in the New York *Commercial Advertiser*, of January 2, 1829, this sort of thing:

The Baltimore and Ohio Railroad Company are calling upon Hercules. They have solicited a subscription of stock from the government. I do not believe that their request will be granted. The company is at present in bad odor. *It is thought that they had no other idea in getting up their scheme than to discourage the Chesapeake and Ohio Canal of which the Baltimoreans are unreasonably jealous.* Their stock, which by dint of puffing was raised to seventeen dollars for one dollar paid in, fell to below par the moment the passage of the bill authorizing the subscription of a million dollars on the part of the government to the Chesapeake and Ohio Canal was known in Baltimore. . . .

To this slur Baltimore lost no time in responding. In the *American* of January 5 we read:

We would caution the author of the [above] paragraph to be more scrutinous when he writes another of the information that is given him. The words in italics contain a notable discovery. This scheme of discouraging the Chesapeake and Ohio Canal must be allowed to be a pretty costly one when it is known that some years have now passed in making surveys of the country betwixt this place and the Ohio by engineers of the first talent in the country, many or most of them in the employ of the government; that the land . . . has been purchased, of course at some expense, by the company; that the location of the road has been established for a considerable distance; and that finally the excavation, bridging and final formation of the road have been commenced and in some places already completed on the first twelve miles and these allowed to present as great difficulties as any other part of the route, even over the Alleghanies. The last fact we assert on the best authority. Other considerable outlays of money have been made and all this only to discourage the Chesapeake and Ohio Canal Company! To this piece of jugglery, too, the corporation of the city of Baltimore and even the state of Maryland, itself, have lent a hand, each having subscribed $500,000 of the stock. If, therefore, the company is in bad odor, it is in the same way that a managing enterprising man gets the ill-will

of less thrifty and judicious neighbors. . . . This *bubble* of a
railroad will take a still gayer hue by the Fourth of July next
when it is pretty certain that the first twelve miles of the railroad will be in complete operation. By that time *Hercules*
may be inclined to give his assistance as we shall have complied
with the required condition of having first "put our shoulders
to the wheel" and that with a vigor which will receive its just
commendation hereafter.

The editor of the *Baltimore American* must have had a
great time when he penned those paragraphs. Even though
the following Fourth of July was still to see the first twelve
miles far indeed from completion. It was something, however,
to have a chance to crack back at the friends of the canal and
the opponents of the railroad.

.   .   .   .

The construction of the line had not proceeded far before a
highly important problem arose: It was found that it was
necessary to adopt a policy, and that at once, in regard to the
construction of bridges upon the new line. . . . There would
be many of these.

Here was an opportunity for fresh discussion—and dis-
sension—right within the ranks of the company itself. Wever,
the superintendent of construction, took a position that, in
each instance, these structures should be built of masonry.
Colonel Long expressed his belief that this was far too expensive a course; he favored the use of wooden bridges wherever
they were possible, and accused Wever of being both "arrogant
and obnoxious in regard to his authority." President Thomas
supported Wever's position; with Jonathan Knight, the
remaining member of the road's board of engineers, hesitating
between them. Eventually, Mr. Thomas resigned from the
board of engineers and left it to fight out its own battles.
Which resulted in its gaining the approval of the company's
directors for stone bridges everywhere upon the first division
of the road, with one exception; Colonel Long was to be per-

THE CARROLLTON VIADUCT NEAR BALTIMORE.

The first bridge upon the Baltimore and Ohio, completed in 1829 and still in use.

From an early print in *Ballou's Pictorial Drawing-room Companion.*

THE EARLIEST TRACK.

Wooden stringers under iron strap rails. A little later, stone stringers were used.

From a photograph of a reproduced model track section.

mitted to erect a wooden bridge at the point where the Washington and Baltimore Turnpike was carried over the tracks of the new railroad, some four or five miles outside Baltimore.

This was Long's opportunity. And how the soul of the skilled army engineer rose to it! Presently he had fabricated his structure, of which he was so passing proud that he named its type, after the President of the United States, the Jackson Bridge, and had it patented.

Forty feet above the level of the railroad, 109 feet in length, and carrying a single eighteen-foot roadway upon its deck, the entire bridge was wrought in fine white pine. It was a delicate-looking affair, its trusses constructed of timbers, for the most part but six inches square; the largest of them did not exceed six by eight inches in width. The connection of its members was effected by means of an intricate system of locking and of splicing; the latter had never been developed before in bridge architecture. . . . All made to the slender appearance of the entire structure.

And yet Long's bridge, costing but $1100 to erect at that time, delicate as it might appear to the layman, stood well to the task it was to bear. It is related that it actually sustained about eighty head of cattle, driven over it in a close gang; and this, without the least apparent yielding in its truss frames. . . . Neither coach nor wagon, heavily laden as it might well be, had to slacken its speed to cross upon it.

.   .   .   .

Nevertheless, Colonel Long's brilliant Jackson Bridge is gone these many years, while the stout Carrollton Viaduct, nearby and builded contemporaneously with it, still stands bravely to the hard tasks imposed upon it. Three-hundred-ton locomotives may today roll over it at full speed, even though the last of its masonry courses was set in place almost one hundred years ago. It is possible that a hundred years hence, or perhaps five hundred, the Carrollton Viaduct still will be carrying the locomotives and the trains of the Baltimore and Ohio.

Because it was the first large bit of bridge construction attempted upon a railroad anywhere within the United States, this viaduct deserves a paragraph or two of attention: It is 312 feet in length; the height of the structure from the surface of Gwynns Falls, which passes underneath, being 51 feet, 9 inches. Two railroad tracks have always crossed upon it, with footpaths upon either side of them.

The structure, into which went some 12,000 perches of stone, is divided into a main arch and a side one. Through the larger opening pass the swift running waters of Gwynns Falls. Through the side arch originally went a wagon road. It is the larger arch, however, which to this day commands the admiration of the engineer, no matter whence he may have come. It was no easy task, setting in place that giant eighty-foot span. Many tons of the heavy granite were laid upon its temporary wooden centers before it finally was keyed and made able to sustain itself. It is written in the records of its construction that the wooden structures finally held 1500 tons before the arch was completed. And yet the centers themselves had not yielded so much as one-eighth of an inch. . . . They were real master builders, those days!

The stone for the building of the Carrollton Viaduct, for the most part, came from the vicinity of Ellicotts Mills; the rest of it from Port Deposit, upon the lower Susquehanna. It was all carefully dressed and measured before being swung into place. And yet, the entire structure, begun about the middle of May, 1829, was practically finished and crossed by a man on horseback on the seventh of the following November. Caspar Wever, who had charge of its construction, and James Lloyd, its architect, worked swiftly, as well as thoroughly.

.   .   .   .

Other stone bridges, some of them of a fair degree of importance, were to come into existence on the line of the new railroad to Ellicotts Mills and beyond; but, until the opening of the Washington Branch and the construction by

Latrobe of the remarkable Thomas Viaduct at Relay House, nothing was to rival the Carrollton Viaduct, either in size or in beauty. . . . Over the first stream that swept itself across its course, the Baltimore and Ohio Railroad achieved a real triumph—nothing less. . . . Wever may have had his disagreeable traits. Eventually, Captain McNeill quarreled with him, bitterly, and finally parted with him, to go with the Susquehanna Railroad. . . . Caspar Wever came from a region—the pioneer Ohio ccuntry—and at a time when diplomacy was a virtue often scorned. But that he was a master builder, no one can deny. . . .

. . . .

One other important stone bridge, long since disappeared, must have attention. It was named after William Patterson, and it spanned the Patapsco about halfway between the Relay House and Ellicotts Mills. History records it as a fine stone-arch structure, of four spans, and in all some 375 feet in length. It was designed by Wever and built under the close supervision of one of his lieutenants, one John McCartney. For many years it carried the main line of the railroad over its first crossing of the Patapsco. When came, ultimately, the revision and the straightening of the line through that rather narrow and tortuous valley, the tracks were carried through a short tunnel in the breast of a protruding hill on the westerly side of the valley and the Patterson Viaduct finally abandoned. . . . It was, in its day, a fairly pretentious structure. The record of it is that it was begun on the sixth of May, 1829, and that upon the following fourth of December it was first crossed by William Patterson, on horseback.

. . . .

That summer of 1829 must have been a brisk one, indeed, upon the Baltimore and Ohio. . . . A season of rather feverish activities. . . . Men coming and men going, all the while. . . . Endeavor. . . . Progress. . . .

"The works at the Deep Cut are being prosecuted with energy," writes a visitor to it, early in July of that year. "A like progress is visible on other parts of the road." . . . A few days later—to be precise, on the Fourth of July—the corner stone of the small viaduct that was to carry the line over the Frederick Turnpike at Ellicotts Mills was being laid; again by the Masons. Again there was speech making, and again a band of music. But the event was in no way even to be compared with that notable one in James Carroll's field, but a twelvemonth before. For one thing, on the Fourth of July, 1829, it rained miserably, most of the day. . . . God spared from such a dire fate the preceding Independence Day. . . .

Prosecuted with energy, and yet not without drawbacks. . . . There were some accidents; a particularly distressing one—the first to be recorded in the history of the road—when four laborers, Patrick Hackett, Edward McCreary, Thomas Hughes and Daniel Ragan, were killed, almost instantly, by the caving in of a high bank of earth under which they were working. Two other workmen were seriously injured at the same time. . . .

There were numerous quarrels among the men; both between the laborers and the contractors, and among the workmen themselves. . . . Baltimore lived that year in a state of almost continuous apprehension. . . . Liquor was freely sold at the workmen's camps, and as freely consumed. Brawls were frequent. Through the heat of August, these seemed to increase, both in number and in violence. Until, on the fourteenth of that month, there came actual rioting, which culminated in the killing of one man and the wounding of several others; among these last, a contractor, a Mr. Elliott, whose house previously had been sacked.

Apprehension in the town over this condition of affairs led to indignation. And no little discussion. . . . A local clergyman furnished this statement to its newspapers:

Messrs. Gardner and Jessop, contractors on the Baltimore and Ohio about two miles west of here, made it known when they entered upon their section that they would receive no man into their employment who would make use of any species of distilled liquor or any kind of stimulating drink. Notwithstanding this unpopular condition these gentlemen procured their full complement of men (all of whom are from York County and form part of the German population of the section of Pennsylvania) and they are now prosecuting their work with exemplary industry and expedition; the hands are all in good spirits and frankly confess that they can do their work better and with more ease to themselves under the present restrictions than they possibly could without it. . . .

Messrs. Gardner and Jessop and their highly model forces must have been very exceptional upon the line of the new railroad, for a day or two later the *Baltimore American* gave a considerable amount of space to the agitation being suffered in that city by the continued reports of outrages committed on the line of "the Ohio Railroad." Its veracious reporter writes:

. . . . It appears that some days since, Messrs. Hahn and Elliott, the contractors on the tenth section of the Railroad, discharged some men in their employ for disorderly and unruly conduct. Finding that they could not get work on any of the other sections these men came to the house of Elliott (situate near the road) and threatened to take the life of himself and his partner. Some damage was done to the property of Elliott. Three of the men were arrested.

It became known, however, that the Sheriff was to go out yesterday morning and when he left the city for that purpose he was followed by a large *posse* of spectators, armed and unarmed, some of whom were influenced by curiosity and others by a determination to aid if necessary in the support of the law. . . . The Sheriff had little difficulty in getting his men. The only difficulty he experienced was in keeping his *posse* within bounds for, having come out to see a fight, they did not want to be disappointed.

In relation to the workmen on the Railroad we are assured . . . that the operations on the various sections are going on with all the regularity and quietness that could be desired by friends of the undertaking. The number of men employed is large and occasionally, through the too liberal use of whiskey, instances of intoxication unavoidably occur. These sometimes lead to broils and fighting among themselves and . . . have given rise to the many exaggerated stories which have been so freely circulated. . .

Strenuous times, indeed. And busy ones. . . . Times of real accomplishments. Here was George Winchester, citizen of Baltimore and president of the Baltimore and Susquehanna Railroad, on the eighth day of August, adding to the celebration of the one-hundredth birthday of the town, by laying, with much ceremony, the corner stone of his line, which was to lead off to the north, on to both York and Harrisburg in Pennsylvania. . . . Still further to the north, another railroad had been begun: the Mohawk and Hudson, leading from Albany to Schenectady, and which was in after years to form a part of the main stem of the New York Central. While, far to the south, was still another railroad, slowly reaching its way from the important port of Charleston, in South Carolina, back to Hamburg, just opposite from Augusta, Georgia, at the head of navigation on the Savannah River. Of a truth, the railroad age was being born! . . . Why, already a line from Baltimore to Washington City—branching from the route of the "Ohio Railroad" at Relay House (then known as Elkridge Landing)—was in contemplation. The Baltimore and Washington Railroad Company, with very much the same directors as the Baltimore and Ohio, had already been chartered and was advertising for subscriptions to its stock. Responses to which came in with at least a satisfying rapidity. . . .

All this, while swift progress on the grading and the masonry of those first twelve miles of the Baltimore and Ohio itself was being made. Quarrels and fights among the workmen, perplexities and disagreements among the engineers, could not really delay the progress of the enterprise. Steadily it moved forward toward its goal. . . .

.   .   .   .

On the first day of October, 1829, the laying of the permanent track began, close to the Mount Clare terminus of the road, and under the general supervision of Major George W. Whistler, U. S. A., superintending engineer, and John Ready, superintendent of construction of the track-laying forces. The actual work was done at the first by Thomas McMachen, foreman, and the following carpenters: Alfred Ray, Nicholas Ridgely, Silas Ficket and Wendel Bollman. The last of these names recurs many times in the history of the Baltimore and Ohio. It is that of a man who, eventually, became its master of the road and one of its best-known bridge builders.

That carpenters should first lay the rails of the Baltimore and Ohio was not particularly surprising. In the vicinity of Mount Clare they were placed upon wooden sleepers. Some of the very first of them were metal straps, laid upon wooden stringers as well as sleepers. This construction followed the principle of a temporary track which had been laid down at Ellicotts Mills, some weeks before, for the ready handling of granite blocks from out of the quarries there. . . .

This entire question of track for the new road was a real problem. Its engineers simply did not know. There were few precedents which they might follow. Major Whistler, together with Jonathan Knight and Captain McNeill, had been sent by the directors to England to make a minute examination of the two railroads already builded there; the Stockton and Darlington, and the Liverpool and Manchester. The ideas that they brought back with them were of importance in the first planning of the Baltimore and Ohio, even though some of them were not applicable to the American road. The solidity of English railway construction gradually evinced itself in the highly substantial workmanship of the first twelve miles of the American road.[1]

Because of the bountiful supply of fine stone roundabout Ellicotts Mills, it was quite natural that a permanent way of that material should be laid down in that neighborhood. . . . One method of laying it was curious, indeed.

In all, some 16,000 granite blocks were cut, each of them about fourteen inches square. In placing them in position, they were brought into continuous lines, with diagonally opposite corners touching. In this way, the rails, or the rail-bars, as they were commonly called at that time, ran diagonally across the face of each stone sleeper, being affixed by metal chairs to their centers. . . . The final effect was not unlike that of an old-fashioned tessellated marble floor.

It is obvious that this elaborate, and expensive, method of track construction could not long be continued. Gradually, wooden foundation structures for the rails came into general use, the rails themselves finally being directly affixed to the sleepers—or the ties, as we call them now—and there was evolved the present simple and efficient form of American railroad construction. . . .

.   .   .   .

[1] " . . . Two plans for laying the rails on the Baltimore and Ohio Railroad have been in contemplation; the one with wood sleepers and string pieces surmounted with the iron rail; the other with the continued stone sill, or string piece on which the iron rail should bear throughout. The English methods, which would have required about three times as much iron, were excluded on account of the great cost in this country of that material. The stone sills were considered next in cost to the English railway, but preferable. The method with wood was adopted on account of its still greater cheapness, especially on the parts where it would have been attended with very great expense and where the road-bed had not become sufficiently settled and firm for the more permanent work. . . .

" It was determined that in laying the part of the track from the city to the Patapsco . . . a distance of about 7½ miles, it should be done with wood sleepers and string pieces, but that the residue of the distance to Ellicotts Mills . . . about 5½ miles, should be laid with stone blocks and wood string pieces. The track has been so laid, accordingly. The comparative advantages of the two methods will of course now be tested by experience. . . ."—Jonathan Knight's report to President Thomas, 1830.

𝕺𝖋𝖋𝖎𝖈𝖊 𝖔𝖋 𝖙𝖍𝖊 𝕭𝖆𝖑𝖙𝖎𝖒𝖔𝖗𝖊 𝖆𝖓𝖉 𝕺𝖍𝖎𝖔
𝕽𝖆𝖎𝖑 𝕽𝖔𝖆𝖉 𝕮𝖔𝖒𝖕𝖆𝖓𝖞,

DECEMBER 22, 1829.

THE HONORABLE *Edward Everett.*

WASHINGTON:

    The President and Directors of the Baltimore and Ohio Rail Road Company, having completed a division of their road near to this city, and being prepared to shew, upon a limited scale, by the application of horse power alone, the advantage of this system of Inter-communication, most respectfully invite you, with such of your friends as may be disposed to honour them with their company, in the Christmas recess, or at any time during the sitting of Congress, which may better suit your convenience, to examine the Rail Road, and to witness such results as can be produced.

    Most Respectfully, &c.

PHILIP E. THOMAS, *President.*
Balt. & Ohio Rail Road Co.

AN INVITATION TO RIDE UPON THE RAILROAD.
Sent by President Philip E. Thomas to the Honorable Edward Everett.
From the company's archives.

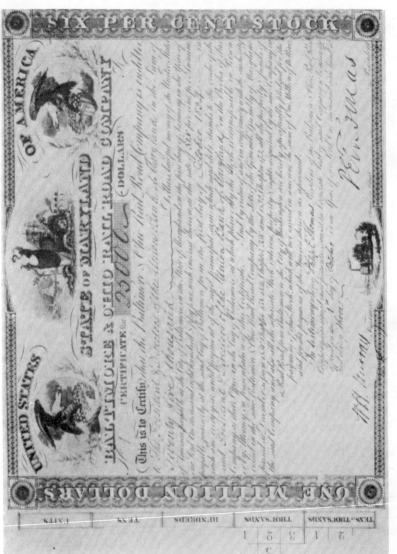

An Early Baltimore and Ohio Stock Certificate.

Issued in 1834 during the presidency of Philip E. Thomas.

From the company's archives.

The question of the proper gauge between the rails was another perplexity. Again there was neither standard nor precedent by which one might be guided. The English railways had followed the gauge ordinarily used in setting the wheels of burden wagons for the highways (itself, in turn, determined by the "draw" or width of the span of horses), a gauge going back to Roman days—specifically, that of the Killingworth wagonway (one of the early railway attempts in England), which had been definitely set at four feet, eight and a half inches. This early became fixed by the British as their standard railway gauge.[1]

In the United States, in the beginning, there was less uniformity. The rails of the Mohawk and Hudson were going down at four feet, nine inches, and those of the railroad in South Carolina at a flat five-foot gauge. The Baltimore and Ohio, for reasons which do not appear at this late date, first determined upon four feet, six inches for its track, but changed from this to the standard four feet, eight and one-half inches, before it began to lay its rails. The Baltimore and Susquehanna chose four feet, nine and one-quarter inches; the New Castle and Frenchtown—a very early road, over in Delaware—also took the present standard, four feet, eight and one-half inches. . . . It was all very confusing. And many years were to elapse before the confusion was to be ended. The first of the important Canadian roads, the Grand Trunk, was originally put down at five feet, six inches; and that monumental work, the Erie, at an even six feet. . . . The Ohio and Mississippi was another six-foot gauge. . . . Such shortsighted practices meant, of course, the greatest interference to through traffic. And, eventually, all the gauge mistakes that had been made upon American railroads had to be corrected, at no little cost.

.   .   .   .

[1] Only one of the British lines, the Great Western, ever had the audacity to depart from this gauge—adopting seven feet as its width between rails—and eventually it was compelled to return to the gauge which slowly has become the absolute standard for nearly every quarter of the world.

The rails for the original line of Baltimore and Ohio were of wrought iron, and after a little time they were being fashioned after the so-called "fish-belly" pattern, the diameter of the bar being widened appreciably between its bearing points on the chairs which fastened it to each of the sleepers. . . . At the very beginning, the rail was imported from England, although at an early date its manufacture, upon a sizable scale, began at Mount Savage, near Cumberland.

Congress having failed to remit the import duties upon rails in favor of the Baltimore and Ohio, they cost, laid down by ship upon the wharves of Baltimore, the very considerable price of $58 a ton.   Yet, the few furnaces in the United States which were able to turn them out at that time had quoted a rate of $90 a ton.   Which, of course, was not to be even considered.   The wrought-iron rails at the outset all came from England, and before the year was ended were costing the company but $54.50 a ton, duty included, and put down in Baltimore. . . .   Cast-iron rails made in that city were purchased in a considerable quantity, however, and used in the branches and the sidings of the new railroad.

.   .   .   .

As the permanent track went down west from Mount Clare toward Ellicotts Mills, it also advanced east toward the waterfront of Baltimore. . . .   After all the arguments and the confusions, the railroad had at last won its right to traverse Pratt Street with its tracks; all the way from Mount Clare through to President Street, which was already being talked of as a beginning point for a railroad toward the East, to reach as far as Philadelphia.   The ordinance of the City Council which permitted the railroad to occupy this thoroughfare—as well as some others—with its tracks, specifically provided that no steam power was to be used in it; animals exclusively. . . . Freight was to move no faster than three miles an hour.   And passengers, no faster than six. . . .

The question of cars or carriages to traverse the rails of

the line still perplexed the directors of the company. Also the more important one of the power by which they should be hauled. The steam locomotive was beginning to emerge from a purely experimental stage into one wherein it was becoming a thoroughly practicable agent of transport. In due time we shall come to it. In the meantime, it is enough to know that the Baltimore and Ohio directors were content to begin the operation of their railroad with horse power, although it was seriously proposed—as we also shall see in a moment—to *sail* the cars, like ships, under canvas. . . .

All these things were vague. . . . Highly perplexing. . . . After all, one knew the power of horses and the best ways of handling them. If it were finally found necessary, the line could eventually be operated all the way through to the Ohio by horse power, with the aid of the inclined planes at Parrs Spring Ridge, and at other mountainous points upon the line. . . . Relay House, eight miles out upon the new road from Baltimore City, gained its name from the fact that here would be the first changes of horses upon the cars. . . . The next would be at some point just a little beyond Ellicotts Mills.

Perplexing days. . . . But tremendous ones. A railroad, a really great railroad, in actual conception. The solidheaded citizens of Baltimore were in the thrills of the beginnings of a real enterprise. . . . More and more they journeyed out the Washington Turnpike to the southwestern corner of the town; to see for themselves this strange new thing that was called the railroad.

Finally, carriages were in operation upon the metals; wagons builded with queer flanged wheels to keep them from departing from the rails. Back and forth they went, in increasingly lengthening distances all the while. . . . Now Charles Carroll was crossing the great bridge which until this day bears his name, and now William Patterson over the viaduct which once bore his name and is now entirely gone. . . . And now a party of distinguished visitors is riding out over the line; not on horseback this time, but actually seated in a railroad car.

It is the first day of January of the year 1830 and the rails are down; all the way from Mount Clare to and across the wonderful Carrollton Viaduct. A remarkably mild and beautiful first day of January—how Heaven did seem to favor the important days of the new railroad enterprise—and many folk to ride in the new carriages; most important of them all, the Postmaster-General, over by the turnpike coach from Washington. On the morrow, the *Baltimore American* is to tell of all of it, after this fashion:

. . . The Honorable, the Postmaster-General, having reached the city the evening before and being desirous of visiting the Railroad, he was accordingly accompanied thither yesterday by the gentlemen attached to the Board of Direction. A carriage having been brought out, the party, consisting of twenty-four ladies and gentlemen, including the Postmaster-General, were drawn to the viaduct by one horse in actually a little less than six minutes! After alighting to visit the magnificent granite structure . . . the party again seated themselves and were convoyed back to Pratt Street in the same brief period or at the extraordinary rate of *fifteen miles an hour!* [The italics are the *American's*.] In order to show the perfect ease and rapidity with which heavy loads can be transported on a well-constructed railroad, three carriages were attached to each other and being filled with more than *eighty persons* were readily drawn by one horse at the rate of upwards of eight miles an hour. Averaging each passenger at 150 pounds weight and estimating the three carriages to weigh together two and one-half tons, it follows that a single horse has drawn a load of at least eight and one-half tons, at the speed of upwards of eight miles an hour. And this extraordinary result was accomplished without any apparent distress to the animal or indeed uncommon exertion on his part.

One week later, the Mayor and the City Council of Baltimore visited the railroad and again there was a task for the

one horse and the carriages.   A large crowd watched the city
fathers on the thrilling journey up to the viaduct and back,
a little more than a mile and a half in each direction. . . .
Every one now wanted to ride upon the railroad. To meet
their desires the president and the directors of the company
decided to operate some sort of regular service and to make
at least a nominal charge for it. . . .   Which brings us to the
next chapter of this book and the beginnings of the commercial
operation of the Baltimore and Ohio Railroad.

CHAPTER VI

TRAFFIC BEGINS UPON THE NEW RAILROAD

Operating for Revenue, at Last—The Perplexing Question of Railroad Carriages—Ross Winans and His Model—The Car That Sailed—The Treadmill Engine—Regular Train Service Begins Upon the Baltimore and Ohio.

ON the seventh day of January, 1830, the Baltimore and Ohio Railroad first began to be productive of revenue. For it was upon that day that, in response to a very genuine demand, the road opened its line from Pratt Street—at Mount Clare—through to the Carrollton Viaduct for public riding. Even though the riding was of a purely excursion sort. Announcements in the Baltimore papers said that the cars would be in operation from ten o'clock in the morning until one o'clock in the afternoon; and again from three o'clock to five o'clock on all days when the weather was favorable. Tickets would be sold for nine cents one way, or three for twenty-five cents. . . . Four cars, with a combined capacity of 120 passengers, were put into immediate operation. And it is recorded that they were kept busy for long weeks afterwards. . . .

This is the first instance in the United States where a railroad was ever operated for public use. The Delaware and Hudson's lines at Honesdale, upon which the first steam locomotive in America, the *Stourbridge Lion*, had operated the preceding August, as well as that at Mauch Chunk and the granite-carrying line at Quincy, Massachusetts, were in every sense private lines, serving but a single purpose. . . .

But the Baltimore and Ohio, at the beginning of 1830, was carrying passengers, for profit. Even though it was not until five months later that the entire first division of the line from Baltimore to Ellicotts was placed in service, with regular passenger trains for the accommodation of the public. Yet even then, no other railroad on this continent was ready for general patronage.

.   .   .   .   .   .

To go to Baltimore and not to have ridden upon the railroad was to have missed completely the chief lion of the town. . . . Several days after the inauguration of the new regular excursion service, the *American* said:

> The interest in relation to the railroad . . . appears to be daily increasing. On every favorable day large numbers of citizens visit the line and since it has been understood that the company have made arrangements to treat visitors to a ride to and from the viaduct for a trifling charge, they have had more applicants for seats in the carriages than could be accommodated. Four cars, capable of containing about thirty persons each, were kept busily in operation yesterday. . . .

On the sixteenth of January, a delegation of members of Congress arrived at Mount Clare and made the customary trip out to the viaduct and back. One horse again hauled all four cars, and it is said that this was a "common wagon horse, which previously had been employed the entire day in traveling on the road."

The fact that such astounding loads were moved by a single horse speaks volumes for the efficiency of the cars. . . . For almost a year the engineers of the Baltimore and Ohio had been working upon them; with no great success, until one Ross Winans, a resident of New Jersey, who had journeyed from there primarily to sell horses to the new railroad, took the problem personally in hand. . . . Winans quickly showed that he was a genius in this sort of thing. The perplexities of devising a carriage for a perfectly new type of highway evidently had no terrors for him.

Remember, if you will, that all this time there was no very serious thought of a motive power other than horses for this railroad; not immediately, at any rate. Despite the efforts that presently were made to introduce the steam locomotive upon it (of which very much more in due time), it was not until after the line had been completed through to Frederick that it ceased to use horses as its chief form of motive power. . . . It was to a horse-drawn wagon that the New Jersey horse trader, Winans, devoted his best thoughts. The problem in his mind concentrated itself toward a solution which would reduce the friction of the axles. . . . The solution, as it came to him, was to have the axles move with the wheels—as against age-old highway practice—and to have the entire rolling portions set in bearings outside the wheels. This, in itself, was a tremendous contribution to railroad invention. Afterwards, Winans took his remarkable idea to England and there he was robbed of it; but in this country he became known rather quickly as the inventor of the "friction wheel," as it was first called.

Dr. William Howard of Baltimore, son of Colonel John Eager Howard—a most accomplished and scientific engineer and architect—had already patented the application of an ordinary friction wheel to a railroad car. In the Howard patent, however, the main journal revolved on the outside periphery of the wheel, a rather awkward and complicated arrangement. . . . Winans arranged to have his wheel held by a projecting flange, on the inner periphery of which the main axle revolved, thus dispensing with lateral guards of any sort and completely solving the problem, at least as far as reasonably slow speeds were concerned. . . . After a preliminary test of 8000 miles, it was shown to have done no damage whatsoever to its wearing parts—under constant use these had merely become burnished, not worn.

Baltimore enthused tremendously over the Winans wheel.

. . . It welcomed its inventor to the town and from that time forward he became conspicuously identified both with its railroad and its other large enterprises. No man was of larger value to the Baltimore and Ohio Railroad in the early days of its existence.

. . . .

The Winans car first was shown, in miniature, upon a tiny track laid down upon an upper floor of the new Exchange. It was there displayed late in the fall of 1828 by Winans and by J. L. Sullivan, an engineer who had assisted him in the details of its construction. "The car is very simple in its construction and seems so admirably to answer its intended purposes as to leave nothing to be desired on the score of transportation," writes one who saw it upon that occasion. . . . The model was built to carry 400 pounds. Yet upon test that day, a half-pound weight, suspended from a pulley in the stair well of the Exchange, had drawn 460 pounds in it, exclusive of the weight of the wagon itself, 100 pounds. . . , The Baltimore merchants who gathered at the Exchange that day, and in the days that followed, were astonished at its ingenuity. . . . Mr. Carroll was finally induced to come to see it; and he marveled greatly at it.

The aged gentleman seated himself in the tiny car and was as pleased as Punch when the small weight, working over the pulley, drew him along the track. . . . Roundabout him were grouped the directors of the railroad, sharing his enthusiasm. They all were for the moment more like a group of boys with a new toy than the grave and experienced bankers and merchants of the town. . . .

So first came the Winans car into existence. . . . It was not many months thereafter before the inventor, having clearly demonstrated his principle of the proper type of railroad wheel and having moved its flange from the outside of the tread to the inner side and having evolved it into a truck, was placing two four-wheel trucks under the car, much lengthened, after the fashion which prevails until this day. With the lengthened car came cross seats. . . . The first passenger cars of the Baltimore and Ohio were open affairs, hardly more, in truth, than the boat-like body of a Conestoga wagon placed upon one of Mr. Winans' trucks. . . . The earliest closed ones were mere wooden boxes, with the seats ranged round-about their edges.

.   .   .   .

The horse car might have its own good position in the future operations of the Baltimore and Ohio Railroad, for the transport of produce and other goods, but it had its distinct limitations for the carrying of passengers. At least, such was the opinion of the impulsive Evan Thomas, brother of the president of the company. So thinking, Thomas entertained a belief that he might design a practicable railroad car which could sail before the wind. . . . And so was evolved the *Æolus*, which, under the charge of an expert sailing master from the Chesapeake Bay, made its first voyage over the rails of the Baltimore and Ohio on the twenty-third of January, 1830. The journey having been achieved without fatal results, it was repeated four days later, with De Witt Clinton, the distinguished engineer who had just completed the Erie Canal across the state of New York, as a passenger. History records the fact that, there being a good breeze abaft the land ship, she sailed nobly out over the Carrollton Viaduct and beyond, but before she could be brought to a sober stop, she ran into a dirt bank at the end of the finished track. The sailing master was not expert enough to strike the sail and apply the brake in time. . . . What eventually became of the *Æolus* is not recorded. The absurdity of the idea as any real solution of the problem for the motive power of the road became apparent. Yet before it had been thrust entirely aside, Baron Krudener, the Russian Ambassador at Washington, had ridden upon it, managing the sail himself. He was so pleased with the excursion that, before he left Baltimore,

THE SAILING CAR *Æolus.*

It refused to go against a head wind.

From a photograph of a reproduction used in the Baltimore and Ohio Centenary Pageant of 1927.

THE TREADMILL ENGINE.
It met its Waterloo when it collided with a cow.

he announced that he would send his suite over to enjoy "sailing on the railroad."

He did more. At his request, President Thomas of the company had a small model made of the sailing car, and equipped with miniature Winans friction wheels; the Ambassador forwarded it to his imperial master at St. Petersburg. . . . As he gave the sailing-car model to Baron Krudener, Mr. Thomas remarked: "Should our present anticipations of the efficiency of railways be realized, a total change would be produced in commercial and social intercourse in every country where these roads might be introduced." And that the discovery promised greater advantages to Russia and to the United States than to any other countries. . . . Mr. Thomas went forward, saying: "Should the Emperor introduce railroads into Russia it would not be many years before a railway would be constructed between the Baltic and the Black Sea, along the rivers Dwina and Dnieper, and such a road would enable Russia to encircle in her arms, not only the northern but also the eastern frontier of Europe, and thus greatly extend her power and influence."

To all of this, the Baron Krudener replied, with a fine diplomatic naïveté:

"My dear sir, you cannot suppose that Russia has any ambition, that she desires either to increase her power or influence! On these points she will remain content with her present position."

And yet, the fact remains that presently Ross Winans was sent for, to go to St. Petersburg and superintend the mechanical installations of the Russian railroads. In the Winter Palace he may have again seen the model of the sailing car. Almost certain it is that Winans and the sailing car furnished the imperial thought that afterwards led to the building of that remarkable direct railway line from St. Petersburg to Moscow.

Another odd form of car was experimented with in the early days of the "Ohio road." It also relied upon horse propulsion. Some genius had devised a scheme to mount a stout horse in a treadmill, upon a car (as they used to saw wood in other days), and by belts and gears to transmit the power to its wheels. . . . The idea seemed to have possibilities. . . . At any rate, the car was built and some of the directors of the road took passage in it out over their new line. According to contemporary versions of that ride, they got on famously for a few miles—until they came to a stout cow which had implanted herself squarely across the track. The cow, quoting from the same highly veracious historian, declined to yield the road to such an outrageous contrivance as the horse-power motor, and, inasmuch as there were no effective brakes, the train ran into the cow and the entire outfit was spilled into the ditch. No physical injuries were sustained, but the incident was made the subject of such atrocious puns in regard to the "cowing" of the party that the horse motor was then and there laughed out of court.

It was not to be until the coming of the steam locomotive that the Baltimore and Ohio was to find any real solution of its vexatious problem of motive power.

· · · · · · ·

Yet, in the meantime, the road was getting on, quite famously, with its horse-pulled cars. And steadily improving the quality of all of these. It became quite a fashion with it, whenever it had succeeded in evolving an improved model of one of these vehicles, to roll it down under the trees in Monument Square in the center of the town and there show it to the admiring multitudes.

There it was—squarely in front of Barnum's Hotel—that Richard Imlay of Philadelphia, in the hot August of 1830, placed his gaily painted new "Improved Passenger Car" for the delectation of the Baltimoreans. They came to it, to see, to admire, and finally to place themselves upon its cushioned seats and fancy themselves riding off to the Ohio on the railroad. Of it, the indefatigable reporter of the *American* wrote:

A number of persons visited Monument Square yesterday, for the purpose of examining a very elegant railroad passenger carriage just finished by Mr. Imlay, and intended to be immediately placed on the road. The arrangement for the accommodation of the passengers is, in some respects, different from any other which has yet been adopted. The body of the carriage will contain about twelve persons and the outside seats at each end will receive six, including the driver. On the top of the carriage is placed a double sofa, running lengthwise, which will accommodate twelve more. A wire netting rises from two sides of the top of the carriage to a height which renders the top seats perfectly secure. The whole is surmounted by an iron framework with an awning to protect from the sun or rain. The carriage, which is named the *Ohio*, is very handsomely finished and will, we have no doubt, be a great favorite with the visitors to the railroad, the number of whom, we are gratified to learn, continues to be as great as it was at the opening of the road.

For already the line was open—all the way through to Ellicotts Mills. This important event had come to pass on the twenty-fourth of May, 1830, after the *American* and the other newspapers of Baltimore had printed this very significant advertisement:

OFFICE OF THE BALTIMORE AND OHIO RAILROAD

20 May 1830.

Notice is hereby given, That the Railroad between Baltimore and Ellicott's Mills will be opened for transportation of passengers on Monday, the 24th inst.

A brigade of train coaches will leave the Company's depot on Pratt Street, and will return, making three trips each day, starting at the following hours precisely, viz.:

Leave Baltimore at 7 A.M. and Ellicott's at 9 A.M.
　　"　　　　"　　　" 11 A.M.　"　　　"　　　" 1 P.M.
　　"　　　　"　　　"　4 P.M.　"　　　"　　　" 6 P.M.

The price for the trip of 26 miles will be 75¢ for each person. Tickets to be had at the present means of accommodation, passengers will be under necessity of going and returning in the same coach, until a sufficient additional number of carriages can be furnished. As soon as this can be effected, of which due notice will be given, provision will be made for travelling a shorter distance than the whole trip.

P. E. THOMAS, President
Baltimore and Ohio Railroad.

Here *was* railroading, indeed. . . . No longer a mere plaything of a trip from Poppleton Street and Pratt just up to the viaduct and back, but a real journey—all the way through to Ellicotts, nearly thirteen miles distant from the city terminal of the road. . . . How all Baltimore must have contemplated the new railroad with surpassing pride that sunshiny May morning! . . . The day had begun with another of the formal excursions that were so excessively popular at that time and generation. Into the cars—the *Pioneer* leading the "brigade" and looking for all the world like a North Carolina shanty, neatly painted—had poured the president and the directors of the company, the Mayor of Baltimore and the City Council, the Senators and the Representatives of the city in the Legislature down at Annapolis, the editors of the city newspapers— the Baltimore and Ohio already had developed its publicity sense—and several strangers in town; among whom were to be noticed the Hon. Mr. Shannon, a member of Congress from Kentucky; Colonel Perkins of Boston; Messrs. Stevens and Sloan of the newly formed Camden and Amboy Railroad, up in New Jersey; Mr. Winter, the president of the Lexington and Ohio; and Mr. Townsend Wood, of Liverpool, England. . . . What stories all these would have to carry home; of the remarkable new Ohio Railroad at Baltimore ready to carry both passengers and produce upon its line! . . . Not the least of these passengers, the venerated Charles Carroll of Carrollton. It was almost his last public appearance. The flame of a long and exceedingly useful life was nearly extinguished. Yet, upon the pages of history it forever would be recorded that he was the only one of the signers of the Declaration of Independence ever to ride upon a railroad train. . . .

And now, the starter's bugle blowing, and the first train upon the Baltimore and Ohio starting punctually upon the appointed moment. What a record of promptness to set for future years! . . . According to prearranged plan, the *Pioneer* leading the brigade and setting the pace for the parade; its horse traveling at only a moderate speed so that the guests that day might the better drink in all the beauties of the line. . . . So many of these! How verdant and soft and beautiful it all was, that bright May morning! And how wonderful! The great new white arch of the Carrollton Viaduct gleaming out against the greenery of Gwynns Run, the excavation of the ridge at the Washington Turnpike, with Colonel Long's spidery Jackson Bridge directly overhead, the Deep Cut, the tremendous embankments at both Roberts and Gadsbys runs, the cutting through Vinegar Hill—all of these to be traversed within the first section or stage of the railroad. . . .

All of this, highly lovely. But hardly to be compared with the natural beauties to follow, in the narrow valley of the brisk Patapsco. Here the railroad on a narrow pathway, fully sixty feet above the bed of the tumbling river, twisting and turning all the way along its tortuous course. More granite viaducts—three of them—before the Patterson, which finally carries it across the Patapsco and up to the new stone station at Ellicotts Mills.[1]

. . . The cars are to halt at the Patterson Viaduct so that the party may alight and wonder at that fine new piece of engineering. . . . But as they swirl along, there is both talking and laughing—and silence. Bantering, as to this and as to that. . . . The silence of contemplation. . . . Here is Elkridge; already they are talking about building the new line to Washington out from the old one, by means of a mighty

---

[1] This station is still standing and in use by the Baltimore and Ohio Railroad for its passenger service.

curved viaduct to cross the Patapsco here. . . . Some of the men are laughing at Evan Thomas and his sailing car. They are talking, too, of Mr. Peter Cooper, recently arrived in town again with his small locomotive, the *Tom Thumb*, for experimental trials upon the railroad. Somehow, they do not laugh so much as they speak of the *Tom Thumb*. Awkward and ridiculous and clumsy as it may seem, it breathes an awesome sense of mystery into the hearts and minds of these Baltimoreans. . . . The men who are silent are thinking of this, perhaps—and wondering what this strange new thing, the railroad, is yet to bring into their lives and into those of their children and their children's children.

. . . Off and away. . . . Even the horses in the spirit of the morn. Why silence, this day? . . . This is the railroad, bright and new and wonderful. . . . The railroad to the distant Ohio. . . . The saviour of a goodly American town. . . . When the party finally is come to the brisk little community that already is springing up on the Frederick Pike about Ellicotts Mills, it will be quite sure to take notice of the construction work rapidly in progress beyond that point. Already the grading and the masonry are finished all the way to the forks of the Patapsco, another full dozen miles on, and Major Whistler is promising to have the track down over all of it before snow flies. . . . The railroad is in swift progress toward the Potomac . . . toward the Alleghenies . . . toward the mysterious and remote Ohio country. . . .

. . . .

For the return from the Mills to Mount Clare, there was no occasion for particular moderation, and speed was made. The trip back—twelve and one-half miles—was made in one hour and five minutes. While the minute examination of both car wheels and axles that followed, showed that not the slightest bit of damage had been done to either. Seemingly, both Mr. Imlay and Mr. Winans knew their business. And knew it well.

. . . .

Travel on the Baltimore and Ohio increased. Its fame spread still further. Folk came to see it from greater and still greater distances. It was a favorite objective for visiting journalists. . . . A correspondent from the *New York Commercial Advertiser* arrived to write of it for his newspaper. They were rather interested in railroads up in New York State those days. Of it he wrote, a day or two later in that same month of May:

> . . . On Tuesday afternoon I walked to the junction of the Fredericktown and Washington turnpikes where, at present, the Railroad commences; although I was on the spot some thirty minutes before the hour for the cars to start, I found the vicinity of the place of embarkation crowded with ladies and gentlemen, anxiously awaiting their turn for a ticket at a small office, similar to the box-office of a theater. I made several fruitless efforts to get a ticket . . . but did not succeed. Finally Mr. Patterson, who is a very large stockholder, got me a seat in the *Pioneer*, the leading carriage. . . . I must give you some description of a railroad stage coach. . . . The body is highly finished and fully equal to the elegant stage recently built at Newark . . . the wheels of iron, very strong, and only about twelve inches high. The body is placed upon a very strong carriage, or what in ordinary stages is called a treble perch. It is drawn by one horse, which is attached to a single pair of shafts, similar to those of a small dearborn. We had sixteen inside passengers and fourteen outside, making thirty to be drawn by one little pony, who stood ready to start the moment the horn sounded. . . . Shortly, the work of stowing the five other cars being completed, the signal was given and we darted off—the road for miles being lined with spectators. At the end of the first stage, seven miles, we found fresh horses awaiting our arrival, and the changing operations were only the work of a few seconds. . . .

Travel upon the new railroad continued in full volume, even after the very first elements of the novelty of it had worn off a bit. A full fortnight after its formal opening, one of the Baltimore papers was observing:

> . . . The railroad continues to be an object of very general attraction. . . . The four o'clock trip to the Mills seems to be the one most in favor at present and in order to be certain of the seats in the carriage at that hour it is necessary to secure them in anticipation. . . .

A few weeks later it was said that in the first thirty days of its operation the road had earned upwards of $1000 a week. The directors were more than gratified at this, as well as at the approaching completion of the second track through as far as Ellicotts, which would permit both a swifter and more reliable operation of the cars. . . . The road was coming on. . . . Faster and faster, all the while. . . . Trains of freight wagons were being added to those of the passenger carriages, as swiftly as was possible. Even then, ten times as much produce and other merchandise was offered the little new road in that summer of 1830 as it possibly could handle. . . . The receipts increased. By the beginning of October, four months after the cars were first put into operation, these had amounted to $20,012.36. This was considerably in excess of the operating costs for this period. . . .

The Baltimore and Ohio was born in a burst of real prosperity. Each year, each month, each week, almost each day, was to show an appreciable increase in its traffic. . . . Increase in accommodations as well. Early in July, 1830, one first finds the following advertisement in the columns of the Baltimore newspapers:

RAIL ROAD NOTICE

A sufficient number of Cars being now provided for the accommodation of passengers, notice is hereby given, that the following arrangements for the arrival and departure of carriages have been adopted and will take effect on and after Monday morning, next, the 5th inst., viz.:

THE PATTERSON VIADUCT.
Between Relay and Ellicotts Mills. It long since disappeared.
From a contemporary lithograph.

THE ARRIVAL OF THE EVENING TRAIN.

The coming of the horse-drawn *Pioneer* was an important event each day.

From a painting by H. D. Stitt.

A brigade of Cars will leave the Depot on Pratt street, at 6 and 10 o'clock, A.M., and at 3 and 4 o'clock, P.M., and will leave the Depot at Ellicott's Mills at 6 and 8½ o'clock, A.M., and at 12½ and 6 o'clock, P.M.

Way passengers will provide themselves with tickets at the office of the Company in Baltimore, or at the Depots at Fleet street and Ellicott's Mills, or at the Relay House near Elkridge Landing.

The evening Way Car for Ellicott's Mills will continue to leave the Depot, Pratt street, at 6 o'clock, P.M., as usual.

N. B.—Positive orders have been issued to the Drivers to receive no passengers into any of the Cars without tickets.

P.S.—Parties desiring to engage a Car for the day can be accommodated after the 5th of July.

.   .   .   .   .   .

Presently, riding on the railroad became a passion. Every one did it. People who were going west from Baltimore over the great National Road took passage on the Baltimore and Ohio for the thirteen miles to Ellicotts Mills, and the stage coach on from that point. . . . There were a few folk who viewed the new railroad enterprise with distrust and suspicion. These were the exception, decidedly. . . . But there were such folk.

The aged John Randolph of Roanoke, Virginia, riding north from Washington to Philadelphia in the early summer of 1833, refused to have anything to do with the railroad. It is a question whether he even took the trouble to gaze upon the construction as he passed over it on Colonel Long's lofty Jackson Bridge. . . . Randolph was a very old man and a very tired one, and for the greater part of the tasking journey he sat huddled in a corner of his ancient English coach, drawn by four horses, a postilion mounted upon one of the leaders. . . . Beside him sat his faithful servant, Juba. . . . The procession into Baltimore and up to the doors of the City Hotel drew throngs of people in the streets and, in consequence, Mr. Randolph was visibly annoyed. He shrank still further back into the cushions of his great coach. . . . The crowd continued to gather about the equipage; until finally it was necessary to bring it to a side door through which John Randolph presently was carried; in Juba's arms.

He probably was the last important traveler to reach or to leave Baltimore by coach-and-four. To Baltimore he never returned. Five days later he was dead. . . . Later travelers came and went by railroad. It was in fine fettle now. The iron horse had already completely replaced the one of flesh and bone as its motive power. The steam locomotive was the newest thing in the land. . . .

We anticipate. We are going too swiftly. To find the beginnings of the steam locomotive upon the Baltimore and Ohio, which are practically the beginnings of the steam locomotive upon the American railroad, we must return once again to that memorable summer of 1830.

CHAPTER VII

THE IRON HORSE ARRIVES

The Coming of the Steam Locomotive—English Developments
—The Rainhill Trials—Peter Cooper and His *Tom Thumb*—
Locomotive Tests on the Baltimore and Ohio—The *York*—
The *Atlantic*—A Railroad University.

IT was in the summer of 1829 that Horatio Allen first brought
the English *Stourbridge Lion* up over the new Delaware and
Hudson Canal into the wilderness of northeastern Pennsylvania; and at Honesdale, upon a crudely builded track, operated the first steam locomotive to turn its wheels upon the
soil of the United States. . . . It was not, however, until
the following year that serious plans upon a sizable scale were
made for the real introduction into this country of this new
and highly practical agent of rail transport. . . . In these
plans the Baltimore and Ohio company was to participate,
in no small degree. In the fall of 1828, Jonathan Knight,
Captain McNeill and Lieutenant Whistler had been dispatched
by the company to England, to make a thorough study and
report of the progress on the first railways being laid down
in that country; giving especial attention to the development
of the steam locomotive.

This is not the time nor the place to trace in any detail
that development; from that crude road locomotive of Cugnot,
which is still preserved in the Museum of Arts and Trades
in Paris, up through the remarkable experiments of Richard
Trevithick and others, to the days of George Stephenson.[1]

[1] Trevithick, a Cornishman, accomplished much. In his "tramwaggon," as
he was pleased to call it, weighing but five tons, he drew ten tons of burthen at a

Stephenson's first locomotive was produced in 1814 at Killingworth, for Sir Thomas Liddell, afterwards Lord Ravensworth. It was, however, hardly more than an experiment. . . . It was not until 1825, when the so-called *No. 1 Locomotive* (the *Locomotion*) of the Stockton and Darlington Railway was first placed in service, that Stephenson may be fairly said to have passed the experimental period of his work. This *No. 1* engine, which has been carefully preserved, may perhaps be said to be the first practical steam railroad locomotive in the world.

It should be understood that in Great Britain the situation at the outset was much similar to that existing here in the United States. Prior to the decade of the 'twenties, railroad development in each of these widely separated nations was limited to small industrial lines, chiefly those builded for the service of collieries, in getting coal out of the mines and to the nearest canal or other water navigation. . . . In the United Kingdom, the Stockton and Darlington, although a coal line, was followed closely by the vastly more important Liverpool and Manchester Railway, which was not a coal line, but a public railroad which marked the beginning of the real rail-transport development of the British Isles.

It was to see these two pioneer railways in a land far overseas that Knight and McNeill, accompanied by Lieutenant George W. Whistler of the Army—who afterwards moved to Lowell, Massachusetts, and became an engine builder there, and the father of a great American artist—sailed in a packet from Baltimore in the autumn of 1828.

---

west-coast colliery, and finally forty tons; thereby winning for himself a bet of 500 guineas. That was in 1804. Eight years later, John Blensinkop and Matthew Murray builded at Leeds an even better locomotive, which cost them £380, including £30 paid to Trevithick for his patent rights. The Blensinkop locomotives, as they became known, were manufactured for a number of years. A model of one of them was sent to the Czar of the Russias and excited a tremendous interest in the palace at St. Petersburg. William Hedley was another English locomotive builder of some reputation; but it was not until the coming of George Stephenson that that industry was really placed upon a firm foundation.

That winter, these three men made a minute inspection of
every railway, finished or unfinished, in the United Kingdom.
The solid construction of the Baltimore and Ohio at the
outset—the stout masonry bridges, the stone sills for the tracks
—was due largely to the impression made upon their minds
by the English railways. That railroad construction most
suitable for Great Britain, even in that day a long-settled and
intensively developed nation, might not be so practicable
for pioneer America, apparently did not occur to them.
But that the solidly constructed British railways weighed
most upon them, was evident when they endeavored to
force the Baltimore and Ohio, hard pressed for funds as it
often was, to lay down a similar sort of line, through a sparsely
settled, almost virgin country, for more than 300 miles—a far
greater distance than that from Liverpool to London.

The greatest attention given by these commissioners from
Baltimore was to the steam-locomotive progress upon the
English lines. Early in 1829, we find them writing back
home to this effect:

LIVERPOOL, February 4, 1829.

. . . We travelled on the Stockton and Darlington Railroad back and forth, with a locomotive engine, passing from
Darlington to Stockton, a distance of twelve miles, with about
80 tons, including the weight of wagons, in about an hour and
a half, and returning the same day with the empty wagons,
weighing about 25 tons—the ascent varying from nearly a
level to about 50 feet per mile. The snow had just been
scraped off the rails so they were not in the best state for locomotion. Some of the curves were nearly as quick as ours on
the Patapsco; the retardation on their account was perceptible,
but not as great as we expected.

Sometime before this and before the snow fell, we called
and witnessed some experiments on a portion (4 or 5 miles)
of this railway which descended in the direction of the load,
say towards Stockton, at the rate of ten feet per mile. The
load was about 70 tons. The locomotive engine descended

with this at the rate of about 15 miles per hour, hauling the train after it.   Then, to shew us the power of the engine, the motion was reversed, and the engine made to retrace its path, pushing the whole train before it up the same ascent at the rate of ten miles per hour.   The road had curves of nearly one thousand feet radius.   We rode upon the wagons, counted the revolutions of the locomotive engine wheels, and marked the time, so as not to be mistaken as to the velocity.   In addition to this, each quarter of a mile is marked upon the road by a post.

Upon the whole we have every confidence that we shall succeed with the Baltimore and Ohio Railroad. . . .

So felt Philip E. Thomas, too.   Yet, when Knight and McNeill and Whistler returned, they found the Quaker president of the Baltimore and Ohio so absorbed in getting even the first sections of his line laid down and completed that little serious thought could be given to the question of its motive power.   Horses were cheap and convenient and close at hand.   It was most logical that the Baltimore and Ohio should have begun its operations with this sort of power.

.   .   .   .

If the commissioners from the road had gone to England but a year later, they might have witnessed there the first dramatic episode in the history of the steam locomotive. This was the competition conducted in October, 1829, by the important new Liverpool and Manchester Railway. . . .   This event assumed almost the proportions of a Roman holiday. For seven days, five small locomotives battled on a short stretch of level track that ran under Rainhill Bridge, some ten miles from Manchester.   The holiday appearance of the affair was given by a band of music which was engaged especially for the occasion and stationed in a field nearby.   There was bunting outside the public houses and a great ado within them.   The directors of the railway wore bits of white ribbon in their buttonholes, and each day a crowd of Englishmen, estimated to be from 10,000 to 15,000, whose sportive instincts had been thoroughly aroused, gathered to witness the contest. Two hundred special constables, with difficulty, kept them off the rails.[1]

The terms for the Rainhill competition were very carefully set down. Each engine must "consume its own smoke"; if it weighed six tons—it was not permitted to weigh more than this—it must be capable of "drawing after it, day by day on a well constructed railway on a level plane, a train of carriages of the gross weight of twenty tons . . . at the rate of ten miles an hour, with a pressure of steam on the boiler not exceeding 50 lbs. per square inch." For smaller engines, which were to be preferred, proportionately lesser loads were set. It was further provided that there must be two safety valves—one completely out of control of the engineer and neither of them fastened down during the contest—and a gauge to show the steam pressure. While fifty pounds of pressure were set as a maximum, the boiler and other equipment must be ready to withstand a pressure of 150 pounds. . . . Other minor details followed. The railway company

[1] Of the five locomotives and the makers that entered the contest (ten were originally promised for it), a contemporary account in the *Mechanics' Magazine* gives the following details. The similarity to a horse-racing entry list will easily be noticed.

No. 1. The *Novelty*. Messrs. Braithwaite and Ericsson of London; copper and blue; weight 2 tons, 15 cwt.

No. 2. The *Sans Pareil*. Mr. Hackworth, of Darlington; green, yellow and black; weight 4 tons, 8 cwt., 2 qrs.

No. 3. The *Rocket*. Mr. Robert Stephenson, Newcastle-upon-Tyne; yellow and black, white chimney; weight 4 tons, 3 cwt.

No. 4. The *Cycloped*. Mr. Brandreth, of Liverpool; weight 3 tons. Worked by a horse.

No. 5. The *Perseverance*. Mr. Burstall, of Edinburgh; red wheels; weight 2 tons, 17 cwt.

The contests were run in heats, similar to a horse race. . . . The Robert Stephenson whose name appears in the above entries was the son of George Stephenson—at this time, the chief engineer of the Liverpool and Manchester—and the founder of the great locomotive works at Newcastle-upon-Tyne which to this day bear his name.

would furnish free of charge all necessary fuel and water for the trials and, in addition to giving a prize of £500 for the winning locomotive, reserved the right to purchase any of the engines for a price not to exceed £550.

.   .   .   .

Out of this great competition, Stephenson's *Rocket* emerged an easy winner. In fact, it was the only locomotive of the five that really met the terms of the contest. While it was agreed that Mr. Timothy Hackworth's *Sans Pareil* gave an interesting account of herself, and that the *Novelty* might have made the tests if it had not been for certain unnecessary defects in her construction, there was no disputing the fact that the *Rocket* far exceeded anything else shown. At that moment, it was the supreme steam locomotive of the world—and the fame of the Stephensons, father and son, was forever established. Later, that fame won at Rainhill was to lead them to attempt to establish a locomotive autocracy, not entirely unlike that established for a time in this country, in steamboat construction and operation, by Robert Fulton.

With the coming of the *Rocket*, the well deserved fame of the Stephensons was indeed firmly launched. News of the Rainhill trials traveled quickly, for those days, to America. And while the directors of the Baltimore and Ohio prepared to have a similar sort of contest here, some of its contemporaries in the United States began importing English locomotives. Not only did the Delaware and Hudson indulge itself in this way, but also the Mohawk and Hudson—just completing between Albany and Schenectady—the Camden and Amboy, the Boston and Lowell, and other lines.

Against this British influx, the locomotive-designing inspiration of the United States was, for the moment, stunned. But not for long. American mechanical wit soon was to pit itself against British. Very soon—a matter to be measured in weeks rather than in months—we were ourselves building steam locomotives in this country. At the historic West Point foundries, in New York, they were making the *Best Friend* which shortly afterwards was sent down to Charleston, South Carolina, for use on the new railroad there. The Mohawk and Hudson also was experimenting with an American-built locomotive and Peter Cooper was building his *Tom Thumb.* . . . The *Best Friend* exploded, but the *Tom Thumb* never did. You almost could have trusted Peter Cooper for that.

This is where Mr. Cooper first comes into this narrative. He was, as most people know, a very great merchant—a man of large ability and ingenuity—of the old city of New York. He had invested in the lands of a terminal and improvement company in Baltimore, known as the Canton Company. Baltimore was then a considerable distance from New York and Cooper worried a good deal about his investment down there. Its success hinged very heavily upon the success of Baltimore. Peter Cooper felt that, if the Baltimore and Ohio Railroad succeeded, both the city of Baltimore and the Canton Company would succeed. . . . But he was not at all sure about this railroad scheme, which was putting down so elaborate a line, seemingly without a definite plan for the motive power by which it was to be operated. . . . He went to Baltimore in the fall of 1829 and managed to get the directors of the railroad company to permit him to build an experimental locomotive for use upon their line.

That they were glad to give him this opportunity is hardly to be doubted. After reading the reports of Knight and McNeill and Whistler and conferring extensively with them, they had decided that the English locomotives were not to be for the Baltimore and Ohio. For one thing—and a most important one—their road was so radically different from those that were being builded in Great Britain. The British lines were virtually straight. Upon some of the early roads this side of the Atlantic, there were curves with a radius as short as 200 feet. Not only was England a more developed country, as has already been said, but her greater wealth had enabled her to build lines of less curvature and grade than was practical in a new land such as this. . . . The directors of the Baltimore and Ohio were quite convinced that an English locomotive, such as had been described to them, would not go upon their track. . . . Neither were they confident that it was adapted to the use of anthracite—a fuel which they felt they would be sure to use. . . . Moreover, they viewed with distrust and suspicion the growing hand of Stephenson upon the locomotive situation over there. The Chevalier von Gerstner, a German engineer who had just finished a short railroad in Russia—from St. Petersburg to Tsarskoe Selo—saw Benjamin H. Latrobe at about this time. Latrobe had expressed his surprise at von Gerstner coming to the United States to engage in railroading when there were so many good opportunities closer home—in England, for instance.

"That is the very thing I want to escape from," quickly replied the German engineer, "this system of England, where George Stephenson's thumb, pressed upon a plan, is an imprimatur which gives it currency and makes it authority, while here in the United States no man's imprimatur is better than another's. Each is trying to surpass his neighbor. There is a rivalry here out of which grows improvement. In England it is imitation—in America it is invention."

Out of this inventive spirit was our American railroad system born.

.   .   .   .

Peter Cooper came to Baltimore in the early autumn of 1829 and there began to build his experimental locomotive. He used the new railroad shop at Mount Clare to set up the device. Its engine he brought down from New York. Although comparatively small in those days—it was the following year that James Carroll generously gave another ten acres, adjoining the original plat, for the extension of the establishment—this shop already was fairly comprehensive. There were several buildings. Among them was a sizable car house, within which the railroad tracks ran at right angles with the road track outside, being connected with it by a crude form of turntable. . . . It was upon one of these lateral tracks that Cooper first began work; upon one of them, that autumn, that his first small locomotive—the *Tom Thumb*—carried for a few feet Philip E. Thomas, the Browns—father and son—and one or two others. While not in any real sense a locomotive run, this perhaps was the first transportation of human beings by an American-built locomotive.[1]

[1] The following is Mr. Cooper's own version of the coming of the *Tom Thumb*, as he told it years afterwards in the columns of the *Boston Herald*, July 9, 1882:

". . . The Baltimore and Ohio Railroad had run its tracks down to Ellicott's Mills, thirteen miles, and had laid 'snakehead' rails as they called them, strap rails you know, and had put on horses. Then they began to talk about the English experiments with locomotives. But there was a short turn of 150 feet radius around Point of Rocks [sic] and the news came from England that Stephenson said that no locomotive could draw a train on any curve shorter than a 900-foot radius. The horse car didn't pay and the road stopped [sic]. The directors had a bad fit of the blues. I had naturally a knack at contriving and I told the directors that I believed I could knock together a locomotive that would get the train around Point of Rocks. . . ."

Inasmuch as the Baltimore and Ohio did not get past the Point of Rocks until some years after the coming of the *Tom Thumb*, Mr. Cooper must have had in mind some other point on the earliest stretch. The quotation, however, is given just as it is printed in the newspaper.

". . . So I came back to New York and got a little bit of an engine, about one horse-power [it had a 3½-inch cylinder and 14-inch stroke] and carried it back to Baltimore. I got some boiler iron and made a boiler about as big as an ordinary washboiler and then how to connect the boiler with the engine I didn't know. . . . I had an iron foundry and had some manual skill in working in it. But I couldn't find any iron pipes. The fact is that there were none for sale in this country. So I took two muskets and broke off the wood part, and used the barrels for tubing to the boiler. . . . I went into a coachmaker's shop and made this locomotive, which I called the *Tom Thumb* because it was so insignificant. I didn't intend it for actual service but only to show the directors what could be done. I meant to show two things: first, that short turns could be made; and, secondly, that I could get rotary motion without the use of a crank. I changed the movement from a reciprocating to a rotary motion. I got steam up one Saturday night; the president of the road and two or three gentlemen were standing by, and we got on the truck and went out two or three miles. All were much delighted, for it opened new possibilities for the road. I put the locomotive up for the night in a shed. All were invited to a ride Monday—a ride to Ellicott's Mills. Monday morning, what was my grief and chagrin to find that some scamp had been there, and chopped off all the copper from the engine and carried it away—doubtless to sell to some junk dealer. The copper pipes that conveyed the steam

Peter Cooper is remembered as an extremely positive character. Yet he was never firmer in any of his beliefs than in regard to his locomotive. He was most sure that it would easily travel the short curves of the Baltimore and Ohio. He was equally sure that the crank—a feature of the early English locomotives—could be dispensed with in the change from a reciprocating to a rotary motion. . . . He built the *Tom Thumb* to demonstrate these articles of his firm faith. . . . It was, indeed, a tiny thing; hardly larger than a railroad handcar of today. It could not have weighed much more than a ton, but the principles that it demonstrated have continued to exist in locomotive building down to the present day.

The boiler of the *Tom Thumb* was no larger than those that are attached to the kitchen ranges in some houses; in fact, although of the same diameter, hardly more than half so high. It stood upright upon the small car frame. The lower part of it served as a fire box, the upper portion being filled with vertical pipes or tubes. Cooper improvised the use of musket barrels for these flues. To force a draught through the contrivance, he devised a blowing apparatus, driven by a drum attached to one of the car wheels, over which passed a cord, which, in turn, worked a pulley on the shaft of the blower. This somewhat cumbersome contrivance once came near being the end of the *Tom Thumb*. Of which, more in good time.

The *Tom Thumb* had but one cylinder, and this but three and a half inches in diameter. The wonder is not that finally

---

to the piston were gone. It took me a week or more to repair it. Then . . . we started—six on the engine and thirty-six on the car. It was a great occasion, but it didn't seem as important then as it does now. We went up an average grade of eighteen feet to the mile, and made the passage . . . to Ellicott's Mills in an hour and twelve minutes. We came back in fifty-seven minutes. Ross Winans, the president of the road and the editor of the *Baltimore Gazette* made an estimate of the passengers carried and the coal and water used and reported that we did better than any English road did for four years after that. The result of that experiment was that the bonds were sold at once and the road was a success. . . ."

PETER COOPER'S *Tom Thumb.*

This small, experimental engine was the first to be built and operated in the United States.

From a photograph of a reproduction shown in the Centenary Pageant of 1927.

THE *York*—1831.

Built by Phineas Davis and the first practical locomotive to operate upon the
Baltimore and Ohio Railroad.

From a photograph of a reproduction shown in the Centenary Pageant of 1927.

the engine ran so speedily, but that it ran at all. . . . Yet, run it did; and bravely, too. . . . Even though not without severe trials and anguish of spirit, both to its inventor and to the railroad directors. . . . For instance, there came a day —early in the summer of 1830—when the *Tom Thumb* ventured out upon the line, all the way to Ellicotts Mills and back. Mr. Cooper, himself, ran the engine. Attached to it was an open car carrying many of the directors of the line. . . . It was an interesting trip. The shortest of the curves were traversed without materially slackening a speed of fifteen miles to the hour. The small engine took the grades with comparative ease. According to Benjamin H. Latrobe, whose narrative of the event has come down through the years, the day was fine, the company in the highest spirits, and some excited gentlemen of the party, when the train was at its highest speed—eighteen miles an hour—pulled out their memorandum books and wrote some connected sentences just to show, apparently, that such a thing was humanly possible.

Yet, the *Tom Thumb* that fine summer's day was due for defeat; for a particularly humiliating defeat—by a grey horse. Let Mr. Latrobe tell the story:

. . . The great stage proprietors of the day were Stockton and Stokes; and on this occasion a gallant grey of great beauty and power was driven by them from town, attached to another car, on the second track—for the company had begun by making two tracks to the Mills—and met the engine at the Relay House on its way back. From this point it was determined to have a race home; and, the start being even, away went horse and engine, the snort of the one and the puff of the other keeping time and tune. At first the grey had the best of it, for *his* steam would be applied to the greatest advantage on the instant, while the engine had to wait until the rotation of the wheels set the blower to work. The horse was perhaps a quarter of a mile ahead when the safety-valve of the engine lifted and the thin blue vapor issuing from it showed an excess of steam. The blower whistled, the steam blew off in vapory clouds, the pace increased, the passengers shouted, soon it lapped him—the silk was plied—the race was neck and neck, nose and nose—then the engine passed the horse, and a great hurrah hailed the victory.   But it was not repeated; for just at this time, when the grey's master was about giving up, the band which drove the pulley which drove the blower, slipped from the drum, the safety-valve ceased to scream, and the engine for want of breath began to wheeze and pant.   In vain Mr. Cooper, who was his own engineman and fireman, lacerated his hands in attempting to replace the band upon the wheel; in vain he tried to urge the fire with light wood; the horse gained on the machine, and passed it; and although the band was presently replaced, and steam again did its best, the horse was too far ahead to be overtaken and came in the winner of the race.   But the real victory was with Mr. Cooper, notwithstanding.   He had held fast to the faith that was in him and had demonstrated its truth beyond peradventure. . . .

Brave little grey horse. Sad little locomotive. And yet how often is the race not to the swift! The victory of the grey horse was the last gasp of a mode of transport that was about to expire upon the railroad and which, within a century, would be battling for its own, even upon the paved highroad. The horse, and the order of things for which it stood, was doomed. . . . Peter Cooper fixed the fan belt upon his blower, you may be quite sure of that. And presently the *Tom Thumb* was out upon the track again—and the grey horse was not.

It was the occasion—on Saturday, August 28, 1830—of the completion of the important Oliver Viaduct, those three stout stone arches over the Frederick Turnpike, at Ellicotts Mills, and the *Tom Thumb* was chosen to draw Mr. Robert Oliver, President Thomas and the other directors of the railroad up to the ceremonies. Twenty-six men were the passengers of the car which was pushed ahead of the locomotive and which was estimated, with its wood and water, as well as with the load of the car, to weigh from four to four and a half tons. . . . A considerable load for a small, one-cylindered locomotive.

And yet, here is the log book of that particular trip; as it was written upon that very day:

FIRST MILE: Performed in 6 minutes, 50 seconds. The steam not being fully raised.

SECOND MILE: Performed in 5 minutes. One minute was lost in altering the switch to pass from one track to the other.

THIRD MILE: Travelled in 6 minutes. Two minutes lost in changing from one track to the other, the switch not being in the right position.

FOURTH MILE: Was travelled in 4 minutes, 30 seconds.

FIFTH MILE: Occupied 5 minutes, 25 seconds.

SIXTH MILE: Travelled in 6 minutes. One minute lost changing to the other track.

SEVENTH MILE: Travelled in 5 minutes, 30 seconds. The engine stopped at the Middle Depot [Relay House] for 15 minutes to receive a supply of water.

EIGHTH MILE: Performed in 6 minutes.

NINTH MILE: Performed in 5 minutes, 45 seconds; the engine traversing an ascent of 13 feet per mile and encountering the numerous curves of this part of the road.

TENTH MILE: Performed in 7 minutes; the engine still ascending at the rate of 13 feet to the mile and the Road much curved.

ELEVENTH MILE: In 7 minutes, 30 seconds; the same disadvantages of an ascending and curved line of Road being still encountered.

TWELFTH MILE: In 7 minutes, 30 seconds; the ascent being here 18 feet per mile and the line curved.

THIRTEENTH MILE: In 6 minutes, 30 seconds. The same disadvantages of an ascending and curved line being encountered as in the preceding mile.

Making the entire passage of 13 miles in the space of 1 hour and 15 minutes.

On the return of the Locomotive Engine at 6 o'clock in the evening the following results were realized—there being four additional passengers, or *thirty* in all, seated in the attached carriage:

FIRST	MILE:	Travelled in	5 minutes			
SECOND	"	"	" 4	"		
THIRD	"	"	" 4	"	6 seconds	
FOURTH	"	"	" 4	"		
FIFTH	"	"	" 4	"	4	"
SIXTH	"	"	" 4	"		

(Four minutes occupied in taking a supply of water.)

SEVENTH	MILE:	Travelled in	5 minutes			
EIGHTH	"	"	" 3	"	50 seconds	
NINTH	"	"	" 4	"	25	"
TENTH	"	"	" 4	"	10	"
ELEVENTH	"	"	" 4	"	40	"
TWELFTH	"	"	" 4	"	50	"
THIRTEENTH	"	"	" 4	"	50	"

Making the entire passage of *13 miles in 61 minutes*, including the 4 minutes lost in taking water at the Middle Depot. If this be deducted it will give 57 minutes as the time which the Engine consumed in travelling the distance. . . . The result under all the circumstances is highly satisfactory and constitutes another triumph of the efforts of American genius.

Yet not a result entirely satisfactory to Mr. Peter Cooper of New York. He knew full well that, at its best, the *Tom Thumb* was but an experiment, and so advised the directors of the Baltimore and Ohio. . . . For some weeks the *Tom Thumb* continued to operate upon the line of their railroad. In September of that same year it carried a group of Baltimore gentlemen who had attended a dinner at Doughoregan Manor, commemorating the ninety-third birthday of Charles Carroll; and came back to the city from Ellicotts Mills, according to contemporary reports, "in quick time."

The directors of the new railroad felt that the time had now come for them to take definite steps toward obtaining the best of steam motive power for it. Just how to take those

steps was puzzling.   Despite the success of Mr. Cooper's first
experiments, the pathway toward the steam locomotive seemed
both difficult and dubious.   Then, as they still were cogitating
as to the best means of securing their ends, came the news of
the Rainhill trials.   Each mail boat brought fresh details of
that great event. . . .   Then they made up their minds.
They would have a locomotive contest, right here in America.
They set to work to plan its details.   And in the *Baltimore
American* of January 4, 1831, one first finds this advertisement:

OFFICE OF THE BALTIMORE AND
OHIO RAIL ROAD COMPANY

4th January, 1831.

The Baltimore and Ohio Rail Road Company being desirous
of obtaining a supply of Locomotive Engines of *American manufacture*, adapted to their road, the President and. Directors
hereby give public notice, that they will pay the sum of Four
Thousand Dollars for the most approved Engine, which shall be
delivered for trial upon the road on or before the 1st of June,
1831—and that they will also pay Three Thousand Five
Hundred Dollars for the Engine which shall be adjudged the
next best and be delivered as aforesaid, subject to the following
conditions, to wit:—

1.   The Engine must burn coke or coal and must consume
its own smoke.

2.   The Engine, when in operation, must not exceed three
and one-half tons weight, and must, on a level road, be capable
of drawing day by day, fifteen tons, inclusive of the weight
of the wagons, fifteen miles per hour.   The Company to furnish
wagons of Winans' construction, the friction of which will not
exceed five pounds to the ton.

3.   In deciding on the relative merits of the several Engines,
the Company will take into consideration their respective
weights, power and durability, and, all other things being equal,
will adjudge a preference to the Engine weighing the least.

4.   The flanges are to run on the inside of the rails.   The
form of the cone and flanges and the tread of the wheels must be

such as are now in use on the road. If the working-parts are so connnected as to work with the adhesion of all the four wheels, then the wheels shall be of equal diameter not to exceed three feet, but if the connection be such as to work with the adhesion of two wheels only, then those two wheels may have a diameter not exceeding four feet, and the other two wheels shall be two and a half feet in diameter, and shall work with Winans' friction wheels, which last shall be furnished upon application to the Company. The flanges are to be four feet seven and a half inches from outside to outside. The wheels to be doubled four feet from center to center in order to suit curves of short radius.

5. The pressure of the steam not to exceed one hundred pounds to the square inch, and as a less pressure will be preferred, the Company in deciding on the advantages of the several Engines will take into consideration their relative degrees of pressure. The Company will be at liberty to put the Boiler, Fire Tube, Cylinder, etc., to the test of a pressure of Water not exceeding three times the pressure of the Steam to be worked, without being answerable for any damage the Machine may receive in consequence of such test.

6. There must be two safety valves, one of which must be completely out of reach or control of the Engine man, and neither of which must be fastened down while the Engine is working.

7. The Engine and Boiler must be supported on springs and rest on four wheels, and the height from the ground to the top of the chimney must not exceed twelve feet.

8. There must be a mercurial gauge affixed to the machine with an index rod, shewing the steam pressure above fifty pounds per square inch, and constructed to blow out at one hundred and twenty pounds.

9. The Engines which may appear to offer the greatest advantages will be subjected to the performance of thirty days regular work on the road; at the end of which time, if they shall have proved durable and continue to be capable of performing agreeably to their first exhibition, as aforesaid, they will be received and paid for as here stipulated.

P. E. Thomas, President.

N.B. The Rail Road Company will provide and will furnish a tender and supply of water and fuel for trial. Persons desirous of examining the road or of obtaining more minute information, are invited to address themselves to the President of the Company. The least radius of curvature of the road is 400 feet. Competitors who arrive with their engines before the first of June, will be allowed to make experiments on the road.previous to that day.

The editors of the *National Gazette*, Philadelphia; *Commercial Advertiser*, New York; and *Pittsburgh Statesman* will copy the above once a week for four weeks and forward their bills to the B. & O. R. R. Co.

   .   .   .   .

Here was indeed a challenge to American inventive genius. That American inventive genius did not respond more quickly to it must have been a disappointment to the directors of the Baltimore and Ohio company. They had hung up a generous prize and had not made the conditions of the contest too onerous.

Yet, truth to tell, there was comparatively little engineering or mechanical talent available in the United States at that time for such work. Again, the further development of England in the mechanical arts in that day and age made it far easier for her to bring forth locomotive builders when she most needed them.

So it came to pass that in the end there was no American Rainhill—no band of music playing in a great field and the directors of the Baltimore and Ohio wearing bits of white ribbon in their buttonholes. Yet, the directors having extended the time for the tests from June 1 to June 27, four locomotives presented themselves for it: the *Johnson*, with a peculiar double fire box, which had been built in Baltimore in the preceding year; the *Costell*, with a vibrating cylinder and built in Philadelphia; the *James*, built in New York; and the *York*, built at York, Pennsylvania.

Of these the *York* is the sole one that has come down in

history as having rendered anything like an efficient performance on that June day of 1831. She was built by Phineas
Davis, a watchmaker in that old Pennsylvania town.[1]   Phineas
Davis labored hard upon his engine, and late in February he
had it hauled down the turnpike to the railroad tracks at
Baltimore.   Of itself, no little task, over those high hills.   As
it went its lumbering way along the pike, it excited sometimes
the derision, sometimes the admiration, but always the interest
of the drovers and the stage drivers. . . .   After a few days
in the Mount Clare shops for final adjustment, it first ventured
out upon the rails on the nineteenth day of February.   Which
gave Mr. Davis several months to get his machine tuned to the
best working order.

The *York*, all told, weighed but three tons and a half.
This first real locomotive upon the rails of the Baltimore and
Ohio was mounted on four wheels, each thirty inches in
diameter, and similar to the "common cars"—all of this in
accordance with the specifications of the advertisement—and
it obtained its velocity by means of gearing, with a spur wheel
and pinion on one of the axles of the wheels.   Despite the
seeming awkwardness of this contrivance, the little engine
actually succeeded in attaining a speed of from twenty to
thirty miles an hour. . . .   It was the first locomotive in this
country whose wheels were coupled, so as to have a double,
instead of a single, pair of drivers.   Mr. Davis's boiler was a
double cylinder, the fire being on the inside of it; and the fire
surface being increased by a cheese-like projection which
hung down toward the heat.   Later, when the engine was
remodeled, this rather unsatisfactory device was removed and
a Peter Cooper type of flue boiler used to replace it.

There was nothing elaborate nor wonderful about the *York*.
Nevertheless, she met the test, and presently was purchased
by the Baltimore and Ohio for regular use upon the line.

---

[1] In this connection it is worthy of notice that another famous locomotive
builder of those days, Matthias Baldwin, the founder of the great locomotive
works that continue to bear his name, also was a watchmaker, in Philadelphia.

And in the *Baltimore American* of July 13, 1831, one finds the following paragraphs:

> By STEAM—We learn from the *Patriot* that the transportation of passengers upon the Baltimore and Ohio Rail-road will hereafter be by Locomotive Steam Engines. The Cars will now be conveyed by the Engine constructed by Mr. Davis of York, Pa.—which, after various alterations, has been rendered efficient and is fully capable of transporting 20 tons (including the weight of the cars) or 150 passengers, at the requisite or desirable rate of velocity. We understand it is intended that this Engine shall make two trips to the Mills daily, leaving the Depot at Pratt Street at 9 in the morning and at 3 in the afternoon. . . .
>
> Since the above was put in type we learn that the locomotive, the *York*, left the Depot at Pratt Street, yesterday evening with a common car as a temporary tender and having the large double-car *Columbus*, on eight wheels, and another passenger car, attached, with about seventy-five persons. The *York* proceeded to Ellicott's Mills in handsome style, at a speed varying from ten to twenty miles the hour and performing the last mile—which besides being much curved is an ascent of thirteen feet to the mile—in four minutes. The *Columbus* was left at the Mills and the *York* brought the whole evening train of five cars and perhaps one hundred and fifty persons to town. Including the *York* and tender the train moved consisted of seven cars. . . . It is understood that the *York* will be constantly employed in the transportation of the passengers for the future.

A large step forward for the Baltimore and Ohio! And one that was not to be retraced. Steadily the capabilities of the small locomotive were extended, until one finds it starting out of the Pratt Street terminal with a loaded train of fourteen cars—some fifty tons, all told. And an excited gentleman who witnessed its departure that day wrote that "it was out of sight of the Depot in about six minutes and the rapid gliding of the immense train was one of the most imposing and beautiful spectacles that I have ever witnessed." They took these things rather seriously in those days.

Eventually, the *York* began hauling the Frederick passenger train, and it is recorded that she did her eighty miles a day without appreciable wear and tear upon her mechanism. . . . Yet, she was regarded as but a forerunner of better engines that were to come. Phineas Davis and his partner, Gartner, kept steadily at work trying to improve the type of locomotive. In the summer of 1832, they placed on the road a second engine, the *Atlantic*, which has been carefully preserved in working order, from that day to this.

In the development and construction of this larger engine, both Ross Winans and Peter Cooper were of great help. The mechanical experience and the natural ingenuity of these two men were of vast assistance to Davis and Gartner. . . . The *Atlantic* was built to ascend the grades of the railroad—in which it met with a real degree of success. A task for which the *York* had shown itself quite incompetent. For the directors of the Baltimore and Ohio already had discarded their highly impractical and extravagant first plan of building a railroad all the way to the Ohio by means of a series of levels and inclined planes. In their surveys for the line beyond the Point of Rocks, the engineers were not hesitating to adopt gradients whenever these were found to be necessary.

The little *Atlantic*—with the *York*, the first of the so-called "grasshopper" type of locomotive—showed herself from the outset most capable. On a single ton of coal she ran eighty miles. She was the most efficient fuel consumer that America had yet seen.

The *Atlantic* had an upright tubular boiler, 51 inches in diameter and 69 inches in height above the grate; the diameter of her fire box was 46½ inches and its height 22 inches; the height or length of her 282 flue tubes was 16 inches and their diameter varied from 1¼ to 1½ inches. They terminated in a hot-air chamber, the upper surface of which was only about three inches below the level of the water in the boiler. The diameter

THE *Atlantic* AND ITS TRAIN, 1832.

Showing also the double-decker coaches built by Richard Imlay.

From a photograph of the original locomotive and reproduced cars.

ELLICOTT'S MILLS, MARYLAND.

As one saw that town in the days when first the railroad came to it.

of this chamber was the same as that of the fire box, 46½ inches, and its height but 6 inches.   The hot air from the air chamber passed through the boiler to the stack, by means of a cylinder 13 inches in diameter.   The top of the stack stood about 14 feet above the surface of the rails.

The locomotive's two steam cylinders stood close to the boiler.   Each was 10 inches in diameter and had a stroke of 20 inches.   The power from the pistons was carried by connecting rods and a shaft to a spur wheel, 28 inches in diameter, which worked upon a 14-inch pinion, attached to the axle of the forward road wheels of the engine, and caused them to advance two complete revolutions for each double stroke of the pistons. . . .   A fan, propelled by the exhaust from the cylinders, was used to supply the forced draught for the fire box.

Crude as this may all seem today, the fact remains that the *Atlantic* was—and still is—a creditable bit of locomotive mechanism.   She was immensely superior to and in every way far outdistanced the English *Herald*, built by the Stephensons, which was imported by the Baltimore and Susquehanna Railroad in that same summer of 1832.   The unfitness of the large wheels of the *Herald* for the short curves of the Susquehanna road soon became apparent.   It ran off the track constantly; and was almost entirely useless until a truck with a horizontal rotation about a center rose-bolt was suggested as a substitute for the forward pair of wheels.   This, accommodating itself to the curves and guiding the drivers, obviated the dangers of derailment.   So was the forward truck, or bogie, born.   And the *Herald*—in other ways a really practical machine—saved from failure.

.   .   .   .

In those days it was all experiment.   Much of it was guesswork.   Devices and practices changed; sometimes, it seemed, almost overnight.   For the guidance of the early railroad makers, there were no rules, carefully upbuilded in the

light of experience, to be set down.   Each problem they must
meet and solve as well as they possibly might. . . .   The
Baltimore and Ohio Railroad was in no small sense a laboratory.   Upon its achievements other roads, other men, were to
build.   It was a pathfinder.   Through the forests it led all
railroad America.

The truth of this is attested to in an editorial in the
American Railroad Journal for 1835, which says:

> We acknowledge the favor by the President of the Company,
> of a copy of the Ninth Annual Report of the Baltimore and
> Ohio Rail Road Company, and cannot refrain from here
> expressing our own, and we believe the thanks of the entire
> Rail Road community, as well in Europe as in America, for the
> candid, business-like liberal manner, in which they annually
> lay before the world the result of their experience.
>
> It will not be saying too much, we are sure, to nominate
> them the Rail Road University of the United States.   They
> have labored long, at great cost, and with a diligence that is
> worthy of all praise in the cause, and what is equally to their
> credit, they have published annually the results of their experi-
> ments, and distributed their reports with a liberal hand that the
> world might be cautioned by their errors and instructed by
> their discoveries.   Their reports have in truth gone forth as a
> text-book, and their road and workshops have been a lecture-
> room to thousands who are now practising and improving upon
> their experience.   This country owes to the enterprise, public
> spirit and perseverance of the citizens of Baltimore, a debt of
> gratitude of no ordinary magnitude, as will be seen from the
> President's report in relation to their improvements upon and
> performances with their locomotive engines, when compared
> with the performances of the most powerful engines in Europe,
> or rather in imagination, in 1829, only six years ago.

Truly, indeed, did the editor of the *Railroad Journal* speak
when he made these comments upon those early annual
reports of the Baltimore and Ohio company.   Each in itself
was a model, not only of succinctness, but of definite detail.

Not infrequently they contained diagrams and tables of figures which Ross Winans and Phineas Davis and Peter Cooper and John Elgar—the inventor of numerous switches, turntables, plate wheels and the like, early placed in service on the line —had found of real value to them and which, though relatively unimportant to the stockholders of the road, were of immense value to the engineers and head mechanics of other railroads. This was the Baltimore and Ohio's unselfish contribution to the common good. This it was that made it very easy to say that for the United States of that generation it was, most truly, a railroad university. Without the slightest exaggeration of the phrase.

.   .   .   .   .   .   o

CHAPTER VIII

THE PROGRESS OF THE IRON TRAIL

Early Railroads Across the Land—The Baltimore and Ohio Advances Toward the Potomac—Problems of Track Construction—Labor Troubles—Caspar Wever and the Whiskey Question—A Fatal Accident Upon the Line—Open to Frederick, at Last.

THE beginning of the fourth decade of the last century saw the railroad fever in the United States fast coming to flood height. From Georgia to Maine, all the way along the eastern rim of the country, new lines were being projected. Most generally, these began at a seaport, or at some river port having direct connection with the ocean, and continued straight inland. There was, as yet, little thought of paralleling the rim of the Atlantic with railroad tracks, even though the Boston and Providence Railroad, which was to connect the two chief seaports of New England, was chartered as early as June 22, 1831; and the beginnings of the Eastern Railroad and the Boston and Maine, both connecting Boston and Portland, followed but a very few years thereafter.

It was not until the late 'forties that New York and Boston were connected by rail. Long before this, however, similar connection had been effected between New York, Philadelphia, Baltimore and Washington. The line from Wilmington to Baltimore—the final link of this connection—was opened July 22, 1837. . . . A few years later, a through rail route, although somewhat indirect, was opened from Albany to Buffalo, at the foot of most of the navigation of the Great

Lakes. The Erie Railroad, extending as a single system from Piermont-on-Hudson, a few miles above New York City, to Dunkirk, on Lake Erie, was not, however, completed and opened for traffic until 1851. The Pennsylvania Railroad Company was organized in 1847, and, five years later, completed its all-rail line between Philadelphia and Pittsburgh. In the following year—1853—the New York Central was first organized and it then absorbed the various separate companies between Albany and Buffalo. It was not until a decade later, however, that it had an all-rail route from New York to Buffalo.

Again, we anticipate. We are talking of the 'thirties, and not of the 'fifties. In the first volume of the *American Railroad Journal*, under date of January, 1832, there appears a list of railroad enterprises in the United States, already under construction.[1] And it is by no means a lengthy list.

[1] "Baltimore and Ohio   Whole length 250 miles, 60 miles completed
     Mohawk and Hudson,   "   "   16 "   12 "   "
     Charleston and
        Hamburg ....   "   "   135 "   20 "   "
     Mauch Chunk ....   "   "   9 "   9 "   "
     Quincy ....   "   "   6 "   6 "   "
     Ithaca and Owego....   "   "   29 "   29 "   "
     Lexington and Ohio ..   "   "   75 "
     Camden and Amboy..   "   "   50 "
     Lackawaxen (Delaware
        & Hudson)........   "   "   16 "

"The following are now making ready or soon to be commenced:

Massachusetts, from Boston to Hudson River	200 miles
Ithaca and Catskill	167 "
Boston and Brattleborough	114 "
Columbia, from Philadelphia to Little York.....................	96 "
Baltimore and Susquehanna......................	48 "
Boston and Providence	43 "
Frankstown and Johnstown (on the Alleghany)...................	40 "
Baltimore and Washington City	38 "
Hudson and Berkshire.........................	25 "
Frenchtown and Newcastle	16 "
Haerlem...	6 "
Richmond and Chesterfield	12 "

In this list the Baltimore and Ohio was easily the longest of all railroads then under construction. Upon its completion and opening to Frederick, December 1, 1831, it became for a season the longest stretch of railroad in the world. An honor of which it was exceedingly proud.

.   .   .   .

Construction work through both to Frederick and Point of Rocks, on the Potomac, was vigorously prosecuted throughout the fall of 1830 and the summer of 1831. In order to give the contractors as much elbowroom as was possible, train operation was not extended beyond the station at Ellicotts Mills until the line was ready all the way through to Frederick. The building of the road west of Ellicotts Mills went ahead, steadily for the most part, yet at times with appalling slowness. Various reasons were ascribed for this. There were labor troubles. And the deliberate method of placing the track upon stone sills was another, and a very important, factor in the delay. The stones came but slowly from the quarries— there also was labor shortage there—and they were not always uniformly good. Once they had arrived at the right of way, many of them had to be rejected. . . . It all was tedious . . . and extravagant. . . . Gradually a tendency to eliminate the stone sleepers in favor of wood showed itself. In consequence of this wise decision, both time and money were saved.

It had been expected that the double track to Ellicotts Mills and the first track to the forks of the Patapsco would be completed in the autumn of 1830, but the delays which have

---

New-Orleans . . . . 6 miles
York and Maryland   ⎫
Tuscumbia   ⎪
Philadelphia and Norristown ⎬ Distance not known
    "   and Chester   ⎪
    "   and Delaware ⎭
Elizabethtown and Somerville Rail-road in New-Jersey."
—*American Railroad Journal*, January, 1832.

just been set down deferred this until the following January; while it was not until November, 1831, that the double track was laid to the Forks—twenty-five miles from Baltimore. Two months later, the single track had been completed to Frederick, and, five months later, to the Point of Rocks; the one sixty-one, and the other sixty-nine miles distant from Baltimore. And this was accomplished only by the elimination of the stone sleepers on the first track beyond the Forks. Presently Jonathan Knight recommended that a similar course be followed with the second track. He made a point of the fact that it would require two or three years for the embankments to settle to a point where they were really ready for the great weight of a stone roadway; in the meantime, the rails could be laid on a wood foundation—temporarily, at least—and the road brought into immediate productivity. Mr. Knight suggested that, with about forty miles of track already laid with stone sills, there was a full plenty for leisurely comparison; both as to first cost, durability, repairs and facility to the motive power.[1]

President Thomas and the directors of the road accepted Mr. Knight's recommendation in regard to the character of the track. . . . The granite and iron rail; the wood and iron on stone blocks; the wood and iron on wooden sleepers, supported by broken stone; the same supported by longitudinal groundsills, in place of broken stones; the log rail, formed of the trunks of trees, worked to a surface on one side to receive the iron, and supported by wooden sleepers; and the wrought-iron rail of British type were laid down and formed different portions of the line. . . . But the trend came steadily to a track formed practically as it is today; and with the gauge set permanently at four feet, eight and a half inches. . . . With the first of the English locomotives to come to the United States, had come also the standard gauge of the railways of

[1] At this late day, it seems strange that the builders of an important railroad should have found it necessary ofttimes to grope so blindly in the dark. It must be remembered that the Baltimore and Ohio was indeed a laboratory at that time. No man really knew. Everything must be worked out—in principle and in practice.

Great Britain. . . . All these things were working through.
In his report of the fall of 1832, Mr. Thomas said:

> Speculation is no longer necessary. Facts now stand in
> the place of opinions—results in place of calculations—and upon
> a full and careful examination, the Board feel no hesitation in
> assuring the Stockholders that the completion of the work to
> its termination on the Ohio, upon the plan first contemplated,
> with a double track of rails, is perfectly practicable within the
> original estimate of twenty thousand dollars per mile, including
> in the average the greater outlay upon the first division of the
> road, and this, too, without the sacrifice to economy of any one
> requisite of durability and excellence.

The University of the Baltimore and Ohio already was
beginning to earn firm laurels for itself.

.   .   .   .

It was not all plain sailing, that summer of 1831. Labor
troubles increased, reaching their culmination near Sykes
Mills—now Sykesville—where one Truxton Lyon had the
contract for the laying of the first track. Lyon had come to
his task well recommended; and throughout all the winter of
1830–31 he had gone steadily ahead. In the spring, reports
began to filter into Baltimore reflecting upon his personal
character, although in no way referring to the quality of his
work. Inasmuch as this continued good, the officers of the
railroad were inclined to let him go forward with it. It seemed
manifestly unfair to take the contract from him, just as he had
completed the hardest portion of it; the preparation of his
materials. . . . So he was permitted to proceed.

Yet, hardly had this decision been reached, when word
came that Lyon's workmen had struck, that he was in their
debt to a considerable amount and that he had gone. The
angry workmen threatened to tear up the track of the new
railroad. . . . The superintendent, Mr. Stabler, went immediately to the men. He succeeded in pacifying them, by a

BUZZARDS ROCK.

Along the original line of the Baltimore and Ohio, near Ellicotts Mills.

From a contemporary lithograph.

THE TARPEIAN ROCK.

An early landmark on the railroad, just west of Ellicotts. Long since removed.

From a contemporary lithograph.

promise that the directors of the road would take care of them.
. . . John H. B. Latrobe next journeyed to Sykes Mills and
entered into a parley with the workmen. They really were in
a sad plight. They were without money, without credit; and
some of them already were becoming destitute and hungry.
Mr. Latrobe, genuinely touched by their distress, distributed
among them some $2000, still due Lyon as a payment on his
work. And returned to Baltimore feeling that the matter was
settled.

Unfortunately, this was not so. It appeared that the sum
really due the workmen was more than $9000, and Latrobe's
disbursements they regarded merely as so many drops in the
bucket. Again they protested to Stabler. They demanded
their pay in full. . . . Cash. . . . Instanter. . . . On the
spot. . . . Vainly Stabler endeavored to explain that he did
not have the funds; that he would have to return to Baltimore
for another consultation with the directors. . . . The men
said that they would not wait again. They marched over to
the track and began wrenching at the rails.

For one more time, Stabler succeeded in gaining a truce.
Again he went to Baltimore, this time post haste. Upon the
advice of Mr. Latrobe, he obtained a riot warrant which he
turned over to the sheriff. That officer immediately called
for a posse, to which only William Patterson responded. Mr.
Patterson, the sheriff and Mr. Stabler went back to Sykes
together. They had not proceeded very far down the track
before they met the workmen, 135 of them, armed with their
stone hammers and other tools, and following an improvised
flag carried on a pole. . . . Hugh Reily, one of their number,
was their captain. Reily came forward and seized Stabler's
horse by the bridle. Hard words were passed.

It was a difficult moment. Three men facing 135. And
the 135 thoroughly maddened and under leadership. The
three capitulated. Again they returned to Baltimore. . . .

There was to be no more temporizing. The time had come
for government to show its strong hand. To Brigadier-

General Steuart the sheriff now turned over his warrant, and at ten o'clock that very evening more than a hundred volunteers from the militia boarded a special train bound for Sykes Mills. (This undoubtedly was the first troop movement by train not only on the Baltimore and Ohio but anywhere.) Despite many delays, the soldiers reached Sykes at early dawn, found the rioters wholly unprepared for their coming, arrested fifty of them, including Reily, and the trouble was over. . . . A new contractor came and finished Lyon's job. Whether his workmen were ever fully paid is not in the records.

. . . .

Troublous times. And yet progress being made all the time. Sometimes the workmen rough. And many times the workmen drunk. Whiskey still at three cents a glass. And Caspar Wever, the doughty superintendent of construction, complaining all the while of it. It was not enough to him that the company, in the making of each of its contracts, had officially prohibited its use by workmen and contractors. Wever went on record in one of his reports, saying:

> . . . It is believed that the work may be executed without the use of this dreadful poison, more advantageously to the interests of the Company, and certainly much more agreeably to its officers and contractors, as well as beneficially to the laborers, themselves. The promised good which its prohibition holds out to all parties, requires that the measure [the contract clause] should be persisted in, at least until it shall have been proved to be an injurious one; this, it is ardently hoped, may never occur. It would indeed be a melancholy reflection, that a public work could not be carried on in a Christian country, without the aid of a maddening poison so destructive of human life and morals as to have been utterly proscribed even in Mohammedan lands.

Mr. Wever, who, it will be recalled, came with Jonathan Knight from the construction of the great national highway across Ohio, seemingly was one accustomed to speaking his mind. A letter, which he wrote to the Hon. John Test of Lawrenceburg (Indiana) in the summer of 1830, reveals something of the thorough quality of the man. After relating the fact that thirteen miles of the Baltimore and Ohio Railroad are now open for traffic and that twelve more will be completed that autumn, he goes on to say:

> . . . One horse will draw . . . 10 tons, or about 100 barrels of flour, at two miles an hour, and forty to sixty persons at six to eight miles an hour—at the rate of ten miles an hour, thirty persons can easily be transported. When the road is finished to the Ohio River, passengers can be convoyed there, by horse power, in 36 hours and by steam power in 24 hours, or less, without the slightest risk of fatigue, but, on the contrary, experience great pleasure from the ride. . . . A great improvement has been effected by the Locomotive Engine in England and the application of friction wheels by Mr. Winans and conical wheels by Mr. Knight. . . . The capital stock of this Company consists of a subscription of stock to the amount of $4,000,000, three-quarters of which is held by individuals and the other by the State of Maryland and the City of Baltimore, in equal shares. The Board of Directors are compelled to limit their calls (for money) by the circumstances of their shareholders. They cannot call on them rapidly without being oppressive. Perhaps one-sixth is as much as prudence would allow in any one year. If I am correct in this supposition it will then require six years to construct the road to Cumberland (nearly 200 miles) to which point it is expected the present capital will carry it. In six years it might as well be made to the Ohio River, as to Cumberland, if the means were at hand. . . .

It is interesting, after all these years, to see the rugged confidence of these old Quakers—Thomas and Knight and Wever—as to the future of their great enterprise. They did not waver. They were not of the wavering sort. . . . Moreover, their railroad, even though operating for patronage for but thirteen miles, was showing some real revenue. Ellicotts Mills was in those days not only something of a pleasure resort

for Baltimore, but a manufacturing center of no little importance. Even after the great novelty of the opening of the line
to the Mills—in May, 1830—had worn off, the travel continued,
to an astonishing degree. It was not until early in January,
1831, that the following advertisement appeared in the Baltimore newspapers:

RAIL ROAD NOTICE

IN CONSEQUENCE of the advanced state of the Season, the
following arrangements will take place on and after MONDAY
NEXT, the 25th inst. for the departure of CARS on the Rail-road,
viz:

From the Depot on Pratt Street there will start.

DAILY

A Car	at 5 A.M.
A train of Cars . .	at 9½ A.M.
A do do . .	at 2 P.M.
The Evening Car . .	at 4 P.M.

And from Ellicott's Mills

A Car	at 8 A.M.
A train of Cars . .	at 11½ A.M.
A do do . .	at 4 P.M.
A Car . . .	at 6 P.M.

. . . .

In the same issues, the Baltimore papers announced that
the Baltimore and Ohio had declared the first dividend upon
its stock, 37½ cents on each share of the common stock.
Whether or not this should have been paid, it was none the
less a great inspiration to those who had labored long and
hard for the enterprise.

It also was just before this time that the first fatal accident
came to pass among the men who were engaged in operating
the road. The driver of the evening car in from the hotels at
the further end of the Carrollton Viaduct—there is no record
of his name—fell from his perch and under the wheels, being

so badly cut and lacerated that he died within the half-hour.
It is related that the car, which had been built in Liverpool for
Mr. Winans to show in that city, and which was supposed to
carry forty passengers, was carrying double that number.
It was a Sunday evening and the excursionists pressing against
the driver's seat are supposed to have caused him to fall to the
rails. . . . The railroad company promptly absolved itself
from any blame in the affair. It said that the car was not
under its management, but had been chartered to Messrs.
Weigand and Chase, the hotel keepers at the Viaduct, who
were therefore solely responsible for the shocking disaster.

.   .   .   .

So progressed Baltimore and Ohio through both 1830 and
1831. . . . It was in the last month of the latter year that it
took another great step forward—in the opening to the public
of its line through to Frederick.

At last, it had a real western terminal. At last, it reached
somewhere. True it was that within a short time Frederick
would find itself off the main line of the railroad, reached only
by a branch, some two miles in length, extending from the
new bridge over the Monocacy. But this mattered but little
to it. Frederick had a railroad. And the Baltimore and
Ohio had a real terminal town. . . . In comparison, Ellicotts
Mills faded. Frederick, situate in the very heart of one of the
finest agricultural districts in all Maryland, was a great center
of trade; rich, social, in all of its aspects.

Throughout the late autumn of '31, preparations for the
opening of the new line went ahead. On the last day of
October, the horse-drawn *Pioneer* went through to the foot of
Plane No. 1, over Parrs Spring Ridge, and the editor of the
Baltimore Gazette, who rode upon it, noticed that stables and
"other facilities" had been erected there to assure a prompt
movement of the trains. The Great Western stages, carrying
the United States mails, and operated by the famous firm of
Stockton and Stokes, announced that upon the completion of

the railroad to Frederick their coaches would deposit their passengers at that town for the rail journey on to Baltimore.

Again, in November, the *Pioneer* made an excursion to Plane No. 1; this time starting from the new downtown depot and warehouse of the railroad in Baltimore, in Pratt Street, close to Light, the City Dock and the *Three Tuns* tavern. The party—a hundred men in all—gathered in the *Three Tuns* and had their dinner in the new hotel at Sykes Mills. They were all amazed at the progress that had been made in the building of the line.

.   .   .   .

The real occasion, however, was that first day of December, when the first regular train went rolling into Frederick, to a tremendous reception.   On the summit of the line, well to the east of the town, a huge decorated arch had been erected over the railroad track.   Within it swung a banner bearing the significant inscription: "To the Ohio—Ça ira—Ça ira." . . . All Frederick was gaily decorated . . . was in festival. . . . Bands playing. . . .   The chimes of the new Catholic church ringing. . . .   More people in Patrick Street than ever before in the history of the town. . . .   And, finally, the great train approaching.

At the head of it, appropriately, the fine new coach *Frederick*—no *Pioneer* for this occasion, but one of Imlay's very best—filled with the Mayor of Baltimore and some of the bigwigs of the railroad.   Then a flat car, upon which had been firmly strapped the Governor's barouche, which had been driven up from Annapolis to Baltimore on the preceding evening and within which sat the Governor of Maryland, himself, that all might see—and admire.   A car with the horses for the Governor's coach, they themselves riding as passengers upon the railroad. . . .   Other passenger coaches. . . .   The *Maryland*. . . .   The *Virginia*. . . .   The *Ohio*.

Now the train is stopping right at the entrance of the proud little city of Frederick.   There are addresses; by the Mayor of the city of Frederick, the Governor of the state of Maryland, the Mayor of the city of Baltimore, the president of the Baltimore and Ohio Railroad. . . . The band plays once again. . . . Then the whole party picks its way across the light covering of snow and into the doors of the hospitable City Hotel. . . . A mighty dinner, of two hundred covers, is served; and, with the unending toasts that follow, consumes four long hours. There is no return to Baltimore that day for the visiting party. . . .

.   .   .   .

Yet the next day—December 2, 1831—the railroad is open for business; all the way from Baltimore to Frederick. . . . Sixty-one miles. . . . You may count them as you go. On the morrow, a new train is added to the time card of the Baltimore and Ohio; leaving the station at the City Dock for Frederick at six o'clock in the morning—in those days they did not seem to mind early starts upon their journeys—and, in return, leaving Frederick for Baltimore at nine-thirty o'clock each morning. A little later, the Baltimore departure also was made nine-thirty A.M. Meals in the hotels at Sykes or at Ellicotts. . . . And connections at Frederick with the Great Western stages.[1]

Of the Baltimore and Ohio Railroad in this stage of its existence, Charles Varle, in his *Complete View of Baltimore*, gives a most excellent picture. In describing a trip over to Frederick in March, 1832—hardly four months after the line had been completed to that point, he says:

We started from the office of the Rail Road Company in Pratt Street at 9:30 in one of four cars running together, the

[1] It is interesting to recall that in that day the ticket system had not yet been invented for the American railroad. The conductor took cash fares and entered the amounts in a book. Such a book, for Train No. 1, bound from Frederick to Baltimore, December 3, 1831, is still in existence. It shows that the train had twenty-nine passengers that day, and each of them is set down by name. Obviously, so complicated a fare arrangement could not long continue. Gradually the ticket system came in upon the Baltimore and Ohio, at a time prior to 1840, for which year a ticket issued by the road is carefully preserved.

number of passengers amounting to eighty, and each car drawn by a single horse. The atmosphere clear and cool, our course due west for about half a mile in that street, in the middle of which a single rail-track has been laid on granite blocks. Reached the old depot, at the upper extremity of the street where we changed our course to a southwest direction. . . . For a distance of eight miles the location of the line runs on a perfect level, except through the three cuts where small summits are introduced to secure the drainage from the road. . . . Passed by the scales on which cars are weighed to ascertain the tonnage of their loads.

Mr. Varle then proceeds to describe in some detail the great Carrollton Viaduct, Colonel Long's Jackson Bridge, and other points along the beginning of the line; and comes at last to the Relay House, where he notes that the horses are changed in but two minutes, and adds that refreshments are kept for the accommodation of travelers. He speaks of the Patterson Viaduct; of the Thistle Cotton Factory, property of the Messrs. Morris; of another cotton factory nearer Ellicotts Mills, belonging to Edward Gray. In another place he refers to the Union Cotton Factory, above Ellicotts.

The scenery at the Mills seems to excite his admiration; also he observes the great difference between the vehicles emerging from the old covered bridge there and passing under the arches of the Oliver Viaduct and "the easy and rapid movement of our cars." . . . At the Halfway House, thirty-one miles from Baltimore and thirty miles from Frederick, the cars stop for dinner. Both the plantation and the tavern belong to a Mr. Sykes, and already the little town springing up around the railroad depot is being called Sykesville. . . . Varle feels that the hotel is well located, being situated between the road and the stream. There is a merchant mill a short way off. . . . Two miles further along the line comes one of the frequent changes of horses.

At the thirty-eighth milepost, there is still another change; and here two horses are added to each of the cars, to make the

THE FIRST TRAIN INTO FREDERICK.

As it pulled into that ancient Maryland town, 1835.

From a painting by H. D. Stitt.

THE OLD STATION AT FREDERICK, MARYLAND.

Built at the opening of the railroad there in 1831, used for many years as a freight house and finally torn down in 1911.

From a photograph.

long ascent over the Parrs Spring Ridge Inclined Plane (No. 1).
No stationary engines nor cables have yet been provided for the
planes; and there is now talk that they never will be provided.
They are beginning to say that this strange new thing that is
coming so swiftly to strength and to power—the steam locomotive—will make these planes unnecessary. Some of the
passengers express their hopes that this is so. It seems a
fearful climb for the horses; up a plane which rises 179 feet in
about a mile and a half. The author of the *View* continues:

. . . We arrived at the summit of the plane called Parr's
Spring Ridge where an area is found, 600 feet in diameter,
where the stationary engine is to be erected. We stayed here
for a minute or two to fix the breakers [brakes] under the body
of the cars for preventing too precipitous a descent. For this
purpose a trusty man is placed behind the Car to assist in the
regulation of the wheels by bearing on them in proportion to
the grades of the descent of the plane. . . . We now descend
240 feet in the distance of one and a half miles by various steps
or grades—having the turnpike road at no more than 500
or 600 feet from us, and we followed it, always in sight, nearly a
parallel line for the above distance. Arrived at the foot of the
plane where the man riding on the breakers left the cars.

We then descended toward the Monocacy river, 11 miles
distant, by various grades, but none exceeding 37 feet per mile,
except in two instances where the grade is 52 feet per mile.
. . . We met a train of cars, loaded principally with flour, and
having but one track on the road we were obliged to retrograde
for some distance until we arrived at a turnout—a circumstance
far from pleasing, but this will not happen when the road shall
have two tracks. . . .

Varle arrived at Frederick at five-thirty o'clock in the
evening, having traversed the sixty-one miles of railroad in
eight hours of what he considered easy travel. . . . He makes
note of the fact that the freight charge westerly from Baltimore
to Frederick is $3.60 a ton, weighing not included. Flour goes
from Frederick to Baltimore at 26½ cents a barrel, and this

rate includes delivery anywhere in Baltimore City. . . . Passengers are carried at three cents a mile.

Flour was now beginning to traverse the road, in increasing quantities. On a typical day, January 28, 1832—not two months after the opening of the line to Frederick—there arrived in Baltimore over the railroad 52 of its wagons, bearing 852 barrels of flour, 12 barrels of glue, 20 tons of granite, 10 tons of wood, and 4 tons of bark. On that same day, there departed from Mount Clare 40 wagons, loaded with a vast variety of iron, bricks, coal, groceries, oysters, shells, dry goods and the like. It was well that the railroad company had provided itself with two hundred new burden wagons before opening its line to Frederick. And new passenger cars, too. Already it was operating seven of these in each direction each day, and on this particular January Saturday, 49 passengers had arrived and 58 departed. Which was, if anything, rather below the average. . . . Yet, that was a particularly hard winter and, during it, travel fell off a bit at times.

The freight traffic increased. Men were astonished to go down into the City Dock of Baltimore and see great ships lying alongside the railroad tracks, receiving from the cars single blocks of granite weighing two and three tons each— all from the quarries in the valley of the Patapsco. Sometimes there were three and four sailing ships all in at once for Patapsco granite, and rumor ran along the docks—and accurate rumor it was—that up at Mount Clare they already were trying to build a car strong enough to bring single granite columns, weighing twenty tons each, down over the new railroad. . . . Added to this, the flour traffic out of Frederick!

Up to the first of March, 1832—just three months after its opening to that point—the road already had carried 32,670 barrels of flour out of Frederick.[1] Yet of the trades that the

[1] Here are a typical April week's ladings in that spring—measured by the arrivals at Baltimore. There came into Mount Clare terminal 213 cars, carrying 1721 barrels of flour, 8 hogsheads of tobacco, 127 tons of granite, 31 tons of iron, 16 of lime, 36 of paving stones, 3 of plank, 3½ of leather, 5 of tanners' bark, and

railroad developed, perhaps none gave a greater satisfaction to the men who had its interests closest to heart than the bringing of fuel wood into Baltimore. It was estimated that because of this new facility, as well as the far lower prices for the wood in Baltimore than in New York or in Philadelphia, the railroad that winter saved the householders in its principal city many thousands of dollars in their fuel bills.[1]

.   .   .   .

2¾ tons of horse feed. Against this traffic, there had departed, in those six working days, 228 carloads of the miscellaneous sorts of freight that already we have seen—some 320 tons all told. In those same days, 488 passengers arriving and 631 departing. In all of these instances, it will be noticed that the passengers departing from Baltimore quite overbalanced those arriving. The trend of emigration into the West was very strong at that time, and the new rail route from Baltimore had achieved an instant popularity.

[1] Of all of this, President Thomas was to write in his sixth annual report to his stockholders, which appeared on the first day of the following October, saying:

". . . Until the first grand division of the Railroad . . . was completed no fair test had been offered to fully ascertain its merits or by which to compare it with the original anticipations of its importance and value. This distance is now completed and tried by the test thus furnished, the Baltimore and Ohio Railroad presents one of the very few undertakings of public works by private means in which no reasonable hope has been disappointed but in which every expectation has been realized. The adaptation of the Railroad system to general traffic—that point so long disputed—has been fully and forever set at rest. Every species of agricultural production, lime, timber, lumber, firewood, even paving stones, have been brought to Baltimore with a profit to those using the road as a means of transportation for articles so bulky and so cheap; and in return and at an enhanced toll, but with equally profitable results, plaster of paris, coal, boards, brick and scrap iron have been sent into the country.

" When articles so varied and some of them of so small value can be carried profitably to their owners and to the Company, no doubt can exist as to the profits arising to both on merchandise and passengers. Neither has the sparse population of the country through which the road for long distances passes—nor its rugged character—had the anticipated effect of rendering it comparatively valueless. On the contrary, the existence of the road has brought into use articles in this very country, which were before valueless to their possessors—and forests and quarries now furnish resources to the landowner which but for the Railroad would have fallen and rotted where they stood or remained forever unknown and undisturbed in the bowels of the earth. In this way the profits of the road have been increased from sources that were unthought of when it was projected and all this in the short period which has elapsed since the commencement of the present year. . . ."

The lateral line to Frederick having been completed and placed in full operation—commerce having begun to thrive through that brisk entrepôt—attention was turned again to the pushing on of the Main Stem. . . . Point of Rocks, on the Potomac, sixty-nine miles from Baltimore, was reached on the first day of April, 1832. Steamboat connection with the important town of Harpers Ferry at the confluence of the Shenandoah and the Potomac rivers, twelve miles distant, was established soon afterwards. While the completion of the Chesapeake and Ohio Canal to this point rendered it now possible for a person, if he so desired, to travel by packet boat from Washington City to Point of Rocks and thence by the train to Baltimore.

It was this same canal that now portended much trouble for the Baltimore and Ohio Railroad. For the narrow impasse just beyond Point of Rocks, both railroad and canal were to contend, bitterly and at great length, before either should finally go forward. . . . At Point of Rocks the iron horse might rub his nose most fretfully against the granite base of old Catoctin Mountain. Not easily was he to be permitted to go beyond that point.

CHAPTER IX

The Canal an Early Antagonist of the Railroad—Conflict Between Them at the Point of Rocks—The Baltimore and Ohio Wins a Drawn Victory—More Locomotives—The *Traveller*—The *Arabian*—The *Mercury*—Better Cars—And, Finally, Harpers Ferry Reached.

In the very hour of its birth, the railroad met a powerful adversary. This was the canal. Particularly true this was in the United States, where this form of waterway, still young itself, was in the flash period of its existence. The completion of the Erie Canal—in those days they had ceased to call it "Clinton's Folly," and were beginning to style it as the "Grand Canal"—across New York State, in 1825, and the season of tremendous prosperity that immediately followed—traffic struggling to get into the narrow waterway, towns springing up as if by magic along its banks, an entire great state being born—had served as a tremendous impetus to similar projects. A few other canals had also been finished and most of these were prosperous. The Delaware and Hudson Company was making a tremendous success of its canal from Rondout on the Hudson through to Honesdale, in the high hills of Pennsylvania. Likewise, the Morris and Essex Canal across New Jersey, from the harbor of New York to Phillipsburg on the Delaware, just opposite the mouth of the Lehigh, was said to be successful. . . . There was a brisk new waterway from Boston to Lowell—this last town already an important textile manufacturing center—and canals either finished or under way in the valleys of the Delaware, the Lehigh and the Schuylkill rivers. The swift development of the anthracite district of Pennsylvania was a tremendous impetus to these. . . . By 1832 many laterals were being planned to the Erie Canal; Ohio was preparing to build an unusually complete canal system of her own; a waterway was under construction from New Haven, Connecticut, to Northampton, Massachusetts; and work was progressing on the Chesapeake and Ohio Canal. Of this last, very much more in a moment.

While most of the important canals devoted primarily to bringing anthracite coal down to tidewater were owned and operated by private companies, the general trend throughout the land was to build and operate these artificial waterways as government works—by the various states that sponsored them. Which possibly gave some opportunities for incompetence, if not for actual dishonesty, in their construction. Not that all the men who were vigorously in favor of canals were dishonest. On the contrary, a great many were the leading citizens of their day; stalwart, upright men who believed honestly and sincerely that a national system of canals, owned and operated by the states, offered the best, if not the only, means of proper transport for the development of the still young nation. . . . Allied with these, however, were others not so honest, either in principle or in act. Business methods in that day were slipshod; particularly was this true of the business methods of many of the state governments. The opportunities for the raiding of their treasuries were tempting. . . . And in their inexperience there were few opportunities for good judgment.

So it came to pass that a great many miles of canal were builded in the United States, in those early decades of the last century, which eventually had to be abandoned; some of them within a pathetically short time. A great deal of energy and money was wasted before it was recognized that, while the canal type of highway might have certain inherent advantages in a national scheme of transport, with its great cost and—in the northeastern United States—its comparatively short open seasons, it was hardly to be compared with the railroad as a swift, all-the-year, economical and efficient transport servant of a nation.

Before this salient principle had been well established, came the canal expenditures, the mistakes, the failures, the recriminations. . . . Long years of warfare . . . guerilla-like. With occasionally a sharp conflict like that which marked the struggle between the Baltimore and Ohio Railroad and the Chesapeake and Ohio Canal at the Point of Rocks in the summer of 1832.

In the preceding chapter we have seen how, after steady construction, the Baltimore road finally reached Point of Rocks, nearly seventy miles from Baltimore, early that selfsame year. . . . Progress and optimism had marked the work most of the way. There was no thought of halting, of turning back. As soon as the railroad had been finished into a town, it was as if a magic wand had touched it; trade and prosperity rolled in upon it.

.   .   .   .

But at Point of Rocks there was to come a real halt. A tiresome and a tedious one. . . . No longer, seemingly, was the country open to the progress of the railroad. While little of it that already had been traversed had formed an easy pathway for it—before the line was well out of Baltimore it was crossing an extremely rugged and rolling terrain—it all was as nothing compared with that which stretched just ahead. . . . At the Point of Rocks, long centuries before, the Potomac finally had broken its way through the mountains in its struggle to find the sea. Laboriously cutting its own deep channel through the high hills, it left but little room for anything else to follow it. Particularly was this true on the Maryland side of the river. The great stone mass of Catoctin Mountain rose with terrific abruptness from the water's edge. There was not enough of a shelf or a bench at its foot to accommodate

even a narrow country road. . . . Twice again this impasse
of the Potomac narrowed before Harpers Ferry, twelve miles
distant, would be reached. At the best, it would have been
difficult to find room for the railroad through that narrow
valley. . . . The demands of the importunate canal company
—not only that it be given a prior right through the pass but
that the railroad be definitely and forever barred from it—
added tremendously to the problem of President Thomas and
his associates. Well they now needed every ounce and every
small grain of their optimism.

.   .   .   .

The prelude to open warfare between the two companies
came in certain whimsical legislation which for two or three
sessions past was repeatedly being introduced in the Annapolis
State House. A curious measure, for instance, was that which
sought to inhibit any bridge of any sort, fixed or open, from
being put across the canal once it had been dug; to allow the
importation of slaves from Virginia to assist in the digging of
the ditch, and to permit the Chesapeake and Ohio company to
purchase in entirety such farms as its canal might cut across.

At these proposals, a storm of indignation shook Baltimore.
That the scheme of buying entire farms would react toward
preventing the railroad from ever crossing them, was patent
at the outset. . . . The idea of constantly ferrying across a
bridgeless canal, but sixty feet in width, was fuel to the flame.
The return suggestion of the canal company, that it proposed
to run "two-storied canal-boats, perhaps even bigger," excited
Baltimore's ribald wit. Washington City came quickly to the
defense of the canal enterprise—at that time a pet enterprise
of the national capital. . . . Taunts followed.

"Why are slaves to be preferred for this *magnificent* public
work," asked the *Baltimore American*, "to the freeborn whites
of Maryland?" And in the next breath added:

"The question is constantly asked us: 'Why do you prefer
railroads to canals?' We think that the Chesapeake and Ohio

Canal Company are now beginning to find out the reasons why. . . ."

The measure was defeated. But not so the canal company. It rolled up its sleeves for a conflict. Its newly dug ditch also had reached Point of Rocks. The temporary ends of canal and railroad rubbed their noses there together against the seemingly impassable wall of the mountain. . . . The iron horse chafed in his uneasiness.

.   .   .   .

In his annual report of 1828, Mr. Thomas had made a reference to the Chesapeake and Ohio Canal Company's claim for a priority of rights in the narrow valley of the Potomac. "This controversy will probably not retard our operations in the least degree," he had then written.

In this optimism, the first president of the Baltimore and Ohio was to be sadly shaken. . . . The canal company had made no reply to his predictions. Secure in its own mind, it probably thought a public answer was not worth while. Yet, it was not asleep in any one of those days or months or years. It did much of its work silently, and in the dark. Early in that same year (1828), the Baltimore and Ohio had made its petition to Congress, begging a subscription to its stock from the federal government. Although committees of both Houses reported generally in favor of such aid being given, it never came to definite legislation; due, it was said at the time, to the opposition of the Chairman of the Committee on Roads and Canals in the lower House. He chanced also to be the president of the Chesapeake and Ohio Canal Company.

.   .   .   .

All this was preliminary to the real battle between railroad and canal just ahead.

Long before the first train had reached the Point of Rocks, the canal company had gone to the Court House in Frederick and obtained an injunction prohibiting the railroad from laying down its track west of the Point, on the grounds that already it had been accorded prior rights along the Maryland side of the valley. . . . That first issue was fought bitterly in the courts, backwards and forwards, and up to the Court of Appeals at Annapolis, which in January, 1832, decided finally in favor of the canal company. It ordered that the railroad should not appropriate nor use the land on the Maryland side between Point of Rocks and Harpers Ferry until the canal company should have located its work between those two points. There was no obligation nor necessity for the canal to hurry to its task.

This was a bitter blow to the Baltimore and Ohio, which had felt that, even with good engineering, there would barely be room for but one pathway—railroad or canal—at the bottom of the mountains. . . . Delays were highly dangerous to the road. It needed to get much further through toward the West in order to become productive in the way that had been promised. . . . Already its energetic young rival off to the north—the Baltimore and Susquehanna—was beginning to talk of building a lateral which should run through Westminster and Hagerstown, and perhaps become the through rail route from Baltimore to the West. . . . Years afterward, the Western Maryland Railroad was to appear almost upon the precise route surveyed and advocated in the early 'thirties. Not merely surveyed and advocated. But some of it actually built. The present Green Spring Valley Branch of the Pennsylvania today represents the physical beginnings of an attempt on the part of the erstwhile Baltimore and Susquehanna to strike an arm off into the West.

.   .   .   .

The irrevocable decision of the Maryland Court of Appeals left apparently but four courses of action open to the Baltimore and Ohio:

It might, if possible, procure the permission of the canal company for the joint construction of the two works from Point of Rocks to Harpers Ferry. Once the latter town was reached, all, seemingly, would be easy sailing. Not only would there be immediate connection with the railroad already building down into the Valley of Virginia, but plenty of diverse routes available for carrying the Main Stem of the Baltimore and Ohio on towards its final destination.

It might construct its tracks alongside the canal, upon such land as remained unoccupied, once the waterway was finished.

It might cross the Potomac there at the Point of Rocks and ascend the south, or Virginia, bank of the river to the Ferry.

It might pierce a series of tunnels through South and Catoctin mountains, and so parallel the course of the river.

All of these possibilities seemed equally hopeless to Thomas and his associates. There was no likelihood of any permission or coöperation from the highly unfriendly canal company. To dream of building on land left by the canal, once it was done with its own work, was almost laughable. That would be sure to be the last thing finished about its enterprise, if ever it permitted it to be officially done. . . . To build on the Virginia side meant, not only an expensive bridge at the outset, but repeated trips to Richmond to gain the necessary rights. . . . The bare costs of tunneling the great mountains rendered the fourth suggestion out of the question.

The Baltimore and Ohio was, indeed, at an impasse.

Yet, the men who stood back of the road in those trying early years were not the sort who easily give up. After much consideration, they decided to attempt the first of these four difficult suggestions; to work with, and not against, the canal company. It was discovered that such joint construction as would be absolutely necessary at stretches before Harpers Ferry would be reached, would cost $14,000—which, normally, might be shared equally by each company.

Because it was in the weaker position legally, the Baltimore and Ohio offered to assume this entire $14,000 cost. The canal company, however, rejected this proposal, holding that injury and inconvenience to the canal would be caused by it, even though at one time—prior to the final decision of the Court of Appeals—it had, of its own volition, proffered almost this same plan to the railroad. The Baltimore and Ohio had then rejected it, unless it could be brought to cover also similar points between Harpers Ferry and Cumberland.

.   .   .   .

The Maryland Legislature now entered the fray. At the instance of William Cost Johnson of Frederick, Chairman of the Committee on Internal Improvements of the House of Delegates, a resolution was passed by both Houses of the General Assembly urging an accommodating spirit on the part of the canal company toward the railroad company, and such a modification of its plans for the waterway as to permit the railroad also to use the right of way between the Point of Rocks and Harpers Ferry. . . . As far as the Baltimore and Ohio was concerned, there was little doubting the real sentiment of Maryland.

The railroad company renewed its proposals to pay all the costs of joint construction at the narrow places between the Point and the Ferry; but again the canal company declined, unless—please mark this modest counter proposition well— the Baltimore and Ohio Company should "*appropriate the yet unexpended balance of their capital to the completion of the Canal to Cumberland, and the abandonment, for the present, at least, of all idea of a Rail Road beyond the Point of Rocks.*"

When the post from Washington brought this communication to them, the gentlemanly Thomas and his associates must have thrown up their hands in disgust.

.   .   .   .

At the next session of the General Assembly, Mr. Johnson's committee took up the entire question once again. It had made a personal inspection of the disputed territory and was prepared and anxious for definite action. . . . But the canal company still stood obdurate, immovable. It was almost impertinent as well, for here it was blandly petitioning the

Legislature, not only for the right to sell its "surplus water" for power, but also begging financial aid of Maryland's governing body. . . .   Baltimore and Frederick together growled back at it. Formally the Committee on Internal Improvements not only refused the requests of the canal company, but stated that it was perverse and unworthy in its attitude toward the railroad. It did more. It recommended a legal inquiry to find out if the Chesapeake and Ohio company had not, by various abuses and the failure to complete within a time limit the first hundred miles of its canal, forfeited its charter.

The committee then proposed, after several constructive suggestions for joint building through the impasse by the rival enterprises, that, if the canal company even now acceded to a genuine coöperative plan, the proceedings for forfeiting its charter should not be pressed and that its request for selling its "surplus water" should be granted.

No matter how this report might—and did—please the citizens of Baltimore and Frederick and the territory that lay roundabout them, it certainly did not conciliate the canal company. That company took fresh umbrage at the findings. The possibilities of compromise between it and the railroad seemed further off than ever. It looked as if the Baltimore and Ohio, having barely touched the banks of the Potomac, might end there indefinitely—at least 250 miles from the nearest point upon the Ohio. . . .   The agitation for the building of a western branch of the Baltimore and Susquehanna as a substitute for the entire Baltimore and Ohio scheme was taken up afresh. . . .   A few timid stockholders felt that President Thomas and his directors might as well decide to end their road at Point of Rocks and so avoid expensive and useless litigation.

.   .   .   .

To the passenger who rides along the line of the Baltimore and Ohio today between Harpers Ferry and the Point of Rocks and who observes the ancient and grass-grown canal that so closely parallels the tracks for almost every mile of the distance, it seems unbelievable that it could ever have been so real an antagonist of the railroad—and for so long a time. That for two long years an important through route to the West should have been held impotent by this shabby competitor.

Yet, two years would have been as nothing, had it not been for the well-nigh indefatigable efforts of the friends of the railroad in the Maryland Legislature. Presently, through the appointment of a new joint committee of the two Houses, these were preparing another agreement. To this, it was assumed that the consent of the warring commercial pathways would be secured. It provided that, this done, both railroad and canal would be put through to Harpers Ferry without delay. In fact, it was specifically set down that construction of the railroad's line west from the Point of Rocks could be begun any time after May 10, 1833. . . . When the road had finally reached the Ferry, it was to subscribe to 2500 shares of the canal stock.

The canal company was to prepare the roadbed through the impasse of the Point of Rocks for $100,000; and to bear, itself, any cost of grading in excess of this figure. The width of the waterway was to be maintained at fifty feet, unless it became impracticable to place the railroad beside it at any point; in which case, the canal was to be further narrowed; to forty feet, if the commissioners, to be appointed to have jurisdiction in the matter, so deemed it necessary.

To the railroad was to be given a breadth of not less than twenty feet through the passes, a curvature of not less than 400 feet radius, and a grade never greater than thirty feet to the mile. All of these points, and any others that might come to an issue, were to be finally decided by the commissioners; three of them—engineers. One appointed by the canal company, the second by the railroad company, and the third by the President of the United States. These were to determine the damages payable by the railroad company to the canal company, if any, for interference upon its right of way.   It was further provided that a tight board fence was to be erected between the canal and the railroad in order to protect the horses on the former from damages by the locomotives upon the latter. . . .   All these things being done, the canal company was to have its coveted privilege of selling its surplus water for power; it being especially stipulated, however, that this power was not to be used for the establishment of grist mills.   At this late day, it looks as if the flouring-mill industry of Maryland had had something at that time to say in the matter.

.   .   .   .

.To this report, which presently was put in the form of legislation, the Chesapeake and Ohio Canal Company acceded. It was about all that it could do.   It hardly had a leg left upon which to stand.   Its bad manners had cost it friends; through a great and populous section of Maryland, public sentiment was strongly against it, and, in consequence, it was having a fearful time trying to raise funds.   The obligatory subscription of the Baltimore and Ohio to 2500 of its shares— which in the end virtually amounted to a purchase of the canal—saved its face.   When finally it was put through to Cumberland—in 1850—nothing more was said about its going further than that point.   In fact, it was Baltimore and Ohio capital that helped to complete it; a tidy ditch all the way from Washington, at tidewater on the Potomac, through to the very base of the Alleghenies, 184 miles away. . . .

How long this ancient waterway will be maintained is problematical.   Its real usefulness as a carrier, if ever it had any, is long since gone.   Annually, the spring floods come and damage it.   Those of the spring of 1924 were especially devastating.   But Baltimore and Ohio has always seen fit patiently to repair the old ditch.   Sentiment enters a little into its policy.   If the vanquished Chesapeake and Ohio Canal were to be completely abandoned through the District of

Columbia, the national capital would lose one of its favorite playgrounds. To canoe upon the old canal, up and out from Georgetown, is a great and perennial joy of the Washingtonians. There is no scene quite like it this side of the English Thames.

.   .   .   .

The provision in regard to the fence between the railroad and the canal westward from the Point of Rocks was never carried through. For a time, the railroad compromised the matter by limiting the operation of its locomotives to the Point of Rocks and using horse power on from there to Harpers Ferry. But only for a short time. Horses upon the Baltimore and Ohio already were doomed, even for the simplest local uses. The steam locomotive was swiftly coming into its own. Already the *York* and the *Atlantic* were hauling the passenger trains between Baltimore and the inclined plane at the foot of Parrs Spring Ridge, leaving only the slowly moving burden trains to be handled by horses.

Presently a third locomotive, much bigger and better, was added to the twain and the road's officers first began to speak of their "locomotive fleet." The newcomer was also built by Davis and Gartner—assisted by Ross Winans—and it was known as the *Traveller*.

In this engine there was a variation from the *Atlantic*, in having the pinion removed from the axle of the road wheels and placed upon a separate axle or shaft about three feet forward from the axles of the driving wheels. By means of a simple mechanical arrangement, this driving shaft could be attached either to one or both of the pairs of driving wheels, as might be desired. In this last way, the locomotive could have greater or less driving adhesion to the rail. . . . So was first born the device which today we know as the booster —an extra pair of drivers carried behind the regular pairs, into which power may be placed for starting the locomotive and on other occasions when extra driving force is needed. . . . The side pieces of the *Traveller* were plated with rolled iron;

CANAL VS. RAILROAD.

When the Iron Horse came to disturb the prestige of his flesh-and-blood predecessor.

From a painting by H. D. Stitt.

THE FAMOUS *Arabian*, 1834.

With engineer William Galloway in its cab.

From a photograph taken many years after its first appearance upon the Baltimore and Ohio Railroad.

her bearing boxes rolled in slides, and the springs were placed above the boxes and underneath the side pieces; all of which devices were supposed to be superior to those upon the *Atlantic*.

Yet soon the *Traveller* was to be supplanted in magnificence—this time by the *Arabian*. . . . The company had turned over a good part of its Mount Clare shops—now much enlarged and improved—to Davis and Gartner, who were giving all their time to building locomotives, and who, in return for the use of Mount Clare, were to give the Baltimore and Ohio precedence in their output. . . . This was considered an extremely good business arrangement on the part of the railroad company.

The *Arabian*, with her sister craft, the *Mercury*, still clung to the short base and the upright boiler—despite the steady developments of the Stephensons and others with the horizontal type. Still, even her upright boiler, 64 inches high, 52 inches in diameter, and filled with 400 flue tubes, represented a considerable advance in power. So did her cylinders, with a bore of 12 inches and a stroke of 22 inches. Things were indeed moving forward. The *Arabian* sent her steam to the cylinders by a pipe through the boiler instead of through the outer air, and thereby saved much condensation. She had her springs fixed above her frame and a device by which the fan wheel, supplying the artificial draught to the fire box, could be controlled by the engineer. . . . The steam locomotive was becoming perfected. More efficient. . . . The mechanical department of our first practical university of railroading was traveling steadily ahead.

.   .   .   .

These five small locomotives—the *York*, the *Atlantic*, the *Traveller*, the *Arabian* and the *Mercury*—in addition to two others still under construction by Charles Reeder of Baltimore, comprised the total motive power of the Baltimore and Ohio as finally it pushed its track up to and opposite Harpers Ferry in the autumn of 1834. Of them, the *York* could now be discounted as being practically worthless. She could not ascend even moderate grades. So she was finally assigned to the local passenger train in service between Baltimore and Ellicotts Mills. The others were considered much more efficient, even though one of the new Reeder engines exploded late in November of that year, killing her engineer and seriously injuring her fireman.[1]

The Baltimore and Ohio was beginning to be a real railroad. With seven locomotives, thirty-four passenger cars and more than a thousand freight cars—or burthen cars as they were then known—it was taking a real position as a carrier. At about this time, the baggage car first came into existence. In his report to the president of the company, dated October 1, 1833, George Gillingham, the superintendent of machinery, says:

> . . . The conveyance of baggage on the tops of passenger-cars has been attended with so much labor and inconvenience in loading, unloading and shifting the baggage at so great a height, added to the manifest injury done the cars in the hurry and bustle of these operations, that the necessity of some improvement on the present plan is obviously indispensable. It is proposed to construct some cars and tenders to the passenger-cars for the exclusive purpose of carrying baggage and in constructing them to make two distinct apartments, one for the baggage going to the ultimate point of destination, which will remain undisturbed for the whole trip, the other for the accommodation of way passengers. . . .

With the coming of the baggage cars, there came also greatly improved passenger coaches, following the example of

[1] The *Arabian* ran with the Frederick passenger train up to Plane No. 1 fifty successive days, eighty-two miles a day, without a lay-off or repairs of any kind, and this was then considered to be something of a record. Her daily expenses came to $13.25; divided in this fashion: 1¼ tons of coal at $6 a ton; oil at 50 cents; the engineer's wages, $2; the fireman's, $1.50; an interest charge of 75 cents; and a contingency fund of $1. It was estimated that she did the work each day that it would have required 113 horses to accomplish; and of course at vastly less cost.

the Ross Winans' *Columbus*, all of them now eight-wheeled. Among these was the *Dromedary*, also a creation of the indefatigable Winans, who was working steadily all the while improving the details of the car truck.   In the *Dromedary*, he connected the axle boxes of the two pairs of wheels together with two strong springs, one on each side.   These, in turn, were connected by a transverse bolster, carrying the swivel pivot socket.   This once done, Winans employed no other frame whatsoever.

The *Dromedary* type was not, in the end, pronouncedly successful.   But the eight-wheeled car was firmly established upon the American railroad.   These had ceased by 1834 to look like stage coaches.   They had end platforms and, although much smaller, were not unlike the open-platform railroad coaches of this day.   Following the custom of the locomotives, they were all named. . . .   Moreover, they were growing in size.   Some of the newer coaches, such as the *Winchester* and the *Comet*, for instance, were capable of seating from thirty-six to forty passengers each. . . .   Gaily painted and curtained, these passenger trains of 1834 indeed bore more than a slight resemblance to those of this day. . . .   Already the American train was beginning to look radically different from its British prototype.   For the English were to stand rather closely by their stage-coach traditions in building their railway carriages. . . .   Even today, such innovations as the corridor and the vestibule have not entirely robbed them of an air faintly reminiscent of the comfortable old coaches that once went on the highroad from London to Brighton or Bath or York or Edinburgh. . . .

The interior arrangements of those new Baltimore and Ohio passenger coaches of 1834 also were similar to those of the day coaches in ordinary use upon the American railroad at the present time.   The seats were ranged on each side of the car in a double row, with a long aisle running between them.   At first, there was considerable opposition to this arrangement.   In deference to an established American institution of that day, it was argued that this aisle would soon become an elongated spittoon. But the aisle came. And deference to an established American institution for many years took the form of frequent cuspidors ranged down it. . . . There was some attempt also in those early days to decorate the interior of the cars—somewhat in keeping with their gay exteriors. Even though the gay and flamboyant car decorations of the 'sixties and 'seventies still were far in the future.

Neither the comfort nor the luxury even of the best railroad cars of that day should be exaggerated. There was little of either, as we know them today. The seats were small, their backs low, the windows small and ofttimes awkwardly placed. There was no monitor nor clerestory along the roof for ventilation, and, with a big iron stove roaring at one end of the car, there were times when the air was terrific. There was no chance for fresh air except through opened windows, and these let in fearful amounts of dust and of cinders. When folk traveled in those days, they put on their dusters and old hats, and then arrived at their journey's end hardly recognizable to their friends.

But it all was a vast improvement over staging over rough roads. The poorest passenger car upon the rails was infinitely to be preferred to the best stage coach on the highway. Not alone for speed, but for just ordinary comfort. And so when, on the first day of December, 1834, the first regular passenger train upon the Baltimore and Ohio pulled up to the temporary station established just across the Potomac from Harpers Ferry, it was an event of real moment for that town. Rail communication was bound to mean much to it.

.   .   .   .

In accordance with the custom which had been followed ever since the road had been opened to Ellicotts, the coming of the first train to the Ferry was made an event of some social importance. And so, upon that memorable first day of December, 1834, a party of distinguished citizens—bigwigs of every sort—

left Baltimore in the early morning and journeyed through to
the north end of the Harpers Ferry Bridge in an even six hours.
The train was hauled by the road's best engine, the *Arabian*,
and it was marked, too, for a great distinction in the fact that it
was the first time that a locomotive had hauled a train west of
Parrs Spring Ridge.

The *Arabian* had gone on a day or two ahead of the excursion train, and had pulled herself up over the planes—with her
tender and two loaded coal cars, together weighing not less
than eleven and a half tons—absolutely unassisted. Which, in
its day, was considered something of a feat. After the dinner
had been concluded at Harpers Ferry, together with the inevitable toasts and speech making which had to follow, she hauled
the entire party back to Baltimore, over the planes and all.
. . . The inevitable abandonment of the extravagant planes
was thus clearly foreshadowed. Although it was seen that,
despite the remarkable performance of the little *Arabian*, a
complete new line would have to be builded roundabout them.
Their grades were quite too steep for any practical form of
railroad operation.

. . . .

The entrance into Harpers Ferry was also a real event for
the Baltimore and Ohio Railroad. The town was a place of
importance. It then ranked with Frederick. Not only was it
a manufacturing center of some pretense for those days—the
United States government maintained a busy arsenal there—
but it was a gateway, both to the upper valley of the Potomac,
as well as to the rich Shenandoah Valley, known poetically as
the Valley of Virginia. Thomas Jefferson had an especial
admiration for the place.[1] George Washington also loved it.

[1] In his *Notes on the State of Virginia*, Jefferson wrote:
". . . You stand on a very high point of land; on your right comes up the
Shenandoah, having ranged along the foot of the mountain a hundred miles to
find a vent; on your left approaches the Potomac, in quest of a passage also. In
the moment of their junction they rush together against the mountain, rend it
asunder and pass off to the sea. The scene is worth a voyage across the
Atlantic. . . ."

And frequently visited it. As long before as 1733, Robert Harper, the original resident of the place, had purchased a land title from Lord Fairfax and established his ferries across the two rivers there. These gave birth to the town. Which grew gradually, until by the 'thirties it was fairly bustling with all of its energies.[1]

· · · · · · ·

The chief value of Harpers Ferry to the Baltimore and Ohio was not that it marked a distinct point of progress in its growth, but rather one of opportunity for swift expansion. Not only was the road now to leave the soil of Maryland for the first time—although eventually to return to it, many miles to the west—but it was in a position to take any one of several routes through to the Ohio. . . . Moreover, at Harpers Ferry it connected with a railroad already well under way toward Winchester, thirty-two miles distant, and one of the chief towns of the Valley of Virginia, a place of considerable importance. This road was the Winchester and Potomac, and its president, John Bruce, had been in Baltimore more than two years before to see and ride upon the new railroad there.

It had even been suggested that the Winchester and Potomac might be acquired by the Baltimore and Ohio, which could use it as part of a route which would go through the valley as far south as Staunton, and then, by way of White Sulphur Springs and the valley of the Kanawha, through to the Ohio. . . . The people of Virginia did not, however, take very kindly to this suggestion at that time. Neither did the railroad group at Baltimore. They stood committed to a far shorter route to

---

[1] A writer in the *Virginia Literary Magazine* for 1829 describes Harpers Ferry at some length. He notices that already a handsome double wooden highway bridge, 750 feet from one abutment to the other, has been built across the Potomac from the town to the Maryland shore. . . . Another is to be begun at once, across the Shenandoah. . . . In the arsenal some 250 men are employed, who earn $2 a day apiece turning out 1400 muskets a month, at an average cost of $14 a musket. The superintendent is paid $1400 a year and is responsible for the safe-keeping of from 80,000 to 90,000 muskets all the while. . . . There are numerous other industries in the town. . . .

the Ohio; one that would have its river terminal many, many miles north of the junction of the Kanawha with that stream. It looked as if, at its best, the line from Harpers Ferry to Winchester would have to be, in effect, and remain, a branch of the Main Stem of the Baltimore and Ohio.

.   .   .   .

To build into Harpers Ferry meant that the Potomac, which had been so closely paralleled for twelve miles, would have to be crossed at last. This meant the construction of a bridge longer and more elaborate than any yet builded by a railroad in America. Because of the scarcity of level spaces about the hillset town, it was decided to combine both the railroad and the highway bridge from Maryland across into Virginia. The joint structure, six spans and nine hundred feet in length, which carried both of these busy pathways, not only across the Potomac but also over the Chesapeake and Ohio Canal—which remains upon the Maryland shore of the river for its entire length—when finally finished, was a most unusual thing. . . . A thing of many twists and bends.

It was not until many years thereafter that the railroad was to cut its present short tunnel through the nose of Maryland Heights, and in so doing greatly strengthen its line. In that beginning day, railroad and canal and highroad somehow managed to find lodgment between the base of the mountain and the swiftly flowing river. Which meant that, even with a decided curve of the great bridge at its eastern end, there still was a fearful turn of the rails to be overcome there. Always a difficult operating matter. And widely known as one of the most unusual bits of railroad engineering in all the United States.

Yet, the complex problem of the eastern end of the bridge was hardly more than the one that existed at its west end. There the two railroads debouched; the Winchester and Potomac turning off toward the left, and the continuation of the main line of the Baltimore and Ohio curving with great sharpness toward the right. . . . A railroad junction in the middle of a covered bridge was a novelty, to put it mildly. . . . Probably no man living today remembers the old covered bridge at Harpers Ferry—it must have been a weird and shadowy and uncertain place with the iron horse coming and going through its all-day blackness, twisting this way and that; off to Winchester, or to Martinsburg, or racing back home to Baltimore. And an important county highway also threading its way through the dark tunnel-like structure, along and across the railroad tracks.

Louis Wernwag, a distinguished early American bridge builder, helped erect that original timber structure at Harpers Ferry, which finally was completed in 1836, nearly two years after the Baltimore and Ohio first had poked its way around Maryland Heights. In 1836, the Winchester and Potomac was finished through to the junction at Harpers Ferry, and, in order to make connections with the Baltimore and Ohio tracks, it was necessary to build the left span of the "Y" section of the bridge. This connecting span, coming close to the center of the main structure, was first built by Wernwag. Fourteen years later it was destroyed.

In the earlier stages of its existence the Harpers Ferry Bridge had a hard time. Twice it fell. Benjamin Latrobe, in his report to the president of October 31, 1837, had complained of the inherent weakness of the original stone piers and told how Wernwag and William Lester had been brought in to help repair them. Because of the great money stringency which followed the financial panic of 1837, however, these repairs were postponed, indefinitely; most unfortunately, as it proved. Because, on the third of September, the old Harpers Ferry Bridge came to real trouble. An engine and tender were crossing one of its center arches, when the entire fabric gave way, precipitating the engine and its crew to the bed of the river. Fortunately, no serious injury came either to the men or to the machine, and travel was resumed after a few hours.

This accident was not, it was discovered, to be charged to

THE LOCOMOTIVE DISPLACES THE HORSE.

Dobbin lost his place on the railroad long before he lost it on the canal.

From a curious contemporary drawing.

HARPERS FERRY BEFORE THE WAR.

Showing—in the foreground—the Chesapeake and Ohio Canal and the famous wooden bridge built by Louis Wernwag.

From a contemporary lithograph.

the piers, but to decaying timbers which could not be observed because of the close wooden boarding of the outside of the bridge. When the arch was rebuilded, this scheme of outer boarding was so changed as to permit frequent inspection of its main timbers. . . . All of which was expensive. The engineer's reports show that the entire repairs to the structure at that time cost some $7500, only $9000 less than the road's surplus revenue for that year.

And, after all was said and done, they might have spent more money and made the job right. For, in the following spring, that selfsame arch again fell, this time under a freight train, consisting of nine house cars (box cars) and eleven gondolas, all loaded with iron and with coal which were being transported over it by the engine *Gladiator*. Fortunately, the engine and tender were clear of the pier and so did not go down. Most of the cars did. The conductor of the train fell among the broken timbers into the river but escaped with slight injuries. Again the bridge was rebuilt, this time at a cost of but $6000. But apparently so well in this second instance that there were no more complaints of it.

Yet, fourteen years after its completion, one finds it disappearing in favor of the first wrought-iron structure at that point, still shaped like a "Y" and still carrying both railroad and highroad.   In these fourteen years, a new builder of bridges had come forward—a man whose name was to go down into history as one of the masters of his craft. . . . This man was Wendel Bollman. We first saw him, in the fall of 1829, as one of four carpenters putting down the first lengths of track for the Baltimore and Ohio—upon its Mount Clare premises. Since then he had progressed rapidly. Swiftly he perfected himself as a constructing engineer.

Mr. Bollman possessed a rare genius in the fabrication of bridges. In this he showed especial vision and daring. Upon the passing of the original timber span of the Winchester and Potomac at Harpers Ferry, Bollman, who had by that time become master of the road of the Baltimore and Ohio, replaced it with a single suspension truss bridge of wrought iron, 124 feet in clear span. This, in its day, was regarded by engineers everywhere as a most remarkable structure. It was tested on June 1, 1852, by running three locomotives and their tenders out onto the span. These nearly covered it, from end to end. Together they weighed 273,550 pounds, or nearly 137 tons—more than a ton for each foot of bridge. . . .

Slowly, cautiously, the engines were moved upon the structure; yet the instruments of its observers showed that the center of the span deflected less than one and three-quarters inches under all of the great weight. Bollman had done his work with a remarkable thoroughness. Truly a triumph it was for this early American builder.

In fancy, one may see Bollman, with his assistant, Albert Fink—also destined to become a figure upon the Baltimore and Ohio—carefully making these metal trusses in miniature; working out, step by step, each detail of their fabrication. It is enough to say that the Bollman bridge builded at Harpers Ferry in the early 'fifties stood stoutly until it was burned and torn down by the armies of the South in the Civil War. At the end of that conflict, it was again rebuilded and remained to its great task of conducting both highway and railroad over the Potomac until 1893, when the Baltimore and Ohio radically changed its track alignment at the Ferry and built its own staunch steel bridge across the river there.

But even then, the old Bollman trusses continued faithful to their work. The highway, increasing vastly in importance with the coming of the automobile, still threaded them. Grown old and to an extent feeble, the ancient bridge met its Waterloo, however, in the disastrous floods of 1924. These swept out a span and marked the beginning of the end of the historic structure, which to this day still shows clearly the path of the railroad upon it, even to that long abandoned and most remarkable junction midstream.

CHAPTER X

THE RAILROAD ENTERS THE NATIONAL CAPITAL

The Washington Branch—Its Peculiar Problems of Financing—
The Onerous Passenger Tax and the Trouble to Which it Led
—Mr. Knight Works Out the Details of the New Line—
"Latrobe's Folly"—Opening the Branch—The Tragic Death
of Phineas Davis.

FROM the very beginnings of the plan to build a railroad
from Baltimore to the Ohio, there had been an element in that
brisk city which had argued that it would be much more
practicable and profitable to construct the first line to the
federal capital on the Potomac; to Washington City, as it was
then quite generally called. The completion of the Chesapeake
and Delaware Canal gave fuel to the arguments of this group.
For now it was possible to travel between Baltimore and
Philadelphia by inland water route—throughout the greater
part of the year—swiftly and comfortably, on a steamboat. A
canal also was in process of construction connecting the
Delaware, at Bordentown, with the waters of New York Bay,
at Perth Amboy; soon one would be able to go in a boat all the
way from Baltimore to New York. Yet, between Baltimore
and the capital city of a growing nation, there stretched forty
miles of toll road, which at its best was none too good—and
which rarely was at its best.

"Why," argued this faction, "endeavor to go through with
this will-o'-the-wisp idea of a railroad through a wilderness to
a wilderness, when so opportune a route lies ready for immediate
exploitation? A railroad from Baltimore to Washington will

at once become a vital link of the most important chain of travel in the country, from New York and the points north of that city to Washington and the great territory to the south of the federal capital."

There was meat in this. So, without for a moment swerving from the high idealism and the great vision of their project to strike a railroad through to the great Ohio country, which was to prove the commercial salvation of their city, the promoters of the Baltimore and Ohio gave an early ear to the scheme for a line to Washington as well. The fact that their railroad, at Elkridge, would be within about thirty miles of the capital, gave the plan additional interest for them. It would be no super-engineering enterprise to put a railroad across from Elkridge to the District of Columbia. And so, accordingly, at an early day in the history of the Baltimore and Ohio company, consideration was given to such a route.

In his fifth annual report—dated October 1, 1831— President Thomas gives expression to the favorable results of this consideration, saying:

. . . A railway is now constructing between New York and Philadelphia, and another across the peninsula between the Chesapeake and Delaware Bays, to connect with the steamboats travelling between Baltimore and Philadelphia; these works are fast approaching toward completion; and will, when finished, ensure an easy and rapid communication between these three great commercial emporiums, reciprocally beneficial to them all, and vastly increasing the travel and intercourse between them. By constructing a railway from Baltimore to Washington this line of communication will be extended from New York to the Capital of the United States.

Impressed with the importance of accomplishing this last object in which the convenience of the whole community is so deeply interested and believing the road, if judiciously located and constructed, would afford a fair remuneration to the Stockholders, the Board have directed that during the present season the necessary examinations and surveys should be made for the purpose of ascertaining the facilities which the intermediate country offers for a Rail Road and the approximate expense of its construction. In this duty the Chief Engineer of the Company, with an efficient force, has for some time been engaged.

The Legislature of Maryland during the last session passed an act which, among other provisions, authorized the Baltimore and Washington Turnpike Company to subscribe $100,000 to the stock of the proposed road to Washington and reserving to the state the right to subscribe for five-eighths of the cost of the road, from its intersection with the Baltimore and Ohio Rail Road to the line of the District of Columbia, amounting perhaps to a majority of the whole proposed expenditure. . . .

. . . .

Maryland moved in no great haste to make her subscription to the Washington Branch. The fact that she had reserved a right to subscribe proved to be quite a different thing from actually turning over a signed check to the treasurer of the struggling railroad company. . . . The delay in receiving substantial returns from her original investment in Baltimore and Ohio shares may have accounted in part at least for her laggardness. On the other hand, there was almost the certainty of a quick return from the Washington Branch.[1]

Pro and con, for three sessions of their Legislature, the solons of the Maryland of that day weighed the entire question. Finally it was thought that the state might assume a share of the cost of the new road (a share then estimated at about five-eighths), provided the experiment was made in the first instance by others and was declared by them to be a profitable one. Maryland was not going to take very many chances in the matter.

The first act empowering the state to subscribe—dated

[1] While the Washington Branch was planned and constructed under the general charter of the Baltimore and Ohio company and always shared its officers and directors, it was for a long time operated as a separate railroad; with its own motive power, rolling stock and accounts, kept quite distinct from those of the parent road, which became known as the Main Stem.

February 22, 1831—was moulded in accordance with this policy. It also allowed preference in the subscription for the branch railroad to the Washington and Baltimore Turnpike Company, which had shown agitation over the whole project and had complained of this new kind of road as being extremely likely to embarrass and thwart its own line and its vested rights.

This first act passed. But came to nothing. It suited no one. The second one came on the fourteenth of March of the following year. It still secured to the state her ultimate five-eighths of the stock, but it modified considerably the narrowness of its predecessor by allowing the Baltimore and Ohio Railroad to take shares not subscribed—after a limited period—by individuals; and, to pay for them, it permitted the railroad company to borrow money by a mortgage upon its property.

Yet, there still were flies in the ointment. For instance, there was in this second measure a clause which allowed stockholders to receive for only eight years dividends from the road to Washington as a separate line; after that, its earnings were to be merged with those of the parent Main Stem. This, of course, was the thing that came to pass, eventually. But at the time it aroused bitter opposition and the bill that embodied the provision also became a dead letter.

They had patience, those men of that day. They needed it. Finally, in the spring of 1833, a measure was passed satisfactory both to the friends and to the fairly numerous foes of the new line to Washington. This third measure definitely authorized a state subscription of $500,000. On condition, however, that bona fide subscriptions of not less than $1,000,000 should come in from other sources—including the city of Baltimore and the Baltimore and Washington Turnpike Company, both of which were empowered legally to subscribe.

Nor was this quite all. Maryland did not propose again to wait an indefinite length of time for dividends. She devised a plan for getting a much quicker return on her money. A rate of fare which had previously been fixed, in the two ineffective bills, of $1.50 in each direction between the two cities, was increased to $2.50 in the final statute. Of this, the state took arbitrarily twenty per cent for itself; fifty cents out of each single fare.

In after years, this particular provision arose again and again to curse the lot of the operating management of Baltimore and Ohio. On one particular occasion, it led almost to an open rupture between the road and the Richmond, Fredericksburg and Potomac Railroad. This last line, then as now, formed a most important single link of the great travel chain north and south along the Atlantic seaboard, to which reference has already been made. In its earlier days, its northern rail terminal was at Quantico; on the Potomac about thirty miles south of Washington; where a steamer connection was made with the capital.[1]

The Richmond, Fredericksburg and Potomac and the Washington Branch of the Baltimore and Ohio were therefore, to every intent and purpose, connecting rail lines; adjoining links of the north and south chain of rails, which in the late 'thirties was made practically continuous all the way from New York and Philadelphia, through Baltimore and Washington, to Richmond and Petersburg, Virginia, and points even further south.

There soon developed a powerful rival to this route—in a steamboat link down the length of Chesapeake Bay, from Baltimore to Norfolk, where the cars could again be boarded on toward the Carolinas. Gradually there came into the minds of the men who were conducting the affairs of the Richmond, Fredericksburg and Potomac, a feeling that the arbitrary high fare of the Washington Branch was doing a serious injury to travel upon their line. Vainly they protested to the president and the directors of the Baltimore and Ohio, who shrugged their shoulders and said that the fare was none

---

[1] It was not until many years afterwards that the Washington Southern was builded to connect through trackage at Alexandria with the railroad at Quantico, and so make in every sense a through rail line from the north to and through Richmond on toward the south.

of their making; that it had been established by the Legislature of Maryland, which alone could unmake it.

By 1844, this quarrel between the two railroad companies had almost come to a head. The Virginia company carried it into open warfare in the Baltimore and Ohio territory, quietly reëstablishing stage-coach routes upon the Baltimore and Washington Turnpike. The fare on these stages was fixed at $1.50, as against the railroad's charge of $2.50, and business upon them became brisk. Gradually it developed that the Richmond, Fredericksburg and Potomac had subsidized these stage routes, by agreeing to pay their proprietors $2.50 in addition to the other fare gained, for each *through* passenger from north to south or vice versa that they carried in their coaches, as well as a flat sum of $5000 in case it asked to have the stages withdrawn. Three lines of coaches were set up, and between June 15 and September 30, 1844, these carried 3419 local passengers, and 889 through ones, as against a total of 13,062 transported by the railroad in that same time.

Against this unexpected form of competition, the Baltimore and Ohio—its hands tied behind its back—struggled, ineffectively. The Legislature had said that it was indifferent to one-day excursion fares, and these presently were fixed by the railroad at $2.50—just half the cost of two one-way tickets. As a strike back, it hardly sufficed to meet the situation, and the Baltimore and Ohio eventually was forced to seek a compromise with the Richmond, Fredericksburg and Potomac. But the rather stiff single fare of $2.50—a little more than six cents a mile—remained in effect until 1871 and the coming of a powerful rail competitor to the Baltimore and Ohio between Baltimore and Washington. This competitor, the Baltimore and Potomac—a subsidiary of the Pennsylvania—had no such impost placed upon its passenger fares. The great injustice done to Baltimore and Ohio in a competitive field was then recognized by the Maryland Legislature, the burdensome tax removed and the railroad left to charge such fares as it saw fit to ask.

In all those years, much damage was done to its fortunes by that bonus tax.   And the firm foundation of the two great passenger-steamboat lines which now ply up and down the Chesapeake Bay was laid in the traffic which came to them in the days of the high Washington-Baltimore fares.   Of this, there seems to be but little doubt.

.   .   .   .

Return to the beginnings of the Washington Branch.

Guesswork there might have been about the plans and necessities for building the original line, the Main Stem of the road.   Certainly there were no precedents by which that group of Baltimore merchants and bankers might hope to guide themselves.   But, by the time the Washington Branch was seriously projected, they stood at least in the light of their own experience.   With great detail and precision, the indefatigable Jonathan Knight prepared for its construction.   First he estimated the traffic that might be expected to pass over the branch, both passenger and freight.   Then he gave thought to the type and quantity of equipment that would be necessary to haul it.

For instance, in regard to the passenger business, he felt that not less than four trains would be required; one to be kept at Baltimore, one at Washington, one to be in motion between the two cities all the while, with provision for a fourth train for relief and repairs.   Similarly he estimated the average freight train on the branch would have—if composed of the so-called friction cars (equipped with Ross Winans' friction wheels)— say, six empty cars and four loaded; if made up of the "common cars"—to use the phraseology of that time—five empty and ten loaded cars.   The first train would haul thirty-six tons of freight, the second but thirty tons.   Count that as a triumph for Ross Winans' first practical invention.

There was little guesswork about any of this.   Knight estimated, for instance, that the daily cost of train operation on the new line would be $33.89; divided among the cost of operating the locomotive, $21.02; the cost of operating the train itself aside from the engine, $4.87; and the prorated general expense of the line estimated at $8.00 for each train. They were beginning even then to develop railroad statistics. Cost sheets already were being born.

Knight's report at this day does credit to the assertion of the *American Railway Journal*, already quoted in these pages, that the Baltimore and Ohio was in truth the railroad university of the entire land. He goes forward to say:

. . . The locomotive engine will convey, when the rails are in good condition for adhesion, a gross tonnage equal to 50¾ tons. The gross weight of a passenger-car containing sixteen to eighteen persons is about 2¾ tons. Consequently the engine would travel with a train of eighteen such cars containing 300 persons. The supply of steam would probably not be sufficient with such a train to maintain a speed of over twelve or fifteen miles an hour, which is not sufficient velocity for the line.

It is not improbable that ultimately 100 persons will be the usual number conveyed in a train; with these the speed may be as great as to comport with comfort and safety; especially in summer when twice that number could be carried with equal ease and facility. . . . Supposing six cars to accommodate 100 persons and that two other cars shall be added to allow for wear and tear of cars partly filled and for baggage, the train will then consist of eight cars. . . .

The daily expense of a locomotive engine and train conveying 100 passengers between Baltimore and Washington, one circular trip each day, will then be as follows:

Engineer, wages	$ 2.00
Assistant, do	1.50
1½ tons anthracite at $7	10.50
Repairs and renewal of engine and tender	8.15
2 spare engines and tenders interest	1.67
Total for engine and tender	$23.82
8 coaches at $1	8.00
Conductor, wages	2.00
General expenses	6.85
Total per day	$40.67

And 4067/100 equal 40⅔ cents per passenger for the circular trip, or for the single passage between the cities, 20⅓ cents, or very little over half a cent a mile.   Adding the conveyance into the city from the engine station, the conveyance per person will be about 24 cents.

With the passenger return to the railroad fixed by the state at $2, there would seem to be, from Mr. Knight's figures, a fair chance for profit for it.   These figures are set down here for what they are worth, certainly not for analysis.   By what process Knight arrived at his primary figures, it is not easy always to discover.   But the figures themselves are ingenious; and, for that day, probably fairly accurate.   He continues:

> One engine, according to the foregoing arrangement, would therefore convey daily 200 passengers and two engines 400 passengers from city to city; and the time employed in performing the transit would be 2½ hours, according to the speed constantly maintained upon the New Castle and Frenchtown Railway across the peninsula between the Chesapeake and Delaware bays, or the velocity might be made to average nineteen to twenty miles per hour and the trip be performed in two hours only.

Today, over that same line of the Washington Branch, it is done daily by regular passenger trains in a fraction less than fifty minutes!

Mr. Knight says that he thinks it probable that public convenience and exigencies would be better served by running three, instead of two, trains daily for the conveyance of passengers.   Although the number of these would, under ordinary circumstances, not exceed 200 a day in each direction at the outset, one of the trains might carry the principal mails at such times as the Post Office Department might require.

> This arrangement by lessening the number of passengers in each train enhances the cost to the Company of their conveyance; yet without doubt the government would pay a just

compensation for the speedy and safe carriage of the enormously bulky mails that must pass upon this route.   The remuneration thus to be received from the Post Office Department will probably more than counterbalance the excess of cost in the conveyance of the passengers.

Mr. Knight makes a résumé of traffic possibilities of every sort along the line of the new branch railroad and then expresses his very sincere doubt whether all of it can be moved by two, or even three, engines.   The reduction in freight charges, bound to come with the completion of the new road, he stresses.   At that time on the turnpike, it took wagons two or three days at the shortest to go from Washington or Georgetown or Alexandria to Baltimore, and these charged about 25 cents a mile per ton or about $9 or $10 a ton for the entire distance.   Sloops took a week, steamboats from twenty-four to forty-eight hours, for the water journey between Baltimore and these cities of the Potomac, roughly speaking some 200 miles distant from the mouth of the Patapsco.   These water craft, in the season of their navigation, charged from $1.62½ to $5.00 a ton.   Yet, despite these high rates, a very considerable commerce already was passing back and forth between Washington and Baltimore, already estimated at paying more than $30,000 annually.

It all looked like a fair field for a railroad.   It was determined that the freight rates upon the Washington Branch should be but 4 cents per ton mile, or $1.60 a ton for the entire haul; considerably cheaper than the average charge either by boat or by wagon.   Mr. Knight, in his enthusiasm, felt that a locomotive would be required for the freight traffic alone; in addition to the three demanded by the passenger business, as has just been seen.   He made a special point of new traffic to be created by the coming of the railroad—of a sort beyond the possibilities of either turnpike or water route.   For instance, there was the Patapsco granite.   Fine new government buildings already were beginning to spring up in Washington, and the new railroad could—and eventually did—bring the building stone for them, in great single blocks, as well as many

THE RELAY BRIDGE.

As it appears today after ninety-two years of continuous service. In the distance, the monument to its builders and the hotel and station at Relay.

From a recent photograph.

ANNAPOLIS JUNCTION, MARYLAND.

As the intersection of the Washington Branch and the line to the Maryland capital appeared sixty years ago.

From a very old photograph.

smaller ones. . . . One can almost feel the tingling enthusiasm of this fine old Quaker citizen of Baltimore as he writes:

The local trade that will be created by all these causes combined, added to the exchangeable products of agricultural and manufacturing capital already employed between the Patapsco and the Potomac and accessible to the line of the proposed improvement, will unquestionably demand the constant work of one, and probably of two engines. And this conclusion will appear moderate upon reflecting that the local trade upon the railway between Baltimore and Ellicott's Mills amounts to about 25,000 tons in a year, and that the water power upon the two Patuxents is abundant, constant and easily improved; and indeed it is already improved to some considerable extent.

Giving due weight to the foregoing considerations, we must conclude that two and even three engines will be inadequate to the trade in commodities upon the Washington railway and that the time is not very distant when four will be required. Whilst the facilities and advantages to be secured to the public in the conveyance of commodities by means of the railway proposed will be very great; yet the Company's receipts from this source will be far less in amount than what will be received for the conveyance of persons and the net profits to remain after paying the expenses of the motive power and the machinery will . . . bear a much greater ratio to the gross receipts in the carriage of persons than of goods. It is from the conveyance of passengers therefore that the great and adequate sources of revenue in this concern must be derived.

The number of passengers traveling the turnpike in regular and extra stages now amounts to about 125 a day, in both directions—and the number now passing is fully double that which passed four years ago. In three of four years hence, therefore, and without any additional facilities and at the same price for the passengers, viz. $3—the number of passengers by the turnpike road will probably be increased to 200 a day. The lessening of the price to $2.50 and the reducing of the time to at least one half, will probably have the effect to increase the number fifty per cent; in that case 300 a day, or 150 in each direction, would pass between the two cities. But we think it probable that from the increase of wealth and population and business, and from the increased facilities of travel to the west, the north and the south, the number will be greater and perhaps not less than 200 a day in each direction. . . .

All travelers upon business or pleasure visiting the Capital of the Union from the states, west, north and east as well as all those from the southern states traveling through the seat of government will pass and repass upon this railway. The improved lines of communication into the interior, westward and northward as well as to the eastward parallel to the coast, now projected or in course of construction by railways, some of which have already been completed, whilst most of them are in progress of construction, added to the increased facilities for travel afforded in steamboats and especially between Baltimore and Philadelphia, will tend considerably to increase the number of travelers upon this line. Doubtless before many years the cities of Baltimore and Philadelphia will be connected by a continuous line of railway, as well as those of Boston, New York and Philadelphia. And this will greatly increase the travel in the winter season, hitherto prevented between Philadelphia and Baltimore unless in stages upon very bad roads and at considerable risk and in cases of urgency and necessity alone. Let communication to Washington by railway be established and whole families will visit the seat of government where single individuals only go now. The southern states will likewise be connected to the seat of general government by railways, whilst the line from Baltimore to Washington will be the link connecting the railways diverging from Washington to the South and Southwest with those diverging from Baltimore to the West, the North and the East. And consequently the railway between Baltimore and Washington must continue to be a great central national highway upon which the quantity of travel will be very great. . . .

Mr. Knight estimates that, with the steady growth of the nation, the time will come when as many as eight hundred or a thousand people will travel daily between Baltimore and Washington; in *both* directions, of course.   He concludes:

> We believe that this will be at a period not very remote. We deem it therefore reasonable to calculate upon 400 in both directions, or 200 in each direction daily as the number of passengers that must be conveyed upon the Washington railway, either immediately or very soon after it shall be open for travel—certainly by the time the second track shall be laid down.   Travel between Baltimore and Frederick has been increased since the formation of the Baltimore and Ohio sixfold.   It ranged from 15 to 20 persons a day before the Rail Road was opened and it is now perhaps 120 a day.   The same rate of augmentation upon the route to Washington would give 750 a day, but so great an increase in so short a time ought not to be expected upon the Washington railway.

The chief engineer of the Baltimore and Ohio argued very well indeed for the success of the projected branch.   So well, that presently the board of directors, having given grave consideration to his detailed report, decided that the line should be builded.   Then it was that application was made both to the state of Maryland and to the city of Baltimore for aid. And while these grave bodies deliberated upon all the whys and wherefores of the problem, surveying parties were sent out into the field to make reconnaissances for the new line.   These brought back the alternative of two routes:

One of them, known as the lower line, would pass in a southerly direction from Baltimore to Washington (somewhat south of the present interurban electric railway connecting the two cities) and through a fine agricultural country.   The other, or upper route, which eventually was adopted, went through a territory, as Knight suggests, rather better adapted for mill sites and manufacturing purposes than for farming. The fact that nearly a quarter of this route, from Baltimore to the Patapsco, already had been built, was an additional point in its favor.

This upper route crossed three ridges between Elkridge (near the present Relay where it diverted from the Main Stem of the Baltimore and Ohio) and Bladensburg; the first between the Patapsco and the Patuxent, the second between the two branches of the Patuxent and the third between the Patuxent and the northeast branch of the Potomac. The altitude of these ridges varies from 200 to 215 feet above the level of mid-tide at Baltimore, and it was estimated that, with the railroad crossing these rivers at an altitude of from forty to fifty feet above their waters, there would have to be cuttings of about the same depth through the crests of the ridges. This done, the grades would be easy and well adapted for swift running by the small locomotives of that day.

Knight suggested that the track should be laid with the sleepers—of wood, by this time—three feet apart, instead of four, as on the Main Stem, and that stringers be placed below, as well as above, the crossties; this last a considerable variation from established practice. On the upper stringers, he proposed to lay a continuous flat iron rail, each rail about fifteen feet long, with a base three and a half inches wide and standing about two inches in height. It would weigh about thirty-two pounds per running yard, or about fifty tons for each mile of single track.

This rail, when finally laid down in accordance with the chief engineer's recommendations, was the first form of "T" rail ever used upon the Baltimore and Ohio—and probably anywhere within the United States. It represented a distinct advance in one of the most important phases of railroad construction.

.   .   .   .

For the crossing of the three rivers between Baltimore and Washington, there would have to be bridges. For the Patapsco, at the point where the new line would diverge from the old, there was planned and built what was, and is even to this day, one of the finest bits of railroad architecture within the entire land. To Benjamin H. Latrobe is due credit for the fashioning of this remarkable stone structure, a curving viaduct seven hundred feet long, of eight elliptical arches, each sixty feet in width and about sixty-five feet above the level of the stream. The care, the thought, and the labor that went into the fabrication of this unusual bridge must have been very great. But that it was well built, as well as planned, the evidence of time itself has gone to show. Over a structure originally designed for the passage of six-ton locomotives with their small trains, there pass today, 300-ton locomotives, with the heaviest of steel trains, both freight and passenger. And this, with no alterations nor repairs to the original bridge, save, from time to time, the common upkeep of pointing its masonry fabric. Mr. Latrobe builded better than he knew. He builded not alone for the Baltimore and Ohio Railroad of that day, but for the Baltimore and Ohio Railroad of many and many a day to come—to at least a full hundred years, and no one knows how far beyond.

In honor of the distinguished first president of the company, he suggested that it be called the Thomas Viaduct; and this suggestion was placed into effect, although for some years the bridge was called, by idle-minded folk, "Latrobe's Folly." This name was taken up for a time by engineers who swore that the bridge could not even be built, that it would not stand under its own weight. The fallacy of these men has long since been exposed; the bridge stands to its work—day in and day out, in all seasons of the year, year after year—today one of the very oldest stone-arch railroad viaducts still in use in all the world.

. . . .

With a single exception, the laying down of the Washington Branch went ahead in a fairly uneventful fashion. The problems of construction were as light as Mr. Knight had anticipated, and with the experience of building the Main Stem to guide them there was but little delay in the work.

A serious disturbance between one of the contractors—a

Mr. Gorman, father of the late Arthur Pue Gorman—and some of his men arose, however, late in the autumn of 1834. Gorman and John Watson, one of his superintendents of construction, were seated talking in the contractor's shanty when eight or ten men, armed and in no light mood, surrounded the place, dragged them out into the night and beat them into insensibility. The next night, the outrage was repeated, in a far more aggravated form. Watson, who was lying on a couch in his office, still weak from his wounds of the preceding evening, was deliberately murdered, in a particularly violent and brutal way. Nor was this all. Two other men, assistants of Mr. Watson— a William Messer and a man named Callon—who came to the assistance of their chief, were also killed. And the shanty rifled and robbed before the cutthroat gang departed.

By this tragedy, so utterly needless, Baltimore and Washington alike were aroused to a high pitch of indignation. That those were other than rough times, it need not be asserted. But gradually there was arising everywhere a decided feeling for law and order. Not only the Baltimore and Ohio had suffered from lawlessness of this sort. The construction of all the early railroads, as well as the canals and other public works, was marked with occurrences such as this. Because they were generally attributed to whiskey, they laid, no matter how unconsciously, the firm foundations for the temperance movements which began, a few years later, to spring up across the land and which were to continue in force and in volume until national prohibition became a matter of statute law.

It was with a deal of satisfaction, therefore, that the people of Baltimore saw the disorder gradually stamped out upon their railroad; even though at great cost—involving the sending of the militia out upon the Washington Branch, which returned presently with no less than three hundred of the recalcitrant laborers. Justice gradually was done and the workmen's camps settled down once again to at least a comparative state of peaceful activity.

.   .   .   .

9th July 1832 8 oClk P.M. Arrived No 157 from Balt°

P. Toomey	418	Red.	1 Trunk
C. A. Gambrill	"	"	1 Piano Forte
C. Wilson & Co	210	"	1 Blo Linseed Oil
Stuart Gaither	418	"	1 Coil of Rope
H. M. Jamieson	210. 418	"	2 Blls 3 pieces Steel
Baldwin & Co	418	"	2 Band Sives
Wm Fischer	210	"	1 Blo Chloride of Lime
Henry Kepler	418	"	6 Bales Deer Skins
H. M. Jamieson	210. 418	"	1 Hhd Sugar
Thos Starr	418	"	1 Box Pipe, 1 package Brass rules
Valentine Thomas	"	"	1 Box
Geo Salmon	"	"	1 Box Lemmons
C. A. Gambrill	"	"	1 Box, 1 Bale, 1 bag pepper ½ box Chocolate
"	"	"	1 Mat Cinnamon 2 packages 1 Hhd Sugar
"	"	"	4 bags Coffee 1 Bale 4 boxes 2 Sacks Salt
"	"	"	1 Box Merchdze
C. Wilson & Co	"	"	1 Nest Tubs 6 Buckets 12 Wooden Bowls
"	"	"	1 Blo, 1 Box & 1 Keg
Wm Fischer	210	"	1 Cask White Lead
A. Fischer	"	"	1 Blo Molasses
Thos Gordon	418	"	1 Barrel
Geo. Salmon	"	"	4 plates Copper 2 pattern pieces 8 Bottoms
			2 Hammers
B. Ellicott	368. 150	L.K.	2 loads empty Blls (free)
C. Grimes	130. 100	P. No 1	1 load Pine plank 27 29 feet
Geo. Hamilton		Dorseys S.	1 lot plank 200 feet
Thos Murry		P.N. 1	1 load Shingles 60. feet

The above is a true and full account of all the
goods and Commodities transported by me between
Baltimore and Frederick in the above described
Transit.   Benj. Stevens

EARLY RAILROAD.

Ohio train of 1832 in the form of a manifest.

original.

And all the while the railroad going forward.

Men laughing . . . quarreling . . . working. . . . Teams and wagons struggling through newly turned earth, blasters with their gunpowder at the hard rock. . . . The semblance of a railroad embankment first appearing. Growing more and more definite all the while. And then the track, spruce and new and bright and clean. There is something immensely dramatic about the building of a railroad, even through gentle territory. One feels that something intangibly great has come across the face of the land; and come to stay.

All the while the railroad going forward.

Until comes that day, in the summer of 1835, when the line is finally completed through the historic little village of Bladensburg—almost upon the District of Columbia line. By that time, it should have been done right into the heart of Washington City itself. But there had been many delays. Chief among these, the non-arrival of the English rails, the last shipload of which never came into Baltimore harbor until the second week in July. . . . After which, there was short shift toward putting down the final links of the track. Until, on July 20, the road was opened to the District line and trains went through to it in one hour and forty minutes. A few days later, one of the reporters of the *Baltimore American* rode upon the new line and said in his paper this·

The trips on the Washington Railroad—that is between Baltimore and Bladensburg—are made twice a day each way. The trains are drawn by locomotive engines whose power and fleetness are not exceeded by any in the world. Of all seasons of the year the present is always the dullest for passenger traveling between this city and Washington and yet, notwithstanding the dullness and the incomplete state of the railroad we learn that the company's receipts have been $300 a day since the opening. A very handsome beginning indeed.

. . . We made, a day or two since, a trip on the railroad, starting with a train of three eight-wheel and very large cars, each capable of holding sixty persons and all drawn by one steam engine. The average speed of the train was about eighteen miles per hour and it frequently exceeded twenty-five, the engine being under perfect command, moderating its gait at the curvatures or in passing over the highest embankments and stopping at short notice. We had the pleasure of witnessing a new application, not exactly of steam power, but of its generator, the boiling water, by the ejecting of which the engineer quickly cleared the road of some obstinate cows.

We take the opportunity of calling the attention of the company to the policy and propriety of accommodating way passengers. People residing on the line have reason to complain if they cannot have the benefit of its construction without the inconvenience of going several miles to one of the few regular stopping places. Such too is the facility of arresting the engine that the delay occasioned by taking in or letting out a passenger is but momentary.

The passage of the cars is a novel sight, which attracts the inhabitants of the country long distances to witness and well it may, for it is enough to excite a special wonder to behold a row of long houses roaring along the road, borne at the rate of thirty miles an hour by the snorting engine. . . .

It is the contemporary press that best gives us the real pictures of these beginnings of the Baltimore and Ohio Railroad. The episodes of the kine, driven from the rails by the hot water from the locomotive, the anxiety of the folk living along the new branch for fear that they will not have a chance to board the cars, the tableau of a "row of long houses roaring along the road," are in the eyes of the folk that saw them at that time. . . . Just as, a month later, we find in the same musty files of the *American* the following formal announcement of the opening of the completed line all the way into Washington:

. . . The spectacle of the passage of the four trains of cars, each with a swift and powerful locomotive at its head, on their way to Washington will be worth a visit to the Rail Road this morning. They can be seen at greater advantage at points west of the Upper Depot [Mount Clare]. The following program has been published by the Committee for the information of the invited guests:

OPENING OF THE WASHINGTON RAIL ROAD

The Committee of Arrangements for opening the Washington Rail Road respectfully inform the invited guests that they have adopted the following regulations to be observed on the occasion.

1. Every gentleman must present his ticket before taking his seat in a Car.

2. Gentlemen will be permitted to introduce not more than ONE LADY. This regulation is rendered indispensable by the limited number of seats.

3. The Cars will leave the Depot in Charles Street at NINE o'clock *precisely*.

4. It is requested that no persons leave the Cars until the arrival of the party at Washington.

5. The party will leave the Depot at Washington at FOUR o'clock P.M. *precisely*.

6. The first two cars are reserved for the Executive of Maryland, Members of the Legislature of Maryland and the Mayor and City Council of Baltimore and other Public Functionaries.

7. Ladies and Gentlemen in returning are requested to take the same Car in which they leave Baltimore.

.   .   .   .

So much for the preparations. All is now ready for the occasion itself. And no little a one is it to be; this entrance of the first railroad train into the capital of the United States.

It is the twenty-fifth day of August, 1835, and a warm summer sun already is shining down upon the heads, the hats and the parasols of the privileged folk who are making their way to the immaculate new cars drawn up in Pratt Street just opposite the Inner Depot at Charles. Nearly a thousand folk come to ride upon this excursion—how paltry the openings to Ellicotts Mills and Frederick and Harpers Ferry now seem!
. . . Sixteen cars are not going to be enough for all this

throng.   A messenger is sent on horseback up to Mount Clare. More cars come sliding down through pleasant, tree-embowered Pratt Street.

Off and away, at last.   Up the long hill toward the edge of the town and the Upper Depot.   And here at the Upper Depot, four brand-new locomotives, spick-and-span and shined almost to the last possibility of human effort.   These engines have been built by Baltimore man power (by Davis and Gartner, who will be recalled as having leased the Mount Clare shops from the railroad company a short time before).   They are also of the upright-boiler type, which, with its huge ungainly rods and arms and joints, is beginning to be known colloquially in Baltimore as the "grasshopper" engine.

These engines—the *George Washington*, the *John Adams*, the *Thomas Jefferson* and the *James Madison*—divide the heavily laden passenger cars among them. . . .

A little delay and then off they go. . . .   By this time, the road up to the wonderful new stone bridge over the Patapsco —curious how these Baltimore folk will persist in calling it "Latrobe's Folly"—is fairly familiar.   But beyond, the country is new to most of the party, save to those who have been steady travelers over the Washington Turnpike. . . .   Bladensburg is the first stop.   The party disregards the instructions in the morning paper and goes tumbling out there.   A trainload of bigwigs over from Washington comes forward to meet the Baltimore trains.   There is no double track as yet, not even a passing siding, and therefore there must be a meeting at Bladensburg . . . handshaking . . . compliments and congratulations. . . .   What a wonderful new thing, the railroad. . . .   And how far back it seems to that Fourth of July seven years ago, when the Masons of Baltimore and Charles Carroll of Carrollton were laying the First Stone in the field just west of Mount Clare. . . .   More compliments . . . a display of wit . . . some more handshaking. . . .   All there in the field beside the new railroad track. . . .   Some oratory. . . .

On the highroad that skirts the hills that look down into the crowded field at Bladensburg, a post chaise stops. It is a pretentious vehicle, with postilions and even an outrider. . . . A flunky opens the door of the carriage. From it an old man steps. He wears knee breeches, a ruffled shirt, a stock, a long coat of black satin, wide-skirted, a wig, a three-cornered hat. . . . He walks slowly, this old man, with the aid of a stick, it seems. . . . The crowd in the field, the smoking locomotives along its edge, seem to irritate him greatly. . . . He chatters to himself, pokes disdainfully with his stick at the mob below. No one catches his words. Few in the busy throng even see him. None is ever to know the identity of this old man, who after a moment turns his back scornfully upon the scene and slowly clambers again into his chaise.

No one is ever to know the identity of this man unbidden to Bladensburg that day. Yet, after all these years, it may be possible to guess at it. He is old man Yesterday. Again and again he shows himself. He was present when the first electric locomotive went its silent way, he ranted in the recesses of his ancient rickety coach when first it drew up to let a snorting automobile go rushing past. He saw the first aeroplane and, willy-nilly, heard the wireless and the radio and saw the television. . . . This is he who looked down into the field at Bladensburg and upon whom the newspapers of that day spent so much time and guesswork.

. . . .

The new depot in Washington at the foot of the hill just back of the Capitol (Pennsylvania Avenue and Second Street) was by no means complete, but the trains were able to approach it and there discharge their passengers who formed themselves behind a military band and proceeded to Gadsby's and Brown's hotels, where there was the customary banquet; and, it is to be presumed, more speeches. . . . At half past four o'clock, the four trains were again in motion, homeward bound. And the record of the memorable day in the annals of the Baltimore and Ohio closes with the fact that the Upper Depot at Mount Clare was reached two hours and twenty minutes later.

.   .   .   .

So came the Washington Branch into existence. With a brisk patronage being accorded it from the outset. And an early passenger upon it writing:

> . . . The cars on the Baltimore and Washington Railroad perform their trips now regularly twice each way in two hours and a half from office to office, including all stoppages. They take in and let out passengers anywhere along the line, losing only one minute in the operation. [The editorial plaint of the reporter of the *Baltimore American* could not have been entirely without effect.] Their common, steady gait is at the rate of a mile in three minutes and when they stop for a passenger they require four. The conductors are active, watchful and accommodating, and the cars, with their broad seats, with high, stuffed, well-inclined backs, are the most commodious we have ever traveled in and we have been in a good many.

It is plain to see that the Washington Branch was not to be regarded as any ordinary sort of railroad.

.   .   .   .

Across the brave, gay start of this new line, the sinister note of tragedy.

The death of Charles Reeder, of the Baltimore and Ohio, upon one of the locomotives which he had builded for the road, has already been noticed. A similar fate awaited Phineas Davis, the watchmaker of York, whom already we have seen quitting his bench to build the first really successful engine for the Baltimore road.

Davis, who was a particularly well-liked man, was helping the celebration that followed the opening of the Washington Branch by taking a party of his workmen on a special excursion train over to the national capital. They all had had a wonder-

Nos		Stage	Balt.
3	Mr Hardy	5 40	Balt
1	Mrs Oliver	1 80	do
1	Sett Lewis	1 80	do
5	Mr Eaton	9 00	do
1	Mr Benland	free	N. M.
1	Mrs Shipman	1 80	Balt
1	Mr Pickard	1 80	do
1	A Ponci	1 80	do
1	S Alexander	33	N. Market
1	Mr Rudd	1 80	Balt
1	Mr Steward	1 80	do
1	S Mahar	51	Shawsone
1	Mr Hills	1 80	Balt

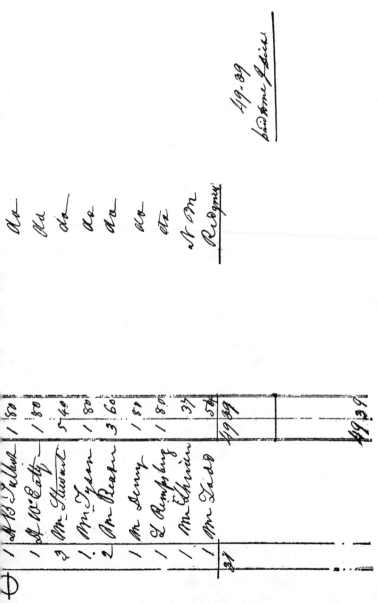

BEFORE THE **DAY OF TICKETS.**

The passenger list of the local to Frederick as a conductor of 1831 compiled it.

From the original.

ful time of it. Travel in the days before the coming of the railroad was not easy and few Baltimore folk had ever had the time or the opportunity to go to Washington, even though it was but forty miles away.

On the return journey Mr. Davis was riding upon the locomotive—it was one of the new engines which he had just constructed for the opening of the branch. The train was running rather better than twenty-five miles an hour, and he was just commenting upon the success of the mechanism when the engine struck a loose rail, which had worked out of its fastenings, and was derailed. The flange of a wheel hit the projecting end and the locomotive went into the ditch. Every one was shaken up a good bit but no one was seriously injured, save Davis, who was killed almost instantly. The wheels of the tender passed over his body, terribly mangling it.

This accident produced a profound effect, not only upon the excursion party, but upon every one who had been connected with the locomotive builder. All Baltimore was saddened by it, but the blow hit hardest upon the railroad. For almost the first time, its management realized that this was no plaything that it had created. It was serious business. A business that easily required all that a man had to give; in patience, in thought, and then, not infrequently, in life itself.

In the ninth annual report of the company, one finds President Thomas paying a tribute to Phineas Davis in these words:

. . . With untiring patience he bore disappointment after disappointment; and the eminent and splendid results which ultimately rewarded his efforts are ample testimonials of his genius, and will identify his name, most honorably, with that great system of internal improvement which is yet to work so many and such important changes in the relations of society. Of a quick and clear perception, in matters relating to his profession, he possessed a calm and discriminating judgment. The warmth and energy of inventive talent were tempered by a prudent foresight and great practical skill. He seldom therefore took a step which was not a secure one; and the success of his suggestions, when put into practice, gave them, from the first, almost the same weight as if they had been the dicta of experience. His private worth and unassuming manners were not less remarkable than his rare abilities. The Board deeply regrets his loss, and holds his memory in sincere and respectful consideration.

CHAPTER XI

THE BALTIMORE AND OHIO OF THE 'THIRTIES

The Chief Engineer of the New Erie Railroad Visits the Baltimore Road—His Flattering Reports upon It—Locomotive Problems—The Vertical Boiler—Black Days—Panic—And a New President for the Baltimore and Ohio Railroad.

THE railroad fever lay hard upon the land. In the middle of the fourth decade of the last century, with less than five hundred miles of track actually laid within the United States, plans were already under way for putting down from ten to twenty times that length of line. The business of railroad promotion had begun. Impressive looking gentlemen, generally silk-hatted, frock-coated, black-moustached, smooth-tongued, went from place to place stirring up sentiment for railroads; with a considerable interest in their own fortunes in so doing. Railroads were projected that never should be built; that never could be built; that never would be built. In a brief period of time, little towns that had struggled against ceaseless adversity since their beginnings, found themselves anticipating metropolitanism, with rail lines reaching out from them in every direction. Poor was the county that did not have at least one railroad planned for it. Busy were the state legislatures incorporating new rail systems. A thousand companies were organized and ten million hopes raised to the high heavens.

After this came the devastating, blackening panic of 1837. Of which, more in good time.

Among the railroads that were being planned in that early

day, and one which was to make a very definite impress upon railroad history in the United States, was a line that would some day run from the west bank of the Hudson River, near its mouth, across the counties of the so-called Southern Tier of New York State, and terminate either at Dunkirk or Buffalo, on Lake Erie. This road, which presently became known as the Erie, also was planned very largely because of the success of the Erie Canal. The Southern Tier counties of New York State had viewed with an ill-disguised jealousy the sudden prosperity that that new waterway had brought to the counties of central New York. They exerted strong pressure upon the State Capitol at Albany and, aided by the city of New York, which had everything to gain and nothing to lose in the matter, the Erie Railroad was chartered at an early day, and in 1835 work was actually begun near Deposit, New York.

The Erie had the advantage of seeing how other railroads were now being built, everywhere along the Atlantic seaboard all the way from Maine to Georgia. Because the great rail enterprise at Baltimore had pioneered so faithfully and apparently so well, the promoters of the New York and Erie, as it was at first called, gave especial attention to its workings. They sent for its remarkable reports, modeled quite largely upon the voluminous pamphlets issued by the Liverpool and Manchester Railway, and finally dispatched one of their chief engineers, James Seymour, to see for himself what had been accomplished at Baltimore and to report at length upon it.

Seymour's report gives a very definite picture of the Baltimore and Ohio as it stood at the beginning of 1836, just seven and one-half years after the laying of the First Stone and a little more than five and one-half years after it had commenced actual operations. He writes that he traversed the line in company with Mr. Thomas, its president, and that they had traveled swiftly up to Parrs Spring Ridge; but that they could have gone faster had not the company's regulations forbidden

a speed of more than fourteen miles an hour along that portion
of its line.   He goes on to say:

> . . . At the time when the road was located over this
> ridge, about the year 1829, it had not been supposed practicable
> to ascend with locomotive engines with loaded trains upon
> grades exceeding thirty feet to the mile, and therefore in order
> to pass this ridge, four inclined planes, arranged for stationary
> engines, were adopted. . . .   Since the recent improvements in
> Baltimore locomotives, much exceeding in power the com-
> paratively feeble engines imported from England, the Baltimore
> and Ohio Rail Road have resolved to locate anew this section
> of their road so as to dispense with these planes, and to adopt
> a more circuitous route over the ridge upon which the grades
> will be reduced to eighty feet and to one hundred feet to the
> mile, and will be passed exclusively by locomotive engines.
> The planes as now located are passed by auxiliary horse power,
> but they have lately been surmounted by one of the Baltimore
> locomotive engines [the *Arabian*] drawing thirty-three pas-
> sengers and other freight.
>   I was informed by Jonathan Knight, Esq., Chief Engineer
> of that road, that it is now proposed to pass the ridges west of
> the Alleghany mountains, lying west of Cumberland, ex-
> clusively with locomotive power, encountering grades of from
> fifty to one hundred feet to the mile, and containing an aggre-
> gate length of fifty-five miles.   The company estimates the
> actual cost of traction on those heavy grades at *two* cents a ton
> per mile and on the grades less than thirty feet to the mile at
> one cent per ton.   The road with the planes as now located is
> very extensively used for the transportation not only of
> passengers and merchandise, but also of flour, lumber, tobacco
> and the general agricultural products of the country.
>   The Baltimore and Washington Rail Road diverges as a
> branch from the Baltimore and Ohio Rail Road at a point
> nine miles west of Baltimore.   The length of this road . . . is
> forty miles, it is traversed by a locomotive engine of seven and
> one-half tons, and cars, which are thirty-four feet long and
> unusually commodious, containing seventy passengers to-

gether with the baggage car, at a velocity varying from sixteen to twenty miles an hour.

On my return from Washington to Baltimore, the same engine drew three of these large passenger cars, containing 140 passengers, together with their baggage and the baggage car at the same speed before mentioned.

The locomotive engines are able however to travel much faster upon this road, having passed a number of times from Baltimore to Washington in one hour and a half, conveying from seventy-five to one hundred passengers, passing over a part of the road at the rate of forty miles per hour upon a straight line. An agreement was made to deliver the President's Message in Baltimore in forty minutes, and it would have been accomplished but for the circumstance that after the engineer had started and obtained the velocity proposed, the fireman became alarmed at the speed and put out the fire. The engines upon the different roads . . . have horizontal boilers and generally burn wood. Those upon the Baltimore and Ohio use anthracite coal and vertical boilers. This plan of engines I consider preferable to those with the horizontal boiler, particularly upon steep grades, as it prevents the water from varying from its place. The use of coal is also preferable, as well on account of its bulk as in maintaining a more uniform and regular amount of steam; and avoiding the smoke and sparks which are found exceedingly inconvenient, unpleasant and even dangerous on the roads where wood is used.

. . . I consider the engines made at Baltimore better than those that are imported from abroad. An English engine arrived in Baltimore a few days since which was destined for a Rail Road in Virginia; but upon being tried upon the Baltimore road ran off the track once or twice. The foreign engines appear to be much better calculated for very straight and level roads than those which must be constructed in this country. The State of Pennsylvania has expended $100,000 for English engines, but has recently concluded to abandon the use of them and hereafter to order their engines made in this country. . . .

Yet, as will be seen in another chapter, the little English engine, *Tennessee*, to which Mr. Seymour here refers, really gave a very good account of herself on the Winchester and Potomac Railroad, frequently doing 128 miles in a day, and so completely winning for herself the hearts of her Virginia owners. . . . Also the vertical boiler was doomed, almost from the beginning. The next group of engines for the Washington Branch, built by William Norris up in Philadelphia, were to follow the conventional design of horizontal boiler, very much the same as in use today; and eventually the mechanical department of the Baltimore and Ohio would bend to the inevitable and adopt that practice for itself, even to the extent of rebuilding some of its existing engines.

For a considerable time, however, it clung rather tenaciously to its own pet type of locomotive. These still continued to be built with vertical boilers. President Thomas, Ross Winans and George Gillingham were a unit in favoring this. Not only did they advance the thought just given by James Seymour that the upright boiler preserved the water at a better level on steep grades, but it was also argued that the English type of locomotive (the early way of referring to the machine with the horizontal boiler) had a way of frequently bursting its tubes; which not only was an expensive sort of business but immediately stopped the engine by drenching its fires and so caused a cessation of traffic upon the line.[1] Jonathan Knight once suggested to Mr. Thomas that brass tubes be used instead of the copper and iron ones that were then rather prevalent practice in Great Britain. And this was done; once or twice.

These men of Baltimore clung tenaciously to that vertical boiler, also to the use of anthracite coal as a fuel (bituminous came a little later)—although the Baltimore and Ohio soon began to stand stoutly opposed to these practices of the others

---

[1] In later years they were to do this rather better. A gentleman who knew some of the Virginia railroads of the early 'eighties still recalls very well the ingenuity with which an engine crew would stop a disabled locomotive in the middle of the open country, hunt around for a bean pole and use it to plug a broken flue. They did not know how to do that in the mid-'thirties.

of the growing family of railroads in the United States. In the one position, they were wrong, and were soon to have to admit the fallacy of their stand; in the other, they were to be proved, although many years afterward, quite right.

From the beginning, these things were part of the distinct individuality of the Baltimore and Ohio—a road which always has possessed a very definite personality. Another radical step for that day was the road's manufacturing its own locomotives; in its own way and in its own shops. After the death of Phineas Davis, Gartner drops out of the picture and these two pioneers are succeeded by George Gillingham—who had held the post of superintendent of machinery—and the indefatigable Ross Winans.

Reference already has been made to the method by which the company had let out its Mount Clare shops. It was a rather ingenious arrangement; not unlike one which is in use today by certain American railroads. Under it, Gillingham and Winans were permitted to manufacture locomotives for other railroads; but the Baltimore and Ohio at all times was to have the prior rights, agreeing to pay $5000 for each engine, as well as prices fixed slightly above costs for other machinery and repairs. The Mount Clare shops at that time had been steadily improved and developed. One hundred men were employed in them and there was a steady output, not only of the "grasshopper" engines—a little later to be succeeded by the "crabs," the first of the Mount Clare engines to be given horizontal boilers—but of cars of every sort.

.   .   .   .

The advocates of the horizontal-boiler type of locomotive steadily increased; the fallacy of arguing in favor of the vertical, simply because of steep grades or of bursting flues, became more and more apparent. Yet neither Gillingham nor Winans was quickly convinced. They answered the growing circle of critics by producing two more grasshoppers—the *Phineas Davis* and the *George Clinton*—far better in type and in construction than any that had gone before. These were placed in service on the Washington Branch early in the summer of 1836 and at once gave good accounts of themselves.[1]

They were die-hards, those old fellows who believed so faithfully in their own type of engine. Winans, in particular, forever showed himself a real invincible. Surrender was never in his soul. Of a tremendously creative mind, he always drove straight to a point; after which, it became extremely difficult to deviate him from it.

To make their position all the stronger, they had succeeded in getting a joint committee from the two Houses of the Baltimore City Council to visit the road earlier in that same year (March, 1836) and make an engine report for themselves. Just what knowledge of locomotive performance the portly aldermen of Baltimore town might be expected to exhibit is not written upon the record. Other things are.

It seems that there was some little delay in starting the excursion. In consequence of which, the locomotive made

[1] Of these engines, Jonathan Davis wrote (1836):

". . . The trains [of four or five eight-wheeled cars averaging from nine to ten tons each] after being put in motion upon a level were made to pass for a distance of about four miles up an ascent at the rate of twenty miles per hour. . . . The *Davis* engine drew up the ascent twelve cars weighing gross, 115 tons, 9 cwt.;but allowing for the weight of the persons upon them 116¼ tons, at the uniform velocity of seven miles per hour. The *Clinton* then drew the same load upon the same ascent at the uniform rate of six miles per hour. In these trials the engines worked expansively, with a cut-off at five-eighths of the stroke. In order, however, to try the effect of the full pressure, the *Davis* was now furnished with cars accordingly, and the ascending road was now traversed with a train of thirteen burthen cars and a passenger car, each upon eight wheels, and weighing, exclusive of engine and tender, 131 tons. This train was not allowed to ascend beyond the straight part of the road upon which the speed was only at the rate of three miles per hour. The *Davis* and its tender were again hitched to the aforementioned train of 116¼ tons, which was then drawn four miles up the ascent in 23 minutes and 45 seconds or at the rate of a full ten miles per hour. In this trial, as well as in the preceding ones, steam constantly escaped from the two safety valves from which it commenced to blow off at a pressure of fifty pounds to the circular inch. . . . The great powers of the boiler to generate steam were here displayed in the evaporation of water at the rate of at least 600 gallons per hour. . . ."

extra efforts to hurry forward to Parrs Spring Ridge. While this was being done, a train of freight wagons was passed upon the opposite track. Alarmed at the speed of the locomotive, the team of the leading wagon sprang before the engine of the special train. Only the utmost efforts on the part of the engineer prevented a collision, with perhaps a loss of human life. . . . After but a little more delay, the train arrived at the foot of Plane Number One.

Instructions had been given to the engineer to stop at this point and, after dropping the long eight-wheeled car, to take the three smaller ones and try with these to make the top of the long climb. Confident, however, in the power of his engine, the man at the throttle went straight ahead up the plane, with the entire train. The momentum of the running start did not, however, it was agreed, carry him more than 300 feet up the slope. After that it was dead pulling against gravity, and yet the little grasshopper (the record does not reveal which of the road's small fleet was chosen for this highly important task) continued straight on toward the summit, at a rate estimated to be between three and four miles an hour. Not only kept on, but actually gained speed as it neared the top. Let the report itself tell the details:

. . . The plane is 2150 feet in length—2050 feet of which ascends at the rate of 197 feet per mile. . . . From the first plane, the train proceeded to the second, which is 3000 feet in length—2800 feet at 170 feet per mile, 100 feet at the rate of 227, and the 100 feet at the summit at 264 feet to the mile. The engine and its train ascended at the rate of from five to six miles per hour to within thirty feet of the summit of this plane, when, on the grade of 264 feet to the mile, it stopped. The three small cars, weighing 5 tons, 1 cwt., were then cast loose, when the engine, starting without assistance on this grade, drew the double car and passengers to the summit with the greatest apparent ease. The steam escaped from the safety valve as well when the engine reached the summit of the plane as when it left the foot.

JOSEPH W. PATTERSON.
President of the Baltimore and Ohio, 1836.

From a painting.

LOUIS McLANE.
President of the Baltimore and Ohio, 1836–1848.
From a painting.

Splendid little engine! What a pity that its name should not have been preserved for the record. Let the document continue:

. . . The weight of 25 tons, 15 cwt., [the total estimated weight of engine and tender, cars and passengers] was drawn up the grades before mentioned, the steepest of which was 227 feet per mile, with much ease and by the inherent power of the engine, without the assistance of impetus of previous high speed—and the weight of 20 tons, 15 cwt., deducting from the above the weight of the three cars cast off on Plane No. 2 was drawn with equal ease up a grade of 264 feet to the mile; the engine starting the train from rest on this grade. At the summit two carloads of pig-iron, weighing each four tons, were attached to the train and the whole, weighing then, 33 tons, 15 cwt., was made to descend the plane . . . by the action of the engine alone and without the assistance of a break [brake] at such speed as the engineer pleased and was several times stopped on the way down to show the command in which the engine was held.

With such results as the above it is unnecessary to add that your committee are equally gratified and surprised; and from what they themselves witnessed, they have no hesitation in expressing their conviction that the engines of the Baltimore and Ohio Railroad are capable of drawing, with ease, at least fifty passengers up ascents of any length, of from 200 to 220 feet per mile. . . . It is now a matter of common parlance to assert that the Alleghanies can be passed by locomotive engines by the Potomac route without the use of stationary power; and your committee entertain no doubt of the fact. It is this which gives to Baltimore the vantage ground in the competition with her sister cities for the western trade, and yet this is owing now more to the geographical depressions of the mountain range than to the engines perfected by the company [sic!] . . . Excepting the engines manufactured by them, there is probably not one in the United States, although some of the best ever made in England have been imported, which is capable of ascending the grades and passing the curves . . . which must occur among the mountains. . . . While nature has done

much to facilitate the intercourse of Baltimore from the West,
the Baltimore and Ohio Railroad Company has not done
less. . . .

Brave words, these. And yet, in the end, they were not,
like a good many brave words, to be of much avail. The
vertical-boiler locomotive was doomed. Moreover, a definite
feeling was showing itself as to whether or not the Baltimore
and Ohio Railroad enterprise, with all its constant experimenting, was not beginning to wear itself out. There were many
doubters; inside the company, as well as without. An increasing number of them. Many to point this way and to point
that. And the shadow of oncoming financial panic was closer
than ever upon the face of the land. The blackening clouds
came all the while, more and more closely together.

Until one day Baltimore read in its newspapers that Philip E.
Thomas no longer was president of the "Ohio Road," as it was so
often called at that time. It was given out that Mr. Thomas
had resigned because of impaired health, as well as an increasing
pressure upon him of his private affairs. The board of directors
passed highly eulogistic resolutions of regret at his going and
pointed out the very great service that he had been to the road
in the first nine trying years of its career. Well might they
pass such resolutions. Philip E. Thomas unquestionably had
given nine of the best years of his life to the service of his
fellow men, through his devotion to the railroad. His unques-
tioned honor and probity, his keen business sagacity and
experience were, beyond all doubt, of vast service to the
Baltimore and Ohio company.

And yet the fact remained that the railroad company
hovered on the edge of bankruptcy. It may have been, and it
certainly was, the railroad university of the United States in a
most difficult and necessary decade of rail-transport history,
but there was little pecuniary reward in that. Its costly
masonry bridges and tracks, its curious experiments with
locomotives, and the fact that it had not immediately led into

a well populated country—in sharp contrast to most of the lines already built or building inland from the Atlantic seaboard—had brought it to the verge of financial disaster. . . . Mr. Thomas's going was an hour of sorrow; in no sense, one of triumph.

He was succeeded, in October, 1836, by Joseph W. Patterson, son of William Patterson, who accepted the presidency of the road temporarily until a man should be found to take permanent charge of it and endeavor to work it to a successful culmination.

Mr. Patterson appears as the author of the tenth annual report of the company. Despite the difficulties into which it had entered, there remains a distinct tone of optimism in that document. He says:

. . . Of the ultimate profit of the Baltimore and Ohio Railroad to the stockholders the Board of Directors can only here reiterate the favorable opinion that they have so often heretofore expressed. To doubt its making a return on the outlay when it shall have been completed to the western waters is impossible, when the probable travel and transportation upon it then is considered. There is hardly a railroad in the country that has been completed, that is not now realizing a handsome return on the cost of its construction; and the chief reason why this is not done by the Baltimore and Ohio Railroad is that it is *not completed*. If it were, at this date, proposed to make a railroad to Fredericktown [Frederick] or Harper's Ferry (supposing the Baltimore and Ohio Railroad to the West not to be projected even) no one would be willing to undertake such a work through so difficult a region; for every one would, at once, doubt its affording an interest on its cost. To expect, therefore, that the Baltimore and Ohio Railroad, which is now, not a road to the West, but a road to Fredericktown and to Harper's Ferry only, should make the dividends declared by the finished railroads of the country were vain indeed. The full extent of its profit can only be realized upon its completion. . . .

Mr. Patterson gives attention—apparently for the first time officially in the history of the company—to the puzzling questions of its rates and charges, and says:

> . . . When . . . the charter of Baltimore and Ohio Railroad was granted . . . it was the first railroad for general purposes that had been projected in the country—and so sanguine of profit were its friends that the charge for passengers was deemed ample at three cents a mile, and for merchandise and produce, four cents [a ton] eastward and six cents westward, making an average, as experience shows, of about 4½ cents. Experience has shown that upon a costly road through a difficult country these rates are too low, upon the limited amount of business that has heretofore been done by the company, and there are but few railroads in the union upon which the charges are not higher.

He proceeds to cite the charges upon some of the important railroads of the United States of that day[1] and then goes forward to say:

> . . . Combined with the low rate of charge to which this company is limited may be mentioned those causes of expenses —the working of inclined planes and the maintenance of an expensive horse power to be used in the city—from which other railroad companies, whose stocks give large dividends, are exempt. . . . The Portsmouth and Roanoke Railroad, for instance, is allowed to charge six cents per mile for the transportation of passengers and eight cents per ton for freight. The Washington Branch makes the same charge for passengers —but only four cents for freight—and has to pay a bonus of

---

[1] Charges on other railroads, as shown by the Patterson report:

	One person per mile	Goods per ton per mile
On the Petersburg Railroad	5¢	10¢
Winchester and Potomac	6¢	7¢
Portsmouth and Roanoke	6¢	8¢
Boston and Providence	5¢	10¢
Boston and Lowell	3½¢	7¢
Mohawk and Hudson	5¢	8¢

one-fifth of its receipts from passengers to the State. Were this bonus not paid and the Portsmouth and Roanoke rates charged, it would be able to declare out of the earnings of last year alone a dividend of 8¾ per cent to its stockholders—and at the same rates, for the same time, the main stem could have declared a dividend of 8½ per cent. When this road is finished to the West there can be no doubt of its productiveness; and even in the meantime, what with the increase of toll already authorized and avoidance of the planes at Parrs Ridge, it is believed that a return may be made to the stockholders. It is the desire of the Board to see the great work finished that is to unite Baltimore indissolubly with the west. They believe that the prosperity of Baltimore depends upon it. The liberality of Maryland, the munificence of the city most interested, have contributed nobly to the enterprise; and the Board cannot doubt that when the surveys shall have ascertained, beyond cavil, the expense of construction, any deficit which may exist will forthwith be furnished.

The plight of the Baltimore and Ohio, the pleas of President Patterson could not have fallen upon deaf ears and unseeing eyes in Baltimore. As the report itself indicates, even before it had been written, the Legislature of the state had authorized an increase in passenger rates upon the Main Stem; of from three cents to four cents a mile. This was done in return for a state subscription of $3,000,000, upon which the railroad company guaranteed six per cent interest annually. Moreover, definite plans at last were being started for the abandonment of the planes at Parrs Ridge, with the expensive horse power that they necessitated. In that autumn (1836) the company still possessed 173 horses, divided into 78 "passenger horses" and 95 "tonnage horses"—in the streets of Baltimore, at Parrs Ridge and out upon the line. Even though that was the autumn that the exclusive use of horse power west of Point of Rocks and up to Harpers Ferry was discontinued.

In the first week of January, 1837, Louis McLane was elected president of the Baltimore and Ohio Railroad Company,[1] and a new era—and a season of house cleaning—was formally inaugurated. His salary was fixed at $4000 a year, a figure which had been carefully calculated to keep him from accepting the presidency of a New York bank. This was slightly raised after Mr. McLane actually became president.

As a personality, Mr. McLane stood in a strong contrast to Mr. Thomas. For the work of his predecessor, he seems to have held but small regard. He looked upon his inheritance as hardly more than an elongated bit of metal scrap. He is reported to have taken a swift look at the condition of the property and to have put his verdict upon it in a terse, "a wreck."

If it was not a wreck, it was something that looked much like it. For a number of years past, the expenses of the property as a whole had exceeded its income. By the spring of 1837, the building of the line west of Harpers Ferry had been suspended; while east of that busy point a neglect to keep it in repair had brought it to a sad state of dilapidation. The motive power and other equipment seemed to be utterly inadequate for the increasing flow of traffic that was coming to the road. The company was heavily in debt, and with but little cash in hand.

"A wreck," was McLane's characterization of it.

.   .   .   .

There began to be hard times; not alone for the Baltimore and Ohio but for all other railroads in the land—for business

[1] Mr. McLane was a Baltimore citizen of no little distinction. Born in Smyrna, Delaware, the son of an officer in the Revolutionary Army, he joined the Navy as a midshipman at the age of fourteen and served under Stephen Decatur on the frigate *Philadelphia*, on her first cruise. Later he graduated from Newark College in his native state and in 1807 he was admitted to the practice of law. Five years afterwards, he was a volunteer soldier in the Second War with England and marched to the defense of Baltimore when it was threatened by the British. He was first a Congressman and then a Senator of the United States, from Delaware. In May, 1820, he became our Minister to Great Britain and later he was successively Secretary of the Treasury and Secretary of State. Clearly a man of parts.

enterprises generally. The shadow of the great panic of 1837 already was upon the country. A tremendous era of expansion —particularly in railroad schemes—and of prosperity was swiftly approaching a disastrous ending. Before good times could return, commercial America would have to scourge herself, unmercifully. Businesses, men, reputations, would have to go down into the dust; some of them never to rise again.

The men of the Baltimore and Ohio kept a stiff upper lip. They joined with the banks of Baltimore in the issuance of fractional paper currency—the "shinplasters" that were to spring up again at another financial crisis in the nation's history. The banks of Baltimore, following the lead of those of Philadelphia and of New York, suspended specie payments, and the little shinplasters of the railroad and the town remained for long months the only reliable small money in general circulation.[1]

Times were indeed hard. McLane's first report as president —dated October 1, 1837—reflects clearly the general depression prevailing throughout the United States. To this was added a crop failure in many sections of the land. The Baltimore road was embarrassed by the expensive repairs upon the troublesome Harpers Ferry bridge, as well as by the complete rebuilding of eleven miles of line around the planes at Mount Airy. The receipts for the preceding twelvemonth, $457,110.26, were shown to have been exceeded by expenditures just $20,330.88. No wonder that certain of the directors were hinting that the president's salary might be reduced again to $4000 a year!

The president's report a year later shows a far better state

[1] For the Baltimore and Ohio, this money was issued in amounts running from 12½ cents up to $100. It was printed from fine steel plates—which have been preserved in the company's vaults from that day to this—and each bill, large or small, bore the inscription: "When presented in amounts of $100 and over, these certificates will be redeemed by the Baltimore and Ohio Railroad Company in Baltimore City stock, drawing six per cent." During the first year of issuance of this money, more than half a million dollars worth of it was paid out. It went into wide circulation in Maryland and in Virginia.

of affairs.   Not that the country was yet out of its financial
fog—a panic such as that of '37 was not to be easily forgotten.
Yet the fact remains that upon the Baltimore and Ohio the
disastrous condition of outgo exceeding income had then
actually been reversed.   For the twelve months ending
September 30, 1838, receipts exceeded expenditures by more
than $7000, and McLane had good cause to congratulate his
fellows and himself.   Perhaps now there would be less talk of
cutting the president's salary.

This result had been accomplished as it was to be accomplished a thousand and more times afterwards in railroad history;
by cutting expenditures down to the sinew and the bone.
Traffic had been increased a bit, but the reversal of the road's
financial condition was accomplished chiefly by economies.   Of
these, the greatest was through the abandonment of the extravagant planes over Parrs Spring Ridge at Mount Airy.   It was
estimated that $20,000 a year was saved at this point alone.

Things were looking up.   The company had effected a real
economy by canceling its lease of the Mount Clare shops and
doing its own work within them.   A new locomotive was to
be built there for the main line and it was not to have a vertical
boiler.   Mr. Winans would have to adapt himself to the
English way of doing the thing.   For the Washington Branch
—which continued to be operated as a separate unit—twenty-
eight burden cars and four locomotives had been ordered; the
last from William Norris of Philadelphia.   These also were not
to have upright boilers.   You could trust Mr. Norris for that.
He already had a good reputation as an engine builder.

Best of all, a fairly definite survey for the continuance of
the line through to the Ohio—always its great goal—had
finally been completed.   McLane makes somewhat extended
reference to it.   He says:

. . . The reconnaissances and preliminary surveys from
Harper's Ferry to the Ohio . . . show the practicability
of locating a satisfactory route . . . embracing both *Wheeling*

and *Pittsburgh* at the maximum elevation of 66 feet per mile and that the cost of construction with a *single* track of the most durable plan to both points will not exceed nine and one-half millions of dollars. . . .

It will be noticed that the fine notions of Thomas and his associates for a double track all the way through to the Ohio now had been tossed into the discard. The road would be fortunate to lay a single pair of rails. But this much it would do; even though Gargantuan difficulties loomed ahead, and the first of its locomotives was not to stand beside the muddy flood of the Ohio until fifteen long years afterwards.

One of the first of these difficulties was with the state of Virginia. She had always proved more difficult to handle than Maryland. For one thing, the entire Baltimore and Ohio scheme was not of her inception; and for another, it was a blow at her capital city of the seven hills rather than any aid to it. Such aid as Virginia had given had been granted grudgingly, indeed.

The time allowed for the occupation by the Baltimore road of any territory whatsoever in Virginia had expired in July, 1838, and a charter of renewal was immediately necessary. Yet, with the growing strength of the Richmond group who quite naturally favored a railroad from the Ohio country down the valley of the James, this became more and more difficult. Finally, however, a law was passed extending the time for the completion of the road upon the Virginia soil five years, but this same statute deprived the Baltimore and Ohio company of selecting between routes either in Maryland or in Virginia for its link between Harpers Ferry and Cumberland; it made an express condition that the Baltimore road should remain entirely within Virginia all the way from the Ferry up to within about six miles of Cumberland itself. . . . It also ordered that Wheeling must be made one of the main terminals of the road. Seemingly, there had been too much talk in the wind about Pittsburgh receiving this honor, to the detriment of the western Virginia river port.

That this arbitrary location of a railroad line by statute law might bring forth embarrassing engineering difficulties, meant nothing to the Richmond legislators. The engineers of the Baltimore and Ohio would have to work their own way out. Immediately west of Harpers Ferry there were but two routes open to them: They could continue up the valley of the Shenandoah for about six miles over the track of the Winchester and Potomac, or they could attempt to secure a narrow right of way from the Secretary of War over the grounds of the United States arsenal. This last route eventually was chosen. The Winchester and Potomac was not particularly agreeable to having its line used by the Baltimore and Ohio. The Secretary of War proved more tractable. Perhaps McLane's political training and influence at Washington stood him well.

At any rate, the line was builded along the edge of the arsenal property next to the river. Its trestle served as a revetment wall and a flood protection to the arsenal buildings. But a fearful turn in the track was necessitated, which was not eliminated until many years after, when the historic arsenal had been burned and a new bridge location secured at Harpers Ferry. . . . The groans of the locomotive making the hard turn at the Ferry meant nothing whatsoever to the gentlemen who sat in the classic Capitol on Shockoe Hill in the city of Richmond.

. . . .

Cumberland now became the immediate objective for the Baltimore and Ohio; and Wheeling, which already had contributed a round million dollars to the capital stock of the new railroad, the second. McLane in his report of 1838 comments upon this:

. . . The connection also between Wheeling and Cumberland by the National Road of a distance of only 131 miles when Cumberland shall be connected by railroad with Baltimore and thence by a similar communication with Philadelphia, will

GOODBYE TO THE VERTICAL BOILER.

The *Thomas Jefferson* (1835) was the first locomotive to operate in the state of Virginia and one of the last to have an upright boiler.

From a photograph made in 1927 of the original engine.

THE HORIZONTAL BOILER APPEARS.

The *William Galloway* is an exact reproduction of the famous *Lafayette*, which made its appearance on Baltimore and Ohio rails in 1837.

undoubtedly supply a vast amount of trade and travel to the Baltimore and Ohio road and restore to it much which heretofore have been drawn into other channels. . . . Although some further time must elapse before the stockholders can receive a dividend from the profits of the present road, the company have commenced the present year with a surplus of revenue beyond their expenses, etc., etc. . . .

Apparently the best sort of an effort to put a good face upon a situation, the real seriousness of which could easily be disguised.

.   .   .   .

In the blackness of 1838, one real ray of sunshine:

Rail communication had been completed between Baltimore and Philadelphia. In this simple statement there was, as McLane has already hinted, a vast promise of hope to the road struggling toward the Ohio. There have been references already in these pages to the construction of what was hoped to be the first rail link of this through route between Philadelphia and Baltimore in the completion of the New Castle and Frenchtown Railroad connecting the Delaware with the headwaters of Chesapeake Bay. This was in fact one of the earliest bits of railroad in the entire United States. Yet its use necessitated two considerable steamboat trips—the one from Baltimore to Frenchtown and the other between Philadelphia and New Castle.

The route that was opened in the autumn of 1838 was rail all the way, consisting at the outset of three railroads: the Philadelphia and Delaware County, the Wilmington and Susquehanna, and the Baltimore and Port Deposit. By the autumn of 1838, these had all been included in a single company which was to bear for many years the honored title of the Philadelphia, Wilmington and Baltimore Railroad, before eventually becoming merged in the Pennsylvania Railroad of today.

The destination of the section of this route that was built

east and north from Baltimore was changed from Port Deposit to Havre de Grace. In those years, there was no thought of bridging the broad Susquehanna near its mouth. In place of a bridge, there was placed in service, in the summer of 1837, what was probably the first railroad train ferry in the world —the *Susquehanna*. This vessel continued in service for nearly twenty years, being replaced in 1854 by the much larger *Maryland*, which remained in use until the completion—toward the close of the Civil War—of the first timber bridge across the Susquehanna between Havre de Grace and Perryville.

The building of the *Susquehanna* made it possible to inaugurate through train service between Wilmington and Baltimore, on July 22, 1837; while the completion of the railroad bridge across the Schuylkill at Grays Ferry, Philadelphia, extended that service through to Broad Street, in that city, in November of the following year.

Gradually the links in one of the greatest of rail-transport chains in all this world were being forged. Soon one was able to go by train from South Amboy, in lower New York Bay, to Camden, directly opposite Philadelphia; and a few years later there would be rail communication from Jersey City and Newark and Trenton across the Delaware and through to Philadelphia. . . . Space was being shortened, if not actually in miles and rods and feet, practically in hours and minutes and seconds. Soon it would be nothing at all to go from New York, the nation's chief city, to Washington, its capital. Twelve hours, perhaps ten. What of that? Cars now to be changed not more than twice—at Philadelphia and again at Baltimore, where one went from the tracks of the Philadelphia, Wilmington and Baltimore.

Yet this last change was not long to exist. A little later, they were connecting the President Street Station in Baltimore of the new railroad to Philadelphia with Mount Clare and the downtown station of the Baltimore and Ohio, by a continuation of the track through the center of Pratt Street. Along this pair of rails, whose original placing had caused so very much discussion and argument, stout horses were to haul the cars, singly, from the locomotive engines of the Philadelphia, Wilmington and Baltimore at President Street, to those of the Baltimore and Ohio at Mount Clare. Along that busy way passed then one of the busiest of the nation's rail highways—growing all the time in vigor and importance. In it, history was to be writ—and the ink of the writing was to be the life blood of human beings. But this anticipates. . . .

. . . .

The connection at Philadelphia was not to be so swiftly improved. A whole quarter of a century later, one finds William Prescott Smith, the master of transportation of the Baltimore and Ohio of the strenuous years of the 'sixties, writing to S. M. Felton, the war president of the Philadelphia, Wilmington and Baltimore, and saying:

I would venture . . . to express the hope that, for the benefit of the route, all the through trains for each way daily be run through Philadelphia. . . . Mr. Cole surprises me with the statement that but one or two out of the four are to be run that way, the passengers of the other trains being still compelled to go through the purgatorial ordeal of changing in Philadelphia, which has become a national dread. . . .

Plain words, these. But the railroaders of those early days rarely hesitated to speak their minds, in plainest fashion.

CHAPTER XII

THE STRUGGLE TOWARD CUMBERLAND

Hard Years, and Troublous Ones—Difficulties in Financing—
McLane's Two Voyages to England and What Came of Them
—Construction West of Harpers Ferry—And Cumberland
Finally Reached.

THINGS began to grow better; not rapidly, but steadily all
the while.

In his report dated January 1, 1840, Mr. McLane reviews
the year which ended on the thirtieth day of the preceding
September. He presents statements which show an increasing
trade and a steadily growing excess of receipts over expenditures. At the end of the fiscal year of 1838, it will be recalled
that the road had turned a rather bad corner and had changed
what today we should call "red ink" into a definite profit of
$7000. Yet the twelve months that immediately followed
showed this last figure increased to $27,000. Not such a bad
showing for hard times that continued unabated! . . . Evidently the economies of operation that had been introduced by
the new administration were beginning to show.[1]

[1] In his report Mr. McLane says:
". . . The means of the company being inadequate to reconstruct the
remainder of the road to Harper's Ferry upon the substantial plan heretofore
adopted, a more thorough renovation of the timber of the present track and the
entire renewal of four miles west of Parr's Ridge became indispensable for the
accommodation of the trade and the security of the passengers; the dilapidated
condition also of the old engines and passenger and burthen cars made it necessary
in some instances to entirely renew them and in others to make extensive repairs.
. . . It became necessary during the year to purchase and put upon the road

During that same fiscal year the road brought 264,033 barrels of flour down to tidewater; exceeding the previous year by 121,521 barrels. No mean traffic, this! Mr. McLane goes on to say that flour is the "most burthensome" and most liable to injury of any article brought upon the railroad and less indulgence is shown to the company for any delay in its transportation than in the haul of any other commodity. It is an article highly important to the commercial interests of Baltimore and yet he has figured it out that it costs the road not less than six cents per ton mile to bring it down; while the charter permits it to charge but four cents for the service. In this respect, he says, both Virginia and Pennsylvania in their charters have done far better for the road than has Maryland.

He reports that, despite the unusually difficult conditions in money markets everywhere, contracts have been let for the extension of the line from Harpers Ferry to Cumberland and that 1495 men and 466 horses already are employed in constructing it. The almost insurmountable financial difficulties in the marts of the United States have been overcome by sending a special commissioner to London, who, despite the accumulation of American securities everywhere throughout Europe, has finally succeeded in getting Messrs. Baring Brothers and

---

five new locomotive engines; and in addition to these, four others have been purchased and will be on the road in the course of the present and ensuing month. During the same period 32 single house cars [box cars] each calculated to contain 25 barrels of flour have been constructed for the main stem and many of the old platform cars heretofore used for granite have been converted into open box cars for the transportation of flour. Contracts have been made for four new passenger cars. . . .

"The new road around the planes . . . has been in operation since June 1st last. . . . Beside the net saving in actual expenditure considerable facilities were afforded to the passenger trains; and in the transit of burthen trains between Baltimore and Frederick and Harper's Ferry there is an average saving of at least 48 hours. The burthen trains are now frequently brought from Harper's Ferry to Baltimore, there discharged and returned to Harper's Ferry within 24 hours. . . ."

This seems to be one of the very earliest instances on record of line revision and the excellent results that may arise from it.

Company, of London, to back the project. . . .   So it was that
money began once again to flow into the coffers of the Baltimore
and Ohio.   If not freely, at least to an extent that justified the
resumption of the pushing of the road through toward the banks
of the Ohio.

This particular financial enterprise—remarkable in the hour
that it was undertaken—deserves a few words at least of further
explanation:

When the state of Virginia, as was seen in the preceding
chapter, compelled the Baltimore and Ohio company to build
the line from Harpers Ferry west on the south side of the
Potomac, instead of the north, the engineers were quick to estimate that more than two million dollars could be subtracted
from the cost of the road as planned for the Maryland side.
Such an amount—an actual capital outlay estimated at not less
than $2,625,400—in those parlous days was no slight sum of
money.   In addition to it, the road gained two large subscriptions—the joint contributions of the city of Wheeling and
the state of Virginia—amounting to $2,358,420; which it would
have forfeited had the stockholders voted to keep the line
entirely within the borders of Maryland from Baltimore to
Cumberland.[1]

Facing the immediate necessity of completing the railroad
through to the Ohio at the very beginning of his administration,
Mr. McLane found, therefore, that his available funds were
about as follows:

Subscription by the state of Maryland . .	$3,000,000
" " " city of Baltimore . .	3,000,000
" " " state of Virginia . .	300,000
Additional subscription by Virginia . .	1,058,420
Subscription by the city of Wheeling . .	1,000,000
	$8,358,420

[1] Later—in 1846—the Virginia Assembly withdrew both of its subscriptions to
the road.

Against this total subscription of about eight million dollars, was an estimated cost of some nine millions and a half for completing the road to Wheeling and to Pittsburgh as well. The problem that confronted McLane was to raise at least $1,139,480; and to raise it promptly.

It was a dark outlook, indeed. Banks, like houses of cards, crashing down; money growing more and more difficult each hour. The new president of the Baltimore and Ohio would have to climb many hard hills and leap many hurdles to get his road to the Ohio. For instance, the subscription of Baltimore City was limited to the terms of an ordinance authorizing its use only on the portion of the railroad between Harpers Ferry and Cumberland. It was payable in cash at the rate of not more than one million dollars a year. To raise the sum, the city planned to issue its own scrip, paying six per cent annual interest. But 1838, 1839 and 1840 were no years to place the bonds of even as wealthy a city as Baltimore had grown to be, with any hope of receiving par for them. Therefore, instead of trying to float this large amount of city securities, the commissioners of finance at first borrowed the money for the installments needed for the extension of the railroad, directly from the Baltimore banks; and in order to meet the interest on the loans, the City Council levied a direct tax to cover the amount of interest for the first year. These loans were then made by the banks upon deposits of city stock as security.[1]

[1] Dr. Milton Reizenstein, in his *Economic History of the Baltimore and Ohio Railroad* (1897), tells in some detail of the interesting but not very successful financial scheme which the later stringency of the markets developed in relation to this subscription. He says:

". . . At a meeting of the directors of the company held in the autumn of 1839, it was decided that something must be done to make the subscription of Baltimore immediately available at the par value of the six per cent city stock. Therefore it was determined to offer to contractors for their work and to the owners of land in payment for the right of way, certificates payable, when presented in sums of $100, in Baltimore City six per cent stock at par. That entire confidence might be felt in these certificates the requisite amount of city stock was to be received by the company simultaneously with each issue of certificates, and be immediately vested in two commissioners in trust for the holders of the certifi-

There came, however, a change in the situation: The certificates, although fundable in city stock at par, were in reality not worth par in the open market. They began to depreciate. Workmen and shopkeepers who had taken them at their face value found eventually that they could not dispose of them in anything like the same values. They fell under suspicion. And then under ban. The City Council of Baltimore added fuel to the flame by repealing (in 1842) an ordinance which it had passed (February, 1841) permitting these Baltimore and Ohio certificates to be received at par in payment of taxes and other city dues. . . . A deal of controversy arose. Which, in times generally troublous financially, was not easily stilled. Finally, meetings of protest were held, and many broadsides printed.

Yet the certificates had played a very definite, and a very valuable, part in permitting the construction of the railroad to go forward in a time when most other large works of internal improvement throughout the land were being partially suspended. They aided, moreover, in sustaining the credit of the state of Maryland.[1]

---

cates. These certificates did not promise to pay money nor were they promissory at all in character. They conferred an absolute authority for the transfer of city stock when presented in the requisite amounts, and when this stock was received, the obligation for which the certificates had been received in satisfaction was finally cancelled. They were not therefore paper money, although they might and did circulate as currency.

"The scheme was at first successful. The contractors and land owners to whom they were offered accepted them without demur. They in turn gave them to their workmen in return for labor. Here they were again accepted and so passed into general circulation and floated the city stock for a while at par. By September, 1840, the payments made through this medium amounted to $515,000. . . . By the autumn of 1840 only 100 certificates for $100 each had been redeemed in city stock. The saving of interest to the city due to the amount of certificates kept in circulation was considerable."

[1] ". . . Before the certificate scheme had been conceived the six per cent city stock had not been regarded as negotiable. Therefore the $3,000,000 subscription of the state of Maryland had been looked to as the means whereby the construction of the railroad was to be carried on. This subscription of $3,000,000 by the state of Maryland had originally been payable to the company in cash to

There was, nevertheless, a deal of quarrel and of conflict in regard to all of these financing arrangements. No less a personage than the Governor of Maryland (William Grason) entered the situation. In his annual message of 1840 he says that the Baltimore and Ohio company

> . . . in entering into extensive operations without money or the certainty of raising it, has abandoned the prudent and cautious policy which has so generally characterized its proceedings . . . that . . . the introduction of so large an amount of Maryland stock into foreign markets for so slight an inducement was calculated to sink, more deeply, if possible, the credit of the bonds which had been unfortunately pledged by the Chesapeake & Ohio Canal Company . . . that . . . in making the arrangement with the Barings the Baltimore and Ohio Railroad Company has entered into the system of hypothecation which has been so disastrous to the credit of the State. . . .

To this, the board of directors of the Baltimore and Ohio took vigorous exception. And, a few days later, they replied to the criticisms of the chief executive of the state, saying:

> . . . The State holds an actual interest in the Baltimore and Ohio Company of $1,000,000, furnished not by the advance of money but by her credit; the City of Baltimore and its citizens are stockholders to the amount of $7,000,000 of which

---

be raised by the sale of state currency bonds bearing interest at six per cent. These bonds were to be offered for sale first in Europe before being put upon any other market. When the attempt was made to put these bonds upon the European market the state's commissioner in Europe reported that it was impracticable to do so and wrote that sterling, instead of currency bonds, might prove more salable. The legislature of Maryland therefore changed the bonds to sterling bonds bearing interest at five per cent and payable, principal and interest, in London. In order to provide for the interest for three years, an amount of bonds equal to $3,200,000 was issued and delivered directly to the railroad company in full payment of the state's subscription, the company giving the requisite guarantee for the payment of interest."—*Economic History of the Baltimore and Ohio Railroad*, Reizenstein.

nearly $4,000,000 was subscribed in money; the State has never been called upon for a dollar, and, by the preference she has secured to herself in the affairs of the road, now receives 6 per cent on her investment. The other stockholders receive nothing and do not expect to receive dividends until the road shall be completed to Cumberland. . . .

All of this controversy seemingly worried McLane but little. Having quickly ascertained for himself that new bonds of the Baltimore and Ohio could not—in the face of times still extremely panicky and delicate—be disposed of to any advantage whatsoever, either in the markets of Philadelphia or of New York, the commissioner of the Baltimore and Ohio decided to proceed at once to London, where there was still a brisk market for American securities. The absence of cables rendered foreign markets far less sensitive to ours.

The commissioner of the railroad was none other than the president of the road himself. McLane, having found himself in an intricate position, determined to sacrifice everything to make a success of the road, and of his administration of it.

He prepared at once for the long voyage overseas. A transatlantic trip in the early 'forties was not only long, but extremely tedious; if one managed to cross within a fortnight, he did exceedingly well. . . . And so it came to pass that before McLane could reach London there had been a reversal in regard to American securities.

"It's too risky; they're flying too swiftly, those Yankees over there," the Britishers were saying to one another. "They cannot unload all their demned securities over here."

There was much truth in this. London was becoming choked with American scrip. With the rather natural result that a depression had come to pass in it. In addition to which, certain of our states had embarked upon the highly perilous policy of repudiating their debts. Others—including Maryland—had boldly suspended interest payments upon their bonds. We were in bad financial odor upon the other side of the Atlantic.

This was the situation that McLane faced upon his arrival in Lombard Street. He came quickly to realize that even to attempt to place the bonds upon the open market over there would be folly.

Instead, he did what turned out to be a far better thing: He arranged with the great house of Baring Brothers and Company of London to take care of the entire issue. That bank agreed to advance to the Baltimore and Ohio company, from time to time, such actual sums of money for the rehabilitation and the extension of its properties as it might require. For these advances to the railroad, the bonds of Maryland were to be deposited as security. Barings were not without vision. They had British commercial acumen. In 1840, they foresaw that the financial recovery of the United States would not only be sure, but swift. So it was that the good name and fame of one of the strongest banking houses in the world went back of the still struggling Baltimore enterprise.

It was arranged that Baring Brothers were to put upon the market—from time to time and in such quantities as it could absorb without the slightest disturbance to its digestive powers—small offerings of the bonds. Before the end of 1840, some of these already had been sold—at 85—and had brought a net of $21,583.68 into the treasury of the Baltimore and Ohio. Not a great sum; but it served a good purpose. It was applied to the payment of accrued interest on some recent bonds; a debt which was causing the company real worry.

.   .   .   .

On the whole, it is to be recorded that on his first trip to London McLane had succeeded, handsomely. He was to return at least once again—in 1844—when he remained nearly two years, trying to secure further financial aid for his company. On this second expedition he was not so successful. Yet it was not to be adjudged an entire failure. For he spent much of these long months in a detailed study of English railways, with the direct result that he brought back to America a system for the reorganization of the Baltimore and Ohio which he placed in effect, and which—with the exception of the term of his successor, Thomas Swann—remained as its permanent plan of management for many years thereafter.

To this rather remarkable scheme, attention will be given in a later chapter. But at this time it seems fit to give full credit for it to the man who was its originator and who caused it first to be placed in actual use.

.   .   .   .

In his report as president of the Baltimore and Ohio company—issued the second Monday in October, 1840—McLane reflects the optimism which he brought back with him from his successful initial trip to England. He calls attention to further increases in traffic on the line, and a continued lessening of its transportation costs. Apparently his forcefulness and his methods were counting for much. . . . And the needed optimism that he brought the board was reflected soon after in a reversal of its announced policy and its decision to declare a two per cent dividend on the stock. Which was followed the succeeding autumn by one of three and a quarter per cent. The next fall (1842) there was no dividend. The folly of even attempting to pay dividends, when the road's treasury was embarrassed to meet the payments of the contractors, was realized. It needed all its available means—more, too—to complete the Main Stem to Cumberland. To do anything less was unthinkable. By that time, more than $2,465,000 had been expended west of Harpers Ferry; and this would have been lost had not the line been continued through to some natural traffic point. At Cumberland it again would have connection with the National Road. But, while it was being continued along the south side of the Potomac through the domains of Virginia, it had lost intermediate connections with that important turnpike.

We anticipate.

We still are considering the fourteenth annual report of the president of the Baltimore and Ohio. . . . It is not all optimism. McLane complains again that the original structure of the road is wearing out and that during the past twelve months it has been necessary to expend about $500,000 in renewing it. Nineteen and one-half miles have been reconstructed "with heavy rails and upon present-day plans," the old water stations have been rebuilt or repaired and "are now in good order." Six new stations have been constructed, and three others are "constructing." In 1837, there were thirteen old locomotives; such of these as were capable of being repaired have been thoroughly refitted and eleven new engines for the Main Stem purchased. Most of the burthen and all of the passenger cars have been repaired and new cars of every sort—costing all told, some $50,000—have been added to the road. Four engines have been bought for the Washington Branch and, for it, cars to the value of $13,000.

The flour traffic for the year has come to a new high point—392,419 barrels (42,383 tons)—and McLane expostulates against the Maryland Legislature, which, the previous year, had permitted an increase of all the rates of the road—*except* those for hauling flour! Flour was then an important product of the state. The legislators of those days were good to their own; as legislators have been almost ever since.

And finally—most important of all, by far—the extension of the Main Stem from Harpers Ferry to Cumberland, after many grievous delays, is making steady progress. The heavy cuttings through North Mountain are well advanced and the Doe Gully Tunnel—between 1200 and 1400 feet in length—is more than one-third excavated.

.   .   .   .

Here then, the most hopeful thing by far in President McLane's report. No longer is the Baltimore and Ohio to falter and to halt at Harpers Ferry, to exist miserably on the traffic of that small manufacturing town, plus that brought to it by the Winchester and Potomac. After the eternal squabblings with the Virginia Legislature down at Richmond, the profferings of state monies from that quarter, and subsequent withdrawals, construction going on apace.

Moreover, the work was being done in a somewhat better style than was at first planned. It was being given greater permanence and, in almost every way, a better appearance; and at less than the original estimates. As is already understood, the line was now being builded in Virginia (the present West Virginia) almost all the way from Harpers Ferry to Cumberland, ninety-seven miles distant. . . . For the first thirty miles west of the Ferry, it crossed the wide Valley of Virginia, almost at right angles, and at a considerable distance inland from the Potomac. In the language of the engineers, it made a general tangent across a wide bow or bend of that river.

It did not return to the bank of the river until it came opposite old Fort Frederick, Maryland, about twelve miles east of the important village of Hancock. It then followed in a general way the south bank and the course of that stream until, as has been said, within six miles of Cumberland, where it recrossed into Maryland soil once again and found a path into the heart of that historic trading town, between the Potomac and the National Road.

Such, in brief, is the location of this all-important section of the Main Stem of the Baltimore and Ohio, which in recent years has come to be one of the busiest stretches of railroad in the United States; which means in the entire world as well. . . . It was a well planned road. The sharp, abrupt, very difficult curves by which the railroad originally had ascended the narrow, twisting valley of the Patapsco from Relay to Ellicotts Mills, were now known to be most impractical. The grades throughout the entire distance from Harpers Ferry to Fort Frederick in no place now exceeded forty feet to the mile; there was not a single curve of less than a thousand feet radius.

From Fort Frederick west to Cumberland, construction was much more difficult. Reference already has been made to the Doe Gully Tunnel; there were two other bores on this section of the line; a short one of but 90 feet, just above Harpers Ferry, and one at the Paw Paw Ridge, 250 feet long. The two longest of these three tunnels were necessitated by bringing the railroad almost straight across the neck of two long and narrow bends of the river which thrust themselves well up into the mountainous heights of Maryland. The path of the Potomac through this part of the Alleghenies is a tortuous one, indeed. Yet the grades of the road were held to an easy maximum and the curves, with a single inconspicuous exception, to the high standard maintained east of Fort Frederick.

In addition to the tunnels, there were numerous viaducts; after the generally prevailing standards of that day, these were constructed of timber mounted upon stout stone abutments. But no longer was there thought of building these bridges all of masonry, save in the single instance of Back Creek. Permanent though it might be, the stone bridge was now regarded as quite too great an extravagance for the struggling Baltimore and Ohio.

There were eleven bridges on the new section of the line, their total length being some 3690 feet. The important structure at Back Creek, with the height of its parapet at sixty feet above the water, consisted of a single fine stone arch of eighty-foot span. The long trestle out of Harpers Ferry, along the edge of the property of the United States arsenal—at that point which we have seen as a compromise after the refusal of the Winchester and Potomac to permit the Baltimore and Ohio to use its tracks for six miles west of the Ferry—reached for nearly 1700 feet. It was built upon a double row of cast-iron pillars set solidly in parallel stone walls, and it was a substantial structure.

Throughout its entire length, the new stretch of the Main Stem was graded and the bridges built to the width of double track. It was anticipated that the need of a second pair of rails would not be far off. . . .   The track itself consisted of a wood undersill and stringpiece, with cross ties and blocks between the ties; the whole fastened together by wooden pins.   The rails were of "bridge" or "H" form, weighing fifty-one pounds to the yard and eighty tons to the mile.[1]   The whole rested on a bed of broken stone, one foot deep.

.   .   .   .

So much for engineering details.

Now consider once again the road in actual construction progress; McLane and his fellows using every energy to hasten it through to Cumberland, where it would at last be in a real strategic position to gain traffic as well as to make the final leap through to the Ohio.   No effort of any sort was neglected.

With the result that on June 1, 1842, the line between Harpers Ferry and Hancock—or rather the point in Virginia directly opposite Hancock—a distance of forty-two and a half miles, was at last formally opened for the reception of traffic and the operation of regular trains.   On the fifth of November of that same year, a similar ceremony was celebrated at Cumberland.   The Baltimore newspapers record the passage of the inevitable special train with all the bigwigs—as well as the lesser wigs that might climb aboard in the always sublime hope of free riding and free food—up to the new west

---

[1] A paragraph in the *American Railway Journal* that summer tells of the arrival of these rails from England:

"Two of the seven shiploads of railroad iron required for the completion of the Baltimore and Ohio Railroad to Cumberland have recently reached Baltimore. The quantity embraced in these two cargoes is upwards of 1300 tons; the five cargoes yet to arrive comprise an aggregate of 2700 tons, making with those just received . . . over 4000 tons. . . .   A gratifying evidence of the earnestness of the Company to complete the road to Cumberland as quickly as possible is shown by the fact that twenty-four hours after the first cargo reached the wharf, a portion of it was in the hands of the contractors beyond Hancock. . . .   Since then rails have been sent to the western terminal of the finished road at the rate of what is equivalent to about a mile of track per day and as the entire line to Cumberland is ready for the reception of the rails they are in the course of being laid down very nearly if not quite as fast as they reach their destination. . . ."

"TWENTY MINUTES FOR DINNER!"

A typical scene upon the American railroad in the 'forties.

From a painting by H. D. Stitt.

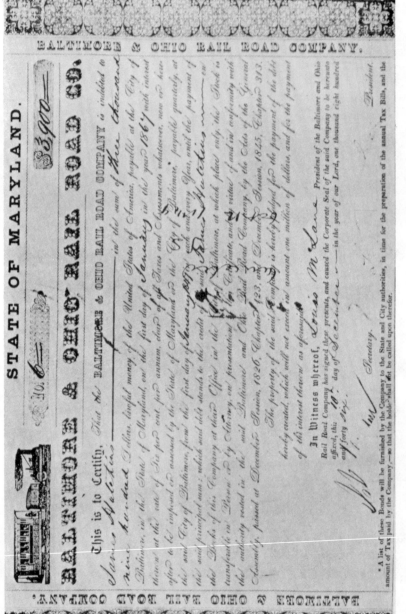

A Bond of a Later Day.

Issued in 1846 during the administration of President Louis McLane.

From the company's archives.

terminal of the line.   We spare the details of this expedition—
so much larger doings were to come a few years later when the
road finally should thrust its way through to Wheeling.

It is far more interesting to record the resignation—on
September 30 of this same year—of Jonathan Knight as chief
engineer of the Baltimore and Ohio.   For sixteen hard years,
perhaps as hard years as might possibly come to the lot of any
railroader, Mr. Knight had served the road.   He had been
with it from the beginning.   He was one of the last of its pioneers to depart from its official ranks.

Mr. Knight served the property faithfully and well.   But he
seems to have had a rare faculty for engaging in bitter dis-
putes, in acrimonious word battles, long drawn out.   He fought
in this way years before with Captains Long and McNeill. . . .
After finally leaving the service of the Baltimore and Ohio, he
became a consulting engineer for the city of Wheeling; and,
upon the entrance of the railroad to that Ohio port, engaged
in a sharp controversy with Benjamin H. Latrobe, his successor. . . .   Despite these things, however, Jonathan Knight
to this day remains one of the commanding figures of the early
days of Baltimore and Ohio.   His Quaker sincerity and honesty
and his undoubted ability rendered him of vast help when
help was most needed—at the very outset of the road's career.

.   .   .   .

Worth mention, too, is the fact that on the fifth of December, 1842, twenty-five days after the line had first been completed, a special locomotive, running straight out from
Washington, and bearing a copy of President Tyler's message
to Congress, made the run to Cumberland, 170 miles, in five
hours and fifty minutes.   And much of it over miles of brand-
new line which hardly had had opportunity as yet to settle
down into its permanent bed, and over which it was not even
hoped to run regular passenger trains in less than ten hours!

At Cumberland, the message was transferred to waiting
coaches—for which you may be sure that on such an occasion

the very best horses and the very best drivers were chosen—
to be whisked off over the National Road; to Pittsburgh, to
Wheeling, to the great and swiftly growing country of Ohio,
of Kentucky, of Indiana and of Illinois that lay beyond these
cities. No longer could one speak of these oncoming states
as wildernesses. Civilization—with a ladder-like wand of
wood and steel that looked dangerously like a link of railroad
track—was waving her hand over them, and great new cities
were having their foundations laid; in Ohio, Columbus, Cincinnati and Cleveland; in Kentucky, Louisville; in Indiana,
Indianapolis; and in Illinois, Springfield and Chicago; with
St. Louis, growing apace, perched close by her southwestern
rim. Between these larger places, hundreds and hundreds of
smaller ones. And, literally, thousands of farms. No longer
was the axe of the pioneer heard in the greater part of these
four states. In its place was coming the silent efficiency of the
permanent cultivation of the land.

The stage was being set, swiftly, for the coming of Baltimore
and Ohio, not merely to the rim of the Ohio River, but over it
and across it and far, far beyond it. Men in the company's
offices in Baltimore began to whisper to one another—ever
guardedly—that some day the road might even aspire to such
distant capitals of commerce as Cincinnati, or Chicago or St.
Louis. Wheeling, like Cumberland, like Harpers Ferry, like
Ellicotts Mills—each in its turn—to be only a momentary
resting place! Stranger dreams than this might easily be
imagined.

We have seen already the eastern terminals of the stage
coaches and the water routes thrust back twice from their
original placing at tidewater in old Baltimore City. Once to
Ellicotts Mills—not much of a thrust, but still indicative of
what the power of the railroad was to mean in some oncoming
hour—and then to Frederick, a far greater retreat. And now
Cumberland was to be the east terminal of through, horse-
drawn traffic upon the highway.

The Baltimore and Ohio was making real preparations at its

new western terminal for the handling of this interchange of traffic, which was to grow in volume each year for fully a decade after the completion of the railroad through from Baltimore. Four extensive brick warehouses were begun in the summer of 1842 and were ready for use when the line was formally opened late that autumn. They were assigned to the local firms of Talbot, Jones & Co., Hollyday & Edgerton, Atkinson & Templeman and Dilly & Edwards. . . . In speaking of them, the *Cumberland Civilian* said, under date of August 19:

> . . . The completion of the road to this point this fall is confidently calculated upon, by which time it is intended to have these warehouses finished to accommodate the anticipated trade which this great work will afford.
>
> The results which have been realized in the few months since the railroad has been in operation to Hancock have been of the most gratifying character. The travel to and from the West has been doubled, having been attracted to this route by the superior advantages of comfort and expedition which it presents over others; and there can be no doubt that when the road is open to Cumberland so that the trip between Baltimore and Wheeling and Pittsburgh can be made easily in twenty-four hours, or probably less, the question of the course of travel between the East and the West will be settled definitely and permanently in favor of this Great Central Route. There is no other that can come into competition with it in any one of the prominent particulars of expedition, comfort or economy, and it must therefore *command* the travel between the Atlantic States and the vast valley of the Mississippi. . . .

In all of its optimism it will be noted that the *Civilian* sounds a single note of slight alarm. Competition *is* coming to the fore. If we examine the contemporary records, we find that in that same year, 1842, the first through rail route between Boston and the Great Lakes, at Buffalo—a group of correlated lines, afterwards to bear the name of the New York Central Railroad—was almost ready to be opened for traffic.

Also the route—a curious combination of railroad and canal—all the way across the state of Pennsylvania from Philadelphia to Pittsburgh, which some day was to be known as the Pennsylvania Railroad, was steadily being bettered. Even though it was not to be until December 10, 1852, that the first through train from Philadelphia was to run through to the head of the Ohio at the growing young city of Pittsburgh.

This last route—curious and incomplete as it then was—was already proving itself a troublesome competitor of the Baltimore and Ohio. Because of this competition, the rates—freight and passenger—that the company had labored so hard with the Maryland Legislature to advance, had to be lowered; in the case of the passenger rates, twenty-five per cent, and in that of the freight, thirty. Yet, oddly enough, this seemed to cause no great alarm. In the annual report of October, 1842, one finds McLane optimistic even in this regard; and expressing his belief that merchandise may easily be carried from Baltimore to the near railhead at Cumberland at fifty cents a hundred; and on to the Ohio River—either at Pittsburgh or at Wheeling—by the highway in thirty-six hours and at a cost not to exceed fifteen dollars a hundred.

Through its president, the board of directors of the Baltimore and Ohio expresses its belief that iron may be transported between Cumberland and Baltimore "at a little more than 3 cents, and coal, if a sufficient quantity be offered, not exceeding 2 cents, per ton, per mile." Here is the first reference in the official records of the company to the possibility of hauling coal eastbound. In fact, a certain definite movement of this sort already had begun, even though there is no official mention of it. Such traffic of this type as had heretofore developed was of coal from the anthracite districts of Pennsylvania, west from Baltimore to the interior. Now the situation was to reverse itself. And the beginnings made of a vast trade that in the future was to rise to a great volume and become the greatest tonnage, by far, of the Baltimore and Ohio Railroad.

.   .   .   .

That day still was afar.   The Baltimore and Ohio had just reached Cumberland.   In truth, it still was merely at the base of the Alleghenies.   Ahead of it, still stood one of God's great walls; a seemingly impenetrable barrier over which man now must crawl, carrying his metal highway with him.   For such an adventure he would need all that he might possess, of resource, of endurance, of energy and of faith.   These things the Baltimore and Ohio, come to the thirteenth year of its actual service as a railroad, would need to buckle on before it might even hope to reach the great goal of its ambition: the swiftly running Ohio, on the far side of the mountains.

CHAPTER XIII

THE IRON HORSE IS BEING PERFECTED

Locomotive Development on the Baltimore and Ohio from 1837 to 1853—The "Grasshoppers" Succeeded by the "Crabs"— Haphazard Design Becomes a Well Ordered Pattern, the Locomotive a Distinct Forerunner of the One of Today.

In earlier chapters of this book we have witnessed the first attempts of the builders of the Baltimore and Ohio Railroad to create and to evolve some satisfactory type of steam motive power for their line. From the experimental *Tom Thumb* of Peter Cooper and the *York* and the *Arabian* of the ill-fated Phineas Davis to the *Davis* and the *George Clinton*, which Gillingham and Ross Winans placed upon the Washington Branch in the summer of 1836, there has been seen a distinct progress in locomotive construction. Even though all these early builders clung tenaciously to the upright style of boiler, despite the belief of Stephenson and other designers of reputation and experience that the horizontal type was the only one fit for the real necessities of the situation.

All this was water that had gone over the dam.

Now—we have returned in our chronicle to the year 1837— a radical change was to come in locomotive design upon the Baltimore and Ohio. After declaring against the horizontal boiler, the road was to adopt it as well as the horizontal type of cylinder—to the exclusion of any other type. . . . Count this as an early achievement for the highly practical administration of Louis McLane.

The reform started with the cylinders. In 1837, and while the road still clung to the upright boiler, these began to be built horizontally. In the company's annual report, issued in the autumn of that year, Jonathan Knight states that a plan has been matured to place and work the cylinders horizontally. "Two engines are being built at the Company's shops," he adds, "and it is expected that they will have some advantages over former engines." Which certainly would appear to be a modest enough assertion.

The plan to which Mr. Knight refers was covered by patents obtained by Ross Winans, in July, 1837. There were five of these, covering, in considerable detail, the various unusual features of the design. These details, however, are now unimportant, particularly so in view of the fact that these engines, which presently became known as the "coal crabs"— even more definitely as the "crabs"—(as distinguished from the original "grasshoppers" of the Baltimore and Ohio) in the long run contributed little or nothing to locomotive design in the United States.

There were eight of the crabs, which, like the grass-hoppers, were built in that prodigious workshop, that untiring font of energy, Mount Clare. In addition to their horizontal cylinders, which were geared through two crank shafts to rods connected to the driving wheels, their most distinctive feature was their cabs, which were placed at the very front of the locomotive, so that the engineer might have the best possible view of the track. A small four-wheeled tender, in type not unlike those in use today, was carried at the rear.

Like the grasshoppers, the crabs were built with extremely short wheel bases, in order that the short 400-foot radius curves, which still prevailed upon the eastern sections of the Baltimore and Ohio, could be traversed without the precious little engines thrusting themselves into the ditch. That they did good work—within their somewhat severe limitations—is not to be doubted. A very few of them were in the switching service of the road up until about 1892. At about that time

they were distributed—almost as museum pieces.   One of them
—the *Atlantic*, the second locomotive of the Baltimore and
Ohio—was carefully preserved by the road and to this day
makes excursions to various historical celebrations and pag-
eants in the territory served by the company.[1]

In 1837, apparently at the instance of Louis McLane,
the road ceased its experimentations in building locomotives,
and went out into the open market to buy engines of standard
types.   The new president seemingly was determined to get the
largest value for his money.

Philadelphia already had become a locomotive-building
center of importance.   Three firms—William Norris, Eastwick
and Harrison, and M. W. Baldwin—were contributing to the
luster of her reputation in fabricating this form of product.[2]

In that day, Norris was perhaps the bright particular star
of that little group.   He had built an engine—the *George
Washington*—which was given a test on the steep inclined plane
of the Columbia Railroad, just west of the Schuylkill River.
This was a complete success, of a most dramatic sort, and did
much toward establishing the practicability of the steam
locomotive in the American mind.[3]   An immediate result of

[1] At the Centenary Exhibition and Pageant of the Baltimore and Ohio held at
Halethorpe, in the suburbs of Baltimore, in the fall of 1927, two of these small
engines—the original *Atlantic* and the original *Thomas Jefferson*—were displayed,
working under their own power.   In addition to which there moved reproductions
of the *Tom Thumb*, the *York* and the *Lafayette*—this last now renamed as the
William Galloway—which Mount Clare had built as close as was humanly possible
to the original engines and which represented its own contribution to the
Centenary.

[2] The last of these three firms continues in Philadelphia to this day—with its
name changed to the Baldwin Locomotive Works—as one of the greatest manufacturers of locomotives, steam, gas and electric, in the entire world.

[3] A contemporary account of the performance—taken from the *American
Railroad Journal*, for July, 1836—is interesting.   It says, in part:
". . .   The engine started at the foot of the plane. . . .   After proceeding a
few feet the wheels were found to slip and the engine returned.   It was said that
the rails were found to have been oiled at this place; but a small quantity of sand

THE *Hercules*—·1844.

Built by Ross Winans at his Baltimore shops.   It follows few of the recognized traditions.

From a water-color drawing.

THE *Philip E. Thomas.*

A William Norris locomotive of 1838, which also pioneered in the horizontal boiler and leading truck.

From a water-color drawing.

this astounding performance—at first received with skepticism —which in due time was carefully reported in the Baltimore newspapers, was that the directors of the Baltimore and Ohio ordered eight locomotives of Norris; each with a horizontal boiler. Delivery of these began with the arrival of the *Lafayette*, which was placed in service on the road in April, 1837. The others continued to arrive at irregular intervals, until the coming of the *Pegasus* in November, 1839. They at once formed an immediate and valuable addition to the motive power of the property.

That indefatigable historian of Baltimore and Ohio locomotives, Mr. J. Snowden Bell, reports[1] the cylinder dimensions of these engines as approximately 10 by 18 to 20 inches. He forms the conclusion that it is probable that they were very much the same as those given in a schedule of so-called "Class B" engines, which was issued by the Norris Works, January 1, 1841, and which follows:

DIMENSIONS

Diameter of cylinder	10½ inches
Stroke of cylinder	18 "
Total length of boiler	13 feet
Length of tubes	8 "

---

was strewn on the spot and the engine proceeded. She regularly and steadily gained speed as she advanced to the very top, passing over the plane in 2 minutes and 24 seconds. . . .

"The length of the plane is 2800 feet; the grade 369 feet to the mile, or 1 foot rise in 14.3 feet. . . . The weight of the engine with water was 14,930 pounds; the load drawn up the plane, including the tender with coal and water, and two passenger cars with 53 passengers, was 31,270 pounds; steam pressure less than 80 pounds to the square inch. . . . It is to be remembered that the rails were wet with dew. As to the oil it was afterwards mentioned that bets were made with the workmen to a considerable amount and those having been lost by the successful performance of the engine on a former day were quadrupled, and to save themselves it is not unlikely that this means was provided to accelerate the descent rather than the ascent of the engine."

[1] *Locomotive Development on the Baltimore and Ohio*, by J. Snowden Bell. Locomotive Publishing Company, New York, N. Y., 1912.

Number of tubes	78
Diameter of tubes	2 inches
Grate area (square inches) . . .	1,050.8
Diameter of stack	10 "
Diameter of drivers	4 feet
Weight, in running order . . .	20,615 pounds
Weight, on drivers	12,781 "

"The statement of grate area in 'square inches,' in a builder's circular," comments Mr. Bell, "appears almost humorous at the present day [1912], at which, after gaining a comparatively few square *inches* by the extension of the fire-box over the tops of the frames, which was made by James Milholland in 1857, we have duplicated and even quadrupled the square *feet* of grate area considered to be large in olden times, by the introduction and development of the wide fire-box properly so called. . . ." To which may be added the thought that the most modern of steam locomotives upon our railroads today not only have fire-box arches, thus greatly increasing their combustion effectiveness, but, on some roads, a real beginning has at last been made in adapting the highly modern marine boiler—of so-called Scotch-tube type—to the locomotive, so increasing its efficiency.[1]

Return for a final moment to the Norris locomotives. Let us quote Mr. Bell at still greater length in regard to them. He says:

. . . It will be observed that the Norris engines contained the first three of the "original improvements" over English

[1] At the Baltimore and Ohio Centenary Exhibition there was shown for the first time a water-tube fire-box locomotive, designed by George H. Emerson, chief of motive power of that road, which was the first engine of this type to be built for the Baltimore and Ohio. To an original Class Q-1 Mikado locomotive, the new fire box had been applied. It consisted of a double row of 2½-inch water tubes, extending from a mud-ring manifold to an overhead steam drum carried in a double-plate tube sheet and a double-plate backhead. The grate area was 73.5 square feet, the heating surface of the fire box 603.2 square feet, the total heating surface 3457.2 square feet, and the superheating surface 842 square feet. Boiler pressure was placed at 250 pounds.

practice mentioned by Colburn, viz.: the "bogie," the use of
four fixed eccentrics and the spark arrester.   The reverse gear
was, as shown, of the "drop hook" pattern, which necessitated
the use of starting-bars; the frames, while light in their proportions, were of the modern "bar" type, and the design of the
engines was, except as to the location of the driving wheels, in
front of the firebox, practically followed in all particulars in
subsequent practice, during the period in which this type continued to be built.   The engines gave as good service as was
within the limits of their capacity, which being soon found
insufficient to meet transportation requirements, no more of
this type were placed on the Baltimore and Ohio Railroad,
and, as early as September, 1839, the four-coupled engine
with four-wheeled leading truck, or 4-4-0 type . . . was
introduced.

.   .   .   .

The first of the 4-4-0 engines was the *Atlas*, built by
Eastwick and Harrison, of Philadelphia, and delivered to the
Baltimore and Ohio in the early fall of 1839.   Four others
followed during the next three years.   The *Mercury* and the
Minerva were designed by Joseph Harrison, Jr., for fast service.
In this they seem to have met with success.   It is reported
that the *Minerva* picked up a long passenger train with great
ease and within a comparatively short distance was able to
carry it forward at the rate of a mile a minute.   Her 60-inch
drivers, as well as her 14-by-20-inch cylinders, were factors of
no mean importance in achieving such a rate of speed.

Each had novel and ingenious forms of reverse gear—an
Eastwick patent—and the *Mercury* a new form of leading
truck—the English have always insisted upon calling this a
"bogie"—on which the side frames were simply long springs,
with axle boxes at their ends and journal boxes atop the
spring-bands, which were fitted to vibrate on the ends of a
wrought-iron bolster, on the center of which the forward end
of the locomotive rested. . . .   That this design must have
stood at least fairly well to the task is indicated by the fact

that the railroad company's annual report for 1844 shows that the *Mercury* in a single twelvemonth ran 37,000 miles; at that time an unprecedented and sensational record.

.   .   .   .

What a pleasant sound those old engine names had . . . *Mercury* . . . *Minerva* . . . *Pegasus* . . . *Vulcan* . . . *Jupiter* . . . all the rest of them! It was a survival of a certain sentiment and courtliness that underlay the rough and ready ways of stage-coach times. The habit became universal all the way across the land. Nor were the names of locomotives by any means limited to those of classical characters. Occasionally, the names of rivers or lakes or mountains were used; and these, especially when of Indian derivation, were both beautiful and appropriate. The *Opequan* . . . *Catoctin* . . . *Youghiogheny* . . . *Tuscarora* . . . all of these . . . and many more . . . were cognomens that did credit to the expression of a small part of the vast store of real romance back of railroading.

Sometimes, the entitling of the locomotives was of a baser sort . . . and then it was that mere men sought to glorify themselves by causing their names to be emblazoned upon the sides of engine cabs. At first this practice was quite innocent. For who would deny the appropriateness of naming a fine new locomotive after the first President of this land—or after any other President of the United States? Or, for that matter, after a Governor of a state or perhaps an unusually distinguished Senator or member of the Cabinet? It was somewhere after that that the custom ran toward the ridiculous. . . . Until finally it came to the point that, local celebrities having been exhausted, the officers and the directors of the railroads caused their names to be advertised to an admiring public along the station platforms by naming the engines . . . after themselves.

Nevertheless, the practice, in the large, was a pleasing one. And when, in the swiftly growing number of engines upon each of the more extensive roads of the land, it became necessary—

or advisable—to drop it, and merely to number the locomotives sequentially, like passenger or freight cars, a distinct something was lost to the American railroad. Something more than a flavor. Something more than a mere bit of sentiment. A something which betokened a personality, and justified the frequent extension of the gender feminine to that huge mass of steel and other metals, the steam locomotive. . . .

.   .   .   .

Coincident with the arrival of the engines from Eastwick and Harrison, came two more from William Norris: the *Vesta* and the *Stag*—numbered, respectively, *25* and *31*. With the exception of their reverse gear and the peculiar spring leading truck, which has just been described, this fine brace of train pullers were much the same in general design as the *Mercury* and the *Minerva*. They, too, had big and speedy 60-inch drivers; their cylinders were 12 by 20 inches. Primarily they were designed for passenger service; but were upon occasion used for hauling fast trains of merchandise freight—a practice just beginning upon the Baltimore and Ohio.

At about this time, although the delivery extended for a few years afterwards, also came five more engines from New Castle, Delaware (built by the New Castle Manufacturing Company), which, with the exception of one—the *Arrow*, *No. 28*—which arrived in February, 1840, were very similar to those of the William Norris and the Eastwick and Harrison factories. The *Arrow* was inside-connected—a true British type which has prevailed in England until this day—and was one of the very, very few of this sort ever placed upon the Baltimore and Ohio.

.   .   .   .

In the meantime, what was Ross Winans doing?

One can imagine him, in great perplexity and no little anger, stroking his immense white whiskers. . . . He who had assisted at the very birth of the locomotive in America. . . .

Winans was not the sort to sit by idly and watch his competitors run amuck over him.   He was of man size and fighting caliber, this trader in horses from New Jersey who had first come to Baltimore years before to sell four-legged equine motive power to the new railroad there, and who developed quickly into one of the most valuable and prolific of early railroad designers and inventors.   He was a man of ideas and he clung tenaciously to them, once he had adopted them for himself. . . .   In the bitter days of the Civil War, he was to espouse the Southern cause, with all the fullness of his vigorous nature.   Because of this, he was to be arrested and to sleep—for a few nights, at least—in the prison of Fort McHenry.   Although for many years a successful and a respected manufacturer of Baltimore —long after he had left the service of its chief railroad—he was to estrange himself from many of its citizens.   And finally to withdraw into his house, there to end his days, very much of a recluse.

All of which anticipates.   Let us repeat the question:

What was Ross Winans doing?

For one thing, he was bringing out three engines of the well-known 4–4–0 type of that day—it might be fair to call it the Campbell type—the *Atalanta*, the *Reindeer* and the *Juno*.

But this he must have regarded as fairly unimportant.   He was not the sort content to follow long the lead of other men. He preferred to think for himself, to strike out along more original lines.   And thus one finds in the eighteenth annual report of the Baltimore and Ohio Railroad Company, dated the second Monday of October, 1844, the following paragraph:

. . . The report of Mr. Knight was submitted and published in 1842, and as early as that period, Mr. Ross Winans, an ingenious mechanic of Baltimore, had not only contrived a far more important improvement in the locomotive, but had actually constructed an engine weighing *twenty tons*, running on eight wheels, all of which were drivers, and with the weight equally distributed over the wheels, so that the bearing upon

The *Mercury*—1842.

Built by Eastwick and Harrison at Philadelphia. This early locomotive developed a high speed in service.

From a water-color drawing.

A "MUD DIGGER."
Another Ross Winans creation. It was designed originally with a vertical boilder
From a water-color drawing.

any one is not greater than that upon the ordinary machine of ten tons weight, capable of hauling over a level and straight road, *eleven hundred* tons; and over grades of eighty-two and a half feet to the mile with curvatures of one thousand feet radius, about *one hundred and seventy* tons, at a speed of eight miles per hour.

This would seem to answer pretty completely the question of what Ross Winans was doing. Assuredly Ross Winans was not asleep.

Twenty tons! Twice the weight of the best American locomotives of that still early day. This, decidedly, was daring. To pull 1100 tons, even though along straight and level track, was a performance with which to reckon. Even today there are not many freight trains weighing more than 5000 tons, gross. . . . Ross Winans was indeed progressing.

He made no claim to being an inventor of the eight-wheel locomotive. It is quite clear that a machine of this type was in use at the Wylam collieries in England as early as 1815, although these British engines were not coupled by connecting or side rods and were propelled by spur gearing. The connecting rods of the Winans engines were their especial feature. Of them, as well as of the other distinctive parts of his design, he says in his claim for a patent upon them:

I claim as my invention the construction and use of a loco-motive engine, having either six or eight driving wheels, the axles of which are placed parallel to each other, and which are permanently to preserve this parallelism during the whole action of the engine, whether running upon straight or curved roads; the said axles having sufficient end play to allow the wheels, when the whole of them are provided with flanges, to adapt themselves to the curvatures of the road; or instead of this end play of the axles, the constructing of two of the pairs of wheels where eight are used, without flanges, the motive power from the steam engine to be transmitted to the first pair of driving wheels, through the intermedium of a fifth axle

furnished with spur wheels, which gear into small spur wheels
or pinions on the axle of the first pair of driving wheels, and
the power from these wheels being transmitted to the whole
system of driving wheels by means of cranks on the axles of
said wheels and suitable connecting rods as set forth. . . .

A road which had persisted in calling its earlier engines
"grasshoppers" and "crabs," must presently find a good
name for these creations of the inexhaustible mind of Ross
Winans. And so this engine—technically of an 0-8-0 type
—soon became known as a "mud digger." It actually
weighed 23½ tons instead of the 20 tons originally planned,
and its eight driving wheels were each 33 inches in diameter.
Cylinders were 17 by 24 inches. . . . As, by reason of the inter-
posed gearing, the main and side rods moved in opposite directions when the engine was in motion, they are reported to have
presented a novel and a somewhat peculiar appearance when
under way. . . . In his original design for the mud diggers,
Winans had clung to the upright boiler. It was a swan song
for that pet idea of his. But when the Baltimore and Ohio
engines were actually built, it is to be noticed that the horizontal
boiler was used. Unquestionably, it lent itself infinitely better
to the lines and type of the modern locomotive.

The record of these engines is a fairly good one. They
were, of course, limited by their very design to slow-moving
heavy tonnage freight. Some of them continued in yard
service until 1865. Because of their proved efficiency—
within their own peculiar limitations—they were used at an
early day by the Western Railroad of Massachusetts (afterwards the Boston and Albany) and the Philadelphia and
Reading Railroad; and these had vertical boilers. Mr.
Baldwin, of Philadelphia, acting in conjunction with Mr.
Winans, built them for the Western Railroad of Massachusetts.

.   .   .   .

Baldwin began building for the Baltimore and Ohio itself
in the middle of the 'forties. Three six-driver engines (0-6-0),

the *Baldwin*, the *Wisconnisco*—originally ordered by the Lykens Valley Railroad—and the *Unicorn*, were built. The drivers of these engines were considerably larger than those of their predecessors—43 inches—but their entire weight ran only from 32,000 to 35,000 pounds. The cylinder size was 13½ by 18 inches.

A distinctive feature of their construction was the use of the flexible beam truck (developed by Mr. Baldwin) by which the first and second driving axles were held parallel to each other, but at the same time were allowed a limited amount of lateral or side motion; the one to the right, the other to the left, or vice versa. This arrangement comprised a pair of vibrating beams which supported the frames through spherical bearings and were fitted to receive cylindrically turned driving boxes. The side rods had cylindrical brasses, thus forming ball and socket joints, so that they could accommodate themselves to the lateral movement of the wheels. This arrangement enabled locomotives with comparatively long wheel bases, and having all their weight on their drivers, easily to traverse curves of short radius—which still existed in considerable numbers on the Main Stem of the Baltimore and Ohio. It came, beyond a doubt, as a development arising because of proved defects in the earliest of the Winans mud diggers.

The fourth Baldwin engine to be builded for the Baltimore and Ohio was the *Dragon*, which came to the line shortly before the arrival of the *Unicorn*. This was a notable mechanism; a direct-connected engine, with the 0-8-0 wheel arrangement, and one of the first to be built for any American railroad. It represented the beginnings of a type which was to supplant the earlier mud diggers in the handling of the heaviest freight and which was to do tremendous service for a score of years to come. According to a recent description issued by the Baldwin works, the *Dragon* had 14½-by-18-inch cylinders and 43-inch drivers. She weighed 41,000 pounds and, although not quite so heavy, was, with her direct connections, a distinct improvement on the curiously geared original eight-wheeled Winans engines.

Progress was being made all this while. Not rapidly, but steadily.

For those who are inclined to follow the technical development of the locomotive in the second and third decades of the Baltimore and Ohio, the following advertisement, taken from the pages of the *American Railroad Journal* of October 23, 1847, may be of interest. It shows what were considered the requirements for a freight locomotive on that road at that particular time.

To Locomotive Engine Builders:

Proposals under seal will be received by the undersigned up to Saturday, the 6th of November, inclusive, for furnishing the Baltimore & Ohio Railroad Co. with 4 LOCOMOTIVE ENGINES, in conformity with the following specifications:

1.   The weight not to exceed 20 tons of 2240 lbs., and to come as near to that limit as possible.

2.   The weight to be uniformly distributed upon all the wheels, when the engine is drawing her heaviest load.

3.   The number of wheels to be *eight*.

4.   The diameter of the wheels to be 43 inches.

5.   The four intermediate wheels to be without flanges.

6.   The boiler to contain not less than 1000 square feet of fire surface, of which there shall be not less than one-fifteenth in the firebox.

7.   The tubes of No. 11 flue iron, with not less than $\frac{3}{4}$ of an inch space between them in the tube sheets.

8.   The firebox, with the exception of the tube and crown sheets, to be of $\frac{2}{3}$-inch copper.

9.   The tube sheets to be $\frac{3}{8}$-inch thick.

10.   The boiler to be of No. 3 iron, of the best quality.

11.   The firebox to be not less than 24 inches deep below the cylindrical part of the boiler.

12.   The steam to be taken to the cylinder from a separate dome on the forepart of the boiler.

13. The frame, including the pedestals, to be entirely of wrought iron, and the boiler to be connected therewith, so as to allow of contraction and expansion, without strain on either.

14. The cylinders to be 22 inches stroke and not less than 17 inches diameter.

15. The cut-off to be effected by a double valve, worked by separate eccentrics.

16. The angle of the cylinder to be not greater than 13½ degrees with the horizontal line.

17. The frame and bearings to be inside the wheels and the direction from the cylinder direct with the back pair of intermediate wheels.

18. The centers of the extreme wheels to be not more than 11½ feet apart.

19. The wheels to be of cast iron with chilled tire.

20. The means to be provided of varying the power of the exhaust in the blast pipe.

21. The engine to be warranted to do full work with Cumberland or other bituminous coal in a raw state as the fuel, and the furnace to be provided with an upper and lower firedoor with that view.

22. The smokestack to be provided with a wire gauze covering.

23. Two safety valves to be placed upon the boiler, each containing not less than five square inches of surface and one to be out of reach of the engineman.

24. The tender to be upon 8 wheels and constructed upon such plan as shall be furnished by the Company, and to carry not less than 3 cords of wood or its equivalent in coal and 1500 gallons of water.

25. The materials and workmanship to be of the best quality, and the engine to be subjected to a trial of 30 days' steady work with freight upon the road before acceptance by the Company.

Payment to be made in cash upon the acceptance of the engine. The four engines to be delivered at the Company's Mount Clare depot in Baltimore—the first on the 1st of February, 1848, and the three others on the 1st of March, April and May ensuing.

The track is 4 feet 8½ inches gauge and the shortest curve of the road is 400 feet radius.

The Company to be secured against all patent claims.

Further information will be communicated upon application to the undersigned, at the Company's office, No. 23 Hanover Street, Baltimore, to which the proposals suitably endorsed will be addressed.

By order of the President and Directors.

BENJ. H. LATROBE,
Chief Engineer and General Superintendent.

Baltimore, September 18, 1847.

To this interesting advertisement, Mr. Baldwin, of Philadelphia, quickly responded. With the result that he was awarded a contract for five engines; not four, as set down in the terms of the advertisement. Yet in the long run, and because of the time limitations of the contract, but three of the locomotives were delivered; for which Baldwin was paid $9000 apiece. These were the *Hector*, the *Cossack* and the *Tartar*.

Little information is available in regard to these three engines, yet it is known that in them the flexible beam truck was omitted, the wheels all being held in rigid frames, and plain tires used on the second and third pairs. Mr. J. Snowden Bell recalls having personally seen them in service, and adds:

. . . The firebox was of rectangular section, with a hemispherical or "Bury" dome on its top, and the back wall was rearwardly inclined from top to bottom, so as to provide larger grate area. . . . The pumps were 11-inch stroke, and were worked by eccentrics on the crankpins of the rear wheels.

According to Mr. Bell, claims having been made by Ross Winans that the use of chilled tires and variable exhaust, which were called for by sections 19 and 20 of the advertisement just given, would infringe upon patents that he held, Baldwin was released from these particular requirements, by a letter from Mr. Latrobe, the chief engineer of the company, in the course of which he said:

. . . You will be expected to direct your best efforts to provide the engines with the best substitute for the variable exhaust as a means of increasing and diminishing the draught at pleasure. The use of rolled iron tires will obviate the chilled wheel patent. I would suggest you to try Mr. Horatio Hines' *twisted* iron for the tires. . . .

Which suggestion presently was put into effect in the new engines.

. . . .

There came, before the beginnings of the Civil War and a great new expansion upon the Baltimore and Ohio, an important type of steam locomotive to which other references will be made in the pages of this book; yet which cannot be ignored completely within this chapter. This engine was the so-called "camel" type, the last great invention from the remarkably fruitful brain of Ross Winans. In all, 119 of these unusual engines were built by Mr. Winans for the road; in addition to three which he had in stock in his Baltimore works in 1863, and the *Centipede*, which was the first 4-8-0 engine that was ever built, when Baltimore and Ohio suddenly found itself in critical need of more motive power. These were then sold to the company, to meet the war-time emergency.

These machines, although of the now familiar 0-8-0 type, represented a considerable advance, both in size and in the perfection of their details, over the mud diggers. They were divided into three major classes—known as the short, the medium and the long furnace. The majority, however, were in the last two of these classes and had 19-by-22-inch cylinders, in addition to the 43-inch drivers, which by this time had become almost a standard upon the road.

All in all, the camels were perhaps the most curious large engines ever placed upon an American railroad. You could trust Ross Winans never to do the conventional thing. Weighing, on an average, some twenty-five tons, they had great pulling capacity, although, of course, no speed whatsoever.

. . . But it was their special features—highly original and highly distinctive—that set them apart from the standard types of locomotives in use upon the railroads of the United States in their day and generation. . . . The front end of the fire box, for instance, was fed through an upper chute, the lower part through a rear door. To facilitate this novel mode of feeding, the tender was built with two decks, the upper for firing the coal through the chute, the lower for firing through the door. . . . Frames, valve gear and other details of these engines presented radical departures from the conventional. The engines had many critics. Yet it cannot be denied that the camels were practical motive power, and they remained in service for many years after their first appearance. This, despite the trouble and extra labor that some of their special features gave to their crews.

. . . .

The question arises as to the performance rendered by these locomotives of the Baltimore and Ohio during the decade of the 'forties. One of its best answers can be found in the company's annual report, issued in October, 1847. In it, Mr. B. H. Latrobe, chief engineer of the road, but in this instance signing himself its general superintendent, states that there are now forty-nine locomotives in service. As a forerunner of present day practice, he proceeds to divide these into four classes, according to weight and to power, as follows:

> 1st class, weighing 23 tons, on 8 wheels, all drivers, 13, rated at 39 of the 4th class
> 2d class, weighing 16¼ tons, on 8 and 6 wheels, all drivers, 2, rated at 4 of the 4th class
> 3d class, weighing 15 tons, on 8 wheels, with 4 drivers, 12, rated at 18 of the 4th class
> 4th class, weighing 10 tons, on 6 and 4 wheels, with 2 and 4 drivers, 22, rated at 22 of the 4th class

Mr. Latrobe then describes the road's engine fleet in some detail. He says, in part:

. . . The engines, various as they are in weight and form, are all useful machines in their various degrees. Those of the first class burn Cumberland coal, for which their furnaces are specially adapted; and so do the upright boiler engines of the third and fourth class. The rest burn wood, or a mixture of wood and coal. The passenger trains on both roads [Main Stem and Washington Branch] were originally drawn by the horizontal six-wheel engines of the fourth class, for which they became too heavy two or three years since, and now eight-wheeled engines of the third class are chiefly used for them; and upon the Main Stem even these are so often inadequate to the duty that the alternative will soon be presented of running more frequent trains, or of using heavier engines, or assistant power, upon the higher grades. . . .

There are . . . at work upon the Main Stem, forty-four engines of all classes, and upon the Washington Branch, five. . . . The duty performed by these engines has been as follows in miles run:

On the Main Stem

13 first class engines, with freight trains, have run	207,586 miles
2 second class engines, with freight trains, have run	24,702 miles
10 third class engines, with freight trains, have run	115,885 miles
The same engines, with passenger trains, have run	129,838 miles
19 fourth class engines, with freight trains, have run	312,984 miles
The same engines, with passenger trains, have run	17,031 miles
44 engines of all classes, with passengers and freight, have run	808,026 miles

On the Washington Branch

2 third class engines, with passenger trains, have run	44,784 miles

3 fourth class engines, with passenger trains,
    have run . . . . 15,925 miles
The same engines, with freight trains,
    have run . . . . 40,652 miles
5 engines of both classes, with passengers and
    freight, have run . . . . . 101,361 miles
49 engines of both classes, with passengers and
    freight, have run . . . . . 909,387 miles

The whole stock of engines have therefore run during the year ending the 30th September, ultimo, nine hundred and nine thousand, three hundred and eighty-seven miles, being an average of 18,559 miles to each engine.

Mr. Latrobe expresses his opinion that the only perfect way of analyzing the performance of a locomotive or a group of locomotives is in the tons hauled one mile by each. He thereby sets a fashion which is in use today by the most accurate railroad statisticians. He goes forward to say:

By this . . . mode of expressing the duty of the engines it would appear that the forty-four engines employed in hauling freight have drawn one mile within the year an average of 652,207 tons upon the Main Stem and the Washington Branch together, excluding the five engines of the third class which have been altogether engaged . . . in the passenger business, and converting the passengers hauled by those engines of the third and fourth class usually employed in the freight business into tons, at twelve passengers to the ton. The forty-four freight engines of all classes being expressed by their equivalent in engines of the fourth or lightest class, would be represented by 75½ engines of that class—of which 72½ would belong to the Main Stem and three to the Washington Branch—and each of these engines would have drawn one mile on both roads an average of 380,094 tons in the period of twelve months. This tonnage includes materials and fuel distributed along the line for the company's use. If that be excluded, and the freight for which compensation has been received be alone considered, the performance of each engine expressed in its equivalent of the lightest class will have been 337,671 . . . which if all the

THE *Dragon.*
Built by M. W. Baldwin at Philadelphia in January, 1848.
From a water-color drawing.

WILLIAM MASON BUILT THIS LOCOMOTIVE.

The noted New England engine builder sent it out of his Taunton shops in 1856. It was known as Baltimore and Ohio *No. 25.*

From a recent photograph of the original locomotive.

engines upon the road had been upon it the whole twelve months would have been increased 4½ per cent or to 352,863 tons one mile.

Railroad operators in the United States today can best appreciate the significance of these figures. Also of the repair costs of the Baltimore and Ohio of 1847, which Mr. Latrobe next explains:

The whole amount charged to this account [on the Main Stem] for the past year is $74,139.51—from which must be deducted $3,119.28—for increase in stock of materials and duplicate parts of machinery—and the net amount, showing the actual outlay for the maintenance of the engines, is $71,020.23. This is greater than the corresponding amount for the preceding year by $14,969.06—and the increase is sufficiently accounted for by the addition to the number of the engines and the work done by them. The average number at work during the year 1846 was equivalent to 53½ of the fourth class, and during the year 1847 was equivalent to 74. Consequently the number of engines is greater by 39 per cent. The duty in tons and passengers carried one mile is also greater by 65 per cent, while the increase in repairs is but 27 per cent. During the past year the "improvements" in the engines were about equal in value to those which took place during the previous year and amounted to some $10,500. By this expenditure, included in the above amount of $71,020.23, nine of the fourth class engines were thoroughly rebuilt, five of them of the old upright boiler four-wheeled pattern of Winans & Davis, and four of the six-wheeled horizontal pattern of William Norris—besides which two other engines, one of the first and another of the fourth class, had copper furnaces applied to them.

In his report the following year—dated October 1, 1848—Mr. Latrobe notes that the road now has fifty-seven locomotives and gives some more details of engine upkeep, which are not without interest today.

. . . The increase of miles run in the year just ended was 14⅓ per cent, and the cost per mile but little more than

one-half of that of the previous year, while the cost of the real
duty performed was not more than two-thirds. . . . The
comparison is evidence of the improved economy in the working of the engines, and is due in part to the improved condition
of the engines already on the road, and of the road itself, and
in no small degree to the relief afforded to the working of the
machines by the enlargement of the stock which has taken
place during the year. This extension has operated well in
several ways. When the engines have needed minor repairs,
they have been taken at once to the shop instead of being run
until they would run no longer. The necessity of working upon
them at night has been obviated, and this most imperfect and
costly kind of work avoided. The engineman has also had
more time to clean and keep his engine in order. The general
condition of the machines being much improved, their power
has been increased. Fewer irregularities in the running of the
trains have taken place, and where spare engines were wanted
to replace disabled ones, they were at hand. It requires . . .
no argument to shew that, in numerous particulars, economy
in the operations of the road must have been promoted. During the year ending October 12, 1847, there was 90 per cent of
the motive power constantly on the road. In the year just
closed the proportion was reduced to 82½ per cent. Upon the
Reading Rail Road 80 per cent of the power is usually on the
road. On the Boston and Worcester Rail Road 75 per cent
has been kept in motion by dint of great exertions—on the
Boston and Lowell Rail Road about the same—on the Georgia
Rail Road from 62 to 75 per cent. I am of the opinion, indeed,
that there should be a spare engine to every two in constant
use. . . .

To this same report there is appended a detailed list of the
locomotives of the Baltimore and Ohio in that year (1848)
that shows not only the names of the engines, but their makers
and the date of their separate arrivals upon the property.
Because of the value of this list in determining the locomotive
situation upon the road in the first two decades of its existence,
it is here given, despite its considerable length:

MAIN STEM

First Class Engines

	Name of builder	When placed upon road
Hercules	Ross Winans	October, 1844
Gladiator	" "	November, 1844
Buffaloe	" "	November, 1844
Baltimore	" "	December, 1844
Cumberland	" "	July, 1845
Elephant	" "	July, 1845
Opequan	" "	July, 1846
Elk	" "	August, 1846
Catoctin	" "	October, 1846
Youghiogheny	" "	November, 1846
Alleghany	" "	December, 1846
Tuscarora	" "	December, 1846
Mount Clare	Balto. & Ohio Rail Road Company	May, 1847
Dragon	M. W. Baldwin	January, 1848
Hero	Balto. & Ohio Rail Road Company	May, 1848
Camel	Ross Winans	June, 1848
Saturn	New Castle Mfg. Co.	June, 1848
Memnon	" " " "	July, 1848

Second Class Engines

Vulcan	Eastwick & Harrison	July, 1840
Baldwin	M. W. Baldwin	November, 1846
Wisconisco	"	December, 1847
Unicorn	"	February, 1848

Third Class Engines

†*Isaac McKim*	Gillingham & Winans	May, 1838
†*Mazeppa*	" "	October, 1838
†*Atlas*	Eastwick & Harrison	September, 1839
†*Vesta*	William Norris	November, 1839
†*Jupiter*	Eastwick & Harrison	February, 1840
†*Philip E. Thomas*	William Norris	June, 1838

†Mercury	Eastwick & Harrison	July, 1842
†Minerva	" "	February, 1842
†Stag	William Norris	May, 1843
†Atalanta	Ross Winans	October, 1843
†Reindeer	" "	December, 1845
†Delaware	New Castle Mfg. Co.	January, 1847
†Juno	Ross Winans	January, 1848

Fourth Class Engines

Arabian	Phineas Davis	July, 1834
†George Washington	" "	October, 1834
Thomas Jefferson	" "	June, 1835
James Madison	" "	June, 1835
James Monroe	" "	June, 1835
John Q. Adams	" "	July, 1835
Andrew Jackson	" "	February, 1836
†John Hancock	Gillingham & Winans	April, 1836
Phineas Davis	" "	August, 1836
G. Clinton	" "	August, 1836
M. Van Buren	" "	November, 1836
B. Franklin	" "	April, 1837
Wm. Patterson	" "	June, 1837
†Patapsco	William Norris	July, 1839
†Monocacy	" "	July, 1839
†Potomac	" "	August, 1839
†Pegasus	" "	November, 1839

WASHINGTON BRANCH

Third Class Engines

| †Arrow | New Castle Mfg. Co. | February, 1840 |
| †New Castle | "   "   "   " | December, 1846 |

Fourth Class Engines

†Lafayette	William Norris	April, 1837
†Wm. Cooke	" "	December, 1838
†Jos. W. Patterson	" "	October, 1838

[† Indicates engines employed partly or entirely in passenger service.]

NOTE—The weight of the several classes is as follows:

1st Class	from 19½ to 23½ tons
2d Class	" 16 " 17 "
3d Class	" 14½ " 15½ "
4th Class	" 10 " 11 "

The power of the four classes is considered as in the proportion of the numbers 3 – 2 – 1½ – 1.

To these engines were added, in 1848, the *Hector* and the *Cossack*, built by Baldwin of Philadelphia; the *Iris* and the *Mars*, by Ross Winans. In January, 1849, came the *Tartar*, by Baldwin; in May, 1849, the *Giant*, built by the Baltimore and Ohio in its own shops at Mount Clare, and the *Lion*, which emerged from Mount Clare in March, 1850.

Thereafter, the pleasant custom of naming the road's locomotives ceased. A system of using numbers almost exclusively for their designation came in the spring of 1851, when twelve camels—ten built by Ross Winans in his own works and two at Mount Clare—went into service upon the line. These were numbered from *70* to *81*, inclusive. The historic and venerated *Arabian* was made *No. 1* of the Baltimore and Ohio fleet.

So, in 1851, there were 81 engines in that fleet; in 1852, 108; in 1853, 167; in 1854, 207. From a mere stripling of a railroad there was growing swiftly a transport giant. A railroad's strength is to be measured—almost always—in its power; in its locomotive energy, if you please. In that energy, the Baltimore and Ohio, at the end of its first quarter-century of operating existence, was not found wanting. As Mr. Latrobe indicates, there had at last been achieved a surplus of power; as we would say it today, engines were in "white lead." The road at the end of its first twenty-five years found the living muscle and fiber of its arms—its locomotives—abundant and able to meet the great tasks just ahead.

CHAPTER XIV

THE OHIO IS FINALLY REACHED

On to Wheeling—After Twenty-Five Years of Persistent Effort the Baltimore and Ohio Reaches Its Great Goal on the Bank of the Ohio—Construction Difficulties—And Those of Politics and Finance.

ON the evening of the fifth of November, 1842, the first train entered the brisk village of Cumberland. On the first day of January, 1853, a similar event came to pass at the city of Wheeling, upon the Ohio. . . . In the ten long years that elapsed between these two dates, a vast deal of history was made for the Baltimore and Ohio.

These were hard years. Terribly hard years. Even in the beginning days of the company, when its entire future was extremely shadowy and uncertain, there was no period the half so difficult, the half so perplexing as this final decade of the first period of the construction of the railroad to the Ohio. No man even had dreamed of the hardships that were to encompass the enterprise; nor that a quarter of a century would have passed before the road should come to its first great goal. If the merchants of Baltimore had foreseen these time-taking difficulties, it is possible that those memorable meetings in the parlors of Mr. George Brown's house would finally have come to naught.

It is well that man should have vision. But not too much of it. He sees undoubtedly just as far ahead as properly he should see. And, so, confidently steps forward within the limits of his vision. In this instance of the Baltimore and Ohio, slowly, but seemingly surely.

To the vast financial difficulties that always beset the early promoters of the road, were being added, in steadily increasing numbers, political ones. The legislatures of the various states through which it was to pass were behaving abominably. Virginia acted in a particularly cavalier fashion. Despite the fact that the road had announced, as its chief western terminus, her most important city upon the Ohio, many of her legislators continued to resent the fact that it was not to descend through the valley of the James and pass through her capital, and so on to tidewater at Hampton Roads. For a long time, the fact that the Baltimore and Ohio had been sponsored within a comparatively small state, geographically, and so would have to go into alien commonwealths before it had proceeded a very great distance, militated against it.

For not only was Virginia first to do the handsome thing in giving state aid to the project and then to turn about and repudiate her own action, but Pennsylvania was to follow in her lead. The fact that Pittsburgh had been announced early as one of the important western terminals of the road, at first had given delight to the residents of the Keystone state. They had seen in it a brisk and valuable competitor to the curious and already antiquated system of state-owned canals and railroads across their commonwealth, and so they were prepared to welcome it. The granting of the first charter to the Pittsburgh and Connellsville Railroad, as the extension of the Baltimore and Ohio to the confluence of the Monongahela and the Allegheny rivers was to be known, they had hailed with acclaim. When, on April 18, 1843, the P. & C. had been authorized to extend its line east and south to the Maryland line, within six miles of Cumberland, there had been loud rejoicings in Pittsburgh.

But not so in Philadelphia.

Philadelphia, after an indifference—real or assumed—to the Pittsburgh and Connellsville project, suddenly arose in acute anger against it. The idea that a rival seaport city might draw for itself and away from her own harbor the trade of the western part of Pennsylvania, inflamed her. She proposed measures of immediate reprisal.

Out of these, the present Pennsylvania Railroad came into existence.

It was recognized that the state's system of combined railroad and canal—railroad from Philadelphia to Harrisburg and canal on to Pittsburgh, save for the short 34-mile stretch over the summit of the Alleghenies, where the Allegheny Portage Railway with its inclined planes and its high levels formed the connecting link—was both obsolete and outworn. State ownership and operation of this inland transport chain across Pennsylvania had failed. It must be replaced by an all-rail route privately owned and operated; and this as quickly as possible.

So was born the Pennsylvania Railroad. It was chartered February 25, 1847. And, immediately afterwards, a board of directors was elected, which, on March 31 of that same year, chose Samuel Vaughan Merrick as the first president of the company. The sale of stock for the new company was a vigorous matter, especially in the parent city of Philadelphia, where the solicitors went from house to house, even though sometimes selling but a half share at a single one of these calls. So slowly was this scrip sold that for a long time it looked as if the entire enterprise would fail and the trade of Pittsburgh would become all but entirely diverted to the port of Baltimore.

For the Baltimore and Ohio was losing no opportunities. The same Legislature that had met at Harrisburg in January, 1846, to pass the statutes that were to give birth to the Pennsylvania Railroad, was giving consideration to the claims of the Baltimore company for a route through from Cumberland to Pittsburgh. The halls of the old Capitol were filled with the partisans for each route. "On the floor of the two houses, in the lobby, under the dome of the Capitol, in the hotel entries, along the board walk, in the boarding houses, at all hours of the day and night, the friends of one or the other of the measures buttonholed the members in advocacy or assailment," writes William Bender Wilson in his official *History of the Pennsylvania Railroad Company*. "The contest at times became very acrimonious and the debates teemed with adjectives of praise or denunciation."

Finally, not one bill, but two, were passed and signed by Governor Shunk; the first incorporating the Pennsylvania Railroad Company, and the second authorizing the Baltimore and Ohio, under the charter of the Pittsburgh and Connellsville, to construct a line east from Pittsburgh to join its existing line at or near Cumberland. Mr. Wilson then goes on to say:

> Under the first mentioned Act, the Governor was authorized to issue letters-patent chartering the Pennsylvania Railroad Company whenever a given number of the commissioners named for the purpose of securing stock subscriptions would certify to him that fifty thousand shares at $50 each had been subscribed and $5 per share had been paid in. The subscriptions came in slowly. . . . The Act of April 21, 1846, granting the Baltimore and Ohio Railroad Company the right to extend its road to Pittsburgh was conditioned upon the proviso that if the Legislature, during the session of 1846, should pass an act incorporating a company with authority to construct a railroad from Harrisburg to Pittsburgh within the limits of Pennsylvania and $3,000,000 should be bona fide subscribed to the stock of said company and 10 per cent on each share be actually paid in and letters-patent be issued by the Governor in conformity to the provisions of the Act within one year from the passage thereof and if thirty miles or more of said railroad should be put under contract for construction and satisfactory evidence be furnished to the Governor on or before the 30th day of July, 1847, then in that case the Governor shall issue his proclamation setting forth that fact and thereupon the act granting the right of way to the Baltimore and Ohio to extend its road through Pennsylvania to Pittsburgh shall be null and void. . . .

It looked as if the "rights" granted to the Baltimore company were very slim indeed. The Pennsylvania finally raised its beginning subscription and Pittsburgh was shut out from

the men of Baltimore, very much to its own disgust and amaze-
ment.   It was not until some time afterward that the Pittsburgh and Connellsville project was permitted to go forward
again; and then only after a sly and subtle bill had been passed
at Harrisburg.   The opponents of Baltimore and Ohio knew
their legislators.   And they were not often asleep at their
political tasks. [1]

We anticipate.

The Baltimore and Ohio's line into Wheeling was built and
ready some years before Pittsburgh finally had been achieved.
The state of Virginia relented the least little bit.   Although
she did withdraw her state subscription (nevertheless authorizing and permitting the city of Wheeling to take stock to the
extent of $1,000,000), she joined Maryland in extending for
twenty years—to July 5, 1863—the period permitted the road
for its completion to the Ohio.   In a little less than half that
time, it reached that destination.

.   .   .   .

All these things took much time and effort.

Here was McLane, as has already been seen, scurrying back
to Europe, to strengthen with the Barings, as far as possible,
the slender credit of his road; and dispatching his smooth-
tongued young lieutenant, Thomas Swann, down to Richmond
to use his talents on refractory Virginia legislators.   Swann

[1] Legislative tactics in those days frequently were sly and subtle.   Penn-
sylvania was by no means an exception to this statement.   Witness, for instance,
the measure passed in that commonwealth in April, 1843, entitled *An Act for the
Relief of the Overseers of the Poor and for Other Purposes.*   For three paragraphs
it pays attention to a legal predicament in which the overseers of the poor in Erie
County had become involved and of which it sought charitably to relieve them.
The second and third paragraphs give attention to local matters in Delaware
County, while in the fifth paragraph one finds the real meat of the statute.   It
says . . .   "That the act to incorporate the Pittsburgh and Connellsville Rail
Road Company, passed on the third day of April, 1837, be revived, extended and
continued in force. . . ."   Two paragraphs further, the company is authorized
to select any route from Connellsville to Smithfield or any other point on the
waters of the Youghiogheny and within the limits of the state. . . .   Politics
eighty years ago was no stumbling infant.

was a deal of a politician, himself. He was suave, plausible, diplomatic. At this stage, he was of great help to the Baltimore and Ohio.

While political and financial troubles were being smoothed out, the vast engineering problems for the extension of the line west of Cumberland were being solved. The peppery Mr. Knight having been succeeded by B. H. Latrobe as chief engineer, detailed reconnaissances of the rough Allegheny country were being made. These were thrust out in a variety of directions. It was felt that this was not the time for carelessness; nor for mistakes of any sort. At best the precise location of the line would be a ticklish matter. It was all a something for the most careful consideration.

In his annual report, dated October, 1844, one finds McLane telling in some detail of the obstacles which, for twenty-four months past, have retarded the further extension of the road. He comments upon the handicaps of its various charters in the three states as follows:

... The original charter by Pennsylvania, as early as 1828, required as a condition of the grant, in case the railroad should not terminate on the Ohio river in the vicinity of Pittsburgh, that the company should . . . construct a lateral road so as to connect that city with the main line. . . . The charter by the state of Virginia, passed in 1827, granted within that state most of the privileges conferred by the Maryland law; and allowed the road to strike the Ohio river at any point not lower than the mouth of the Little Kanawha; but in a subsequent act passed in April, 1838, renewing the grant for a longer period, the company was required to construct the railroad to the city of Wheeling. . . . Until recently the construction of the road from Cumberland to Wheeling without using part of the territory of Pennsylvania was deemed by those supposed to be best acquainted with the subject altogether impracticable; and it is not unreasonable to conclude that this impression after the act of Virginia of 1838, limiting the termination of the road to Wheeling, had a material influence in imposing the onerous conditions of the Pennsylvania law passed in the following year.

That law, the reader of these pages already has seen. The Baltimore and Ohio seemed all the while to be caught between opposing fires; chiefly between the shrewd and ofttimes unscrupulous politicians of alien states. McLane in his report again refers to the difficulties that he had encountered in Virginia, particularly in regard to time limits for construction, which Swann had been sent to adjust; and goes forward to say:

. . . Accordingly in the summer of 1843 they [the board of directors of the Baltimore and Ohio] directed a particular reconnaissance of the country between the Potomac and Ohio rivers, at various points upon the latter between Wheeling and Parkersburg in order to ascertain the facilities for extending the railroad through Maryland and Virginia, and through Virginia alone, without touching Pennsylvania; and also to ascertain the most practicable and advantageous connections with the trade of the state of Ohio and through it of the Western states in general.

The general result of the reconnaissance has satisfactorily shown the practicability of constructing the railroad through the states of Maryland and Virginia . . . by various advantageous routes from several points on the Potomac at and west of the South Branch to sundry points on the Ohio river between Wheeling and the mouth of the Little Kanawha.

All the routes embraced by this reconnaissance . . . have three principal terminating points upon the Ohio river; namely, the mouth of Fishing creek, the mouth of Middle Island creek and the mouth of the Little Kanawha at Parkersburg. By extending the road along the Ohio river any other intermediate point within the above range, such as *Sistersville* and *Marietta*, might, if desirable, be made the terminus.

The italics are McLane's. They bespeak the early importance of two river towns that never have lost their charm,

THOMAS SWANN.
President of the Baltimore and Ohio, 1848–1853.
From a photograph.

CHEAT RIVER VIADUCT.

Built *circa* 1850 and considered at that time a notable piece of American railroad engineering.

From a contemporary lithograph.

nor their importance. The president of the Baltimore and Ohio continues:

These routes might commence either at Cumberland or at the crossing of the North Branch of the Potomac six miles below.

If at Cumberland they would proceed up the North Branch; and if at the North Branch crossing six miles east of Cumberland they would pass, by a tunnel, through the Knobley Mountain and falling again into the valley of the North Branch reunite with the former routes eight miles above Cumberland —shortening the distance (from Baltimore $8\frac{1}{2}$ miles)[1] and thence continue up the North Branch of the Savage River and Crab Tree Creek to the summit of the Youghiogheny Glades. At this summit two main routes diverge; one leading to the mouth of Fishing or Middle Island Creeks, and the other to Parkersburg at the mouth of the Little Kanawha. Of these there are many branches, which by their connections and combinations will produce a variety of routes, of which the most important may be stated as follows:

First—A route from Cumberland via Fairmont to the mouth of Fishing Creek, 40 miles below Wheeling.

Second—A route via Bridgeport to the mouth of Middle Island Creek, 66 miles below Wheeling.

Third—A route to the last named point via Clarksburg.

Fourth—A route to the last named point via Shinstown.

Fifth—A route to Parkersburg, at the mouth of the Little Kanawha, 96 miles below Wheeling, by way of either Weston or Milford.

These several routes would pass about 60 miles through Maryland and the remainder of the distance, varying from $126\frac{1}{4}$ to 163 miles, through the state of Virginia. . . . The mineral and agricultural resources of that part of the state of Maryland that would be penetrated by the railroad constructed are of considerable value, and, if developed, as they

---

[1] Those men had vision. Many years later, this short cut south of Cumberland, a tangent between two points at the extremities of the bend of the North Branch, finally was brought into being. It is now known as the Patterson Cut-off.

would be by this improvement, would become of great importance to the state. The reconaissance, however, shows several routes quite feasible through Virginia alone, avoiding altogether both Pennsylvania and the state of Maryland.

Of these, the shortest would commence at the crossing six miles below Cumberland and proceeding by the valley of the North Branch [of the Potomac] pass around Fairfax's Stone at its head spring; and would be little greater in length than that to Parkersburg by Milford and Weston.

During the past summer and after the Board had been induced to direct a further examination of the country . . . they were informed that a recent examination by Jonathan Knight, Esq., under the employment of the authorities of the city of Wheeling, had resulted in the discovery of another route terminating at that city and, by passing around the southwest corner of Pennsylvania, avoiding the use of any part of that state. . . . The route this presented is intended to diverge from the line to Fishing Creek . . . at a point upon Buffalo Creek and to cross the hilly country between the head of that stream and Wheeling Creek.

Praises be to Jonathan Knight! His old skill as a surveyor and his long-time knowledge of the Ohio Valley country had indeed served him in good stead. This last route, with some variations, was the one a little later chosen for the Main Stem of the railroad from Baltimore through to the Ohio bank. Mr. McLane dilates upon it at some length:

It would elongate the distance to the Ohio River (compared with that to the mouth of Fishing Creek) about 19 miles and encounter very high grades and extensive excavations. . . . Of the facilities of connection from the terminus of each of the foregoing routes with the trade of the state of Ohio and of the states west of it, extensive examinations were made comprehending several different lines; one from the mouth of Fishing Creek by Sunfish Creek and Wills Creek and Salt Creek to the Muskingum near Zanesville. For the extension of the route beyond Zanesville, northwardly toward the Lakes and westwardly through Columbus, the capital of the State, toward Indiana, Illinois and Missouri, the country affords great facilities.

Another line has been examined from Sistersville, nine miles below Fishing Creek, by the Little Muskingum in the same direction; another from Marietta by the Great Muskingum toward Zanesville; another from Wheeling by Indian Wheeling Creek and Stillwater and Wills Creeks and Dunlap Creek and Tuscarawas River toward Coshocton, 30 miles north of Zanesville; and another from Parkersburg through Athens and Chillicothe to Cincinnati.

In due time, many of these roads were to be built; although not in every case for the Baltimore and Ohio, or even for its eventual operation. Most of them followed logical routes through the valleys of small rivers or creeks on either side of the Ohio, and then for considerable distances beyond.

Louis McLane, president of the Baltimore and Ohio company, returned from his second trip to Europe in October, 1846, and, even though he had been unsuccessful in his attempts to finance the company there, he set himself to the task of completing the road from Cumberland to the Ohio River. The fact that the earnings of the finished portions of the line, both freight and passenger, were steadily increasing, was an encouraging one. . . . There still remained the grave question, however, almost as vital as the political and financial ones, as to whether the first terminus of the road should be at Pittsburgh or at Wheeling. The news that the new Pennsylvania Railroad Company had finally succeeded in making the necessary initial subscriptions to its stock, was discouraging enough. Moreover, at a meeting of his stockholders held in April, 1847, McLane read to them a communication over his own signature, saying that the Pittsburgh and Connellsville, which had been founded at the instigation of the Baltimore and Ohio, had swung about; it now not only refused to accept any further subscription from the Baltimore company, but declined even to treat with it; unless, before a certain designated day, it would consent to assume the responsibility of completing the entire connection to Pittsburgh by its own individual energies; and without the expectation of receiving any assistance whatsoever from Pittsburgh!

One does not wonder that, despite the vacillations of Virginia, it was decided first to build to Wheeling.

On the first day of July of that same summer, Mr. Latrobe, with three corps of competent engineers, started forth to lay out the definite route over the mountains from Cumberland to the Virginia river port. Before the close of that season, Latrobe had sixty-five miles of the extension of the line surveyed in detail and ready for contract. In the following summer, aided by John Child of Massachusetts, and Jonathan Knight, as consulting engineers, he continued the detailed laying down of the route, straight into the city of Wheeling, coming to the left bank of the Ohio about a dozen miles below that thriving town. The three men satisfied themselves that the construction of a railroad across this rugged country of the Appalachians was not only possible, but entirely practicable, and with grades quite within the power of the improved locomotives of that day.

.   .   .   .

It was on the seventh day of January of the following year (1848) that the *Baltimore American* printed a letter which McLane had just addressed to his stockholders on the status of the plan for immediately extending the road to the bank of the Ohio. This letter recapitulates the various possible resources of the company—Maryland and Virginia state bonds and the like, which ought to be available at once but which unfortunately are not—and recommends the adoption of a pay-as-you-go system which should permit the work to go ahead, speedily and without interruption. . . . McLane estimates that it will cost $6,300,000 to complete the road to Wheeling. He was a good guesser. Actually, the extension finally cost $6,631,721, which made the entire cost of the line from Baltimore to Wheeling—including the new Camden Station and the Locust Point terminals at Baltimore—$15,628,963.24.

Commenting on these estimates, the *American Railway Journal* said, a few days later:

> . . . Assuming these estimates to be correct, it will require the income of about 7½ years, at $850,000 a year, to complete the work, but we don't hesitate to say that if this plan shall be adopted the work may as well be completed in five as in seven years and if the stockholders will cheerfully adopt this course and receive the amount of their dividends in stock instead of dividing the net earnings of the road they will be able, after three years earnings of $2,500,000 shall have been expended and fifty or sixty miles of new road shall be in use, to dispose of the bonds of the state on terms acceptable to the company and thus be enabled to push on the work with renewed energy. . . .

This was the thing that presently came to pass. The three per cent dividend of September 30, 1847, already had been paid in bonds; the annual ones from 1848 to 1853 (respectively, 3½, 5, 7, 7, 7 and 3 per cent) were paid in scrip—in the capital stock of the company. It was not until May, 1856, that another cash dividend was ventured. Yet the record is of little complaint on the part of the stockholders of the company. Their faith surely was an enduring one.

. . . .

As Latrobe and Knight and John Child labored in the field, a strange series of letters began appearing in the *Baltimore Patriot*. Baltimore always has been—is to this day—a town where folk are uncommonly fond of writing their troubles to the newspapers. These particular communications, signed "A Large Stockholder," attracted much attention and approval. They gently criticized the management of the Baltimore and Ohio for its dilatoriness in prosecuting the extension of the road into the West. They called attention to the swift progress made in completing the rail routes across New York and across Pennsylvania, and showed in unmistakable terms the commercial stagnation that might be expected to be visited upon Baltimore, should its own rail enterprise be permitted to drag in this fashion.

Soon it began to be noised about in the streets of Baltimore who "A Large Stockholder" really was. None other than Thomas Swann, the capable young man whom McLane once had sent to Richmond to argue with the Virginia Legislature and who, in the preceding year, had, with some other Baltimore men, made a pilgrimage to Wheeling to interest that town properly in the coming of the railroad. Swann was, always, a well rounded politician; suave, diplomatic, oratorical. Carefully he planned his campaign.

In October, 1848, he was elected a director of the Baltimore and Ohio company. He came in frankly as a friend of McLane and lent him a loyal support up to the end of his administration. Swann was a worker. He thrust himself into every forward movement of the board of directors and lent especial help to its president, who was beginning to feel the burden of the tremendous labor that for eleven years he had undergone in behalf of the road. In every delicate emergency that demanded more than ordinary energy and ability, McLane called upon Swann. Who was both ready and willing.

In October, 1849, McLane retired and Thomas Swann became president of the Baltimore and Ohio Railroad.

.   .   .   .

Now was the opportunity come for Swann to put his preachings into practice. An almost superhuman task was immediately ahead. To build a railroad whose credit was almost nil (its stock now was quoted on the Baltimore exchange at twenty-eight cents on the dollar and no considerable amount of its bonds could be marketed at any price whatsoever) over two hundred miles of rough mountainous country at a cost roughly estimated as exceeding six million dollars, was a task requiring all that there was of energy and ability in any man.

To it, Swann went. All was not black in the picture The completed railroads across New York State—the first to reach the inland country from the sea—were proving themselves from the outset highly profitable. Pennsylvania was looking forward eagerly to the completion of her all-rail route. Even the incomplete Baltimore and Ohio, without having as yet reached into a real traffic territory, was making a good showing. The coal business out of Cumberland was booming. The efforts of the Chesapeake and Ohio Canal, which now also terminated at that gateway city, to divert it to the Cumberland Valley Railroad, which it intersected near Hagerstown, were not bothersome. Most of the coal moved over the Baltimore and Ohio, which presently had to complete its double track all the way east from Cumberland, as well as to again completely rebuild the line from the Point of Rocks to Baltimore; this time discarding the strap rail laid on sills and substituting for it T-rail on cross ties, after the present fashion.

These things, as well as the building of the first Locust Point freight terminals in Baltimore, cost much money. But they made money. Moreover, it was estimated that the growth of Baltimore in the mid-'forties had been swifter than ever before in her unusual history. The $3,500,000, which she originally had subscribed to the building of the railroad, had been more than returned to her in the enhanced value of her real estate, to say nothing of the influx of population that came in anticipation of the completion of the Baltimore and Ohio.

Upon these things, Swann played—and cleverly. Daytimes, he sat in his office or in the offices of the Baltimore merchants and bankers; nights, he continued publicly to argue in favor of the immediate completion of the line to the Ohio. A substitute proposal to build only a portion of it beyond Cumberland and to await increasing earnings from it, he dismissed as being entirely unworthy. There had been too much piecemeal effort upon the property already. Now it was to be Wheeling or nothing; which meant that it was to be Wheeling.

The man's energy was untiring. His devotion to the principle of a complete line, unwavering. On one occasion one finds him saying:

> . . . It has seemed to me . . . that whatever is proposed to be done toward securing the original object and purposes of this enterprise should be done promptly and without further delay. The anxiety of the great interests west of the Ohio River to open a continuous line of communication with some available point on the seaboard is daily becoming more and more apparent in the plans which are being projected and the efforts now making to form a junction with this road. These interests, once in motion, cannot be induced to pause. To suppose that the active and restless spirit of our western people can be lulled into inactivity by deferred prospects, however flattering, when so many rivals are in the field striving for the mastery, with all the attractions of overweening capital, would be to underestimate the progressive character of that population. The leading cities of the seaboard are already in motion. They cannot shut their eyes to the value of the stake for which they are so eagerly contending. Their roads are extending toward points where, by prompt action, it is hoped to overcome the obstacles which nature has interposed and entice from its legitimate market a trade which nothing but inactivity and indifference on the part of our own citizens can drive beyond the attraction of the city of Baltimore.
>
> It may be well for us to consider whether the risk is not too great to stand quietly by and see this current diverted from its natural channel in the hope that, at some future day, we may repair the injury and win back the prize which a too tardy policy had permitted to pass into other hands. The avenues of trade, when once established, often become fixed and permanent, whatever original difficulties it may have been necessary to surmount in the effort to make them available. . . .

Mr. Swann's references to the united rail lines, behind which Philadelphia and New York had put their shoulders, are unmistakable. Addresses like these, as was the case with his

earlier letters to the *Patriot*, fired Baltimore to a new zeal for
its own railroad enterprise.   As in the very earliest days of that
railroad, it again came to the aid.   In a noble fashion.   Bonds
were bought generously.   Actual work building the line west
of Cumberland was begun.

With the result that, at the end of Swann's first fourteen
months in office, not less than 165 miles of the extended line
were in various stages of construction, while in the following
year the laying of rails was begun.   In June, 1851, the road
was complete and ready for traffic to Piedmont, twenty-eight
miles west of Cumberland, where an engine house of sixteen
stalls and other facilities were provided for the trains which
here would begin the long ascent of the mountains.

There were many reasons for making an operating point of
Piedmont, near as it was to Cumberland.   The chief of these
—more important even than supplying the extra motive power
to carry trains over the stiff mountain grades—was that there
the coal trade of the richest part of the great Cumberland basin
was concentrated.   The Phoenix Company had just opened
its mines on the Maryland side of the Potomac and finished the
necessary bridge and connecting tracks to the Main Stem of
the railroad.   The Georges Creek Company also had completed its iron mines and works at Lonaconing, eight miles up
that creek, and connected with Piedmont by a branch railroad.

These industries, as well as the iron one at Mount Savage,
back of Cumberland, were to play a large part in adding to the
revenues of the Baltimore and Ohio at the very time when such
revenues most were needed.   Indirectly they helped materially
toward extending the road to its destination.

.   .   .   .

Yet the work was not being accomplished without great
difficulties other than those that nature had provided against
it.   The young city of Wheeling was taking its turn at behaving rather abominably.   Feeling its oats, as it were.   It expressed grave dissatisfaction with the route chosen by the rail-

road for entrance to its borders, fearing that, if the road should turn too far to the south, it might be left wholly upon a side line. It finally went even so far as to bring the matter to the Virginia Legislature. Eventually Swann, with his tact and his forcefulness, was able to compromise the matter by slightly changing the original route; but not until the progress of the completion of the road had been delayed for nearly half a year.

Financial difficulties became more portentous than squabbles of this sort. Three or four years of abundance had brought Swann and his fellows to a false sense of security and prosperity. They had embarked upon a construction program, in size and scope almost unprecedented, with a feeling that things had changed for the better. Even a debt of a quarter of a million dollars in the current funds of the road's treasury had not discouraged them. For, lo and behold, that deficit apparently was changing into surplus. The traffic from the great Cumberland coal basin was turning the scales. Money was rolling into the treasury. . . . Work upon the railroad over the mountains was multiplied in its vigor.

Five thousand men and 1250 horses were engaged in it by the fall of 1851. The paymasters were giving out $200,000 a month in pay rolls alone. To meet these amounts meant increasing effort on the part of the men in Baltimore; constant appeals to its pride, to the necessity of the city's accomplishing its own salvation through the completion of its own railroad. To those rich centers of capital—Philadelphia and New York —it need not look for aid. They had their own rail enterprises. The failure of Baltimore's railroad would be money in their pockets. England and the rest of Europe had been drained dry. Baltimore must look entirely to her own resources.

It is to her eternal credit that she did this thing. She dug more deeply than ever into her pockets. The Baltimore and Ohio sold fresh bonds at eighty-seven and considered itself lucky. . . . A new generation of merchant princes and bankers, highly prosperous, was arising in Baltimore town.

THE SHOOFLY TRACK OVER PETTIBONE.

By which trains made the steep ascent over the Alleghenies before the completion of Board Tree tunnel.

From a contemporary illustration in *Harper's Weekly*.

CLOSING THE LINE AT ROSEBY'S ROCK.

When it was done, Christmas Eve, 1852, the Baltimore and Ohio stretched in unbroken rails from the Chesapeake Bay to the Ohio River and the dream of twenty-five years had finally been accomplished.

From a painting by H. D. Stitt.

Men like Johns Hopkins and Robert Garrett, who showed themselves not only willing but anxious to help the railroad struggling for its very existence. They determined that they would not let it fail.

The old generation, the men who first had planned the Baltimore and Ohio and who, with resolute faith, had first begun its construction, were nearly all gone. Only George Brown, in whose house had been held the meetings that led to the birth and incorporation of the company, still remained in official connection with the road. For twenty-five years he had been one of its directors, a man honored by his fellows as an older statesman of the property.

.   .   .   .

Had there been none of these great financial and political difficulties—if the way of the Baltimore and Ohio had been ever smoothed by large monied resources or by the united force of a single far-reaching state—the physical task of surmounting the Alleghenies still would have remained a vast problem. To build a railroad across an important mountain range means traversing most of its valleys and ridges at right angles or close to that angle. And the Alleghenies—the very backbone of the Appalachians—are nothing if not an important mountain range.

The route finally chosen for the Baltimore and Ohio west from Piedmont—as its name indicates, at the very foot of the mountains—began with a long steady ascent, seventeen miles in length, which brought the road in a single climb to its highest altitude—2626 feet—on the very summit of the ridge which divides the watershed of the Potomac from that of the Ohio. In theory, it would have seemed to be simple enough to carry the road down the valley of the nearest stream that led to the Ohio. But such theory would not only have taken many more miles, but no heed at all of the fussy activities of the legislatures of Virginia and Maryland. So it was that other mountain ranges remained to be crossed. That, after descending a little way into the valley of the Youghiogheny River and crossing and following that stream for a while, there must be for the railroad more ascent! Some of it through the Cheat River Valley. This last, to this day, remains one of the most dramatically beautiful spots upon the entire Baltimore and Ohio system. For four miles the railroad clings high to the side of a precipitous chasm. In two places its foothold is made firm only by great lengths of solid masonry wall, builded up to the level of the track. And so well builded by Latrobe and his men, back there at the beginning of the 'fifties, that it continues to remain a firm foundation for the heaviest engines and trains known to American railroad practice.

Ranking as a dramatic feature of rail construction with the Cheat River Grade was Kingwood Tunnel, some seven miles to the west. At the time of its completion, this was by far the longest tunnel—4100 feet—upon the North American continent. (The great 4½-mile Hoosac Tunnel in western Massachusetts still was many years in the future.) It marked another important summit on the line, from which the drop into the valley of the Monongahela was swift and comparatively easy, until Tygarts Valley Creek was reached at its junction with Three Forks Creek. Here was a place set apart for a rail junction with the new Northwestern Virginia Railroad, already building to Parkersburg; of which more at another time. It is enough now to say that this double junction —of river and of railroad—soon became a flourishing town, to be known to travelers for many decades as Grafton.

From the site of the present Grafton down the Tygarts Valley River, a distance of twenty-one miles, to its junction with the Monongahela and then across that river upon an iron bridge, 650 feet long and 39 feet above the surface of the river at low water, into Fairmont, already a brisk and growing village. No thought of stone viaducts in that day of the development of the Baltimore and Ohio. For one thing, they took too much time. And for another, too much money. Moreover, Albert Fink, who has appeared before in the pages of this history, quite prided himself upon his facility in the fabrication of iron bridges. He had a curious way of going at the problem. In that early day, there were few recognized accurate formulæ for the construction of metal bridges. The rule-of-thumb methods that were used in the creation of so many early wooden spans, were hardly to be trusted in the making of iron ones. So Fink would go to work with pieces of tin and wire, building up trusses in miniature, testing strains and stresses carefully upon these, and from such experiments making his deductions and formulæ for the construction of full-sized spans. . . . Three of these, each of approximately 215 feet, formed the original structure at Fairmont. At the time of its completion, it was the largest iron bridge in America. That it stood for many years and carried an increasingly large burden upon its broad back is the proof that, both in design and in workmanship, it was fundamentally correct.

    .   .   .   .   .

A mile and a half below Fairmont, the route of the Baltimore and Ohio left the valley of the Monongahela, this time through the winding and picturesque ravine of Buffalo Creek. The peak of this last great summit before Wheeling also was to be marked by a tunnel—Board Tree, 2350 feet long. From this point, the line descends 220 feet in four miles, crosses Fish Creek, and then rises 315 feet in five miles to Welling Tunnel, a bore of 1250 feet, from which point the descent is steady through the valley of Grave Creek to Moundsville, on the bank of the Ohio, eleven miles below Wheeling. . . . The path up the broad valley of the Ohio to the first important terminal of the road was ease itself.

    .   .   .   .   .

Yet there was little of ease in the construction of the greater part of the line west of Cumberland. For seventy miles it crossed one of the boldest mountain regions in all America, so stupendous that one wonders anew at the audacity of those early Baltimoreans who even considered building a railroad over it. It is doubtful that, had they possessed all the riches of an imperial kingdom, they could, in the era of the 'twenties or even of the 'thirties, with the limited locomotives and tools then at their command, have built those portions of the line. Eleven tunnels—in length aggregating 11,156 feet— had to be bored between Cumberland and Wheeling; 113 bridges—which, placed end to end, would have stretched 7003 feet—had to be built. And all of this in addition to huge tasks of excavation and fill, of which the Cheat River embankment was but a single item.

In twenty years there had been much progress in methods and tools of railroad construction. Locomotives and cars had increased in size; mechanical devices of many kinds had been invented and perfected. And a B. H. Latrobe had come forward at an hour when most he was needed. When no machinery nor high explosives were available, drilling was done by hand, while black powder was used to blast out rock. The material was loaded on carts by hand and then was drawn to the place of deposit by horse power.

Latrobe's swiftness was dazzling, his thoroughness astounding. As Swann worked in Baltimore to maintain the enthusiasm of the owners of the property, Latrobe worked in the field to keep up the morale of the construction gangs. Through the wilderness these 5000 men and 1250 horses worked unceasingly. Sometimes they were paid promptly, more often they were not. But it was Latrobe's task to see that, money or no money, the work went steadily ahead. Any great engineer might have builded the Baltimore and Ohio—with financial resources back of him. It took a Latrobe to build it —at all times cursed with thin financial support.

He did it. Without slackening. When they came to him and told him that it would be a matter of long months —if not of several years—to bore the Kingwood Tunnel and place a track through it, despite the fact that they were working at it not only from both portals, but from three intermediate shafts, he replied that he could not wait. A temporary line must be laid over the top of the mountain at once, in order to get engines and cars and heavy materials to the sections of the line that lay beyond Kingwood.

And so was builded, in a mere matter of weeks, one of the most remarkable stretches of railroad ever laid down in the United States. It had been said, and at the time generally believed, that the practical limit for a steam locomotive was a grade of 116 feet to the mile (2.2 per cent). So firmly in fact was this credited, that 2.2 per cent finally was fixed as the maximum grade for the entire Baltimore and Ohio system. And more. When, in later years, Congress began granting charters for the great transcontinental railroads to the Pacific Coast, it fixed in these documents as a maximum grade, 116 feet to the mile. And so were the Union Pacific, the Central Pacific and the Northern Pacific graded and builded; because, in the first instance, Benjamin H. Latrobe had so decided to grade and build the Baltimore and Ohio.

One hundred and sixteen feet to the mile then was a permanent maximum. But Latrobe was quite willing to try his hand—and his locomotives—on the temporary track over Kingwood Tunnel at a grade of 500 feet to the mile—nearly ten per cent. The experiment was completely successful. Not only during the two years within which the tunnel workmen removed some 90,000 cubic yards of earth and rock from the bore, but at a later season, when there was trouble with soft earth in the roof of the tunnel, and it was found necessary to close and completely line it.

Over this temporary track, composed of "Y" switches and steeply ascending tangents, the powerful camels, which Ross Winans had built for the road, could push one and sometimes two cars at a time. Which, in that day, was considered quite a remarkable performance.

So successful was the device, that a little later, when Board Tree Tunnel promised to present another delay to the prompt completion of the line, Latrobe caused a similar zigzag to be built over it. Which was continued in service for a time, even after the formal opening of the road to Wheeling.

An early traveler, who passed over this last temporary track in a passenger train, describes the experience in this fashion:

> . . . Pettibone is the name of the first contractor to cut this famous tunnel. He gave his name to the place and failed in his contract. Including the deep cut at each end, with the tunnel itself, it is a little less than a mile through the body of the mountain. For the present . . . a temporary structure absolutely ascends the mountain on one side, attaining an elevation of 2500 feet above tidewater, and descends on the other, the distance being nearly four miles by the zigzag course of the road.
>
> We arrived at the tunnel a little after sundown, and in view of the lofty range to be surmounted, the necessary preparations were made for the appalling enterprise of transporting five hundred human beings fastened up in railroad cars right over the summits of old Alleghany.
>
> The train was divided into ten sections, each drawn and pushed by a huge, black, unearthly looking machine, ten of which (beside the two with the trains) were found waiting for us with steam on at the foot of the eastern slope.
>
> The ascent and descent of this mountain range is accomplished by a most masterly piece of civil engineering. The Rail Road is laid in the form of a letter "Y" many times repeated on the side of the mountain, thus the cars ascend the main stem of the "Y" in an oblique direction along the mountainside and running off into the tail of the "Y" change direction and ascend the oblique arm of the letter, then taking the main stem of the second "Y" and proceeding in the same manner, ascending all the while on one side of the mountain or descending all the time on the other. Never can I forget the scenes and the circumstances of this memorable night. When crawling up the sides of the mountains, crossing the frightful gorges, mounted up on the highest summits amid the clouds

in a Rail Road car I was so full of admiration there was no room for fear. The laborers in the tunnel have fixed their rude huts in the dingles and ravines of the mountains and as the cars were passing, each, with a phantom looking torch, stood out in the valleys and along the mountain sides, giving to the scene the appearance of magic. . . .

Another traveler upon the train contributes his impressions to the record of the years. He says, in part:

. . . The scene was grand. We were composed of nine or ten caravans each attached to one of the most powerful engines. I was in the third and night was settling on the broad landscape as we began the ascent. Before us were two parties slowly climbing their zigzag way far above us, upon different elevations, and their panting iron horses, as if angry with their load, spit out volumes of black smoke and sparks against the blackened sky as from the crater of a deep volcano. The summit gained, we halted a short time which gave us an opportunity of surveying the picture. What a magnificent scene! Around and beneath us were stupendous hills, far as the lurid shadows of evening could be pierced, while far down the mountain side from terrace to terrace the upheaving locomotives glowed, and then away in the deep valley a hundred torches gleamed from the hands of workmen leaving their allotted task in the depths of the tunnel below.

We now descended the western slope of the mountain which is more precipitous than the eastern. . . . It seemed as if the children of Babel were winding down from the huge mountain pile. The locomotive screamed, to us an unmeaning sound, while the deep dells below threw it back in echoing mockery. . . . Many of our party were in ecstacies of delight and enjoyment but others more fearful walked the crooked way, while some who remained on the cars trembled like the aspen leaf.

In those days they took their pleasures rather seriously. While the railroad had already assumed a romance it could not easily lose.

. . . .

The line was completed to Fairmont, June 22, 1852, and the regular operation of trains to and from Cumberland and Baltimore was begun immediately. On Christmas Eve of that same year, the last rail was placed, the last spike driven that connected the levee of the Ohio at Wheeling with tidewater at Baltimore, 379 miles distant.[1]

Mr. Swann had promised the burghers of Wheeling that the railroad into their town would be completed and ready for business on the first day of January, 1853, and it was in keeping with this promise that regular service over the entire line was deferred for eight days. The formal celebration of the opening was further deferred—another eight days—in order to give the folk of Wheeling opportunity to prepare a reception that would do their town credit.

The record has it that that celebration more than did Wheeling credit. The five hundred Baltimoreans who spent eighteen hours in journeying out to the end of their own wonderful railroad were received uproariously. There was a vast amount of speech making—led by Mr. Swann, Governor Lowe of Maryland, Governor Johnson of Virginia, the two Latrobes and the venerable director of Baltimore and Ohio, George Brown. Factional differences were buried and forgotten. Harmony was in the air. And so was the music of the bands. And the waving flags. After the oratory, the entire company repaired to the McLure House, where, in the

---

[1] The exact closing of its tracks was at a place in a narrow valley, eighteen miles east of Wheeling. A great glacial rock, close beside the rails, was named after Roseby Carr, who had charge of construction forces in the immediate vicinity, and this inscription was carved in deep letters into it:

ROSBBY'S ROCK

Track Closed
Christmas Eve
1852

This huge stone, despite the misspelling of the name of the man it commemorates, for many years has been a landmark upon Baltimore and Ohio. It will continue to remain as a reminder of the completion of a pioneer era in the building of the railroad.

ROSBBY'S ROCK TODAY.

It still stands (1927) close beside the track, eighteen miles east of Wheeling.

From a recent photograph.

THE LEVEE AT WHEELING, VIRGINIA.

As it was in the days soon after the Baltimore and Ohio reached the town.

From an early photograph.

sumptuous upper and lower dining halls of that redoubtable hostelry, there was more music, more oratory. Such food! Such drink! It is possible that some gentlemen went under the table; probable that the following day there were many aching heads in Wheeling. . . . But what of that? It was not every day that an important trunk-line railroad was finished and opened to the public.

One desists from further details in regard to the celebration at Wheeling. There will have to be recorded the celebration that followed at Cincinnati four years later; and, because this last was the sublimest of all festivals that ever commemorated the completion of a railroad, a few adjectives must be held in reserve. It is enough to state that the affair at Wheeling was complete and that in every way it did both the railroad and the town proud.

.   .   .   .

After twenty-five years of effort, twenty-five years of accomplishment, twenty-five years of discouragement, the Baltimore and Ohio finally had reached its goal, at the edge of the yellow flood of the Ohio.

Now, what was Wheeling?

In 1853, a brisk river town, with small red brick houses closely lining neatly paved streets; a town whose chief lions were its expansive market house and the remarkable suspension bridge of 1000-foot span, which John A. Roebling had completed but a few years before and which carried the National Road over the Ohio, or at least over the channel of the river that ran to the east of the "island" that rests in the middle of the stream at that point. At Wheeling there were many steamboats—sometimes. For there came days and weeks when the river was low in its stages and the steamboats could not move at all. Then it was that Wheeling was no more than Cumberland; a junction between railroad and highroad.

From Pittsburgh, into which the new Pennsylvania Railroad already was running trains from the East, there already stretched a railroad to Cleveland, a pleasant port town upon Lake Erie, for whose future there seemed to be some fair promise. A railroad—or rather a series of railroads—stretched east from Cleveland to Dunkirk, where it connected with the Erie; and to Buffalo, with connections there with the string of railroads across central New York, which, in this selfsame year of 1853, were to become merged as the New York Central.

West from Cleveland, they already were building a railroad; through to Toledo and on to Chicago. Southwest from Cleveland, other lines already were operating; to Columbus, to Springfield, to Dayton and to Cincinnati. With all of this growing network of lines across Ohio and into Indiana, the trunk lines to the north connected. But not the Baltimore and Ohio. The plan for the Central Ohio, which should run west from Wheeling to Zanesville, Newark and Columbus, where it would enjoy connections for Dayton and Cincinnati, still was vague and nebulous, even though a sporadic sort of construction had been begun upon this line.

Had the Baltimore and Ohio made a mistake? Why Wheeling, anyway?

The answer was the Northwestern Virginia—that line which we already have seen planned to start west from Three Forks Creek (now Grafton) and which Latrobe was busily engaged in surveying and plotting in fine detail, even as the banqueters passed the glass over the mahogany of the famous old McLure House. At Wheeling, it would always be difficult to bridge the Ohio with a structure stout enough to carry heavy railroad trains; eventually, the idea was abandoned completely. But at Parkersburg, the bridge problem—sooner or later to arise—was simpler. While, from the other bank of the yellow stream, the long reaches of the state of Ohio promised easy railroad construction; not only to Cincinnati, but on toward St. Louis, far beyond.

Wheeling achieved, faith having been kept with the sovereign state of Virginia, Parkersburg became the next goal of the men from Baltimore. Parkersburg also was in the state of Virginia, as it existed in those days before the Civil War. Any railroad that found its way to that river port—on the Ohio a full ninety miles below Wheeling—was bound to have the friendly support of the Old Dominion.

To Parkersburg, then, the Baltimore and Ohio, flushed with its new growth and importance, turned its immediate attention.

CHAPTER XV

RUNNING A RAILROAD IN THE 'FIFTIES

The Baltimore and Ohio of 1853—The Organization and Operating
Methods of That Day—The Washington Branch Sees the
First Telegraph Line in the World—And the First Electric
Locomotive—The Coming of Camden Station.

WHAT manner of railroad was this ambitious line, which,
at the very beginning day of 1853, finally had finished its
tedious climb over the steep slopes of the Alleghenies and
accomplished its great goal of the brink of the Ohio?

For some time past, these chapters have been given to
the financial and constructional difficulties of the still struggling
line; to the gradual changing of its personnel; to the passing
of the original generation of its promoters and actual operators
and the incoming of the succeeding generations. Young men
were taking the places of the older men. . . . Always so it
goes. The passing of the generations. But the railroad,
the living thing, the undying thing, watching them pass;
through the march of the decades.

.   .   .   .

Gradually the service of the completed portions of the
Baltimore and Ohio was being improved; not rapidly, but
steadily. In a preceding chapter has been shown the rather
swift development of the motive power; the coming, at last,
of real locomotives, well calculated to lift sizable trains up
over the stiff mountain slopes. Cars were much better, too,

and there were many more of them. And with increased rolling stock came also increased train service.

No large additions were made to the time-tables of the Washington Branch in the few years preceding the completion of the road to Wheeling. From the outset, the line had been generously provided with trains. But, on the Main Stem, where conditions were very different, a real effort finally was being made to improve the service.

In the early spring of 1848, this consisted chiefly of the trains known as the *Great Western Mail*, which left Baltimore at half past seven and Cumberland at eight o'clock each morning, passed one another and arrived at the opposite ends of the Main Stem at half past five o'clock the same evening. But, in March, 1848, there is found in the columns of the *American Railway Journal* the following announcement:

NOTICE! GREAT CENTRAL ROUTE, via Cumberland and Baltimore—To facilitate travel upon this route, the Baltimore and Ohio Railroad Company, in conjunction with the line of stages upon the National Road, will commence on Monday, the 27th of March, to run a SECOND DAILY TRAIN OF CARS AND LINE OF COACHES over the route, leaving Baltimore at 4 P.M. and Cumberland at 7½ P.M. on every day of the week.

The coaches upon the National Road will henceforth leave Wheeling regularly twice a day at 6 A.M. and 6 P.M. and Cumberland at the same hours, connecting regularly each way with the morning and evening boats at Brownsville. By this arrangement passengers arriving at Baltimore from Philadelphia at 2 P.M. may proceed Westward after a delay of but two hours, instead of lying over until the next morning. Passengers coming Eastward and arriving at Wheeling or Pittsburgh or Columbus too late either for the morning or the evening line will be detained but twelve hours at the most, instead of twenty-four as heretofore. Great additional despatch will thus be given to travel upon this route, already the most expeditious between the East and West and the passenger may always make his choice between the day or night for passing over either the Railroad or the turnpike section of the route.

By order, WILLIAM S. WOODSIDE,
Master of Transportation
Baltimore and Ohio Railroad.

Here was a definite order indeed, signed by an officer, who, on the railroad of that still early day, ranked in authority next only to the president himself. The effect of the competition already being offered Baltimore and Ohio by the rapidly completing through routes to the north, was showing itself in this announcement. Baltimore and Ohio was beginning to struggle for the through business. It further advertised its through passenger rates as being but four cents a mile; the fare from Baltimore through to Cumberland being seven dollars, and on to Wheeling and Pittsburgh by coach, eleven and ten dollars, respectively.

.   .   .   .

The master of transportation, as has just been stated, was a man of sweeping powers, and responsibilities. Slightly outranking in importance the general superintendent or master of the road or the master of machinery, he was the general manager of the Baltimore and Ohio of that day; and then something more. He solicited business as well. In fact, many of the duties of the present-day traffic manager were also thrust upon his shoulders.

The actual everyday working of the line was under the authority of the general superintendent, who had, as today, division superintendents working under and reporting to him. Already—we are speaking of the Baltimore and Ohio now come close to the twenty-fifth year of its working existence—definite rules and regulations had been evolved for the guidance of the train forces. Thus one finds that

. . . every train and engine before starting must be closely inspected, either by the conductor or engineman, or a person specially appointed for the purpose, and attesting the fact in person at the time of starting. If the engineman of a tonnage train thinks any car unsafe to be run, he must have it off from his train at the first opportunity, unless overruled by the supervisor of trains, or foreman of machinery, or an officer still higher in rank.

These things—many others, too—all were set down definitely in the book of rules of that day. For instance, that volume said that there must be a bell cord, and that this cord must remain attached from the beginning to the end of the train throughout each moment of its operation. Each train and engine, when running, also must have a red flag by day and a lantern by night, for signaling purposes; while the man who runs back with the rear signal must either continue until he meets an oncoming train or until his signal may be seen by its engineer a full half mile from the one that is stalled. The clean accident record of the Baltimore and Ohio apparently came only by careful planning for it. This portion of the rules continues:

A lantern must always be placed and remain at night (and by day in the tunnels) on the rear of every train on the road—*red*, when such can be procured. Every engine when running at night must also show a good bright light *in front*, and if without a train, in the rear also.

All road parties making local repairs must place a red flag at sufficient distance each way from them on the track to be seen by the engineman, when he is at least three-quarters of a mile from the point of danger. . . . Although the provision and the use of flags, as above, is obligatory on all—the *absence* of a flag in any caution given to an engineman will not justify his proceeding—*but he must stop as soon as possible* and learn the meaning of any earnest signal made on the road; there must be no *taking this or that for granted*, and the disregard of such notice will be reckoned a reason for discharge.

Apparently, slipshod methods were not to be tolerated. . . . The rules continue:

Conductors and brakemen of tonnage trains, excepting of empty coal cars, must ride on the top of their cars that they may see better, and be able to use as many brakes as possible.

.   .   .   .

Trains following each other must be kept *one-half mile or more apart*—and no train may leave a station within five minutes of another, unless it be for a short distance to a hauling place, to enable another train to obtain needed accommodation at a station, or for some like purpose.   Road repairers and station agents are required to report every breach and neglect of this rule which may come to their notice, and to give all practicable caution and assistance to their engineman [?] for its observance. . . .

.   .   .   .

It will be remembered that all of this was before trains upon the Baltimore and Ohio began to move under telegraphic orders.   Indeed it was not until 1851 that Superintendent Charles Minot of the Erie Railroad had sent over the slender new strand of copper wire that stretched along that broad-gauge track what is said to be the first railroad telegraph order ever given in the world.   In fact, it was but a few years before (1844) that, on a telegraph wire placed alongside the Washington Branch of the Baltimore and Ohio Railroad, Professor S. F. B. Morse had dispatched the first long-distance message ever to be sent by electricity anywhere in the world.

Return to the rule book of the early-day railroader.   One finds it saying:

Enginemen running in the wake of other trains are required to stop and enquire often enough to be sure of the distance at which they are from trains in their advance.   In taking sidings they must pull in at the switch first reached; and in approaching all stations they are required to check their speed, so as to avoid all possibility of collision with trains or cars occupying the track.   All wooden and iron bridges must be passed at half the usual speed.   They must sound the whistle

CAMDEN STATION, BALTIMORE.
As one saw it in the days of the Civil War—and even before.
From an early photograph.

CAMDEN STATION AT A LATER DAY.

The tall spire had been taken down and the historic building greatly refurbished.

From a photograph.

on approaching all stations, switches and road crossings and have their trains in perfect control, especially at the turnpike crossings. Along all dangerous places, or such as would render an accident very serious, trains must be confined to half speed —as at the Narrows of Harper's Ferry and Point of Rocks, the Cheat River and all high bridges or side cuttings. Great care is especially required at the crossing of the main stem of the road by the Washington branch, at the Patapsco viaduct. Main stem trains only must whistle there, but the trains on both roads must run very slowly, the Washington branch trains from Baltimore coming to a dead halt before reaching the crossing, unless the switchman at the viaduct signify by a known signal that the way is clear. Those from Washington reduce their speed to that of a walk, till the way is seen to be perfectly free to allow the crossing of the other track.

The general superintendent, in his circular of instructions to his subordinate officers, agents and conductors, speaks also after this fashion:

All persons in the employ of the Company are admonished that positive carefulness is expected of them at all times; and that no man ought to remain in the service unless he is willing to comply with this requisition to the fullest extent. *In all cases of doubt*, take the side of safety. . . .

In another place in the same circular, he calls attention to the necessity for "entire sobriety" on the part of the road employés in train service, saying:

. . . No man who uses intoxicating drinks at all can thus rely upon himself, or be relied upon, and it is intended as far as possible to deny employment to all who use them. It is hoped, therefore, that those who desire to remain in the service will avail themselves of this notice and abstain entirely from a habit which is full of evil to themselves as well as to their employers, and is now acknowledged to do no one any good. . . .

In this day and age of a pretty full development of railroad operation—both in theory and in practice—,it seems odd indeed to note the simplicity and yet the meticulousness of the regulations set down for the Baltimore and Ohio of 1853 for its men in their daily work. . . . Take, for instance, the single important question of time: We have standard time in this country and have had it for so many years now that it seems hard to realize that once there was a day—and that a bare fifty years ago—when Boston had its local time and Springfield and New York and Philadelphia and Baltimore each had its separate time, and different. Which brought many problems. And nowhere more troublous ones than in the difficult business of operating a long-distance railroad.

For the guidance of the Baltimore and Ohio man of 1853, it was set down plainly in the book of rules that the clock in the new Camden Station in Baltimore was to be the standard for the entire system; and each passenger-train conductor was solemnly adjured to make sure that his own watch was in absolute consonance with that master clock. The book of rules goes on to say:

> In order to afford like facility to the enginemen and to the conductors of other trains as well as to all such as do not have regular opportunity to examine the regulating clock, each passenger train conductor must inspect the clocks which he has opportunity to see, notifying the agents on every outward trip of their error, if any; and on his return to Baltimore report the state of each clock as he found it. . . . The clock at Mount Clare is kept in conformity with the standard by the agent at that station. . . . All enginemen and conductors must wear good watches, approved by the master of transportation and correct them daily by the facilities thus afforded them.
>
> . . . .
>
> Where two tracks are in use, the engineman is required to keep to the right unless otherwise specially provided for. Where the same track must be used in common, the trains

are classed, as to priority of right, as follows:—First, all passenger trains; second, Ellicott's Mills, tonnage, coal and stock trains. Between trains of the same class going in *opposite* directions, the following rules are enjoined: One hour's advantage shall be given to eastward bound trains over those of the same class going westward; thus, when an eastward bound train arrives promptly at the regular meeting point, and the other *does not* arrive, the former may proceed on its time and have the prior right to the track until it shall, by losing time, become *two hours late* when it shall stop and give the track to the other train—provided only that the Frederick train shall wait its hour for the day passenger train.

If the westward bound train gets first to the meeting place it shall wait its hour, and *then* proceed; having, in its turn, a prior claim to the track—until, by losing time, *it* shall become two hours late, when it must lie by and give the track to the other train—provided that the westward bound Cumberland train will *not* wait its hour for the Frederick train east. Neither the eastern nor the western train, however, when short of the meeting place, and proceeding upon finding the other two hours late shall go beyond the meeting place without a man far ahead with a flag or lantern.

In skimming this old-time book of rules, one comes to an inevitable conclusion that the railroader of its generation must have had at least a modicum of human brains. No numskull could easily have solved such operating riddles as these.

Phraseology of railroad operation has changed greatly in seventy years. No one longer speaks of *convoys* of trains. Yet the old-time Baltimore and Ohio rule book uses the word, saying:

Several trains running in company are called a convoy and their number must always be announced on a list carried by the foremost train, in order to avoid verbal messages which may, in no case, be sent to a train, and will not be acted on for the purpose of affecting its movement or management. Parties are required to write their notices or messages so as to admit of but one meaning and an exact copy must always be kept. . . . Trains in a convoy are numbered in succession— the largest number in the lead; and the number appropriated to each will, as soon as the fixtures can be prepared, be exhibited conspicuously on the engine for the information of road repairers and others who cannot see the written list. The last train of a convoy will thus always carry the No. 1. . . .

Into greater detail than can possibly be reproduced in these pages, these old-time rules run. Not only are operating instructions set down for the train crews as a whole, but special ones for each member of it. Thus the engineer is specially prohibited from allowing any one but the conductors of passenger trains (seemingly always a privileged class) and officers of "higher rank in the company's service" from riding in the cab with him, while he is very strictly enjoined at all times to conform absolutely to the speed set down by the time-tables, "whether there be a train behind him or not." The rules further say:

In respect to speed he [the engineer] is held directly and wholly responsible at all times. It is a particular part of the engineman's duty to sound his whistle in turning abrupt curves, road crossings, switches, water and other stations. . . . Also, to stop and learn the meaning of all earnest signals, taking nothing for granted.

Apparently it had once been the practice in American railroad operation to take very much indeed for granted. . . . Here is a rule that is well kept in mind on the Baltimore and Ohio to this very day:

Great caution is required in regulating trains at stations or stopping places to avoid violence to the cars.

Nothing, however, was said in those days to the engineers about violence to passengers who were in those cars.

.   .   .   .

There now enters into this picture that highly important figure of the early American railroad—the old-time conductor.[1] One does not have to close one's eyes and look very far into the background to visualize him—with his whiskers, his lantern on his arm and his general air of benign authority.

[1] Typical of the Baltimore and Ohio railroaders of that early day was one Henry Gassaway Davis, afterwards destined to become a distinguished member of the United States Senate—from West Virginia—and a candidate for Vice-President of the United States.

At the request of Dr. Woodside, the master of transportation of the road, Davis, in his twentieth year, had become a freight brakeman at thirty dollars a month; which, a little later, was raised to forty dollars, and, when he had become a conductor, to sixty dollars. He began as a brakeman in 1842. In his life, as written by Charles M. Pepper, Mr. Davis is quoted as saying of his early railroad days:

". . . We coupled our freight cars with bars about eighteen inches long, wrought, with a hole in each end. These were held by bolts, one dropping down through the bumper of each car. Passenger cars were coupled with bars of similar shape, but made of wood and having iron ends. The wood was used so that, in case one car should overturn, the coupling would snap and leave the other cars upon the track. . . ."

When young Davis first became a brakeman, the daily traffic requirements of Baltimore and Ohio were adequately supplied by three freight trains. These were run in sections—a few minutes apart—and rear-end collisions were ordinary incidents. . . . At a later time he became a passenger conductor upon the road. He ran one of the very first night trains upon the line. Many famous men rode with him; notably Henry Clay.

On one of these trips of the Great Commoner, a pathetic incident occurred. As the train stopped at Harpers Ferry, it became known that Clay was aboard and a crowd of townspeople gathered to demand a speech. He was about beginning to speak, when a man pushed forward and said, "Mr. Clay, I want to tell you something about your boy, Henry. He died in my arms." The man had been a soldier in the Mexican War in the storming of Chapultepec, at which the younger Clay had been fatally wounded.

"The appearance of this comrade of his son," records Pepper, "and the word he gave was too much for Clay. He threw up his hands, reeled, cried out 'My God!' and, as he sank back into a seat, beckoned the man to him. The crowd fell back in silent sympathy while Mr. Clay heard from a comrade the story of his son's death. . . ."

In a later year, Davis visited Clay at his home in Ashland and became his ardent supporter. By this time, the railroader was a superintendent and one of the best liked and most efficient men upon the line. It was said of him that he could get twice as much work out of the train crews as any other superintendent upon the road.

(In a still earlier day, he had a penchant for wearing a tall hat of beaver fur.) The book of rules naïvely admits that the duties of the conductor are "extremely varied and responsible." And then adds:

> He will, on no account, start a train on its trip without having previously been instructed to do so by the station agent. But it is distinctly understood that, from the moment of the starting of the train, the entire responsibility of its condition devolves upon him. . . . He is expected to keep up a friendly and a harmonious intercourse with the engineman; but should occasion require it, no false delicacy is to intimidate him from reporting any want of coöperation on the part of that or any other individual to the master of transportation.

For tonnage (freight) conductors, still further special instructions are set down; in a considerable detail. They are told how to receive, to make out and to deliver manifests; how to describe the amount and the nature of the tonnage under their care; the number of cars, if any, that may have been left along the road because of insufficient motive power, the number and description of empty cars which are wanted by the "second class station agents" and how to designate any accidents or delays to their trains.

The passenger train conductor has a chapter of the book of rules of his very own. With an almost brutal frankness, it starts by saying:

> The duties of passenger train conductors are of a higher grade than those of tonnage trains and much more responsible in their character. He must, as an essential requirement, carry a first rate watch always set to the true Camden street time. He must be on duty before his passengers begin to muster, to see that his cars are all in order, early enough to get others if any be not so—that the water cans are well supplied—the lamps freshly filled and trimmed with *new* wicks—that the couplings are as they should be, etc. . . . He must meet his passengers on the platform and see that

they are all seated, taking care to anticipate a demand for extra cars, but preventing the monopoly of two seats by one person in any instance; *to be always in a thoroughly good humor and polite to every one he meets* [the italics are all of the old book of rules as printed]; to be cleanly and tidy about his person, in all respects and habited as a gentleman. When on the way to repeat all the courteous attentions as far as practicable. On arrival, or before, to see that his passengers understand all arrangements made at the station for their comfort, especially as to coaches, omnibuses, the "through car" in Baltimore, meals and baggage wagons for the conveyance of baggage.

It is evident that even in those days the Baltimore and Ohio placed the comfort and convenience of its passengers high in the category of the essential duties of its agents. For the regulations for the proper conduct of the conductor—the captain of the train—continue:

. . . In examining his train he must see that all necessary tools for relief in case of a breakdown are on board and in good order; to light the lamps before passing through long tunnels, as well as at night; to see that passengers obey the rules against standing on platforms and putting their feet on the seats, etc.; to see that passengers *first occupying* a seat are given a prior claim to it until they voluntarily shift to another; to notify all passengers in season of all stoppages and of arrangements for meals and other accommodations; to keep newsboys and *other annoyances* out of the cars; to report himself to the station agent when going on duty and to leave duty at the end of the trip only with the express assent of the agent there. He will see that no train be started or run with any passenger on the platforms, under any circumstances whatever, but there must be room provided for all in the cars. Whenever on duty he must wear his badge conspicuously so that strangers may be at no loss in addressing themselves for information and assistance and to require his baggage master and brakeman to do the same. . . .

He must report promptly to the master of transportation

and to the local agent where his trip terminates, whatever affects the success of his trains—the usual returns of passenger and way money, and a correct table of his actual running for comparison with the time tables.

The method of handling tickets and ticket money had been worked out but six years before. Reference has just been made in these excerpts from the rule book to "second class agents." This means all stations other than those at Pratt Street and Mount Clare in Baltimore (and, after 1853, the fine new Camden Station), Frederick, Harpers Ferry, Cumberland and Washington (to which, of course, Wheeling was soon to be added). In 1847, it was ruled that all passengers' tickets were to be sold from Pratt Street only (afterwards from Camden). All tickets when sold were to be entered at once upon the station waybill, for the system was still quite prevalent of putting the names, residences and destinations of passengers upon a manifest which was carried by the passenger train conductor on his run and then turned into general offices for check and record. . . . It was further ruled that all unsold tickets at each station should be sent back to headquarters at Baltimore by the conductor of the last passenger train going in each evening; a fresh supply being returned by the secretary of the company on the earliest train the next morning. Similarly, all monies were to be returned from every second-class station to Baltimore each night, and sent out again in the morning; strong tin boxes, properly lettered, being provided for this purpose. Access to these was only by duplicate keys; one held by the station agent, the other by the treasurer at Baltimore.

An irritation then, and for many years thereafter, was the deadhead rider. Many men, and men of good position, considered that it was very smart to cheat the railroad out of its just dues for carrying them. Sometimes they went to extreme lengths to accomplish this. Not infrequently, they connived with the conductors. In addition to which, the free passes which were granted in the course of an average twelvemonth came to a staggering total. . . . It was not until the passage of the federal Hepburn Bill, as recently as 1906, that the free pass nuisance and burden to the American railroad was brought under proper control. And a great leakage of income stopped.

.   .   .   .

The officers in charge of the Baltimore and Ohio at the beginning of the decade of the 'fifties had man-sized jobs cut out for them. But, despite all their problems, they were accomplishing some very definite things. And not the least of these was real railroad organization—along the lines which have just been set down here. . . . Also, some very interesting other things were being achieved on the Baltimore and Ohio. Of which, not the least were things electrical.

The artist from New York City, Professor S. F. B. Morse, who was to come to fame eventually as a great inventor rather than as a great painter, had seen fit to choose the Washington Branch of the road for the installation of his first telegraph line—in those days they referred to it invariably as the "magnetic telegraph." He had found the officers of the railroad both interested and highly coöperative. Much more so, for instance, than those of the New Jersey Railroad, which bluntly refused permission to the Magnetic Telegraph Company (as finally incorporated by the Maryland Legislature) to place its line along its tracks, giving as its reason that, if the telegraph were successful, it would hurt the railroad by enabling folk to do business by wire instead of by traveling. . . . The management of the Baltimore and Ohio was of a far wider vision. And Morse and his associates were readily granted permission to build their line along its right of way.[1]

[1] In his *Reminiscences*, Judge Neilson Poe, at that time a director of the Baltimore and Ohio, recalls the meeting of the board at which Morse was given permission to lay his lines alongside the Washington Branch. B. H. Latrobe had endorsed the project. John Spear Nicholas had introduced a resolution to permit the laying of the line, provided "that it can be done without injury to the road and without embarrassment to the operations of the company, and provided Mr.

This was as far back as the summer of 1843. In the autumn of that same year, the materials for the new telegraph line began arriving in Baltimore. These consisted chiefly of a lead pipe, with an interior bore half an inch in diameter (in truth, much like the modern conduit system for conveying electric wires underground) and copper wire, covered spirally with a cotton thread-like wire which had been treated with a special solution to insulate it properly from contact with the surfaces of the pipe through which it was to be strung.

For this beginning telegraph line was of the most modern approved type of today—laid under the surface of the ground. In the Mount Clare shops of the Baltimore and Ohio, there had been devised a special type of ploughshare, which, drawn by sixteen oxen, at a single operation, cut a trench two inches wide and twenty inches deep beside the track, into which it dropped the lead pipe, inside of which the copper wires already had been drawn. . . .[1] In this way, the first telegraph line was laid all the way from Mount Clare to Relay. At this last point, a snag was struck; the line there was heavily ballasted in stone. The ingenious ploughshare would work no more; and so recourse was had to stringing the copper wire overhead; at first as a temporary expedient. But it worked so well and

---

Morse will concede to the company the use of the telegraph upon the road without expense, and reserving to the company the right of discontinuing the use if, upon experiment, it should prove, in any manner, injurious. . . ." "Whatever may be our individual opinions as to the feasibility of Mr. Morse's invention," Mr. McLane had added to the discussion, "it seems to me that it is our duty to concede to him the privilege he asks and to lend him all the aid in our power, especially as the resolution carefully protects the company against all present or future injury to its works and secures us the right of requiring its removal at any time. . . ." After a slight opposition, the resolution was passed and Morse went ahead with his project.

[1] The ploughshare by which this trench was cut was cast in the moulding room at Mount Clare. It not only cut the furrow, but dropped the lead pipe into it. On the beam of the plough was a cylinder holding some sixty feet of the pipe, which uncoiled and passed down to the earth-cutting line. A plumber with his fire pot and soldering irons followed immediately in the rear and, as the supply on the cylinder ran short, would set up, wind on a new section and join the ends; and thus keep up the operation of laying the line.

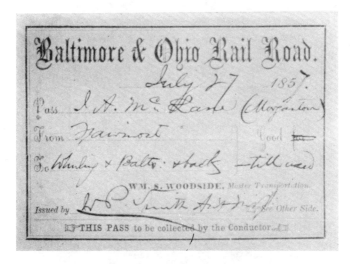

AN EARLY RAILROAD PASS.

It bears the name of William S. Woodside, Master of Transportation, and is countersigned by William Prescott Smith, afterwards Master of Transportation, and a distinguished early historian of Baltimore and Ohio.

From the company's archives.

A HALT FOR PICTURE MAKING.

A group of journalists and photographers made a trip over the main line of the Baltimore and Ohio on a special train in the summer of 1857. Some of them posed for this picture.

From an early photograph.

cost so little, comparatively, that it presently became standard everywhere.

In fact, the underground section had been so poorly insulated—so slight was the understanding of these things in that early day—that it quickly was adjudged a failure. . . . In December, 1843, Professor Morse announced in a card to the public that "the lateness of the season embarrasses further operations until spring." The announcement went on to say that, pending the perfecting of plans for insulating the overhead wires, tests had been made on the section of the line laid beneath the surface of the ground and these had proved that it was not good. The $15,000 (half of the original Congressional appropriation) that had been expended upon it was a total loss. Morse was discouraged.

Yet, in the spring he went again at his task. It was now decided to adopt the overhead system all the way from Baltimore to Washington. The wires were to be carried on unbarked chestnut poles, which were notched to carry four wires; although only two were strung at the outset. . . . To establish the electric current properly, these wires were grounded in huge sheets of copper; one was buried in the Pratt Street dock in Baltimore, the other in the dry dust of the basement of the Capitol at Washington.

May 24, 1844, the Baltimore and Washington telegraph line was formally completed and first opened to business. On that day, magnets and sending and recording instruments were first put in place and attached to the two terminals of the line; in the Pratt Street Station of the Baltimore and Ohio Railroad in Baltimore and in the Supreme Court Chamber of the United States Capitol at Washington. Miss Anne Ellsworth, daughter of the Commissioner of Patents, who had happened to be the first to inform Professor Morse of the passage of the original $30,000 federal aid appropriation, was given the honor of framing the first message to go by telegraph. She took a quill pen and slowly wrote a message which has come down the long ages:

"What hath God wrought."

Professor Morse, himself, immediately transmitted this to Baltimore. On its heels went another; a message of love from Dolly Madison to her very dear friend, Mrs. John Wethered, wife of the Congressman from Baltimore at that time.

. . . .

Quickly and successfully established from the first, the telegraph spread, not only into wide popularity, but into great commercial value. Over its copper strands came, in rapid succession, business messages, personal messages, the dispatches of the press. The first of these last was transmitted the day after the Baltimore and Washington line was formally opened. The *Baltimore Patriot* printed a telegram from the Capitol, saying that the House had just decided to go into the committee of the whole to discuss the Oregon question.

In June, 1846, communication by telegraph was established between Jersey City and Washington; messages being taken across the Hudson into New York City by ferryboat. While a full month earlier the *Baltimore Sun* had published the President's message, transmitted in full for the first time by the telegraph. . . .[1] Three years later, the new means of swift communication had reached Cincinnati. From that time forward, its progress was limited merely by the time required for its construction. In 1863, it had reached itself all the

[1] According to Judge Poe, the telegraph played its first important rôle in politics at the Democratic National Convention which was held in Baltimore in 1844. At that convention, an effort was being made to stampede the nomination of Silas Wright, then a Senator from New York, for Vice-President. It was felt that his name would add great prestige to the ticket. The Whigs also felt this way. Some of them thought of the new telegraph line leading over to Washington and quickly brought it into play to discover Mr. Wright's actual wishes in the matter. These were definite. He did not choose to run. Word of his positive declination was telegraphed back to Baltimore. And the distinguished New Yorker then and there lost his opportunity to become Vice-President of the United States.

way across the North American continent. Long since, it had become one of the valuable essential utilities of the land.

. . . .

Along the right of way of that selfsame historic Washington Branch of the Baltimore and Ohio, there came, not long after the telegraph, another electrical device, which, although developing far more slowly at the outset, eventually was to become as valuable a servant of mankind even as the telegraph itself.

For it was in April, 1851, on the rails of the Washington Branch, that there operated for the first time in the history of the world an electric railroad locomotive.

Incredible as this statement may seem at first, it is true. Dr. Charles Grafton Page, of Salem, Massachusetts, also aided by a Congressional appropriation and working in coöperation with the Smithsonian Institution and the officers of the Baltimore and Ohio, on the twenty-ninth day of April of that year, first ran his electric motor—from Washington to Bladensburg and back. This was an enlargement and perfection of a model which he had completed the preceding year.

The Page locomotive—if such a crude thing might fairly be called a locomotive—ran on storage batteries, the sequence and development of Alfred Vail's important discoveries in 1845. While it ran easily and was a source of great interest and wonderment to the thousands who saw it, it was by no means practical. The great weight and expense of the storage batteries, to say nothing of the difficulties in charging them, weighed against its possible success. Dr. Page found it impossible to interest capital or Congress in it further, and so dropped it. . . . As a forerunner of a practicable electric locomotive, it really amounted to little. Yet it earned its right to its position as a pioneer of a form of rail tractive power coming into rapidly increasing use these years.

. . . .

The Baltimore and Ohio of 1853. . . . At last a real railroad, its first great goal accomplished. A road of fancy, of initiative, of very real progress. A fine public highway, of which any town, or group of towns, might well be proud.

Such a real highway demanded a real gateway at its chief terminal, at the proud city of its birth. Pratt Street Station, at best, was but a makeshift. As the business of the road increased, it became ridiculously inadequate. It was obsolete. And, in the autumn of 1851, the directors of the company decided to build a new depot in Baltimore City that, in size and dignity and beauty, would do full credit to the railroad that they headed. No finer station had been attempted, anywhere.

So came into existence Camden Station. In June, 1852, one finds the board authorizing the purchase of three entire city squares between Eutaw and Howard streets, at an estimated cost of nearly $500,000, as a site for the great new station, which was to serve for both freight and passenger trains. Architects and engineers were brought into consultation. It was decided that something monumental—worthy of the city as well as of the railroad—would have to be done; something that would approximate the magnificence of those new London stations—Euston and King's Cross and Paddington—which were just then coming into being. At the time of its completion, Camden Station was the largest in America; one of the largest in the world. Even though, a few months later, Isambard Kingdom Brunel's masterpiece for the Great Western Railway of England—Paddington—was to be finished and so to wrest the honor of the "very biggest" away from its Baltimore rival.

·   ·   ·   ·   ·   ·   ·

As originally planned, Camden Station was to have been wrought in a Normanesque type of architecture; with a tower, not unlike the Smithsonian Institution over in Washington. However, the Baltimore and Ohio of 1853 was seriously embarrassed for funds—the extension to Wheeling had cost it a pretty penny, indeed. More than once during the construction of Camden Station, the more cautious of the directors denounced it as a piece of extravagant folly and demanded that work on it cease, and at once. Once or twice, work did halt, but only for a little time. . . . The elaborateness of the plans was eliminated. In fact, for a time, but two of the station tracks were laid down. . . . Later, the other tracks were put in place, the long triple train shed erected and such valuable operating appurtenances as engine houses, turntables, water tanks and the like added to the equipment of the terminal.

But the tower feature was retained, although changed in its details. For many years, the great spire of Camden Station—not unlike that of some proud New England meeting house—loomed high as a local landmark over the little red brick houses of a great portion of Baltimore. . . . A few years ago, however, the tall tower became somewhat unsafe and it was taken down and replaced by a cupola of more moderate proportions.

.   .   .   .

What a fascinating place in these early years, this fine, new Camden Station, with the long, long rows of yellow railroad coaches tightly emparked within it; with huge balloon-stacked locomotives now and then and again cautiously feeling their way into the great and shadowy train shed! . . . Long beams of misty light coming down obliquely from the interstices of the giant roof. . . . A place of many, many noises. And varied. Of ceaseless comings and goings. . . . Of farewells. Of greetings. . . . What a stage for tremendous drama; what a setting for the unending comedy of human life!

Camden Station still stands, little changed from the plans of its original architects. It is an important integral part of the Baltimore and Ohio of today. True it is that the imposing chief offices of the road, with their mahogany-topped desks and their great chandeliers and mirrors, went their way from its upper floors these many years ago; but the railroad still uses it as one of its most important stopping places. Nation-famed trains, such as the *Capitol Limited*, still are proud to regard it as their starting point or their destination. . . . Through the ceaseless passing of the long years, it has lost nothing of dignity nor of importance. . . . It has been carefully, even lovingly, preserved. In the entire land, there is not a station better maintained nor more carefully than this Baltimore veteran. If it were to pass out of existence, Baltimore would lose a historic monument which today ranks in her memory alongside the Shot Tower or the great grey shaft in Mount Vernon Square erected a full hundred years ago to the memory of the Father of His Country. . . . Baltimore loves monuments. From them she long since took her popular and colloquial name. But, of them all, there is none with which she comes in closer contact in her everyday life than this ancient, comfortable terminal of her very own railroad.

CHAPTER XVI

DAYS OF SWIFT EXPANSIONS AND REJOICINGS

West from the Ohio—The Northwestern Virginia Railroad . . .
And the New Hotel at Grafton—The Marietta and Cincin-
nati—Trials and Tribulations of the Ohio and Mississippi—
A Happy Outcome and Thirty Mad Days of Rejoicings.

WHY Wheeling? This was the question that the stockholders and chief promoters of the Baltimore and Ohio began
asking each other; not only after their railroad had actually
achieved that neat Ohio River town, but even before. . . .
That Wheeling was a nice town, no one seemed anxious to
argue; the floods of oratory that had accompanied the formal
opening of the railroad into it would have indicated that the
gentlemen of Baltimore had nothing but the greatest enthusiasm for that western terminal, the original goal of the line.

But that Wheeling was the proper place for the chief west
gateway of a system destined to as great a place in the sun
as the already world-famed Baltimore and Ohio Railroad, was
open to a bit of question. By cool-headed gentlemen, not
indulging in banquet feasts, but sitting in the chilling atmosphere of their counting-houses. . . . The upper Ohio is
notoriously temperamental; even so today, after locks and
dams and other artificial works to aid navigation have been
applied to it, prodigally, by a paternal government. . . . In
the early decades of the past century, when the hinterland
was vastly more dependent upon it, the Ohio was more difficult
to navigate safely. There were weeks, even months, when
sizable craft could not penetrate to Wheeling. And the

Baltimore and Ohio seemed likely to be left dependent upon wagon traffic as a sole means of intercourse toward the West; at least until some of those little rail lines that already were struggling across the roughly broken surface of southeastern Ohio could be brought to make a connection with it.

Even Pittsburgh, despite the fact that it was still further up the river, would have been better. The contenders for it at Baltimore in the 'forties and 'fifties had somehow seemed to sense the prescience of the mighty Pittsburgh of today. . . . Its strategic location had appealed greatly to them. They saw even then, in the struggling town at the confluence of the Allegheny and the Monongahela with the Ohio, what today we would call a key city.

Yet Pittsburgh was not to be for the Baltimore and Ohio —not, seemingly, at that particular hour of its history. It has been shown how the embryonic Pennsylvania Railroad, also struggling its way through to the Ohio at the beginning of the sixth decade, had staked Pittsburgh as its very own. As an exclusive gateway. The great power and prestige of the Pennsylvania in the state whose name it so proudly bore would fight to hold Pittsburgh as its exclusive principality. Already that had been shown, clearly. And the Baltimore and Ohio of 1853 was in no position to fight for the town.

Farther down the Ohio—at a point where navigation at all seasons of the year was fairly dependable—was a town whose name in the 'fifties was more often on the lips of men than was Pittsburgh. This was Cincinnati, which already they were beginning to call the "Queen City of the West." In that sobriquet there was not the least hint of irony. Cincinnati was not only a busy town, but it was a pretty one. The distinguished Charles Dickens, traveling on his memorable journey through the United States in the early part of the 'forties, had called it such. The neat pattern of its streets, the cool green trees that line them, the tidy red brick houses with their green blinds—all of this had made large appeal to the English novelist. Who was by no means prone to admire all that he saw in America.

Even before Mr. Dickens visited it, Cincinnati had had the promise of a railroad—although a fairly vague one. As far back as 1836, there had been chartered a company to be known as the Louisville, Cincinnati and Charleston Railroad. Its probable location was indicated by its title, and so impressed was the Kentucky Legislature with the plans of its promoters that it granted it a free right of way for its entire course through the state, and then all hands had adjourned for a mighty celebration.

This line was planned to connect railroads running north and west from Cincinnati—some of which were presently to appear, on paper—with the Atlantic seaboard at the important South Carolina port of Charleston. The promoters likened it to "the trunk of an immense horizontal tree," whose branches were to be northern connecting lines. Yet even before those roads of rail, dimly hinted at, could appear, an artificial waterway had been builded down into Cincinnati, already growing, not merely as a brisk young weed, but in fairness and in beauty. This was the Miami Canal, which, in 1828, had been opened from the Ohio through as far as Dayton; being extended, a few years later on, to Piqua and to Defiance, where it connected with the Wabash Canal, and so opened a through water route all the way from the Ohio to Lake Erie.

The Miami Canal was not then to be laughed at—nor for a long time thereafter. In the first three decades of its existence, it prospered vastly. As late as 1851, it brought 117,655 tons of merchandise into Cincinnati and took 42,784 tons out—all in a single summer. It was a vast stimulus to the town. And it is to be doubted if the railroads, within a short time, ever gave a greater impetus to its growth than once came from the newly completed Miami Canal.

. . . .

In that summer of 1851, three railroads were building out of Cincinnati, and the prestige of the canal already was approaching its end. These three lines were: first, the Little Miami, which already had been completed to Springfield, where it connected with the far earlier Mad River Railroad through to Sandusky on the Lake—another rail connection at Xenia, led by way of Columbus to Cleveland; second, the Cincinnati, Hamilton and Dayton; and, third, the Ohio and Mississippi. Of this last, much more in due time.

The Cincinnati, Hamilton and Dayton was chartered March 2, 1846, as the Cincinnati and Hamilton Railroad; it took its full title three years later. On the nineteenth day of September, 1850, it was opened for business. . . . It was notable among the railroad enterprises of that decade from the fact that it was built entirely without township aid, and without state aid of any sort. Within less than a month after the first train had run out upon the line, the citizens of Cincinnati had completed payment of a total of over $750,000 in cash on first subscriptions for its stock. The rest of the stock and the first series of bonds were quickly disposed of in New York. All in all, as clean and as quick a bit of financing as the land had ever known, and almost without a parallel in its railroad history.

Cincinnati meant business. It already had the push, the enterprise, the vision that later were to distinguish many another Western city of increasing growth and importance. Its citizens had erected, in 1851, the Burnet House, which, for the next twenty years or so, was supposed to be one of the finest hotels in all the world. While, above the neat pattern of the downtown streets, there rose the graceful stone spire of the new Roman Catholic cathedral, then and now one of the best specimens of Georgian architecture in America. . . . All in all . . . no mean town, this Cincinnati.

Why Wheeling?

True it was that the Central Ohio Railroad, running from Bellaire (opposite Benwood, four miles down the Ohio from

Wheeling) through Zanesville and Newark to a connection with the Mad River road at Columbus (and also connecting at Newark with a line to Sandusky, likewise destined to be a part of the Baltimore and Ohio system), was already under construction, while rumors were in the air that a direct railroad would be builded from Bellaire through to Cleveland.

After something of a struggle, because it was felt that it afforded a far better point for the eventual bridging of the Ohio, Bellaire, rather than Wheeling, was chosen as the terminal for these lines. No island lay midstream at Bellaire, as at Wheeling. While the collapse, in a severe windstorm, of the first Roebling bridge, which carried the National Road over the river at the larger town, made men more than ordinarily timorous about attempting any other bridge structure at that particular location.

.   .   .   .

Why Wheeling?

The question persisted. Why, asked the merchants of Baltimore, so indirect a route to Cincinnati as would be afforded by Benwood, Bellaire, Zanesville and Columbus? Why not a far more direct connection with the Main Stem of the Baltimore and Ohio; say, by way of Parkersburg, already a fairly important port on the Ohio? . . . The idea gained favor. So quickly that, well before the opening of the main line into Wheeling, there was incorporated in the state of Virginia— February 14, 1851—the so-called Northwestern Virginia Railroad. This road was to be builded from the Main Stem of the Baltimore and Ohio, at a point near the junction of Tygarts Valley Creek with the Three Forks Creek, through to Parkersburg, where there would be a steamer connection with Marietta and the Marietta and Cincinnati Railroad, already incorporated and with construction about to begin. In this way, a rail route from Philadelphia, Baltimore and Washington to Cincinnati (and soon after to Louisville and St. Louis), many miles shorter than that by way of Wheeling and Columbus—and with lesser grades—would be created.

Thus was retribution finally done. Wheeling had played clever politics indeed—at the expense of Parkersburg—in the Virginia Legislature and had prevented McLane and Swann and Latrobe and their associates from creating their first Ohio River terminus at the precise point where their own best judgment always told them it should be located. But stupid legislation rarely ever blocks economic trend for any great length of time. And so it came to pass that, despite legislation and a long and unsuccessful lawsuit waged by the city of Wheeling, the Northwestern Virginia line was chartered and was already under construction before the first regular trains were running into that city.

James Cook was the first president, and George Neale, Jr., Jefferson Gibbons, Jonathan M. Bennett, William Logan and Joseph Spencer the first directors of the Northwestern Virginia. Most of these men lived in or around Parkersburg. The original subscriptions to the stock were taken in that village. But it was not many months after, that the line came under the direct control of the Baltimore and Ohio; Mr. Swann being elected its president and Benjamin H. Latrobe its chief engineer. Mr. Latrobe quickly completed his reconnaissances. And in December, 1852, actual construction was begun. Despite the great financial difficulties under which the parent company was laboring at that time, work continued without ceasing, for the next five years—pay rolls and other disbursements frequently exceeding $100,000 a month. . . . It was a better planned and better located road than the Wheeling one, having maximum grades of but one foot in a hundred and somewhat more moderate curves. Yet to get such a line through more than a hundred miles of rough, mountainous country meant some exceedingly heavy construction. Twenty-three tunnels—the longest a bore of 2700 feet—were found necessary, as well as some considerable bridge and trestle work.

But none of these problems was unsurmountable, none of them, in fact, quite so great as those that had been overcome by the Cheat River Grade and the Kingwood Tunnel. The

INSIDE CONNECTED WAS *No. 207.*

Fairly typical of the Baltimore and Ohio of the 'fifties is this small passenger locomotive.

From a very old photograph.

ALONG THE LINE IN THE 'FIFTIES.

Showing one of the balloon-funnel locomotives typical of its day and generation.

From an early photograph.

Baltimore and Ohio organization was becoming well accustomed to heavy work, and the building of the Northwestern Virginia came to it as hardly more than part of its original task.

. . . .

The newly created town of Grafton was recognized from the beginning as an important junction point. Here would intersect the trains bound east from Wheeling and Columbus (and a little later from Chicago) with those from Parkersburg and Cincinnati. At all times, many travelers would be coming and going. It was proposed to build a hotel in connection with the depot to take good care of these folk, as well as to give meals to the through passengers who did not find it necessary to change cars there. . . . So, presently, there appeared the station hotel, modeled rather closely after those which the English railways were finding it expedient to build at their own important junction points.

Of this hostel, a correspondent of the *Cincinnati Enquirer* was to write (in 1857):

One of the greatest comforts and luxuries in a good railroad is a first-class hotel station where a good, well-prepared meal can be enjoyed. The Baltimore and Ohio Railroad Company appreciating the necessity of this have recently at very great expense erected large and commodious hotels along the line of their route at which the traveling public are supplied with that which is essential to the wants of the inner man, including all the viands and delicacies of the season and, if needs be, comfortable rooms and beds for a night's rest and everything requisite to the convenience of a first-class hotel in a large city. The hotel at Grafton, the junction of the Parkersburg branch, is one deserving of particular notice. . . . One of our prominent citizens . . . says, in speaking of this hotel:

"In point of convenience, beauty and all the *et cetera* that go to make up a hotel *par excellence*, the one at Grafton is not to be surpassed upon any line of railroad in this or any other country. The edifice is a grand structure, composed of the

Gothic and Corinthian style of architecture and in the point of extent of dimensions and beauty of its appearance will compare favorably with many hotels in larger cities. The first thing that attracts the attention of travelers on entering the spacious main hall is a large ante-chamber with a double row of washstands extending throughout the entire length of the room. The water is supplied from the pelucid waters of the Monongahela which is contiguous to the premises. Clean towels are immediately at hand and no one is compelled to suffer the second application of that valuable auxiliary to cleanliness. The dining room is extensive in its dimensions and is supplied with an array of tables capable of accommodating an immensity of humanity. Everything about the hotel wears the air of neatness, cleanliness and purity—tables, dishes and even the attentive waiters. The parlors are gorgeously furnished; the bedrooms the acme of comfort; the gas for lighting this extensive hotel is manufactured on the premises. The scenery surrounding is grand and sublime; and upon the whole I look upon the hotel as one of *the* institutions of the country."

To such a description, what more remains to be added about the hotel at Grafton? Save, perhaps, to say that in these mundane days, while it still stands, it has been shorn of its erstwhile grandeur. The dining car has supplanted the most valuable assistance it once proffered the traveler. And Grafton, itself, has more modern hotels and a handsome, modern passenger station, some distance down the track.

·   ·   ·   ·   ·   ·   ·

In the Cincinnati newspapers of the summer of 1857, one finds the advertising columns almost bursting with announcements of the various rival rail routes to the East. The completion of the new short line, by way of Parkersburg, is heralded, indirectly, but unmistakably, by the grandiloquent announcements of its competitors. A single one of these will suffice to show the tenor of the rest:

NEW ROUTE
from
Cincinnati to the East

SHORTEST AND MOST DIRECT ROUTE TO NEW YORK, PHILADELPHIA, BALTIMORE, WASHINGTON, PITTSBURGH, WHEELING, ZANESVILLE, AND INTERMEDIATE POINTS
is via the
CINCINNATI, WILMINGTON AND ZANESVILLE
EASTERN
SHORT-LINE RAILROAD

TWO DAILY TRAINS (Sundays excepted) leave the Depot, East Front St., Cincinnati, O., at 5.50 A.M. and 3.30 P.M.

FIRST EXPRESS TRAIN leaves Cincinnati at 5.50 A.M., arrives at Zanesville at 12.30 P.M., at Belair at 4.30 P.M., connecting with the train on the Baltimore and Ohio Railroad at 4.45 P.M.; arriving at Baltimore at 10 A.M., at Washington City at 11 A.M.; at Baltimore the train connects with the trains for Philadelphia and New York direct; at Washington for Fredericksburg, Richmond, etc.

SECOND TRAIN leaves Cincinnati at 3.30 P.M., arrives at Zanesville at 12.10 A.M., two hours ahead of any other route; arrives at Belair at 6.30 A.M.; connecting immediately with train on Baltimore and Ohio Railroad, arrives Baltimore 2.45 A.M. (same connections as above).

Fare as low as by any other route.

(Signed) E. GEST,
President and Superintendent.

J. T. MARLATT,
General Ticket Agent.

The same newspaper that carries this announcement also advertises the Little Miami Railroad, with lines running by way of Columbus, Newark, Zanesville and Wheeling. It had two trains a day, also except Sundays, and claimed to carry passengers into Wheeling and Baltimore more quickly than any other route, a claim which the time-tables do not, however, substantiate.

But the two announcements in that yellowed issue of the *Cincinnati Enquirer* of the spring of 1857 that have the largest interest to the student of the fortunes of the Baltimore and Ohio follow:

MARIETTA AND CINCINNATI RAILROAD

Open through to Marietta

On and after Monday, April 20, 1857, trains will run as follows:

GOING EAST—Mail Train leaves Cincinnati at 5.50 A.M., Accommodation at 3.50 P.M.

GOING WEST—Mail Train leaves Marietta at 6.15 A.M.

These trains make close connection at Hamden with the trains of the Scioto and Hocking Valley Railway for Portsmouth.

Through express trains for Baltimore, Philadelphia, New York and all points east will commence running on Monday, May 4.

GEORGE BARNES, Superintendent.

The other is the modest advertisement of the Ohio and Mississippi Railroad, signed by W. J. Stevens as master of transportation, which shows that the *Louisville Express* will depart from the Mill Street Station at 10.20 A.M., a local at 5.40 P.M. for Delhi, North Bend, Lawrenceburg and Aurora; and at 7 o'clock each morning a freight for Louisville. . . . This announcement was succeeded but a few days later by the following:

NEW ROUTE OPENED

THE OHIO AND MISSISSIPPI

(Broad Gauge)

RAILROAD

On and after Monday, May 4, regular trains commence running between

Cincinnati and St. Louis

Two Trains Daily

First Train—Louisville and St. Louis Mail—Leaves Cincinnati 9 A.M.

Second Train—Express for St. Louis—Leaves Cincinnati at 7 P.M. Accommodation train for Delhi, North Bend, Lawrenceburg, Aurora and Cochran leaves Cincinnati at 5.40 P.M.

No change of cars to St. Louis on the route.

Andrew Talcott,
Chief Engineer and Superintendent.

I. O. Gesner,
Passenger Agent.

Back of these announcements rests the story of the first development of Baltimore and Ohio in its great southwestern territory. But this anticipates.

The Belpre (afterwards Marietta) and Cincinnati Railroad Company was organized at Chillicothe on Wednesday, the eighteenth day of August, 1847, with Felix Renwick as president, William Rose as treasurer, and Seneca W. Ely as secretary. Its formation was marked at the outset by a real tragedy. Mr. Renwick, on his return home in his carriage from one of the first meetings of the board, was killed, almost instantly, by a falling tree. He was succeeded by Allen Latham, of Chillicothe, who in turn was followed by W. P. Cutler of Washington County.

Archibald Kennedy, who lately had been engaged in the construction of the Central Vermont Railway, was secured as the locating engineer of the Marietta and Cincinnati. He seems to have developed a real reputation for this sort of work. The territory to be traversed by the new line afforded him real opportunity for the exercise of his wits. For in the so-called "Mineral Region" of southern Ohio, in fact in the entire country east of the Scioto River, the terrain is semi-mountainous. To project a line of good railroad over such ground, with a maximum gradient of fifty-two feet to the mile and minimum curves of 2600 feet radius, and with but eight short tunnels to tax the resources of the company, was something of an accomplishment.

With all of these early railroads, money was a most vital factor. True it was that civic aid did come to the Marietta and Cincinnati; Ross County alone subscribed $300,000; its then small county seat of Chillicothe, an additional $50,000; and Athens County, $200,000. A little later, the city of Cincinnati extended $150,000 as a portion of a fund that it had subscribed for the aid of all struggling enterprises making their way toward it, while the Pennsylvania Railroad and the city of Wheeling together put up their own stocks and bonds to the extent of $1,000,000 in aid of the Marietta and Cincinnati. When, even after the work of construction was under way, it halted—seemingly indefinitely—just west of Athens, more aid was given. Washington County contributed $200,000; the little town of Hamar, $50,000; and Marietta— the charming town by the Ohio which New England taste and good culture had founded and which still bears the evidence of its aristocratic origin—found $1,000,000 available for the road. . . . In addition to all of this, about $2,000,000 was subscribed to the stock of the company by private capital. While three issues of mortgage bonds supplied several millions of dollars for construction purposes. With the result that, from the outset, the road was well builded and started its career with not less than fifty locomotives and seven hundred cars, of all types.

Fifty passenger cars for the Marietta and Cincinnati were constructed in Buffalo, New York, and of them a western New York paper said:

> One of the new cars [for the Marietta and Cincinnati] which is to be presented [?] to the directors . . . is . . . already completed. . . .   The car is splendidly constructed, painted a handsome cream color, and is ornamented with Gothic panels.   There are four separate compartments, each of which

THE HOTEL AND STATION AT GRAFTON, VIRGINIA.

In its day regarded as an architectural triumph.   The Main Stem passes to the right; the Northwestern Virginia to the left of the building.

From an early photograph.

CROSSING THE ALLEGHENIES.

An early Baltimore and Ohio passenger train shown atop one of Wendel Bollman's famous bridges.

From a very old photograph.

has sleeping facilities which equal a stateroom on a steamboat in beauty and comfort. In the center of the car is a snug little parlor, in which repose easy chairs and other articles of luxury. There are oval mirrors and mahogany cabinets in this room which is carpeted and otherwise made comfortable.

.   .   .   .

The beginnings of the Ohio and Mississippi, which was to extend west from Cincinnati to a point on the great river directly opposite St. Louis, with a branch from North Vernon, Indiana, to Louisville, were marked by no such magnificences. A railroad between the then two most important cities of the West was dimly projected as far back as 1832, but it was not until sixteen years later that the Ohio and Mississippi actually was chartered, first by Indiana and then by Ohio and Illinois.[1] The preliminary survey of the road was commenced on the first day of November, 1848. By the terms of the charter granted by the Legislature of Indiana, the company was authorized to locate and survey a railroad on "the most direct and practicable route between Lawrenceburg, on the Ohio River, and Vincennes, on the Wabash River." This idea was rapidly expanded. Professor O. M. Mitchell of West Point— that distinguished military institution that had furnished the brains for the first engineering problems of the Baltimore and Ohio—made a reconnaissance of the entire country between Cincinnati and St. Louis, and reported that at no point would a grade exceed forty feet to the mile. He estimated the entire cost of building the road and equipping it at a little over $5,000,000. Experience showed that this figure was extremely modest. The line when completed cost over $20,000,000.

The organization of the Ohio and Indiana portions of the new line was effected in 1850; Abner T. Ellis, of Vincennes, being elected president, and a number of substantial citizens of Cincinnati and Vincennes and the intermediate towns being chosen as directors. Both towns and private capital came

[1] The Ohio and Mississippi Company was chartered by Indiana, February 14, 1848; by Ohio, March 15, 1849; and by Illinois, February 12, 1851.

quickly to the aid of the new enterprise; $2,000,000 in capital stock being subscribed.   Which led to the letting of a contract, January, 1851, for the building of the road between the Ohio and the Wabash.

This initial $2,000,000 was rapidly exhausted. And, because times became unpropitious for the raising of further immediate capital in the United States, Professor Mitchell resigned his post as active chief engineer of the company, and went to London, where he sold $2,750,000 of its stocks and bonds. George Peabody, the American banker there, purchased the greater portion of them, and the ease and rapidity with which Mitchell sold them excited the envy and admiration of the financial world.

Erastus Gest, who soon was to become president of the Ohio and Mississippi, took Mitchell's place as chief engineer. He made an elaborate survey and report of his own and added, as a probable cost, nearly $5,000,000 to the original five estimated by Mitchell.   These last figures staggered the directors and for a long time they were not made public.   Yet the fact remains that the contract given to H. C. Seymour and Company, of New York, for constructing and completely equipping the line from Cincinnati to East St. Louis, 335 miles, was for an even $9,000,000. The contractors obligated themselves to finish the work in five years. They were to build "all depots, station houses, turntables and machine-shops required on a first-class railroad and finish as they might be wanted, forty locomotives, forty passenger-cars, five hundred freight-cars," etc.   For this, they were to be paid $3,500,000 in cash, $2,750,000 in stock and $2,750,000 in bonds.   The charter of the state of Illinois provided that work on the western division should be begun before the twelfth of February, 1852. Three days before that appointed time, ground was formally broken at Illinoistown—as the small settlement just across the Mississippi from St. Louis then was known. By special arrangement with the contractors, this western division, through to Vincennes, was to be finished in three years from

July 1, 1852. The cost of this division was to be $3,000,000 of the total $9,000,000.

Page and Bacon, of St. Louis, took the financial responsibility for the building of this portion of the line. Henry D. Bacon of the firm finally was able to save the entire project from collapse. For the Seymour firm had showed its utter financial unfitness to carry out its huge contract. When, under the increasing stress of financial troubles through the land, many of which had been brought on by an era of railroad speculation and over-expansion, it was the Page and Bacon firm, although under another name, that took up the work. In January, 1855, this concern also went down, and upon Mr. Bacon's own shoulders fell the self-imposed task of completing the railroad. He seemed indomitable. By his own efforts, he raised half a million more dollars. And on July 11, 1855, the entire western division of the Ohio and Mississippi—from Vincennes to Illinoistown—was completed and opened to traffic. In a little less than two years, the remainder of the line was done. There was then a railroad in operation between Cincinnati and St. Louis—which meant, with its connections, between St. Louis and the seaboard.

.   .   .   .

The cost at which the new line had been achieved was very great. There came, just before the dawn of its completion, a Dark Age indeed in its affairs. A contemporary account of its troubles in the middle of the 'fifties says:

. . . It was beset by pecuniary difficulties. The western division of the road, though "finished," was not in first-class working order. Mr. Bacon, though supporting the road and sustaining himself with gigantic energy, was embarrassed and perplexed. . . . The affairs of the eastern division were, if not in confusion, in a condition of terrible depression. The stock sunk disgracefully low. The name of the Ohio and Mississippi, from being that in which Cincinnatians took pride, became a by-word. Its glory was under the rubbish of unfortunate financing. . . .

Out from all this mess, a solution gradually was evolved. The city of Cincinnati found a way to contribute half a million dollars to the road at the time of its greatest crisis. Other aid came from New York, from a group of men headed by William H. Aspinwall, whose name was to be forever linked with the successful railroad enterprise at Panama. These men took up bond arrearages and unpaid current bills and received a new mortgage bond, of sweeping powers, in exchange. They saw the railroad through. Saw it to its final completion, incidentally at a cost of twenty millions instead of the five which Mitchell had estimated, or the nine for which the unfortunate Seymour firm had set out to build it. But it was done . . . and it was, in most respects, a fairly good railroad.

.   .   .   .

A fairly good railroad, the Ohio and Mississippi, save in a single aspect. Following the example of the Erie and one or two other well heralded roads, the rails were set at a width of six feet—hence the name, "broad gauge." The real incentive for this step went much further back, to the stubborn stand taken by I. K. Brunel and the other promoters of the Great Western Railway of England, for a broad-gauge track. They had builded their important line at seven-foot gauge and this extreme figure was adhered to on that railway for many years (until 1892). In the meantime, such railroads of the United States as had originally adopted the broad gauge, and which in consequence were extremely embarrassed in their traffic relations with their fellow lines, were compelled gradually to return to the standard gauge—four feet, eight and one-half inches—at no small cost to themselves.

.   .   .   .

No matter what had been the cost, no matter how much trouble and ill-feeling had been engendered, the important fact remained that there now existed, in connection with the Baltimore and Ohio, a fairly well located and direct line of railroads from St. Louis, Louisville and Cincinnati through to the seaboard, at Baltimore, at Philadelphia and at New York. While some of these companies in the beginning were separate entities, they came more and more closely into harmony with the parent company which had inspired them, until finally they were to be part and parcel of it, eventually bearing its name; so that the Baltimore and Ohio might say in a future hour that it ran upon its own rails all the way from Chesapeake Bay (later from the Delaware River) through to the bank of the Mississippi; some nine hundred miles of well builded and well knit railroad.

Even before the name "Baltimore and Ohio" was to be actually lettered upon the cars and engines west of the Ohio River, the route was to take a sort of common cognomen; the "American Central Route" was the name then often given it. The completion of the great bridges over the Ohio, both at Parkersburg and at Bellaire, which followed a number of years afterward, enabled the running of through cars and trains with great ease between Baltimore and Cincinnati and St. Louis. But, even before these structures were done, ferrying across the Ohio was accomplished, usually swiftly and easily. And the route, from the outset, came into great popularity, both for passengers and for freight. And formed the full and reasonable answer for "Why Wheeling?"

.   .   .   .

This chapter must not close without an account of the remarkable ceremony, or series of ceremonies, with which the new route formally was opened in June, 1857.

It was an age of ceremonials. Public oratory today seems to be a well developed and fairly flourishing art; but it is as nothing when one compares it with its heyday there in the middle of the last century. Then it was that the after-dinner and the full-evening speaker flourished and fattened; at the expense of other men. Upon any and every occasion they burst forth—inimitable, unlimitable. They and their kind. A dozen speeches an evening . . . twenty to thirty interminable toasts were as nothing. For the auditors, no suitable means of defense had been found.

It was a fact patent from the outset that, in addition to the inevitable dinners, there must be an excursion. Rail travel, in the swift expansion of the American system, was coming into a vast new epoch of popularity. All classes joined in it. None too proud to go riding on the cars; particularly if the aforesaid riding cost nothing. For this was still well before the day when grim statutes were to frown on railroad passes. So it is that, upon the lists of those who received—and accepted—the invitation of the Baltimore and Ohio and its affiliated railroad companies, to ride upon the new route between Baltimore and St. Louis, one finds the names of many a really distinguished man of those days. Politicians and newspaper men, quite naturally, dominated the roster. But there were many others, from many other ranks of life; several hundred persons—men, women and children—at six o'clock in the morning were on the excursion trains when they left the resplendent new Camden Station, Baltimore, June 1, 1857, for the long trek to the Mississippi.

The President of the United States—the Hon. James Buchanan, whose strenuous term of office had just begun—could not go; but he sent his Secretary of State, the Hon. Lewis Cass, of Michigan, as his personal representative. Henry Ward Beecher could, and did, go; took Mrs. Beecher and a friend with him. So went George Bancroft, and William H. Aspinwall, and Charles A. Dana, and Henry C. Bowen, and Abram S. Hewitt,[1] and Commodore M. C. Perry, and William G. Fargo, and the French Ambassador at Washington and his suite. . . . The list of those who not only accepted, but who actually went, runs to far too great length to be repeated here. While that of those who were invited was fully three times as long. The invitation roll was nothing if

---

[1] Son-in-law of Peter Cooper of New York, designer and builder of the *Tom Thumb*.

not comprehensive. It embraced, seemingly, all the chief folk of the land. Most of these wrote appreciative letters of declination. Washington Irving said that he would have gone if his invitation had not been delayed in the mails until a moment too late to permit of his acceptance; and the editor of the *Knickerbocker Magazine* penned a feeling little note which said that the publisher had elected to go in his place. Most of the newspaper men accepted; they came from a vast range of towns; large and small, and some of them far removed from the territory of the Baltimore and Ohio and its allied lines. Some folk who were not invited, invited themselves. Until, finally, the railroad authorities called a halt; the absolute limit of their train accommodations had been reached. As it was, when the excursion trains reached Grafton, there was room only for the ladies of the party in that magnificent new hotel there; the men had to content themselves in the hard bunks of the crude sleeping cars—the sun of George M. Pullman had not yet arisen.

The party had left Baltimore very early on a rainy June morning and had halted at the Relay House, where the Hon. Lewis Cass, wearing a magnificent silk hat, joined, with other notable Washington guests. Chauncy Brooks was on the station platform to greet these late arrivals. Mr. Brooks had just become president of the Baltimore and Ohio, succeeding William G. Harrison, who in turn had succeeded Thomas Swann, right after the formal opening of the line to Wheeling. Of these changes, more at another time. At the moment, we picture the special trains speeding west all that June day, until they pulled up at Grafton station at nine o'clock in the evening. A long day, but apparently a pleasant one, because of it one historian writes:

There were also quite a number of ladies in the party whose refining influence added not a little to the pleasure of the occasion. By the aid of the officers of the railroad company, the excursionists soon became acquainted with each other and the

usual annoyances of travel were speedily forgotten in busy
scenes of social and friendly intercourse. . . . Never did time
pass more rapidly on a railroad trip. Each member of the
party seemed brimful of happiness and precisely in condition
to enjoy everything enjoyable and turn minor drawbacks
even into elements of hilarity. . . .

.   .   .   .

Little time was afforded, however, for a detailed look at
the magnificence of the hotel at Grafton, for at six o'clock the
next morning the special trains were due to be off for Cincinnati.
Clarksburg—where a throng of folk had assembled to greet the
excursionists—was reached at 6:52, and Parkersburg at 10:20
o'clock. At this point, steamboats were taken to the historic
village of Marietta, thirteen miles up the Ohio, where there
was a formal party, the guests being welcomed by the Governor
of the state, Salmon P. Chase, in an extensive oration to which
Secretary Cass replied; in an even more extensive one. There
were several more speeches, after which the party ferried across
the Muskingum to Harmar, the temporary terminus of the
Marietta and Cincinnati (the bridge across the Muskingum
into Marietta not having yet been completed). All that
afternoon the party traveled across Ohio, until Chillicothe
was reached. This county town being then somewhat deficient
in hotel accommodations, its warm-hearted citizens entertained the greater part of the party in their comfortable homes
over night.

In Chillicothe, more speeches and a parade of the fire
companies headed by marching bands of music and the local
dignitaries. "But," confesses the historian, "our horde of
eastern guests entering the town at so late an hour and the
excitement raging very high, a formal reception ceremony was,
by common consent, dispensed with and an indiscriminate
but whole-souled welcome fitly substituted."

For there was need of a good night's rest. Cincinnati was
to be reached the next day at noon, and rumors already had

filtered forward to the train of the magnificence of the welcome that was to be tendered there. . . . The trains began arriving at the station of the Little Miami Railroad (over the tracks of which the Marietta and Cincinnati then ran, from Loveland) at a little after one o'clock and were greeted by vast numbers of people. Not only the fire companies, but the militia, were out and there was a superabundance of band music. More speeches . . . and then the entire party sweeping into the great rotunda of the Burnet House, where there were still more speeches. . . . Again the hotel accommodations, even of a very considerable town, were exceeded and private houses once more came generally into play. It was estimated that twenty thousand folk came by rail from afar to the celebration at Cincinnati; and the entertaining of these was no easy matter for the town.

In the morning, before the arrival of the excursion specials, the fire department and the militia had paraded through streets gaily caparisoned for the stupendous event. Some of the stores had shown a ready wit in preparing their individual decorations. Thus the hardware establishment of Tyler, Davidson & Co., which displayed:

THE IRON TRACK IS THE ONLY TRUE BOND OF UNION

THE RAILROAD STORE

D. W. Fairchild had an inspiration when his retail mart put forth in huge letters:

A LOCOMOTIVE IS THE ONLY GOOD MOTIVE FOR
RIDING A MAN ON A RAIL

.　　　.　　　.　　　.　　　.　　　.

The greater part of the outdoor form of the entertainment that day was contributed by the Cincinnati Fire Department. In fact, there were times when it was somewhat difficult to distinguish whether the celebration was in honor of the opening of the new railroad or the acquisition by the fire department of several new steam fire engines. At four o'clock in the afternoon, the firemen having paraded all the morning and so worn off their excess energy, the fire bell sounded and all the bright new engines responded. Again we give way to the words of the official historian—Mr. William Prescott Smith:

> . . . The engines, each drawn by four powerful horses, speedily came, like flaming heralds, from every direction; huge volumes of heavy black smoke pouring from their chimneys. Ever and anon they gave a shrill shriek as if to challenge each other to the mighty contest. Fifth Street market place [Fountain Square] was already filled with crowds of people and house tops, fences, and carriages were loaded with additional spectators. In just two minutes the ladders arrived, and in less than another minute were raised against the highest buildings in the neighborhood—five stories high—and the firemen were on the roofs. In less than three minutes after the signals, the hose carriages came dashing through . . . and in four minutes the first water was on and the pipe from which it issued was on the roof of a five-story house. . . . In less than six minutes from the first tap of the bell, steam was up and six engines were throwing streams. . . . The multitude shouted at the appearance of every new jet but the firemen worked in perfect silence. . . .

To any one knowing volunteer firemen, this last statement is a little hard to believe. It taxes credulity to think that fire-company rivalries should have descended, in the Cincinnati of the 'fifties, to afternoon-tea pleasantries. . . . We turn from Mr. Smith's account for the moment and find the dispatch sent that night to the *Chicago Times* from its correspondent on the spot. He also paints word pictures; and uses little restraint in them:

> . . . Fifth Street market place presented a spectacle worth crossing the ocean and climbing mountains to see. Nothing since the Roman emperors looked down upon armies

WILLIAM G. HARRISON.
President of the Baltimore and Ohio, 1853–1855.

From a painting.

CHAUNCY BROOKS.
President of the Baltimore and Ohio, 1855–1858.

From a painting.

of gladiators butchering each other in the Coliseum had been seen like this. The housetops all around the square were densely covered. Every window was filled. The square seemed walled in with human faces. Hundreds of banners fluttered from the windows. Shawk's engine took position at the western side of the place. Latta's institution, *The Citizens' Gift*, was at the east side. Other engines had position in Main and Sycamore streets, two or three squares away. . . . Soon half a dozen streams were being thrown, hissing amid a cloud of rainbows. *The Marion* threw a stream so long and strong it excited vast admiration. *The Citizens' Gift* threw a ponderous volume of water but was said to be saving her strength. Shawk's engine was slow in getting to work but finally threw a stream as muddy as the Ohio on a spree and as powerful. . . .

We desist. But must pause long enough to record a note of tragedy. The new silk hat of Mr. Cass, the Secretary of State, was the victim. One of the resplendent fire engines—history does not record whether it was *The Marion* or *The Citizens' Gift* or the unnamed, but powerful, Shawk's contraption—threw an irreverent stream into the carriage where sat the great man, alongside Mr. Wilson, the new president of the Marietta railroad; and the silk hat of the Secretary of State went rolling down into a Cincinnati gutter, an irretrievable wreck. Neither is there record exactly what the Hon. Lewis Cass said on that trying occasion, but the newspapers are a unit in saying that he soon recovered his composure. Whether he recovered the hat is not stated.

There were not one, but many, formal dinners in Cincinnati that night. Vast amounts of food . . . and drink. Speeches, not merely by the dozens, but by the hundreds, perhaps by the thousands. . . . None of them shall be repeated here. . . . Playing bands all over the town. And, finally, in the classic shades of the Burnet House, a great ball that was to live for long years in the annals of the place.

.   .   .   .

Some of the eastern guests—possibly a bit wearied by all the excitement and the entertainment—turned homeward after Cincinnati; but enough remained, together with new recruits, to still make a respectable party—respectable but tired—of some twelve or fifteen hundred persons to continue on west over the hard-fated Ohio and Mississippi to St. Louis. . . . Illinois-town, the western terminal of the road, was not reached until midnight . . . It was a hard and wearisome trip. But the inhabitants of the large and growing city just across the Mississippi had waited up long hours for the coming of the party. There were fireworks, torches, the shrieking of the whistles of the many, many steamboats tied up at the St. Louis wharves—triumphant, powerful in their momentary glory, but slowly to go down to death under the relentless competition of the iron horse.

At St. Louis, more parades . . . more banqueting . . . more speeches. . . . The St. Louis Fire Department was in the background, but the wonderful new Court House in Fourth Street, with the slave block conspicuously in its front, was put forward as the chief local lion. While the following evening, in the huge Varieties Theater, there was a grand "railroad" meeting . . . with more speeches.

.   .   .   .

It seems incredible that so elaborate a program should have been followed less than forty days later by one quite as extensive; yet such was the case. The Easterners had seen the West; it was equally necessary that the Westerners should see the East. And so, on the fifteenth of July, more files of special trains made their laborious way eastward over the rails of the Ohio and Mississippi, the Marietta and Cincinnati, the Northwestern Virginia and the Baltimore and Ohio railroads. The receptions given the excursionists—who consisted of representative folk of Cincinnati, Louisville, St. Louis and the towns that lay between them and beyond them—at the intermediate points vied with those that had been extended to the outbound parties. . . .

But it was left for Baltimore—Baltimore, forever recognized as a center of unbounded hospitality—to attempt to outdo the efforts of the interior cities. Baltimore had not merely oratory, a cuisine of unrivaled excellence—she had gastronomy. She had other things too; a thoroughly spectacular and combative fire department, and an artistry in decorating herself upon occasion. Yet not since the visit of the Marquis de Lafayette and the laying of the First Stone of the Baltimore and Ohio Railroad, twenty-nine years before, had she exerted herself as she did upon the occasion of the arrival of the special trains over her own railroad from the West. . . . There was an excursion down the harbor to Fort McHenry, and one notes that Edwin Forrest, the tragedian, was of the company. . . . There was a wonderful parade; not too much fire department, but a magnificent display of soldiery; plenty of speeches; and in the evening of the second day a vast dinner at the Maryland Institute . . . with more speeches. . . . Of these, there shall still be no record. But of the real strength of the dinner, the magnificence and the abundance of the food and drink, there must be preserved a bit of knowledge. With the menu card of that affair this chronicle of entertainment ceases:

BILL OF FARE

Soups

Green Turtle   Soup a la Julienne

Fish

Boiled Salmon, Lobster Sauce
Boiled Sheepshead, White Sauce
Striped Bass, Baked, Genoise Sauce
Chesapeake Bay Mackerel, a la Maitre d'Hotel

Relishes

Worcestershire Sauce	French Mustard	Assorted Pickles
Apple Sauce	Currant Jelly	Cucumbers
Olives	Anchovy	

Boiled

Ham   Lamb   Spring Chicken

Entrees

Filet de Boeuf, Madeira Wine Sauce   Mountain Oysters, Sauce Royale
Petites Pates, a la Reine   Beuder a la Richelieu, Tomato Sauce
Sweet Bread, Larded, Gardinere Sauce   Lamb Chops, Soubaise Sauce
Filets of Veal, Perageaux Sauce   Timbale de Macaroni, Milanaise
Vol au Vent, a la Financier   Galantine de Poulets
Young Chickens, Maryland Style

Maryland Course

Roast Saddle of Mountain Mutton, Currant Jelly Sauce
Soft Crabs, Fried, Butter and Parsley Sauce
Soft Crabs, Broiled   Green Goose, Apple Sauce
Hard Crabs, Deviled   Roast Ham, Champagne Sauce
Summer Ducks, with Olives

Vegetables

Stewed Tomatoes   Baked Tomatoes   Green Peas
Green Corn   String Beans   Boiled Potatoes
Boiled Beets   Cymlings

Cold and Ornamental Dishes

Ham on a Pedestal, decorated with Jelly
Boned Turkey on a Socle, French Style
Poulets Truffe a la Belle Vue   Salade de Poulets, Historee
Boeuf Sale en Presse   Buffalo Tongues, Garnished   with
Lobster Salad, Mayonnaise   Jelly
Pate of Liver Jelly   Sliced Tomatoes, a la Harden
Aspic d'Huitres   Crab Salad, Baltimore Fashion

Ornamented Pieces and Dessert

Emblem of Commerce   Punch Cakes
Ancient Cornucopia   Vanilla Ice Cream
Corbeille Renaissance   Almond Ice Cream
Corbeille Antique   Strawberry Ice Cream
Pyramides la Amors   Orange Ice Cream
Pyramide la Dolphin   Raspberry Ice Cream
Nougat Casket   Pine Apple Ice Cream
Pyramides Dessert   Caramel Ice Cream
Bisquet Glacee au Creme Caisse Plumbier
Charlotte Russe   Bisquet Glacee au Chocolade
Maraschino   Fancy Cakes
Charlotte Russe (Lemon)   Jelly Rum Maraschino
Madeira Wine

Fruits and Flowers

Water Melons   Apples   Oranges   Pine Apples   Pears
                    Bananas   Apricots   Raspberries
          Pyramids, Bouquets and Baskets of Flowers, in every Variety

.   .   .   .

Somehow, amid all the excitements of a little more than thirty days, a new railroad route had actually been thrown open.

CHAPTER XVII

THE TUMULT AND THE SHOUTING DIE

The Beginning of a New Era—And the Men at the Helm of the Baltimore and Ohio Face Large Problems—New Faces in the Board Room—Johns Hopkins and John W. Garrett.

IN the hall of the final banquet, the last toast had been proffered . . . the last fervent speech finished . . . the last guest gone . . . tables cleared . . . the final tired waiter dismissed . . . lights dimmed . . . and out. Celebrations were over. A large event had not gone unnoticed. A new and highly important national pathway was, at last, properly dedicated. . . . Yet, after the gayety and glimmer of the evening, there comes, presently, the cold grey of dawn; the unimpassioned reckoning of the morn that follows. . . . So to the Baltimore and Ohio, after a season of great gayety, this inevitable day of reckoning. Of coolly balancing this thing . . . and that.

Unquestionably, the road had expanded with a vast rapidity in the few years which had immediately preceded 1857. So, in that same period, had most of the other railroads of the United States. It was, everywhere, a time of vast expansion. Of over-expansion. Of splurge. Of financial wildness. There was a cold grey hour of reckoning to come for all of it. Which, in after years, was to be known as the great panic of 1857.

Curious it is that three of the greatest financial crises in the United States during the last century should have come at almost even twenty-year periods—1837, 1857, 1877—and that these three serious business trials for the land should have risen very largely, although not entirely, from over-expansion in its building of railroads.   From ordinary business judgment, a whole nation seemingly gone completely wild.   From men, in seasons of vast prosperity, losing their heads . . . men reaching . . . and over-reaching . . . and then falling helplessly into the mire.

The cold fact faced by the Baltimore and Ohio and its connecting roads to the West—the Northwestern Virginia, the Marietta and Cincinnati, the Central Ohio, and the Ohio and Mississippi—was that a great many miles of track had been put down without any immediate increase in traffic returns to justify the vast initial outlay.   Various causes contributed to this; competition was not the least of them.   The important trunk-line rivals of the Baltimore and Ohio—the Erie, the New York Central and the Pennsylvania—also were expanding, as swiftly as they might possibly bring it about, into that great and growing central section of the United States just west of Buffalo and Pittsburgh and Wheeling.   In the flush mid-'fifties, they found plenty of encouragement for their coming. . . .   Not only states, but towns, villages and cities . . . all not only willing but anxious to bond themselves to aid railroad projects, until the thing became so very wild that many states were forced to pass laws forbidding this sort of community subscription.

So swiftly went down the rail lines through the 'fifties that breath hardly could be taken between their building.   A railroad mileage of 8590 miles in the United States of 1850, by 1860 had become 30,794 miles.   In the state of Ohio alone, by 1855, there were 2233 miles of completed railroad and 1992 more miles approaching completion.   The promotion of new railroads rapidly was becoming an art, although many times not a particularly creditable one.   New roads were being incorporated; nearly every twenty-four hours.   Frequently, their shares sold like wildfire.   Frequently, too, they were allied with other highly speculative enterprises: rolling mills, from which were to come their iron rails; new shops, where were to be builded their cars and their locomotives; and, most often of all, model towns, where there were to arise great cities, devoted both to railroad and other industrial enterprises . . . cities, which not only did not ever become great, but which frequently died a-borning, whose well-mapped sites for seventy years have served as very pleasant cow pastures and meadowlands.

'Fifty-seven was preceded, in 'fifty-four, by a sharp warning. The extreme fluctuations within a single decade that these two years brought are shown in the number of miles of new road built in each twelvemonth from 1850 to 1859. In the first of these years, 1261 miles were completed; in 1851, 1274 miles; in 1852, 2288 miles; in 1853, 2169 miles; in 1854, 3442 miles; in 1855, 2453 miles; in 1856, 1470 miles; in 1857, 2077 miles; in 1858, 1996 miles; and in 1859, 1707 miles. In other words, in the fifth year of the decade, more than twice as many miles of line were laid down as were laid in the tenth year. Very gradually the warning was being heeded.

President Franklin Pierce in his annual message to Congress, given December 4, 1854, referred at some length to the problem just then beginning. He said, in part:

When we reflect that since the commencement of railways in the United States, stimulated, as they have been, by the large dividends realized from the earlier works, they are the great thoroughfares and between the most important points of commerce and population, encouraged by state legislation, and pressed forward by the amazing energy of private enterprise, only seventeen thousand miles (at the end of 1854) have been completed in all the states in a quarter of a century; when we see the crippled condition of many works, commenced and prosecuted upon what were deemed to be sound principles and safe calculations; when we contemplate the enormous absorption of capital withdrawn from the ordinary channels of business, and extravagant rates of interest paid at this moment to continue operations, the bankruptcies, not merely

in money, but in character, and the inevitable effect upon
finances generally, can it be doubted that the tendency is to
run to excess in this matter?

Another bit of testimony from an accurate source completes
the rather depressing picture of the condition of the railroad
generally in the middle of the last century. In the *American
Engineer*, for August 29, 1857, one reads:

> The financial world is in the midst of a panic. There have
> been a portentous number of failures. Erie stock (a gauge
> for most fancy stock) has touched 20—the banks are hauling
> in, and the large grain crop being sent forward does not prom-
> ise either ready sales or high prices. The largest part of this
> condition has been owing to the simple delusion that railroads
> could be worked for fifty per cent of their gross receipts. . . .
> There are one thousand million dollars invested in railroads
> in the United States, and where it has been believed that this
> property could pay $70,000,000 yearly, it does not pay
> $40,000,000—a yearly deficit of more than $30,000,000. This
> is a good deal of money to be wasted yearly, but the country,
> if it does not plunge still deeper in debt, will soon outgrow
> it. . . .

One does not wonder that the third decade of Baltimore
and Ohio—aside from the feastings and the festivals—was a
season of great perplexity and worry. Of a swift succession of
presidents. . . . Mr. Swann retired from the executive control
of the road April 13, 1853, and was immediately succeeded as
president by William G. Harrison. . . . Swann was never a
real railroad man. He was more essentially a politician who
had been placed in office through the efforts of the directors
representing the city of Baltimore and the state of Maryland
—in those days always a majority of the board. It was as a
politician that he was most valuable to the Baltimore and Ohio
in a season when it needed a powerful friend in the many halls
of legislature. . . . Soon after he retired from his railroad
post, he was elected Mayor of Baltimore, a position which he

continued to hold, despite bitter political attacks, for a number of years.

Neither was Mr. Harrison essentially a railroader. He was a business man of rather quiet and unassuming aspect. And, at this day, one suspects that the presidency of the Baltimore and Ohio was thrust upon him, rather than sought. It certainly could not have been desired for the salary that it paid at that time—$3000. As much as this was being given to railroad superintendents up in the North and East. But the Baltimore and Ohio of that day was not distinguished by high wages. Its four thousand employés drew relatively small pay. A passenger conductor was paid $62.50 a month; an engineer (freight or passenger), from two to three dollars a day. Day laborers received as low as a dollar a day, and were glad to get it.

Mr. Harrison retired as president after two years in office and was succeeded by Chauncy Brooks. Already we have seen Mr. Brooks as a more or less prominent figure in the tedious celebrations that marked the opening of the Baltimore and Ohio route to Cincinnati and St. Louis. He needed whatever stimulating effects such festivities might render to his soul. For his administration of the road was marked by much trouble. Morale fell to a low ebb; in the fiscal year which ended September 30, 1855, there were not less than sixty-one casualties reported from the various divisions of the line east of Wheeling and Grafton. Thirty-six men had been either instantly killed or fatally injured; twenty-five more had suffered severe injuries, such as the loss of an arm or one or both legs. Of this number, however, but two were passengers, and both of these were stealing rides. Forty-six of the list were employés of the road. Seven were drunk.

No wonder then that, amid all the hurrahs and excitement of that memorable and festive summer of 1857, there had come, back of the scenes, a disagreeable strike, whose memory was to last for a considerable time thereafter. The company had, for most obvious reasons, ordered that the doors of its merchandise cars (box cars) be sealed when in transit. The men, particularly the freight conductors and their crews, had resented this ukase. Mr. Ross Winans, with a personal quarrel and much bitterness toward the existing management of the road, encouraged their efforts. So sharply that, by the twenty-seventh of April of that year, they gathered at Martinsburg and made forcible efforts to prevent the operation of the railroad. With a degree of success.

For two or three days, no freight trains were operated at all on the eastern sections of the line. On May Day, an effort to open the line for freight, which was congesting to an embarrassing degree, was met with resistance. It was found necessary at Ellicotts Mills, to call out both a sheriff's posse and a troop of militia from Baltimore. Before order was restored, a pitched battle ensued, in which a train was thrown from the track and one of the strikers was killed by a flying bullet. The entire affair assumed the proportions of a considerable riot.

A third and even greater anxiety confronted Chauncy Brooks. This one was financial. To the perplexities of an hour which steadily was growing darker, to the almost continuous conditions of monetary embarrassment in which the Baltimore and Ohio found itself in the earlier years of its career, was being added a deal of confusion in its accounts. . . . Of a most delicate and difficult sort. . . . In those days there was but little system in railroad accounting; certainly as it might be compared with accepted methods of the present day. Revenues and expenditures alike were carelessly handled. If not for dishonesty, there was much opportunity for incompetence. As a single instance, such a thing as a railroad purchasing agent, honestly and scientifically supervising a very great avenue of railroad expenditure, was as yet unknown. Heads of departments did their own buying, in their own way; which frequently was a very poor way.

So wonder not that the last month of 1856 saw the appointment of a special committee of five directors of the company to examine its accounts and bring forward, if possible, a true balance, and also to pay the stockholders monies which it was generally felt were due them.

.   .   .   .

Into the board room of the Baltimore and Ohio there had slipped quietly, in that stirring decade of the 'fifties, two men, of young middle age, whose exceptional qualities were to make permanent impress, not only upon the fortunes of the road, but upon those of the fine and growing city whose chief servant it remained. One of these young men was Johns Hopkins, and the other was John W. Garrett. The first was to leave his name perpetuated through the years by the institution of learning which he founded and which was to carry the fame of Baltimore to every corner of the world. The second made his monument in Baltimore and Ohio. Until it was to be said by waggish tongues that the entire history of the road could be divided into three main epochs: before-Garrett, Garrett, and after-Garrett.

Quite natural it was that these two men should become members of the special committee; young Garrett its chairman, stating with little hesitation that he had taken the post as the champion of the stockholders who had a right to inquire into what was being done with their property. Celebrations— marching fire companies and elongated banquets—were to mean little or nothing hereafter to the real owners of the property. Neither were elaborate statements as to the future prospects of the line. What they wanted was assurances of personal returns, to themselves, if you please, and at no greatly deferred day.

.   .   .   .

On the other hand, it must be admitted that, as a result of its swift extension into the new central portions of the land, the fortunes of the road finally were beginning to show some improvement. In October, 1852, just upon the eve of the completion of the line to Wheeling, the twenty-sixth annual report of the company shows the receipts for the fiscal year (ending on the last day of the preceding month) to have been $1,325,563.65—a decrease of $23,659.10 from the year before. Of this, the net earnings were assumed to be $615,384.43, from which contented stockholders had been paid a dividend of seven per cent upon the common.

The following year had brought trouble. The Ohio fell to unprecedentedly low stages at Wheeling. For months that summer, the river gauges showed less than thirty inches of depth. What a mistake it had been to locate the chief west terminal of the road at that point! More questions . . . more trouble for the administrators of the company!

Yet the first six months of 1853—immediately following the opening of the line to the Ohio—showed gross receipts of $1,218,834.99, which compared more than well with the entire twelve months of the last fiscal year. These earnings were maintained right through to the end of the fiscal year of 1853, when twelve months showed a gross of $2,033,419.80. Assuredly, it had been no mistake to build the road through to the hinterland. Wheeling was the only question.

The report of the following year shows, for the first time, the results of the working of the line to Wheeling for a full twelvemonth. The Board Tree Tunnel had been completed, and the extensive "shoofly" track over it, over which one rode but a little time ago, had been abandoned. The gross revenues of Baltimore and Ohio had reached $3,645,609.43; an astonishing increase of $1,612,189.63 over the preceding year. The stockholders of the company should have warmed to such a figure. Yet they did not.

For income means but little until one places it alongside outgo. The expenses of conducting the road in that same fiscal year (ending September 30, 1854) also had taken a generous rise. They were $2,026,211.69. In the preceding year, they had been $1,235,227.01, when the road had been worked at a fine fraction over sixty per cent. The editor of the

American Engineer apparently had been right when he said that it was a delusion to expect railroads to be operated at fifty per cent.

.   .   .   .

With all of its increased earnings, the Baltimore and Ohio company, in the fall of 1854, continued to be seriously embarrassed for lack of sufficient working capital. It had fallen into the bad habit of borrowing on short-term notes, sometimes even to meet current expenses. These, the banks shaded rather neatly for it. But the money that the road most needed should come in larger quantities. To meet the rapidly growing coal traffic, sidings were essential; it was considered highly necessary, too, to complete the double-tracking of the line, at least as far as Piedmont. To add many more miles of siding and passing tracks and—most urgent of all—to line many of its tunnels,[1] long and short, required much money.

To the city of Baltimore, its staunch ally and chief employer, the road once again appealed for help. Very plainly it stated its physical needs. In the meantime, business Baltimore shivered at the very thought that its chief commercial artery might be closed for a time—short or long—by a collapse of one or more of these tunnels up in the mountains. And it carried its anxiety to the doors of the City Hall.

To this anxiety the City Council responded; a loan of $5,000,000 to the road ($4,500,000 for the railroad company, and $500,000 for a sinking fund for eventual retirement) was passed. It was decided that $2,000,000 of this grant should go to meet the company's most pressing debts, another $2,000,000 should pay for additional track, the final $500,000 for lining the tunnels. . . .

---

[1] By rock constantly falling from their ceilings, these bores were giving a vast deal of trouble and worry to the operators of the line. Safety of life, as well as a complete tie-up of the road, was endangered. Finally it became necessary to close Kingwood Tunnel for a full year and to revert to the abandoned and highly difficult shoofly track over the mountain. Before Kingwood was reopened, it had been relined from end to end, and so rendered perfectly safe.

It was one thing for the Baltimore City Council to order
$5,000,000 in bonds struck off the printing presses and quite
another for the city treasurer to go out and sell these bonds in a
badly upset money market.   The credit of Baltimore was not
so good then as it is today, and, after some long months of real
effort, only about $1,200,000 worth of the bonds had been sold.
Which gave the Baltimore and Ohio company barely enough
to meet its most pressing debts and to keep going.   The lining
of the tunnels was deferred, until there came a day when a
portion of the ceiling of Kingwood collapsed.   After which,
the money to line all the bad tunnels *had* to be raised—and
was raised.

.   .   .   .

Neither did the fall of 1855 show any great improvement
in the situation.   The gross had risen to $3,711,453.85, a
fractional increase over the previous year.   Yet, the operating
ratio, which had dropped in the preceding twelvemonth to 55
per cent, had again increased—to 56 per cent.   (In the following two years it was to drop to 54 per cent, and then rise again,
to 60.)

So runs the record of those hard years.   'Fifty-six, with
Chauncy Brooks as president, saw substantial increase in the
gross—to $4,385,951.87—with a holding in check of the
expenditures; so it finally was possible to quit issuing promissory notes, hit-or-miss, and to pay cash at least for pay roll and
for ordinary supplies.   In '57, the gross again climbed—this
time to $4,616,918.95.   The Baltimore and Ohio was begin-
ning to be quite a railroad.   Traffic was increasing upon it,
all the while.   Even the Wheeling line began at last to show
real returns.   The Central Ohio Railroad had been completed
from Bellaire through Zanesville and Newark to Columbus,
where it enjoyed large connection facilities.   Between Bellaire
and Benwood—four miles south of Wheeling—there had been
put into operation a ferry with a daily capacity of several
hundred passengers and at least a thousand tons of freight.

The result of this was to bring to the Wheeling line, in the first twelve months of operation of the Central Ohio, 86,000 tons of freight and 21,692 passengers.   Moreover, the Cleveland and Wellsville Railroad, which previously had ended at Wellsville, forty miles up the Ohio from Wheeling, had just been extended to Bridgeport, Ohio, right across the river and easily reached by the Roebling suspension bridge.   Wheeling at last was beginning to give some justification for its choice as a railroad terminus.

All of this was prior to the devastating panic of the autumn of 1857.

That crash fell with full force upon the struggling Baltimore and Ohio.   Direct reference to it is to be found in the company's annual report (the thirty-second) issued under date of October 1, 1858.   In a brief word, it notices the effect of the unprecedented financial crisis through which the country has passed during the past fiscal year, as well as the "injudicious competition between the four great Atlantic lines (the Pennsylvania, the Erie, the New York Central and the Baltimore and Ohio)."   This last was as much responsible for the troubles of all four roads as the financial crisis itself.   In fact, it had not a little to do with bringing about that crisis.   There was, of course, in those days—and for many and many a year thereafter—no state regulation of railroad rates.   The point where the roads were finally forced to abandon cutthroat competition and to come together and make agreements in their own behalf had not yet been reached.   But was being approached.

This same report (1858) shows most clearly the effect of national depression upon the Baltimore and Ohio's earnings. In a year, they had fallen over three quarters of a million dollars. The Northwestern Virginia, which had been opened from Grafton to Parkersburg and which now was under the full ownership and operation of the Baltimore and Ohio, took in within the year a gross revenue of $248,000.06, and cost $253,252.79 to operate.   Not much opportunity for the stockholders in such a condition as that!

The chief trouble under which that particular line labored was the lack of proper connections to the west at Parkersburg. The ancient town of Marietta, a few miles up the Ohio River, had grown alarmed at the possibility that she might not find herself upon one of the new through railroad routes. Carefully had she planned, therefore, not only that her own through rail route to Cincinnati should depart from her own borders, but also that it should manage to avoid comfortably the immediate neighborhood of Parkersburg. . . . That this was shortsighted and a very great mistake was quickly shown. And, within two or three years, a branch track of the Marietta and Cincinnati was laid down to the water's edge at Belpre, opposite Parkersburg. A ferry was established—which ten years later was superseded by a long high bridge over the Ohio —and the Northwestern Virginia Branch of the Baltimore and Ohio came into its own.

.   .   .   .

All of these things—and many others—had been placed before the Garrett committee. It delved deeply into the finances of the road; yet, when all was said and done, it evolved the somewhat remarkable special scrip dividend which was passed in 1856. This radical step was, at the time, the source of much criticism, and eventually it produced a sharply contested legal action which was carried into the high courts. In brief, it provided that the stockholders of the company should be reimbursed; $3,500,000 on the twentieth of the following January; in scrip, fundable in bonds of the company, bearing six per cent interest. These bonds were to be convertible into stock at par value, at the pleasure of the board upon a two-thirds vote, or upon a majority of the stockholders in general meeting, to be called upon a thirty days' notice.

This resolution was passed December 1, 1856. On the seventeenth of the same month, both the city of Baltimore and the state of Maryland as stockholders went into the courts and secured an injunction restraining the railroad company from

taking this dividend action. The result of this official step
was greatly to arouse the private stockholders, who, under the
leadership of Mr. Garrett, charged that both state and city
interests had too long dominated the management of the road.[1]
. . . For four long years, the entire scrip-dividend matter
held in the courts. Eventually it was determined in the
United States Circuit Court (November 1, 1860) that it was
entirely proper and legal. The case was not appealed. Both
city and state withdrew their opposition and the distribution
was made in actual stock; 1853 shares to the state, 12,415
shares to the city, and 11,594 shares to the private stockholders.

This was one of the early triumphs of John W. Garrett.
Slowly but surely his sun was rising into the picture of the
Baltimore and Ohio. At a later time, he was to succeed,
despite great opposition, in reorganizing the board so that the
private interests would have twenty-three directors, or a
majority of five over state and city combined. After which,
his first triumph was to be rendered complete.

·   ·   ·   ·   ·   ·

In the meantime, Mr. Garrett, Mr. Hopkins and their
investigating committee were having other experiences in the
finances of Baltimore and Ohio. Theirs had become a minority
committee of the board. A majority one, composed chiefly of
stockholders who represented the interests of the city and the

[1] "At the time when Mr. Garrett was made President of the great Maryland
Railway, and for many years thereafter, the State of Maryland really owned
the road and the state and city Directors were in a majority on the board. In
order therefore to maintain his influence in the management, Mr. Garrett, realized
that he must have a dominant influence in the State Government, and that,
most important of all, he must have a Governor who would be guided by him
in all matters pertaining to the affairs of this great property, which was then,
as it is now, the greatest asset Maryland possessed. To that end, his agents
were busily engaged in politics from one end of the state to the other, and to
the day of his death, the word of the President of the Baltimore & Ohio was
law to Governors, all state officials, including senators and members of the
National House of Representatives."—From *Graphic Sketches from the History
of the Baltimore and Ohio Railroad* by Paul Winchester.

JOHN W. GARRETT.
President, 1858–1884.
From a contemporary likeness.

"Railway Cars in America."
An early English idea of them.

From a drawing in the *Illustrated London News* for April 6, 1861.

state, had, on April 14, 1858, rendered a report showing that the floating debt of the company, on the nineteenth day of the preceding February, was $1,707,957, with available assets on hand to meet it of $138,283. The majority committee suggested that President Brooks be instructed to make no charge to the construction account, except for arching the tunnels—a work which was then nearing completion.

To this report, great exception was taken by Mr. Garrett, Mr. Hopkins and their committee. A minority report was filed, which characterized the other as "unjust, incorrect and injudicious in its entire scope, spirit and tone." It asserted that the Parkersburg Branch (Northwestern Virginia), which was to have cost approximately $3,500,000, had actually cost $5,000,000; and that, if the Baltimore and Ohio had not advanced from its own treasury $1,415,986 to complete that line, it would not be seriously embarrassed financially. The minority committee agreed that further expenditures should be limited to completing the tunnel linings, and expressed its belief that, with rigid economy in the administration of the road, all of its pressing obligations would be met.

This report, as might have been expected, made a good impression on the merchants and bankers of Baltimore, as well as the other private stockholders of the company. It also helped make John W. Garrett its president.[1] He was hailed as the saviour of the situation. And on the seventeenth of November, 1858, he was elected its president—at a salary of $4000 a year.

.   .   .   .

John W. Garrett was the son of Robert Garrett, a Baltimore merchant of high standing. He was a man of vast powers and

---

[1] Oddly enough, it had been Garrett who had gone to S. M. Felton, then president of the Philadelphia, Wilmington and Baltimore Railroad, to ask him to become president of Baltimore and Ohio. This honor Felton declined. But, in declining, Mr. Felton urged that Mr. Garrett himself accept the presidency of the road from Baltimore to the West. Which, a little later, was done.

abilities. Of huge size, he usually dominated the men round-about him, both physically and mentally. He possessed all the great qualities of leadership. He had, when he needed it, real charm. He could, upon occasion, be as tactful and as diplomatic as he was, upon other occasions, brusque and commanding. Seemingly, he could bend as easily as he could remain firm; and he was the personification of firmness itself.

Of the old order of the large men of the Baltimore and Ohio, he was the last. And the greatest. For twenty-six years he ruled the road as its president; with an iron hand. Until it became known colloquially as "Garrett's road," just as the Pennsylvania of those days was known as "Tom Scott's road," and the New York Central as "Vanderbilt's." That was, indeed, the era of personal railroading. Of doubt and disaster in rail transport giving way to soundness and large profits; of men reaching for the smaller and the weaker roads and gathering them into their larger combinations; not so much with thought for the public weal as for the aggrandizement of their own properties. . . . It was the era that immediately preceded the coming of strict regulation; both state and federal. It was the era of fine pickings. Of sharp business. In all of it, the Baltimore and Ohio forged still further forward.

.   .   .   .

The first annual report which carries the signature of Mr. Garrett as president was the company's thirty-third, and it bears the date of October 1, 1859. It shows the country still to be in a state of considerable financial depression, the after-math of the great panic of the fall of '57. The Baltimore and Ohio territory was not exempt from these hard times. The gross earnings of the Main Stem alone, within a year, had declined $237,867—and this was to be charged to the general depression. . . . But this was not all of the story of the year's operations. The end of the chapter was one of triumph; the net earnings of the company actually had increased, radically. By sharply cutting down expenses. A fundamental railroading principle used many times thereafter when a property began to drift shoalward.[1]

A real triumph, this, for Mr. Garrett; in the first year of his presidency! (Incidentally, the road had been operated for a twelvemonth at a ratio of about 45 per cent.) The way that all of this was done is best shown in the president's own words, in his first annual report. He says, in part:

At the commencement of the year it was palpable from the general prostration of business and the large financial engagements of the company that, in order to produce satisfactory results to shareholders and the taxpayers of the city and the state, every judicious economy in management should be effected.

Accordingly, the attention of the officers of the company was directed to careful supervision of the economy of detail in the expenditures of their respective departments and the great reform of reduced and slow speed with heavy burden trains and moderate and safe speed in passenger trains was introduced.

The fruition of the system has been presented and is alike most satisfactory and remarkable, although inaugurated during a period in which, in numerous cases, unprecedently low rates of transportation prevailed and a serious conflict with the

[1] The following table shows the division of income and outgo for the twelve months ending September 30, 1859:

REVENUES

	1858	1859	Decrease
Main Stem	$3,856,485.79	$3,618,618.45	$237,867.34
Washington Branch	469,422.92	442,219.53	27,203.39
Northwestern Virginia	248,004.06	240,171.29	7,832.77
	$4,573,912.77	$4,301,009.27	$272,903.50

EXPENSES

	1858	1859	Decrease
Main Stem	$2,531,199.29	$1,684,997.84	$846,201.45
Washington Branch	202,453.64	173,679.25	28,774.39
Northwestern Virginia	253,252.79	198,270.58	54,982.21
	$2,986,905.72	$2,056,947.67	$929,958.05

Total increase of net earnings for the system, $657,054.55.

great rival Atlantic lines was maintained effectively and successfully by the Baltimore and Ohio company in sustaining the cardinal policy of protecting and promoting the business interests of Baltimore.

The speed of heavy freight trains was reduced nearly forty per cent, viz.: to eight and nine miles per hour; of passenger trains to twenty and twenty-five miles per hour. In this connection the subjoined extract from the report of the Master of the Road is interesting: "Of both the Main Stem and branches it is proper to remark that a general reduction in speed has produced a most favorable effect in maintaining our road at greatly diminished expense, as well as a great diminution in the number and extent of casualties."

The black record of but a few years before was still sharply in the minds of the operating department of the road.

.   .   .   .

Economies. . . . Efficiencies. . . . The extravagances of the past being wiped out. But not that there was anything small or mean in the mind of John W. Garrett as, at the end of September, 1859, he contemplated the future of Baltimore and Ohio. That mind leaped to large vision. The road was going to operate, and operate successfully, all its new miles of line. . . . It was going to add to them. It was going to rectify the error of preceding years and it was to enter Pittsburgh; at once. The long somnolent Pittsburgh and Connellsville Railroad project was being revived, with B. H. Latrobe at its head—as president and chief engineer. . . . Already forty-eight miles of that line, along the valley of the lower Monongahela, were in use—from Turtle Creek, where there was a connection by the Pennsylvania into Pittsburgh, twelve or fourteen miles distant, into Connellsville. The road was preparing to gain its own entrance into Pittsburgh; and it was being builded east from Connellsville to connect with the then Main Stem of the Baltimore and Ohio at Cumberland. The great summit tunnel, thirty-three miles west of Cumberland and 4650 feet in length, which afterwards was to be known as the Sand Patch, already was under construction. Some $200,000 had been expended in work upon it. . . . Its beginnings had been halted by the panic of '57. But now ways and means were being found somehow for a swift resumption of the work.

The Baltimore and Ohio, vastly expanded during the decade of the 'fifties, was, none the less, just entering upon its period of real expansion. Not only was the Parkersburg line within ninety days of an adequate ferry connection with the Marietta and Cincinnati, but Mr. Garrett already was making his tentative plans to capture that road, as well as the Ohio and Mississippi and the Central Ohio, in order that some day they might become appendages, instead of mere connections, of the parent Baltimore and Ohio.

There was, indeed, nothing small about the mind of that president. All the while, he visioned great things. Sleeping cars came within his ken. In coöperation with President Felton, of the connecting Philadelphia, Wilmington and Baltimore, through cars of this type now were being run between Philadelphia and Washington. This obviated the time and nuisance of changing cars which hitherto had been necessary at Baltimore; and sometimes at Havre de Grace.

The use of sleeping cars upon the Main Stem also was being extended. Two day coaches of the Washington Branch and two which had been purchased from the Hempfield Railroad were being refitted with berths, for night use. It was a real idea. Yet America still awaited the coming of that ingenious carpenter from western New York, George M. Pullman, with his magnificent vision of comfortable sleeping equipages upon the railroad. In the meantime, the operating heads of the Baltimore and Ohio and its competitors were doing their best with the material closest at hand.

All these ideas, John W. Garrett formulated; and still others. He was going to make Baltimore, nearly two hundred miles distant from the open sea, a great ocean port; a world port, if you please. That would mean, not merely vastly improved docks and warehouses for his road at the waterside of its chief town, but a Baltimore and Ohio steamship line, whose vessels would find their way to all the important ports of the seven seas.

Seemingly, there was little limit to the vision of the new president. And yet, with it all, he was hard-headed, sagacious, shrewd. His feet were planted firmly on the ground. Rome was not built in a day. It would be, in hard fact, nearly twenty years before the dreams of John W. Garrett for a vastly enlarged Baltimore and Ohio would finally come true. . . . In the meantime, step by step . . . steady building . . . and firm.

But the worst had been passed. A property, which for years had stood in dire need of real leadership, finally had attained it. The clouds were rolling back. The sun was brightly shining in Maryland that autumn of 1859 as the first annual report of Garrett came rolling off the presses. . . . When suddenly there flashed from under the fingers of the telegraph operator at Monocacy a message which was to reverberate around all creation and send millions of men into the mightiest conflict the world had ever known.

CHAPTER XVIII

RUMBLINGS OF APPROACHING CONFLICT

The John Brown Raid at Harpers Ferry, October 17, 1859—The
Road's Telegraphic Record of the Stirring Event—The Putting
Down of an Insurrection—Progress of the Garrett Adminis-
tration.

IT is early morning . . . the morning of the seventeenth
day of October, 1859. Grey and misty dawn has given way
to the definite coming of another day. . . . It is the telegraph
room of Camden Station. The night operator sits at his desk;
dozing but uneasy. For some hours past, the telegraph line
has been out of order. Something must have happened to it;
up the road. He wonders what may have been the trouble.
Yet does not let it worry him too much. It has a way, at
times, of going out of business. The night operator is more
interested in knowing whether his day relief will come in
promptly.

Then, suddenly and without announcement, his sounder
begins to click. He looks automatically at the great round
face of the clock just over his head and notes the time. He
will do well to remember this hour; in all of its details. For it
is one in which history is being made.

The sounder clicks its message, distinctly. It is a telegram for William Prescott Smith, master of transportation
of the Baltimore and Ohio Railroad, and the right hand of its
president, John W. Garrett. The operator dips his pen in the
inkwell and begins writing, quickly—after the fashion of all
telegraph operators. And this is what rolls from under his pen:

MONOCACY, 7.05 A.M., Oct. 17, 1859

W. P. SMITH
    Baltimore

Express train bound east under my charge was stopped this morning at Harpers Ferry by armed Abolitionists.   They have possession of the bridge and of the arms and armory of the United States.   Myself and baggagemaster have been fired at and Hayward, the colored porter, is wounded very severely, being shot through the body, the ball entering the body below the left shoulder-blade and coming out under the left side. The doctor says he cannot survive.   They are headed by a man who calls himself Anderson and number about 150 strong.   They say they have come to free the slaves, and intend to do it at all hazards.

The leader of these men requested me to say to you that this is the last train that shall pass the bridge, either east or west.   If it is attempted it will be at the peril of the lives of those having them in charge.   When daylight appeared we were finally permitted to pass, after having been detained from half past one o'clock to half past six.   It has been suggested that you had better notify the Secretary of War at once.   The telegraph wires are cut east and west of Harpers Ferry and this is the first station that I could send a despatch from.

A. J. PHELPS.

Phelps is the conductor of the eastbound night express, coming down from Wheeling. . . . Obviously, his telegram is that of a man laboring under great excitement.   The night operator reads and rereads it, finds a messenger and dispatches it to the home of Mr. Smith.   It is probable that a copy also goes to Mr. Garrett.   There are, of course, in that day, no telephones; and sending dispatches by messenger is a slow and cumbersome business.   But, nevertheless, it has to be done.

Mr. Smith has apparently lost little sleep—or breakfast— over the alarming telegram from Conductor Phelps.   For the telegraph files of the railroad company show that he did not take the trouble to reply to it until nearly two hours later.

Apparently, the message from Phelps annoyed him, not a little. For we find his answer to it, reading:

BALTIMORE, Oct. 17, 1859. 9 A.M.

A. J. PHELPS
    Conductor of the Express East at Ellicotts Mills

Your despatch is evidently exaggerated and written under excitement. Why should our trains be stopped by Abolitionists and how do you know they are such and that they number a hundred or more? What is their object? Let me know at once before we proceed to extremities.

W. P. SMITH.

Not an easy message to be received and answered, accurately and graciously, by a man already much perturbed. We can imagine Mr. Phelps biting the end of his lead pencil and trying to control his overwrought feelings as he replies:

ELLICOTT's MILLS, Oct. 17, 1859

W. P. SMITH
    Baltimore

My despatch was not exaggerated, neither was it written under excitement, as you suppose. I have not made it half as bad as it is. The Captain told me that his object was to liberate all the slaves and that he expected a reinforcement of 1500 men to assist him. Hayward, the negro porter, was shot through the body and I suppose by this time is dead. The Captain also said that he did not want to shed any more blood.

I will call at your office immediately on my arrival and tell you all. One of my passengers was taken prisoner and held as such for some time. I will bring him to see you also.

A. J. PHELPS.

After which, it may be assumed that Mr. Smith lost but little further time in getting in touch with President Garrett, who promptly took up the matter with the military authorities at Washington. There was no telling what this "Captain" (it quickly developed that he was not "Anderson," but one John Brown of Osawatomie, Kansas) would do, if he were not curbed, and quickly. . . . As Mr. Garrett telegraphed the Secretary of War, the following message—a press dispatch—was coming by telegraph into the newspaper offices of Baltimore and the other large cities of the land:

FREDERICK, MD., Oct. 17, 1859

To the Baltimore Newspaper Press

Information has been received here this morning of a formidable negro insurrection at Harpers Ferry. An armed band of abolitionists have full possession of Harpers Ferry and the United States Arsenal. One of the railroad hands, a negro, was killed whilst trying to accompany the express train from Wheeling to Baltimore through the town.

They have arrested two men who came in with a load of wheat and took their wagon and loaded it with rifles and sent them into Maryland. They are led by about 250 whites with a gang of negroes fighting for their freedom. They gave Conductor Phelps notice that they would not allow any more trains to pass.

The telegraph wires are cut east and west of Harpers Ferry. This intelligence was brought by the train from the west. Great excitement here. The leader told Conductor Phelps of the Baltimore and Ohio Railroad train that they were determined to have liberty, or die in the attempt.

Their object in stopping further trains is to save bloodshed by preventing the arrival of troops. One of the passengers was interrogated by them for half an hour.

So, in the faded telegraph files of the Baltimore and Ohio, is told the story of the ignition of one of the greatest conflicts of all time. . . . For a long time, this mine was being prepared. Only the most foolish sort of an optimist could have seen anything but vast trouble impending in the long continuing and steadily increasing dispute between the states of the North and those of the South; over, not merely the question of slavery, but also that of states' rights, which was so hopelessly entangled with it. Fate gave old John Brown the lighted match by which the mine was kindled and set afire. Some other actor might have been chosen for beginning the mighty tragedy. It had to be some one. And John Brown chanced to be that one.

. . . .

Of the political events that led up to that memorable October morning of 1859, one gains a good knowledge from the columns of the Baltimore newspapers of the time. Even though, prior to that day, these give no inkling of the particular trouble that was brewing right at Harpers Ferry. For it was not news worth recording that a tall, bent, bearded man—his speech and manner betraying clearly that he was a stranger to the Maryland country—eight months earlier had appeared at the little village of Sharpsburg and had rented the old-time Kennedy farm near there. Brown—although that was not the name he gave at the beginning—had told the neighbors that he was something of a miner and was prospecting in the neighborhood. The fact that he frequently was seen carrying around bits of rock in his great hands gave credence to his story. . . . The large double wooden boxes which arrived at the Kennedy farm were said to contain mining machinery, and so they might easily have done.

The country folk about Sharpsburg were inclined to regard this mild-mannered stranger with kindliness. They did not take much stock in his belief that the earth under them was to give forth rare minerals. Yet they felt, somehow, that, if the newcomer did meet with success eventually, in some way they would share it with him.

Those boxes, opened secretly, yielded no mining machinery; but two hundred fine new rifles, an equal number of revolvers, and, oddly enough, a thousand spears and tomahawks. It was quite a war for which old John Brown of Osawatomie was preparing. Apparently, his imagination conceived the idea of no larger stand of arms, at least until he should overpower and seize the rich prize of the nearby government arsenal at Harpers Ferry. After which, there would be abundant weapons for the negro army—which he and his fellows were so soon to equip and put into action. . . . Brown seems to have thought all this out quite carefully.

. . . .

It was a few minutes after midnight on that early Monday morning of the seventeenth of October that he began to put his plan into action. The eastbound night express on the Baltimore and Ohio was due to come through Harpers Ferry not long after that hour. (The westbound train had passed the small village on its way to Wheeling some hours before and had been given no suspicion of the vast deal of trouble that was brewing there.) The passenger station, then as now, stood right at the west portal of the bridge; save that the turn of the track from the structure of those days was far more abrupt than it is today.

As the express train, grinding under its old-fashioned hand brakes, came to a slow stop on the curve, both Phelps, its conductor, and William McKay, its engineer, noticed suddenly that both sides of the track were lined with men, all armed, and some of them carrying lanterns or torches. There were no other lights to be seen in the village. . . . Jacob Cromwell, the baggage-master of the train, after a moment, climbed down from the car and, with his lantern in hand, went forward, alongside the locomotive and just ahead of it. . . . Two men stepped forward out of the throng and stopped him, at the points of their rifles.

From this point forward, there seems to be some confusion in the different chronicles. For, at that very moment, there came the sharp crack of a rifle through the dark, and Hayward Sheppard, the colored porter who had been attached to the station for some ten or twelve years, fell upon the ground. . . . There was other fighting, back in the dark toward the town. Fontaine Beckham, station agent of the Baltimore and

Ohio at Harpers Ferry since first the road had been builded through there, mayor and a man of parts in the community—at one time he had been deputy sheriff—was instantly killed, at a single shot. . . . A freight train lay upon a nearby siding and its crew joined in the battle. Evans Dorsey, of Martinsburg, who was one of these, was severely injured. . . . It was very dark and the fighting seems to have been of a desultory order.

In the meantime, Phelps had ordered McKay to back the train out of the bridge entrance and down beside the station. The conductor then went forward and met Brown—who, he understood, was named Anderson. Phelps told Brown that his train carried the United States mail and that, therefore, no one had the right or the authority to stop it. Brown listened attentively and finally told the conductor that he would give the train five minutes to pass through the bridge and be off and on its way. . . . But Phelps hesitated. All the way throughout that passage, armed men stood. And he feared, moreover, that the bridge structure itself might be cut or otherwise weakened, so it would go down under the weight of the train.

He decided to wait until dawn; and wait he did, while the armed men stood quietly roundabout. He found his way in the dark to the Wager House, where the hotel clerk gave it as his belief that really serious trouble was stirring in the town. Then Phelps went back to his train and helped stand guard over it until dawn. It was very, very dark. Not only were there no lights in the village, but Brown's men had ordered the lamps in the cars extinguished. The few passengers in the day coaches huddled together in the dark, in fear and trembling.

At five in the morning, dawn faintly began to show. Phelps then decided to go forward. . . . The train crossed the long bridge very carefully and slowly, nor did its engineer see fit to resume full speed until he was well out of the danger zone and the dense foggy grey of the very early morning had given way to definite daylight. . . . Not until they reached the Monocacy bridge could they find a telegraph office open and manned.

And there they woke up sleeping Camden Station with their astounding message of alarm.

.   .   .   .   .

So, in a few paragraphs, may be told the story of the beginnings of the John Brown Raid as they affected the Baltimore and Ohio. All the details of that dramatic day are not pertinent to this narrative—daylight slowly breaking, the neighborhood aroused and piling in and toward Harpers Ferry, awakened and armed and angry, but thoroughly unorganized. . . . Desultory fighting all that Monday. . . . Stray shots . . . being increased all day. Rumors of a countryside thoroughly aroused. Of bands of men—whites and negroes—being hastily recruited and armed and on their way. . . . All day long, the shooting increasing. Men making their perilous way across the stones jutting up from the rough surfaces of the Potomac and the Shenandoah. One of them falling into the stream, shot and instantly killed by a bullet in his back, and drifting down the swift current. . . . The women of the town opening their houses and tearing sheets into long, thin strips, for bandages. . . . The serious business of war. . . . And John Brown and his men managing to make a small, but seemingly impregnable, fortress for themselves in the engine house of the arsenal; a small, stout brick building just inside the gate of the government reservation.

One can easily imagine Mr. Garrett, sitting in the elaborate old President's Room of Camden Station, consumed with rage at this hocus-pocus on his line, and his own impotency in regard to all of it. . . . The Main Stem of the road completely tied up and out of business. (How many more times there were to come in the next six years when a similar fate was to be visited upon the Baltimore and Ohio!) One can see Mr. Garrett sending for his master of transportation and faithful "man Friday," William Prescott Smith, and pouring upon his defenseless head the phials of his wrath . . . the telegraph operators sending orders, this way and that, as far as their blocked wires will permit.

Washington is sending the Marines—the good, old, faithful Marines—ninety of them in all. . . . Also that brilliantly seasoned colonel, Robert E. Lee, who is to assume command of the entire ridiculous situation at Harpers Ferry. In the meantime, the militia of Baltimore—that faithful standby in time of trouble in the town and roundabout it—is again being mobilized. Passenger cars and a sturdy locomotive to draw them are waiting under the train shed of Camden, ready to take them up to the scene of the insurrection.

.   .   .   .   .   .

After all, it is the Marines that finally save the day for old Law and Order. The hardest fighting comes at about half past three o'clock Tuesday morning. . . . Lee, who already is upon the stage of a theater of conflict afterwards to be familiar indeed to him, at last is in command of the United States forces. Before he begins to fire, he offers surrender to John Brown, and to him and his men the protection of the troops against mob violence, until the pleasure of the United States in the entire matter shall be known. With cool courage, Brown refuses to surrender. He will die in his tracks. . . . Rifles and battering-rams are brought to bear against the stout bulk of the little engine house. There is an hour . . . two hours . . . nearly three . . . of terrific fighting, until Brown, sorely wounded and surrounded by the bodies, dead or nearly dying, of the insanely brave men who accepted him as their leader, finally is compelled to give up. . . . He falls, bleeding and exhausted, almost into the very arms of Lee.

.   .   .   .   .   .

The rest of the tragic story is to be told in even less compass. Lee returns to Baltimore, is met and congratulated by Garrett —the beginning of a friendship which is not to terminate until long years later.

Brown goes to the county jail in the little nearby shire town of Charles Town to await trial. . . . The trial is swift and terrible. Justice rushes in on fleet heels. The entire nation—North and South—is arousing, as never before it has been aroused; men, and their organizations, their communities and their great broad states are aligning themselves for the great conflict that is to follow—inevitably. . . . John Brown is either hero or else—contemptuously—"old Brown," just according to the corner of the land in which you happen to find yourself. No one is neutral—either in regard to him, or seemingly in regard to anything else. The nation is mad, unstrung . . . in battling mood.

The verdict of the jury in Charles Town Court House also is inevitable. The man from Osawatomie must die; must be hanged by the neck until he is dead. The sentence of the court is carried out—in the same swift measure. At eleven fifteen o'clock on the morning of Friday, December 2, 1859, in the presence of long lines of troops drawn up, and ten thousand white faces held tense behind them, John Brown ascends to the gallows platform, speaks a word of prayer to his God, the noose is adjusted, the trap sprung, and the long body held inert suspended in mid-air. The record is made that, for thirty-five minutes after the execution, his heart continues to beat. It is hard indeed to kill old John Brown.

And hard to kill the memory of this day. In the North, the churches have been open all night long, their auditoriums crowded with kneeling folk, praying and crying, the church bells wailing out their pæans for the dead man. . . . In the South, the excitement is of a different sort; but it is not less. The anger of the Southerners also knows no bounds. The stage is indeed set for the greatest tragedy that the world has ever known. And there is to be little holding back of the curtain.

·　　·　　·　　·　　·　　·　　·

In such an hour, in such an atmosphere, it is hard to speak calmly of the mundane things of the Baltimore and Ohio. The reports of the company that follow seem to be in all of their many details—large or petty—but empty and useless things. And yet, as a matter of historical record, as well as

JOHN BROWN'S FORT.

The engine house of the United States Arsenal at Harpers Ferry, which stood near the Baltimore and Ohio tracks and which John Brown used as his last stronghold.

From an old photograph.

THE UNITED STATES ARSENAL AT HARPERS FERRY, VIRGINIA.
As it appeared before the Civil War.

From a contemporary photograph.

of fairness to the beginning of the remarkable administration of Mr. Garrett, it should be noted that in the short interval between the John Brown Raid and Fort Sumter—and the stupendous events that followed in its train—great progress was being made by the new management of the company. With the old political control beginning to be eliminated, and a businesslike one substituted. The decline in gross receipts from the year ending October 1, 1858, to that ending on the same day in 1859, had been changed to a perceptible increase within the next twelvemonth—$303,584.49, to be exact—; bringing those total receipts up to nearly four million dollars ($3,922,202.94). At the same time, operating expenses had been still further cut; $68,382.23. The result of all of this, quite naturally, was to place the road in a stronger financial position than it had enjoyed for many years past. It not only began making all of its purchases for cash, but, because of its vastly improved position, it was able to cut its interest charges; $16,746.64 as compared with the preceding year, and $79,383.96 with the one that preceded that. As an earnest of its good position, it resumed dividend payments upon its common stock, paying two semi-annual dividends of 4½ per cent each. And this, in addition to the long deferred and much discussed extra dividend of more than three million dollars.

All in all, Mr. Garrett would seem to have large opportunity for pride in the beginning of his stewardship. A few excerpts from his report, dated October 1, 1860 (the thirty-fourth annual report of the company), will show the real progress that was being made. He says:

> . . . The careful cultivation of the local trade begins to effect favorable results. The charges upon way traffic have been arranged at rates materially under the average tariffs of other roads; and the board have the satisfaction of witnessing a marked development of business, population and prosperity in the sections of Maryland and Virginia traversed by the road and its branches.

The number of tons hauled on the Main Stem in 1859 was 882,076, whilst during the past year the aggregate is 1,005,837 tons. The largest tonnage in any former year was in 1857, viz: 895,401 tons. The excess of tonnage for the past year, over any previous year, is therefore 110,436 tons. . . .

The quantity of bituminous coal, paying freight, transported during the year has been 427,793 tons—an increase compared with 1859, of 84,064 tons, and compared with 1858, of 94,996 tons. . . . The demonstrated economy of the use of this excellent fuel by northern railroads and for steam purposes generally adds constantly to the demand.

The shipments of cotton for the markets of Europe, and the Atlantic coast have been made, until recently, via New Orleans. In 1859, 6888 bales sought the Baltimore and Ohio route; and during the past year, these shipments have swelled to 14,182 bales. . . . A desirable outlet is offered for this extensive trade via Parkersburg, in view of its advantageous location on the Ohio River, barely 200 miles south of Pittsburgh. If proper facilities for export be afforded via Baltimore, large shipments of cotton will be attracted via this port. . . .

More and more was Mr. Garrett giving thought to the development of Baltimore as a large ocean port; as an entrepôt for Europe, in particular. In connection with his report of the fall of 1860, there is a sizable appendix in reference to a definite plan for assisting in the establishment of such a port at Baltimore. This will be noticed in detail in a later chapter of this book, when the entire connection of the large enterprise of the Baltimore and Ohio in establishing import and export trade through its principal city is considered at length.

It is in this same annual report that Mr. Garrett also gives a paragraph of attention to the upbuilding of a summer resort business—a thing which, up to that time, had attracted but scanty thought on the part of the average American railroad executive. He becomes interested in the tourist possibilities of the beautiful Alleghenies, and says:

The salubrious climate and beautiful country among the highlands of Western Maryland have elicited much attention during the past season; but the absence of adequate hotel accommodations has materially checked the tendency to seek these Glades for summer homes. Arrangements are being made for additional hotels; and a large population from the South, East and West will probably hereafter select this singularly picturesque and attractive region for summer resort. A considerable increase of local travel may be anticipated from this source.

Yet before the magnificent mountains of western Maryland could be made available to much travel, many things were to come to pass upon the lines of the Baltimore and Ohio that were to delay greatly any such tourist influx. The season of quiet between the exciting days of the late autumn of 1859 and the more strenuous ones of April, 1861, was but a short one indeed . . . and much disturbed. There was but little, if any, opportunity in it for Garrett and his associates to accomplish much of a constructive nature. Soon they were to be put to it to maintain their line as an open and secure line of transport, let alone make any improvements to it. The theater for the tremendous drama of the American Civil War finally had been arranged. And the Baltimore and Ohio ran squarely across its stage.

CHAPTER XIX

OPEN WARFARE AT LAST

The Beginnings of the Civil War—President Lincoln Passes Through
Baltimore—And so Does the Sixth Massachusetts—Rumors
and Alarms—Bloodshed—The Baltimore and Ohio Becomes
the Theater of Conflict.

On the twelfth day of April, 1861, the guns of the Confederacy blazed out upon old Fort Sumter, and one of the
mightiest wars of modern history was begun. It all was
tragedy—tragedy sublime. Compared with it, the dramatic
John Brown episode at Harpers Ferry was as a mere curtain
raiser to a main drama. Much of the latter also was to be
enacted within that marvelously beautiful natural amphi-
theater, held between the hills of Maryland and those of
Virginia. As early as the sixth day following Sumter—April 18
—a detachment of United States soldiers, guarding the arsenal
in that village, quickly accomplished the thing that old John
Brown had attempted; they fired the long brick buildings,
thoroughly, then marched out in good order, evacuating the
town and the historic rifle factory. At ten o'clock that same
evening, the Virginia state militia—forerunners of the growing
army of the Confederacy—marched in and assumed command
of the burning buildings, salvaged what they could out of them.
They placed a guard of infantry and artillery upon the double
bridge that carried railroad and highroad together across the
Potomac, and so practically severed communication upon the
Baltimore and Ohio.

From that very minute forward, the Baltimore and Ohio Railroad really began to assume its important rôle in the great modern tragedy of United States history. Through the four long years of the conflict, the railroad suffered, and suffered repeatedly. . . . For whole months at a time, it was out of business; a severed railroad, with its important Main Stem helpless . . . impotent. . . . Twice General Robert E. Lee led his grey hosts up to and over the Potomac, and on across the Baltimore and Ohio, which suffered very greatly.

The longest of these interruptions came in the very first year of the war—1861. It was marked, as we shall see presently, by a wholesale destruction of the railroad where it made its long crossing of the Valley of Virginia. Here it was that General Stonewall Jackson wreaked his fine strategy against it, confiscated its locomotives, either took or burned its cars, and tore up and utterly ruined its track. . . . Eighteen hundred and sixty-two brought with it the second serious interruption to the Main Stem; due to the invasion of Maryland by Lee in his Maryland čampaign. . . . 'Sixty-three was almost equally disastrous to the road. Again the indefatigable Lee moved menacingly toward the North; until the defeat at Gettysburg caused him to turn about and retreat to his own side of the Potomac. The year 1864 was marked by no such prolonged interruption of the Baltimore and Ohio; yet it was, in all, more fruitful of alarms or difficulties, actual or threatened, than those of any preceding twelvemonth of the war. It was remembered as presenting the greatest number of interruptions and difficulties from invading armies, guerilla attacks and the like that the war had yet brought forth. To this may be added the fact that the Potomac, which remained on bad behavior during much of the war, exhibited a restlessness within its banks, such as never before it had shown. It indulged in repeated freshets, which did great damage to the railroad property and called for almost unceasing efforts on the part of its workers.

Through all of these disquieting and violent scenes, the great figure of John W. Garrett walked, with an almost utter imperturbability. Like many of the important citizens of Baltimore at the outbreak of the Civil War, he had found much sympathy in his heart with the cause of the South. . . . The feeling of Baltimore for the states of the Confederacy was an entirely natural one. The great trading city close to the head of the Chesapeake Bay was, in no very large sense, of the North. Not only were many of her trade relations with the South, but her folk had intermarried with the Southern folk. Her climatic and social conditions were enough like those of the states well to the south of her so that she well might understand their problems and their perplexities. At the outbreak of the Civil War, Baltimore distinctly was a city of Southern sympathies. A thousand things pointed that way.

Mr. Garrett, at that time, made no secret of his own personal feelings. "Our Southern friends," was his way of speaking of the leaders of the Confederacy; in its beginning weeks and months. Sometimes, not often, he prefixed the adjective "misguided" in using this phrase. . . . Gradually it disappeared from his conversation. "Rebels" is a word that crept into his vocabulary. There are those who say that he, occasionally, as the war wore on and the property damage to the railroad that he headed began to mount to a pretty figure indeed, used fairly strong adjectives to give stress to "rebels." He was always an outspoken man. When occasion demanded, he never minced words.

Yet in the long run—and in fact the time was not long in arriving—he proved to be a mighty friend indeed of the North. At no time—even at the beginning—did he, by outer action or expression, show the slightest disloyalty to the Union. Some Baltimore people—and, at that, prominent Baltimore people —did show such disloyalty; and were promptly carted off to jail; at Fort McHenry, or elsewhere. In fact, one of John W. Garrett's regular tasks became the releasing of his somewhat rash friends from prison, after they had been there long enough

to repent of their hasty words.   One of these was Ross Winans.
Garrett forgot the old locomotive builder's continued animus
against his administration of the railroad long enough to help
him in his plight; although, to the end, Winans remained bitter,
a more or less outspoken adherent of the South.   He was to
keep himself, much of the time, locked within his house; away
from the looks and intercourse of other men.

To put the matter affirmatively, Garrett became not only a
strong adherent of the North and of the Union, but a large
power in helping it through to eventual victory.   In this, a
fortuitous circumstance aided greatly.   His friend, Edwin M.
Stanton, of Ohio, became, under Lincoln, Secretary of War
and, by the very nature of his position, a tremendous force in
the Lincoln Cabinet.   The ties that bound Garrett to
Stanton were more than those of friendship alone.   The
lawyer from the mid-West had been general counsel of the
Ohio Central Railroad, which, at the beginning of the Civil
War days, already was being merged into the parent Baltimore
and Ohio structure.   Garrett liked Stanton.   And Stanton
not only liked Garrett, but he had an abounding faith in him.
Hence his willingness to comply, whenever it was possible,
with Garrett's wishes and suggestions.

.   .   .   .

The actual and real relationship between Abraham Lincoln
and the Baltimore and Ohio began several weeks before Fort
Sumter.   It was in the fortnight just prior to his first inauguration; when his important journey from his home at
Springfield, Illinois, to the White House was to terminate in the
forty-mile trip over the Washington Branch from Baltimore to
Washington.

Elaborate preparations were made for this trip.   It was
arranged that Mr. Lincoln, accompanied by Mrs. Lincoln and
their three small sons, as well as a delegation of personal friends,
secretaries and the like, was to leave Springfield, February 11,
and proceed east by way of Indianapolis, Columbus, Pitts-

burgh, Buffalo, Albany, New York, Trenton, Philadelphia, Harrisburg and Baltimore to Washington. At these, and other points, he was to make more or less formal addresses. . . . The journey, in its earlier stages at least, was easily accomplished. From the notebook of Captain George W. Hazzard, who was detailed to accompany the President-elect to Washington, one gains these illuminating snatches:

. . . Mr. Lincoln is by no means ugly; he is one of the most excessively pleasant men I ever saw. . . . Don't get disheartened about secessioners; Mr. Lincoln is just the man for the emergency. . . . I believe that we shall get to Washington without any trouble, but all preparations to avoid difficulty will be made. . . .

From Buffalo, Captain Hazzard wrote to his wife:

Horace Greeley came with us yesterday from Conneaut to Erie. He talks very much like a Quaker. . . . We came into Cleveland through Euclid Street, and the scene was gorgeous. . . . Do you recall the finest house in that street, in fact the finest in Ohio? A brownstone Gothic, with observatory and spires on the roof? It is on the side of the street near the lake, and is the residence of Mr. Stone, president of the Lake Shore Railroad. Colonel Sumner, Judge Davis, Mr. Lamon and myself dined there on Friday evening. . . . There was a terrible jam at the depot yesterday. Mr. Hunter came very near having his arm broken. . . .

Every village sends a reception committee of twenty or thirty and some of them bring their wives, so that not only are all the seats in the car taken, but the passageway is filled with people standing. Neither the president nor his wife has one moment's respite and they are evidently tired of it. . . . It is probable that we shall be in Baltimore on Saturday, the 22nd. . . .

Yet, as the journey began to near its end, a new complexity showed in it. Southern soil at last was being approached;

slowly but surely. Philadelphia and Harrisburg were but a few miles north of Mason and Dixon's Line; Baltimore actually was below it. The men in the Lincoln entourage grew increasingly uncomfortable as they neared the last leg of the trip. Rumors, extremely disquieting, came to their ears. At Harrisburg, where Lincoln addressed the members of the Pennsylvania Legislature, it was whispered to the men close to him that the line of the Northern Central Railroad, between that city and Baltimore, had been mined, that the bridges had been weakened and that armed men lay in the bushes back from the railroad waiting for the Lincoln train to be wrecked, so that they might rush in and either kill or take prisoners those who were riding upon it. General Winfield Scott, the hero of the Mexican War and at that time in command of the United States Army, who had assumed charge of the party, finally spoke of these rumors to Lincoln. At first he scoffed at them. And when Scott first suggested that a secret and unheralded entrance be made into the Federal capital, Lincoln refused to hear of it.

"What would the nation think of its President stealing into the capital, like a thief in the night?" he said.

And yet, Lincoln finally gave way to the judgment of these advisers. He accepted the escort of Colonel Ward H. Lamon, who had accompanied him all the way from Springfield, and preparations were made for the journey on to Baltimore by the roundabout route of returning to Philadelphia over the main line of the Pennsylvania Railroad and thence over the Philadelphia, Wilmington and Baltimore. Under the personal guidance of Presidents Thomas A. Scott of the one road and Samuel M. Felton of the other, quick and imperative orders for the movement of a special locomotive and car from Harrisburg to West Philadelphia were given—and all telegraph wires immediately cut.[1]

---

[1] Few details of precaution were omitted. Mr. Felton arranged a clever plan to make sure of Lincoln's safe arrival in Washington. He gave instructions to the general superintendent of the P. W. & B., Mr. H. P. Kenney, that an important package was to go through on the night train on the evening of February 22, from

Throughout the night of February 22, Lincoln traveled, wrapped in an overcoat and a great shawl over it ; with Lamon as his companion and bodyguard. The special ran swiftly from Harrisburg to West Philadelphia. At Philadelphia, the eleven o'clock night express on the P. W. & B. for Baltimore was being held. The President-elect boarded it, almost unseen. . . . There was no incident on the trip to Baltimore, which was reached at a little after three in the morning.

It will be remembered that, in those days, through pas-

Philadelphia to Washington.   Conductor Litsenburg of the train was informed that, under no circumstances, was he to start his train until this package had been delivered personally into his hands.   He—Felton—was to be advised of the delivery of the package at Willard's Hotel, Washington, upon the following morning.

The plan worked.   The "important package," really consisting of nothing more valuable than a packet of old railroad reports, was handed to Litsenburg at his train as it stood waiting in the old P. W. & B. station at Broad and Prime streets, Philadelphia.   Just prior to that time, a tall man had alighted from a carriage and had entered the sleeping car of the train.   As he handed Litsenburg the tickets that provided for the transport of himself and his two companions on the sleeping car that night to Washington, the conductor remarked, lightly: "Well, old man, it's lucky for you that we've got to wait for some despatches; we're half an hour late now."   The tall man smiled in return.   He was none other than Abraham Lincoln.

So it was that Lincoln was safely embarked at Philadelphia.   He was well guarded in the sleeping car.   Not only by Pinkerton and by Ward Lamon, but also by one unknown to either of them, George Stearns of the railroad's own forces.   As the train left the station, the conductor drew Stearns aside and said to him: "George, I thought you and I were old friends.   Why didn't you tell me we had Old Abe aboard?"   Stearns, thinking that the secret had leaked out in some way, acknowledged that Mr. Lincoln was aboard and asked the conductor to share his responsibility.   "Yes," replied Litsenburg.   "I will, if it costs me my life."   So the two watched through the night, one at each door of the car.   It turned out afterwards that the conductor had mistaken his man.   A person, strongly resembling Mr. Lincoln, had boarded the train about half an hour before it had started; and this man the conductor had mistaken for the President-elect.

Neither did S. M. Felton sleep that night.   In the morning there came to him a message.   The telegraph wires between Philadelphia and Baltimore, which had been severed during the night, were rejoined at eight o'clock.   The first words they bore were from Washington and they were: "Your package has arrived safely and has been delivered."

sengers from Philadelphia, New York and other eastern points were transferred across Baltimore, from the President Street Station of the Philadelphia, Wilmington and Baltimore to the Camden Station of the Baltimore and Ohio, by means of the single-track road through Pratt Street. The cars, including the sleeping cars, were detached from the locomotive at the one station and were hauled, singly, by teams of horses, to the awaiting locomotive at the other.

While Baltimore was awaiting the coming of the newly elected President with ill-disguised interest, there was in the old Southern city little or no preparation for his entertainment. The Maryland Legislature had not asked him to address it, neither had the councils of Baltimore. The proprietor of the Eutaw House and the president of the Northern Central Railroad, Mr. Gittings, had offered him the hospitality of their roofs; but that was all. Baltimore was a town to be passed through quickly. There was no doubting its underlying sympathies. There would be crowds in the streets, but they might be unfriendly. It would be dangerous to take too many chances.

. . . .

At the early hour of morning in which Lincoln actually passed through the heart of Baltimore—three o'clock—there still were people abroad in its streets. But none of these knew that the through sleeping car, making its nightly trip through Pratt Street and across the town that night, bore the person of the President-elect of the United States. Not even the railroad employés knew it. As far as can be learned, Lincoln did not even awake as he passed through Baltimore. Quietly, as was the usual way, the sleeping car was turned into the shed of Camden Station. It was the work of but a very few minutes to couple it to the Baltimore and Ohio train there, waiting to go on to Washington; and which had merely been given imperative orders not, this night, to miss the Philadelphia connection—which sometimes it must have done. . . . In a very short time, the train was off and away again, fast disappearing down the line toward Washington.

Of the arrival in Washington, early that Sabbath morn, we have the excellent account in Elihu B. Washburne's *Reminiscenses of Abraham Lincoln*.   Mr. Washburne writes:

. . . I planted myself behind one of the great pillars in the old Washington and Baltimore depot where I could see and not be observed.   Presently the train came rambling in. . . . I could not mistake the long, lank form of ,Mr. Lincoln, and my heart bounded with joy and gratitude. . . .   The only persons that accompanied Lincoln were Pinkerton, the well-known detective, and Ward H. Lamon.   When they were fairly on the platform, a short distance from the car, I stepped forward and accosted the President:

"How are you, Lincoln?"

At this unexpected and somewhat familiar salutation, the gentlemen were apparently somewhat startled, but Mr. Lincoln, who recognized me, relieved them at once by remarking in his peculiar voice:

"This is only Washburne."

Then we all exchanged congratulations and walked out to the front of the depot, where I had a carriage in waiting. Entering the carriage, we drove rapidly to Willard's Hotel, entering on Fourteenth Street, before it was fairly daylight. . . .

Mrs. Lincoln and the boys followed the itinerary as originally laid down for the presidential party.   A telegram, "plums delivered nuts safely"—of which the code translation was "Lincoln's in Washington"—reached her Sunday morning at the breakfast table at her hotel in Harrisburg; and great relief was felt.   The coming of day dispelled the absurd rumors about the dangers that lurked along the line of the Northern Central, and the special train came through quickly and easily.   Neither were there any unpleasant manifestations amongst the crowds stationed in the Baltimore streets.   Baltimore was a little dis-

MR. LINCOLN ARRIVES AT WASHINGTON.
On his way to his first inauguration, February 23, 1861.
From a painting by H. D. Stitt.

The Seventh Regiment of New York Arriving at the Baltimore and Ohio Station, Washington, D. C., 1861.

From a contemporary sketch in *Frank Leslie's Weekly*.

appointed not to have its curiosity relieved with at least a passing glimpse of the President-elect, but it paid a courteous attention to his wife and sons as they rode across the city. In those days, the connection between the Baltimore and Ohio and the Northern Central was handled very similarly to that with the Philadelphia line. A track ran through Howard Street from Camden Station to the so-called Bolton Station of the Northern Central (located not far from the present Mount Royal Station). Down this street came the Lincoln car, and Mrs. Lincoln was received courteously—with here and there slight manifestations of applause. Her trip on to Washington over the Baltimore and Ohio was without incident.

.   .   .   .

But the passage of the Sixth Massachusetts Regiment through the streets of Baltimore, less than two months later, was far from being without incident. It was thrilling, dramatic, tragic to the extreme. In the course of it, the first blood in the American Civil War was spilled. Riot and mob rule, coming for a time almost to anarchy, momentarily gained the upper hand; and upon Baltimore were fixed the eyes of an excited and overwrought nation.

It is not the province of this book to go into the condition of affairs that brought forth the Civil War and Baltimore's important rôle in it. The intention here is only to set down these things as they pertain directly to the record of the Baltimore and Ohio Railroad. Yet even to understand this —and the attack of the Baltimore mob upon the men of the Sixth Massachusetts was a very colorful and important event in the history of the railroad—one must again recall the strong sympathetic feeling that the town held for the South in those beginning days of the Civil War. Maryland had, at no time, declared for secession—although there were to come times when the friends of the Union feared that she was about to take that radical step; but she had shown little enthusiasm over the cause of the North. To the appeals from Washington for men, her Governor, Thomas H. Hicks, had issued a perfunctory call for four regiments, but had stipulated that these were to be used for the defense of the national capital, and for no other purpose whatsoever. In the meantime, hundreds of Marylanders were joining the ranks of the rapidly swelling army of the Confederacy. In that army, a Maryland Line—following the traditions of the days of the Revolution—already was being organized.

The Sixth Massachusetts was not the very first regiment of troops from the North to pass through Baltimore. On the day previous (April 18), several companies of soldiers—about six hundred in all—had arrived from Pennsylvania over the Northern Central. They had had a mixed sort of reception. If the delegation had been composed entirely of regulars (there were two companies of stout artillerymen from St. Paul), there probably would have been but little trouble. For the town recognized quite generally that it was the business of the United States Army to go wherever it was ordered. But militia regiments were different; particularly militia regiments from the North. In some curious way, the coming of these across Maryland was regarded by many as a sort of invasion of the sacred doctrine of states' rights. And, so, was greatly to be resented.

The six companies from Harrisburg arrived in Baltimore about two o'clock in the afternoon of the eighteenth. Efforts had been made to keep their coming secret, but the news escaped and large crowds gathered that afternoon, both at the Calvert and the Bolton depots of the Northern Central. But the soldiers left their special train at a point out on Howard Street, and formed in a column to march toward the Mount Clare Station of the Baltimore and Ohio, where fifteen freight cars, with board seats laid in them, had been prepared for their transport on to Washington. Of their reception in Baltimore, that accurate historian, Scharf, writes:

. . . Upon the troops disembarking they were jostled and pushed about considerably by the crowd. . . . From the commencement of the march to the close of it, they were greeted with groans, hisses and other indignities, and with cheers for Jefferson Davis, South Carolina, the Southern Confederacy and Virginia. But for the efficient police arrangements there would undoubtedly have been a collision between the populace and the military. On reaching the cars, the troops took possession of them, while many of the crowd clambered on top, hooting while others pelted them with stones. They soon departed for Washington and the crowd dispersed.

This, then, was the temper in which Baltimore awaited the coming of the Sixth Massachusetts on the morrow. A citizens' meeting that night, led—let this be marked—by Ross Winans, passed resolutions of protest against Northern troops coming through the town; resolutions to be forwarded at once by messenger to President Lincoln at Washington. The Mayor —George W. Brown—and Governor Hicks both issued proclamations calling upon the people of Baltimore to preserve order and to obey the law. . . .

In the meantime, there were being made efforts to shut off Union troops reaching Washington over the Baltimore and Ohio from the West. On that very day (the eighteenth), a messenger arrived at Mr. Garrett's office from the Mayor of Charles Town, Virginia, with a note demanding guaranties from the railroad that no troops would be permitted to pass over the Main Stem and that no munitions of war should be taken by trains from the arsenal at Harpers Ferry. If these guaranties were not given at once, the messenger was authorized to say that the bridge at Harpers Ferry would be blown up.

To the eternal glory of John W. Garrett, it is related that he made instant and indignant refusal even to entertain such a proposition. The messenger withdrew. The incoming Virginia militia, by blowing up the great bridge at Harpers Ferry a few weeks later, however, finished a large job of destruction there.

.   .   .   .

It was at about eleven o'clock in the morning of the nineteenth of April that the much heralded special trains of militia

troops from the North began to arrive at the President Street
Station of the Philadelphia, Wilmington and Baltimore.   They
consisted of thirty-five cars and carried more than two thousand
men.   For, in addition to the Sixth Massachusetts, there were
six companies of the First, and four of the Second Regiment of
Pennsylvania Volunteers, and about half of the Washington
Brigade of Philadelphia.   To the Massachusetts men—on the
first of the trains to arrive—there had been distributed, just
prior to their arrival in Baltimore, twenty rounds of ball
cartridges; and Edward F. Jones, their colonel, went through
the cars, ordering them to cap and load their rifles.

For a time, the crossing of the city—which was attempted
in the horse-drawn cars through Pratt Street (today recognized
as a very grave military error)—proceeded without serious
disturbance.   There was an enormous crowd in the streets—
by common consent all business had been suspended; but it
seemed content to hiss and groan at the Northerners and to
give cheers for the Confederacy and its leaders.   In this way,
nine cars passed safely.   And the men who felt themselves
responsible for the good name and the good order of Baltimore
began to breathe a little more freely. . . .   Then came the
tenth of the cars, and trouble—of a real and vital sort—began.
Again we quote from Scharf:

. . . As the tenth [car] arrived opposite Commerce Street,
the brake . . . became disarranged by some means and the
car was consequently stopped, when a man standing upon the
sidewalk threw a stone into one of the windows.   This was a
signal to all assembled, and in an instant the stones were
flying thick and fast.   The driver of the car becoming frightened, attached his team to the opposite end and drove rapidly
toward the Philadelphia depot, the car being stoned until it
disappeared from view.   After the lapse of a few minutes spent
in cheers and groans, the crowd, which by this time had increased to the number of about eight hundred, proceeded to
tear up the street for the purpose of blockading the track, to
prevent the passage of any more of the cars.   Picks and

shovels were soon procured and in a short time the entire street, for a distance of about fifty yards, was entirely torn up, the bridges over the gutters were taken up, and the paving stones thrown in large piles in the center of the track. About this time some one among the party discovered several large anchors lying upon the wharf nearby, and a rush was immediately made to gain possession of them. A number of negroes, employed as sailors upon the schooners hailing from the South, came ashore from their vessels and rendered every assistance in their power, hauling the immense anchors to the center of the railroad tracks, with cheers for the "Souf" and "Massa Jeff Davis." By their assistance some eight of the anchors were piled upon the track. A cart loaded with sand happened at the time to be passing, and it was also seized upon, and being backed up, the contents were emptied upon the center of the track.

Rapidly, indeed, the Baltimore corner of the stage was being set for a vital scene in the great national tragedy. Danger was in the air. . . . Rumor ran her way quickly amidst the crowd. "The Boston men are forming at President Street, and are going to march to Camden," she whispered to it. . . . And the mob made its way to the President Street Station. As it moved, it gained size and momentum. When it was beside the train shed of the old Philadelphia depot, it already numbered more than two thousand men (and probably looked like ten times that number). It gazed angrily upon the long lines of yellow cars, and the white faces that peered out of their windows. . . . The crowd yelled. But the troops were strangely silent. And, for a full fifteen minutes, made no effort to get out of the cars. . . . Scharf again:

During this delay among those in command, the crowd became furious with excitement and were about to force an entrance into the cars, when a large detachment of police under the charge of one of the captains made their appearance and rushing forward . . . succeeded in preventing the attack upon the cars. The order being given by the captains of the various companies of the troops, six carloads of them proceeded to alight from the train. As they descended, single-file, into the crowd, they were hustled quite violently and were hooted at and hissed by all assembled, but finally succeeded in pushing their way, with the assistance of the officers, to the footway alongside the depot, where they formed in double-file, awaiting further orders. . . .

Not much fun that morning being a young militiaman of Massachusetts, enlisted for battle in the open, and suddenly and unexpectedly facing an angry mob in the streets of Baltimore. . . . Knowing that, for more than a mile, one must march past that mob through the narrow streets of a strange town, with firing likely to come from any one of those alien roofs. . . . The narrative continues:

. . . The arrangement having been perfected for a march, the order was given. . . . Finding it impossible to proceed they wheeled around and started in an opposite direction, when cries of "head them off" were re-echoed through the vast assemblage, and a rush was made to the southern end of the depot. At this point they were completely surrounded and for several minutes it was found to be impossible for them to move in any direction. . . .

The black cloud of tragedy formed itself. A Confederate flag, about which there had been desultory fighting between the police and the mob for a half hour past, was brought to the head of the forming line, and, as the troops moved forward, it was, for a time, carried ahead of them. This was a matter of much contention . . . followed by hand-to-hand fighting. Finally, several Union sympathizers in the crowd along President Street succeeded in tearing it down. For their own protection, they then ran into the lines of soldiers.

. . . This action exasperated the entire mass of citizens to such an extent that an attack was immediately made upon the troops with stones and such missiles as could be found. As the attack began, one of the soldiers, a man named William Patch from Massachusetts, was seen to fall . . . having been struck in the back with a large paving stone. As he fell upon his side into the gutter, his musket was seized by a portion of the crowd . . . who set upon him, and before the police could prevent them, beat the unfortunate soldier most unmercifully. . . .

The situation grew worse. . . . The officers of the troops began to lose their heads. One of them called out an order to run and the militiamen broke into a dogtrot down President Street and into Pratt. Here it was that the street had been almost completely blocked; that paving stones had been piled up for ammunition. . . . The troops halted for a moment. Their young officers looked about them. The crowd menaced. Stones already were beginning to fly. "Fire," came the order. . . . These Northern muskets blazed. Two or three Baltimoreans sank to the ground. Scharf continues:

> As those who were shot down by the soldiers continued to fall, the citizens, who were almost entirely unarmed, wavered somewhat, and giving way before the fixed bayonets of the troops, opened a passage, and the troops were again in motion, running rapidly up Pratt Street toward Camden Station. Mayor Brown, who had joined the troops near Pratt Street bridge and marched at the head of their column, finding that his presence was of no use, left them about Light Street, but immediately after, Marshal Kane [the head of the Baltimore police], with about fifty policemen from the direction of Camden Station, rushed to the rear of the troops, formed a line across the street, and with drawn revolvers checked and kept off the mob. This movement was perfectly successful, and without a doubt saved the soldiers from extermination. In the meantime, the nine cars which the mob had allowed to pass along Pratt Street, arrived at Camden Station, where the soldiers were greeted with hisses, groans and insulting threats of every description.

.   .   .   .

The scene shifts again . . . from President Street to Camden Station. For nearly an hour—it must have seemed like an eternity—the soldiers from the first nine cars have been sitting in the closely guarded train in the Baltimore and Ohio terminal. The din that comes up from Pratt Street must be horrible. . . . There are thirteen passenger cars in the train for Washington; and, into the waiting places of these, come the first of the panting, dusty, torn and disheveled militiamen who have (literally) run the Pratt Street gauntlet. The station is well guarded, and the ragtag of the crowd that tries to force its way into the train with them is kept off. . . . And, sullenly roaring its rage, goes off and away down the track, to see if it cannot tear it up. But this is a heavier line, by far, and its efforts are desultory. The few rails that are wrenched away are hastily replaced.

At a quarter before one, the train pulls out and disappears on its way to Washington. Those thirteen cars, crowded to the utmost with the men of the Sixth Massachusetts, are all that get away from Camden this day. The remaining cars at President Street—filled chiefly with the men of the Pennsylvania companies—after being threatened by the mob, are drawn off and away and back toward the North again. Other oncoming troop trains—bound toward Baltimore over both the Philadelphia railroad and the Northern Central—are reached by the telegraph and are either halted or sent back.

In the meantime, Baltimore gives the rest of the day to a sort of mob rule. There are excited meetings in the streets— the chief of which is beside the Battle Monument in Monument Square, and which is addressed by Governor Hicks, who says that he is a Marylander and would sooner have his "right arm cut off than raise it against a sister Southern state." In some of the houses of the old Maryland city, there is singing, laughing, rejoicing, that night; but in many of them, there is mourning. In the rambling, running, chaotic fight along Pratt Street, four soldiers have been killed; and twelve citizens of Baltimore. Thirty-six of the Northern militiamen have been wounded; but no one will ever know just how many of the Baltimoreans.

.   .   .   .

In the musty files of the Baltimore and Ohio (such as were not destroyed in the great fire of 1904), one finds reference to those exciting days of April, 1861. William Prescott Smith— remembered always as the highly efficient master of transportation, unofficial historian of the company, and right-hand man of Mr. Garrett—on the day of the Baltimore riot, telegraphs Samuel M. Felton, the president of the Philadelphia, Wilmington and Baltimore Railroad; after this fashion:

April 19, 1861   4.00 P.M.

S. M. FELTON
        Philadelphia

This day will be historical. It is evident that, whatever our Authorities may want in Maryland or at Washington, the people of this state will fight to prevent any Northern troops passing through. I never risked my own life so sadly before. The first regiment got off with greatest difficulty, our street tracks were obstructed in every form, and also for five miles out of town, through all which the troops had literally to fight their way.

We could not return our teams for your second train, and its troops while remaining at President Street were attacked violently while in cars there—the greater part of police being yet on western border of town with Boston regiment.

Some of troops hurt with stones and other missiles, and as they fired on the crowd repeatedly at different points, from five to ten citizens of Baltimore are killed and many others wounded.

We consulted the Authorities and Governor Hicks and Mayor Brown jointly advised that troops at your station be returned northward beyond borders of Maryland. They also telegraphed Mr. Lincoln to let no more troops come through our state as excitement was fearful, and uncontrollable unless cause was thus removed. Our local military are called out and martial law is about being proclaimed. A general town meeting being held in Monument Square. In this state of things, we cannot undertake to carry any more Northern troops over any part of our road.

W. P. SMITH.

Two hours later, the master of transportation of the Baltimore and Ohio sends the president of the Philadelphia, Wilmington and Baltimore this dispatch:

April 19, 1861   6 P.M.

S. M. FELTON
  Philadelphia
  Town meeting in Square this afternoon attended by entire populace—apparently unanimous that Northern Volunteers shall not pass through.   Gov. Hicks and most popular public men of all parties united and concurring.   The change of feeling here is most startling.
  I suppose you know the position of your road in Maryland.

W. P. SMITH.

It is to be assumed that Mr. Felton did know the position of his road in Maryland.   At any rate, it was not many hours thereafter—after the Pennsylvania troops had been carted ignominiously north again—before Isaac R. Trimble, superintendent of the P. W. & B., with a group of men, slipped out of Baltimore and burned most of the road's many bridges between Baltimore and the Susquehanna River.   It was felt that this was far more effective than any form of protest to Washington.

This act, which aroused great indignation in the North, was performed not merely with the acquiescence of Governor Hicks and Mayor Brown, but with their actual coöperation. A squad of Baltimore police accompanied Trimble on his errand of destruction.   They carried pickaxes, crowbars and a goodly supply of turpentine. . . .   While they were at their task, a similar squad was destroying the bridges on the Northern Central; at its Relay House and also at Cockeysville. . . .   When both groups were done, Baltimore was very effectually cut off from the North.   And what was even more to the point, so was Washington . . . already being seriously menaced by the swiftly growing army of the young Confederacy, which was even then encamping itself upon the

Virginia hills within fair view of the new dome of the Capitol.
. . . A serious situation it was, indeed. The North writhed
in its anger and suspense.

A serious situation for Baltimore, too. Which continues
from the nineteenth into the following day, and into the day
following on that. On the twenty-first, Mr. Garrett telegraphs
Mayor Brown, who has gone to Washington for a personal
conference with Lincoln and General Scott and members of the
Cabinet, saying:

> Three thousand Northern troops are reported to be at
> Cockeysville. Intense excitement prevails. Churches have
> been dismissed, and the people are forming in mass. To pre-
> vent terrific bloodshed the result of your interview and arrange-
> ment is awaited.
>
> JOHN W. GARRETT, President.

Mayor Brown at once, upon the conclusion of his interview
at the White House that Sunday morning, replies to Mr.
Garrett:

> We have again seen the President, General Scott, Secretary
> of War and other members of the Cabinet and the troops are
> ordered to return forthwith to Harrisburg. A messenger goes
> with us from General Scott.

. . . .

For three anxious days, Washington and Baltimore remained completely severed from the North. When actual
communication was restored, it was through a different route.
The Seventh New York went by steamboat to Annapolis, and,
with its efficient help, a through rail route was immediately
opened, by way of the Maryland capital and Elkridge Junction,
thence over the Baltimore and Ohio into Washington. After
which, the Seventh went on to Washington, and, on the twenty-
fifth of April, marched in review in front of the White House.

The new route was well safeguarded, but it was slow.

Troops were detrained at Perryville, from the P. W. & B. (at that time there was no bridge of any sort over the mouth of the Susquehanna); and the efficient ferryboat, *Maryland*, which hitherto had carried passengers of every sort between that town and Havre de Grace on the other side of the broad river, lengthened its trips all the way to Annapolis. In this, it was aided by river steamboats, detailed to the service.

An open pathway, but a very awkward and a tedious one. Demands began to be voiced in the North for an "air line" railroad route which would connect New York (Jersey City) and Washington and completely avoid both Philadelphia and Baltimore and all their transportation perplexities.[1] Such a route was never builded. But the threat led to a complete double-tracking of the existing railroad lines between Jersey City and Washington, and the construction of the first bridge over the mouth of the Susquehanna, so that there might be an easy and unimpeded flow of rail travel over the most important link of the nation's entire system of inland transport. . . . All of this was completed before the close of 1864. Yet, long months before then, troop movements from the North had been resumed through Baltimore. The military and

[1] This was not the first time that this suggestion had been raised. In a dispatch from Washington to the *New York Herald*, dated January 19, 1853, one reads of a bill introduced into Congress for a "direct line" from New York to Washington. Of it, the *Herald* correspondent writes:

"This is an important measure, for two reasons—it would create competition, by which the present monopoly would be destroyed, which renders the route between New York and the capital of the Union that every person from the north must travel who has business at the capital, the worst conducted, most inconvenient and dearest line in the Union, and would greatly shorten the distance. At present, a traveler has to pay $7.50 for a distance of only 238 miles, when he can go from New York to Montreal, which is 387, for $6.50. [The present fare, 1927, from New York to Washington, is $8.14; from New York to Montreal, $14.01.] It is true that the states of Maryland and New Jersey pick the pockets of the public by exacting each of them fifty cents as a toll from travelers; but even with this imposition the fare should not exceed six dollars. The tax is an unconstitutional one and were it resisted, it would cease, but the companies pay it whose interest it is to propitiate the state legislatures, which, in their return, secure them a monopoly."

political strategy that made this possible is not germane here.
. . . The Northern troops passed through easily. The
hospitality of Baltimore began to exert itself in their behalf.
It became famed as the town where the ladies met the cars and
gave the soldiers all manner of creature comforts. Thus was
the stain of April 19, 1861, slowly wiped out.

.   .   .   .

In those days of April, 1861, when Baltimore itself was like
a giant powder mine just awaiting a mischievous spark to set
it completely afire, Mr. Garrett was harassed from still other
quarters. From up the Main Stem . . . letters . . . threats
. . . alarming reports poured themselves into his office in
Camden Station. One of the earliest of these reads:

April 19, 1861.

Mr. JOHN W. GARRETT
    Dear Sir:
    It is my duty to inform you that all Republicans must be
removed from your road. Stationed and beginning at Monocacy Bridge, West to Harpers Ferry. (We consider all your
stationed men to be such between those respective points.)
If they are not removed, your *Road will be made one continuous
ruin.*
    By order Committee Fifteen Hundred Western Maryland
Men.

SEC.

    To JOHN W. GARRETT, ESQ.
    B. & O. R. R.

Here, in itself, was an almost continuous problem for the
president of the Baltimore and Ohio; throughout the earlier
years of the war, at any rate. From Baltimore to Harpers
Ferry and Martinsburg, at least the majority of the rank and
file of the road were avowed Southern sympathizers. At the
outbreak of the conflict, no small proportion of them left their
tasks, crossed the Potomac and enlisted in the army of the

Confederacy.   Many of them made excellent fighting records in that army.

Nevertheless, by sheer will power and force of energy, to say nothing of unceasing wit and tact, Garrett not only held his road and himself loyal to the Union, but kept both of greatest service to it.   This has been attested; time and time again. Yet, at the outset, the enormity of his problem is shown, most clearly, by the following long telegram sent in the morning of April 20, 1861, from J. B. Ford, the road's agent at Wheeling, to William Prescott Smith, at Baltimore:

> The following has just been put in circulation in Wheeling. It looks like a special design upon our Road—viz:
>
> Narrative of the Special Reporter of the *Philadelphia Enquirer;* The Special Reporter of the *Philadelphia Enquirer* has just reached here from Washington by Harpers Ferry and has telegraphed the following information to Washington and the principal cities.   He also states that when he left Washington orders had been given for the stoppage of all mails over the B. & O. Railroad, as they had refused to allow the Federal Government the use of the road for carrying troops and had tendered it to Virginia and Maryland.   The most intense excitement exists in Washington.   The wires are so obstructed that no reliable information can be received from the South or Harpers Ferry.

The statement of the "special reporter," chiefly interesting as giving a contemporary picture of the vast excitement ranging along the Baltimore and Ohio at that moment, is appended to the telegram.   It reads:

> "Left Washington at 2.46 P.M. Friday afternoon (the nineteenth).   On reaching Junction of B. & O. Rd., we learned there of the riot at Baltimore and from passengers who had seen it learned that the United States Volunteers had been attacked by a mob and returned fire.   The report of killed varied from 6 to 13 citizens and 4 to 7 volunteers.   A perfect panic was reigning.   Maryland troops were ordered out, the

firemen are ringing the bells and the Railroad Company refused
to carry the troops and turned them back. About 800 got
through before the riot. These will get through to Washington
and make the force there five thousand. The balance, said to
be about four thousand, are retained north of Baltimore.

"Left Junction of B. & O. R. R. at 4 P.M. on Friday. Train
cars full. Along the route I found business stopped. All was
excitement at Ijamsville. There was a crowd around the
flagpole with the American flag. Cheering at Point of Rocks
for the Confederate flag. On reaching the bridge at Harpers
Ferry the train was stopped by Virginia soldiers with loaded
cannon planted in front of the cars. On the conductor assur-
ing them that no United States agents or soldiers were on board,
or any reporters, the train was allowed to cross the bridge
there. We were again stopped, by loaded cannon, pointed
obliquely at the cars so they could demolish the whole train,
with men at the touch-holes ready to fire. As soon as the
train stopped, the soldiers rushed to the sides of the cars and
commenced to search them. The conductor was told to ask no
questions, that orders had been given to allow no one to land,
and men with drawn swords and loaded muskets asked what
is the news from Baltimore. A member of the Richmond
Convention stepped on the platform and shouted, 'Go on,
boys, first blood for Baltimore. The United States troops have
fired into an unarmed crowd of citizens and every man in
Baltimore was now going to stand by his state and shed his
last drop of blood sooner than have abolition hordes come
down there to murder them.' The mob cheered him and
the conductor finding nothing could be done, told them the
road would carry none but Southern men and started the
train. Men followed the train with swords so long as they
could keep up, to prevent any one getting off.

"On the Armory flagstaff rests the Virginia flag and over
the remains of the Arsenal a piece of the U. S. flag. About
3,000 men are in and about the Arsenal, mostly armed and
equipped. The Arsenal and a part of the factory are burned
to the ground. Several volunteers had got on the train. We
asked one what all this means. He said he had orders not to
tell. . . . On Thursday night the United States Artillery

Company set the Arsenal on fire and fled for Carlisle. The citizens rallied and put out the fire, but not until the arms were all burnt. . . .

"The wildest excitement rages there. Troops are pouring in from all parts of the surrounding country. . . . At Martinsburg we stopped for supper. Here there was a great crowd, a repetition of the speech the member of the Virginia Convention (Armstrong) had made at Harpers Ferry and assurance given that the railroad would carry none but Virginia and Maryland men. A number of Union men are here, but will soon be gagged.

"A Lieutenant of the Hedgesville Blues and ten men got on the cars here and came to North Mountain saying they would not fight against the United States flag until Maryland seceded. At Cumberland cheers were given by a crowd for the Union and groans for the traitors. At Wheeling orders were received from Governor Letcher (of Virginia) to seize the Custom House, but Wheeling is strong for the Union and last night it was guarded by the Mayor for the United States. The citizens in Wheeling are in great excitement for the news and announcement that the mail will be stopped on the Baltimore and Ohio Rail-road. . . ."

J. B. FORD.

So was marked, most definitely, the entrance of the Baltimore and Ohio Railroad into the great American conflict.

TECHNOLOGY AND SOCIETY

An Arno Press Collection

Ardrey, R[obert] L. **American Agricultural Implements.** In two parts. 1894

Arnold, Horace Lucien and Fay Leone Faurote. **Ford Methods and the Ford Shops.** 1915

Baron, Stanley [Wade]. **Brewed in America:** A History of Beer and Ale in the United States. 1962

Bathe, Greville and Dorothy. **Oliver Evans:** A Chronicle of Early American Engineering. 1935

Bendure, Zelma and Gladys Pfeiffer. **America's Fabrics:** Origin and History, Manufacture, Characteristics and Uses. 1946

Bichowsky, F. Russell. **Industrial Research.** 1942

Bigelow, Jacob. **The Useful Arts:** Considered in Connexion with the Applications of Science. 1840. Two volumes in one

Birkmire, William H. **Skeleton Construction in Buildings.** 1894

Boyd, T[homas] A[lvin]. **Professional Amateur:** The Biography of Charles Franklin Kettering. 1957

Bright, Arthur A[aron], Jr. **The Electric-Lamp Industry:** Technological Change and Economic Development from 1800 to 1947. 1949

Bruce, Alfred and Harold Sandbank. **The History of Prefabrication.** 1943

Carr, Charles C[arl]. **Alcoa, An American Enterprise.** 1952

Cooley, Mortimer E. **Scientific Blacksmith.** 1947

Davis, Charles Thomas. **The Manufacture of Paper.** 1886

Deane, Samuel. **The New-England Farmer,** or Georgical Dictionary. 1822

Dyer, Henry. **The Evolution of Industry.** 1895

Epstein, Ralph C. **The Automobile Industry:** Its Economic and Commercial Development. 1928

Ericsson, Henry. **Sixty Years a Builder:** The Autobiography of Henry Ericsson. 1942

Evans, Oliver. **The Young Mill-Wright and Miller's Guide.** 1850

Ewbank, Thomas. **A Descriptive and Historical Account of Hydraulic and Other Machines for Raising Water,** Ancient and Modern. 1842

Field, Henry M. **The Story of the Atlantic Telegraph.** 1893

Fleming, A. P. M. **Industrial Research in the United States of America.** 1917

Van Gelder, Arthur Pine and Hugo Schlatter. **History of the Explosives Industry in America.** 1927

Hall, Courtney Robert. **History of American Industrial Science.** 1954

Hungerford, Edward. **The Story of Public Utilities.** 1928

Hungerford, Edward. **The Story of the Baltimore and Ohio Railroad, 1827-1927.** 1928

Husband, Joseph. **The Story of the Pullman Car.** 1917

Ingels, Margaret. **Willis Haviland Carrier, Father of Air Conditioning.** 1952

Kingsbury, J[ohn] E. **The Telephone and Telephone Exchanges:** Their Invention and Development. 1915

Labatut, Jean and Wheaton J. Lane, eds. **Highways in Our National Life:** A Symposium. 1950

Lathrop, William G[ilbert]. **The Brass Industry in the United States.** 1926

Lesley, Robert W., John B. Lober and George S. Bartlett. **History of the Portland Cement Industry in the United States.** 1924

Marcosson, Isaac F. **Wherever Men Trade:** The Romance of the Cash Register. 1945

Miles, Henry A[dolphus]. **Lowell, As It Was, and As It Is**. 1845

Morison, George S. **The New Epoch:** As Developed by the Manufacture of Power. 1903

Olmsted, Denison. **Memoir of Eli Whitney, Esq.** 1846

Passer, Harold C. **The Electrical Manufacturers, 1875-1900.** 1953

Prescott, George B[artlett]. **Bell's Electric Speaking Telephone.** 1884

Prout, Henry G. **A Life of George Westinghouse.** 1921

Randall, Frank A. **History of the Development of Building Construction in Chicago.** 1949

Riley, John J. **A History of the American Soft Drink Industry:** Bottled Carbonated Beverages, 1807-1957. 1958

Salem, F[rederick] W[illiam]. **Beer, Its History and Its Economic Value as a National Beverage.** 1880

Smith, Edgar F. **Chemistry in America.** 1914

Steinman, D[avid] B[arnard]. **The Builders of the Bridge:** The Story of John Roebling and His Son. 1950

Taylor, F[rank] Sherwood. **A History of Industrial Chemistry.** 1957

Technological Trends and National Policy, Including the Social Implications of New Inventions. Report of the Subcommittee on Technology to the National Resources Committee. 1937

Thompson, John S. **History of Composing Machines.** 1904

Thompson, Robert Luther. **Wiring a Continent:** The History of the Telegraph Industry in the United States, 1832-1866. 1947

Tilley, Nannie May. **The Bright-Tobacco Industry, 1860-1929.** 1948

Tooker, Elva. **Nathan Trotter:** Philadelphia Merchant, 1787-1853. 1955

Turck, J. A. V. **Origin of Modern Calculating Machines.** 1921

Tyler, David Budlong. **Steam Conquers the Atlantic.** 1939

Wheeler, Gervase. **Homes for the People,** In Suburb and Country. 1855